Reflective Planning, Teaching, and Evaluation: K–12

Second Edition

Judy W. Eby

San Diego State University

Merrill, an imprint of Prentice Hall
Upper Saddle River, New Jersey   Columbus, Ohio

Library of Congress Cataloging-in-Publication Data
Eby, Judy W.
    Reflective planning, teaching, and evaluation, K–12 / Judy W. Eby.—2nd ed.
      p. cm.
    Includes bibliographical references and indexes.
    ISBN 0-13-496480-2
    1. Teaching. 2. Thought and thinking. 3. Educational tests and measurements.
    4. Educational planning.   I. Title
    LB1025.3.E28   1998
    371.1′02—dc21   96-40427
                                              CIP

Cover photo: © 1996 PhotoDisc, Inc.
Editor: Debra A. Stollenwerk
Production Editor: Christine M. Harrington
Photo Editor: Dawn E. Garrott
Design Coordinator: Julia Zonneveld Van Hook
Text Designer: Pagination
Cover Designer: Brian Deep
Production Manager: Pamela D. Bennett
Electronic Text Management: Marilyn Wilson Phelps, Matthew Williams, Karen L. Bretz, Tracey
    Ward

This book was set in Transitional 511 by Prentice Hall and was printed and bound by Quebecor
Printing/Book Press. The cover was printed by Phoenix Color Corp.

Photo credits: Scott Cunningham/Merrill, pp. 1, 25, 123, 151, 227; Anthony Magnacca/Merrill,
p. 337; Barbara Schwartz/Merrill, pp. 183, 205, 281, 309; Anne Vega/Merrill, pp. 63, 251; Todd
Yarrington/Merrill, p. 87.

Printed in the United States of America

10 9 8 7 6 5 4 3 2 1

ISBN: 0-13-496480-2

Prentice-Hall International (UK) Limited, *London*
Prentice-Hall of Australia Pty. Limited, *Sydney*
Prentice-Hall of Canada, Inc., *Toronto*
Prentice-Hall Hispanoamericana, S. A., *Mexico*
Prentice-Hall of India Private Limited, *New Delhi*
Prentice-Hall of Japan, Inc., *Tokyo*
Simon & Schuster Asia Pte. Ltd., *Singapore*
Editora Prentice-Hall do Brasil, Ltda., *Rio de Janeiro*

Preface

When I was a student teacher, I recall trying to live up to the high expectations of my master teacher, who seemed to do everything with such ease. She had a warm, comfortable rapport with the students in her classroom, which I doubted that I could ever duplicate. She planned exciting projects that allowed students to investigate and research topics in small groups. When I tried to create my own curriculum unit, my inexperience showed at every turn.

Perhaps the most embarrassing moment was when I planned a unit on animal behavior and asked students to bring in cages to hold mice that I planned to get for them at the university. According to my plan, each student would have his or her own mouse and would plan experiments to investigate mice preferences or behavior. The students brought in leftover gerbil cages, bird cages, and other small containers. On the first day of the new unit, I brought in the mice and put one in each cage. But the mice were much smaller and more agile than I had expected. They began squeezing out through the holes of the cages and running around the classroom.

Of course, I was embarrassed. Why hadn't I thought about this? What could I do now? I had to think quickly and take action in front of the now chaotic students. I asked students to try to catch the mice, and we put the ones we caught into a glass aquarium. Now I would have to rethink the entire plan. After school, my master teacher was able to laugh with me about the whole event and allow me to decide on what to do next.

That night I planned how we would identify the mice by dots of ink on their fur so that the individual experiments could proceed. But the next morning when I came in, what I found was carnage in the aquarium. Baby mice had been born during the night and had been eaten by others of their own species. Some adult mice were wounded. None of them looked ready to be handled by eager sixth graders in pursuit of scientific knowledge. Again, I had to think fast, before the students came pouring into the classroom. I decided to change the entire unit. I took the mice out of the classroom and substituted mealworms for our individual animal behavior investigations. Although some students were disappointed, others were obviously relieved when they listened to my new plan.

The unit went on to be reasonably successful. Students tested the mealworms' preference for various colors or for cornmeal versus oatmeal, tried to get them to travel through a maze for various rewards, and charted their growth. I learned a lot from that experience. I learned that I ought to plan ahead as carefully as possible, but I also learned an even more important lesson: that unless a teacher sticks with routine day in and day out, unexpected events are bound to occur. I learned to laugh at my embarrassing mistakes rather than panic and crumble. I learned that I would always need to think on my feet and be ready to come up with new ideas for problems. After that event, I learned to expect the unexpected in my teaching career.

Conceptual Framework

I have designed this book to alert you to the many complex issues that you will be responsible for as a classroom teacher and to assist you in considering some of the possible effects of your decisions before you put them into action so that your embarrassing moments are few and far between. In Chapter 1, I have proposed a *model of reflective action in teaching* that encourages you to consider the consequences of your actions, take an active role in gaining new knowledge as you perceive the need for it, and communicate with your colleagues to improve your own teaching performance.

New to this Edition

I wrote the first edition of *Reflective Planning, Teaching, and Evaluation: K–12* to encourage beginning teachers to become reflective, caring, and creative in all aspects of their work with children. This edition has a similar purpose but has been expanded to provide more strategies that teachers need today in order to meet the needs of an exceptionally diverse student body.

1. *LEP.* In many school districts, English is a second language for large numbers of students and their parents. New programs have been developed to meet the needs of Limited English Speaking (LEP) children, and I have included descriptions of these types of programs and the types of teaching strategies that teachers are using today to stimulate cooperation, interaction, and mutual respect and appreciation of differences among children from very diverse backgrounds.

2. *CLAD.* In California, where I teach, many teacher education programs have developed new Crosscultural, Language, and Academic Development (CLAD) teacher credentialing programs that address the needs of students from very diverse households. I supervise student teachers who are completing their CLAD credential and work with first- and second-year teachers in a program designed to support their best efforts, encourage them when they feel trapped or overwhelmed with minutia, and assist them in developing strategies to develop into the reflective and caring teachers they want to become. I identify with student teachers and first-year teachers because I remember my own experiences in both those roles so vividly.

3. *Professional portfolio.* Another new emphasis in this second edition is on the development of a professional portfolio that allows you to clarify and communicate your educational philosophy with prospective employers or colleagues. At the end of each chapter, there are suggestions for reflective actions that you can use to document the many accomplishments you have made and the strengths and talents you have to offer. Your professional portfolio will be quite impressive if you take the time to clarify your goals, create unit and lesson plans, collect, and reflect on the issues and materials that you choose to include in it. You can take your portfolio with you on employment interviews and then add to it over the years as you build your repertoire of teaching strategies and classroom materials.

Acknowledgments

I would like to express my appreciation to the many reflective and creative classroom teachers, students, school administrators, and colleagues who contributed ideas, materials, curriculum plans, and personal experiences to this book. They include George "Rick" Bailey, learning disabilities specialist, Crystal Lake School District No. 47, Crystal Lake, Illinois; Virginia Bailey, Barrington School District No. 220, Barrington, Illinois; Chris Chiaverina, New Trier High School, Winnetka, Illinois; Tim Curbo, second-grade teacher, Hawthorne School, San Francisco Unified School District; Conchita Encinas, first-grade bilingual teacher, Chula Vista School District, Chula Vista, California; Cliff Gilkey, fifth-grade teacher, Frank Paul School, Salinas, California; Jim Hicks, science teacher, Barrington High School, Barrington, Illinois; Godwin Higa, fifth-grade teacher, Dingeman Elementary School, San Diego Unified School District; Susan King, kindergarten teacher, Hamilton School, San Diego; Pam Knight, mathematics teacher, Twin Peaks Middle School, Poway School District, Poway, California; Sandra Krakow, first-grade teacher, Woodland School, Barrington School District No. 220, Barrington, Illinois; Vernice Mallory, fifth-grade teacher, Edison Elementary School, San Diego Unified School District; Jean Malvaso-Zingaro, sixth-grade teacher, School No. 6, Rochester, New York; Laurie Mednick, sixth-grade teacher, Kellogg Elementary School, Chula Vista, California; Carleen Mullenix, student teacher, San Diego State University; Mary Finkel, history teacher, Crystal Lake South High School, Crystal Lake, Illinois; Ruth Reyes, sixth-grade teacher, Washington Elementary School, San Diego Unified School District; Sylvia Rimm, Ph.D., educational psychologist, Watertown, Wisconsin; Ylianna Romo, fifth-grade teacher, Washington Elementary School, San Diego Unified School District; Lori Shoults, second-grade teacher, Seth Paine Elementary School, Lake Zurich, Illinois; and Judy Yount, first-grade teacher, Woodland School, Barrington Unified School District No. 220, Barrington, Illinois.

I would also like to acknowledge the contributions made by the reviewers of this book, whose perspectives guided me in making many important revisions in this edition: Noble R. Corey, Indiana State University; Michael A. James, Wichita State University; Karen Kusiak, Colby College; Norman Lederman, Oregon State University; and Helene T. Mandell, National University.

This book is dedicated to Richard Eby.
Thank you for your steady love and encouragement,
which have been essential to my growth
as a teacher and a person.

Brief Contents

CHAPTER 1   REFLECTIVE ACTION IN TEACHING   1

2   PLANNING A HEALTHY, SAFE ENVIRONMENT FOR LEARNING   25

3   PERCEIVING AND MEETING STUDENTS' NEEDS IN A DIVERSE SOCIETY   63

4   HOW TEACHERS PLAN SCHOOL PROGRAMS   87

5   PLANNING THEMATIC UNITS FOR AUTHENTIC LEARNING   123

6   LESSON PLANNING AND SEQUENCING   151

7   AUTHENTIC TEACHING AND LEARNING   183

8   DISCUSSION AND QUESTIONING STRATEGIES THAT MAKE LEARNING MORE AUTHENTIC   205

9   COOPERATIVE LEARNING STRATEGIES   227

10   USING TECHNOLOGY AND OTHER TEACHING STRATEGIES TO INCREASE AUTHENTIC LEARNING   251

11   AUTHENTIC ASSESSMENT   281

12   RECORDING AND REPORTING STUDENT ACCOMPLISHMENTS   309

13   REFLECTIVE TEACHERS AND THE SCHOOL COMMUNITY   337

Contents

CHAPTER 1   **REFLECTIVE ACTION IN TEACHING   1**

Teachers' Many Roles and Responsibilities   3

Processing Information   4

How Teachers' Thinking Affects Student Learning   6

Definitions of Reflective Thinking and Action   7

Reflecting on Your Ethics and Principles   9

A Model of Reflective Action in Teaching   12

Perceptiveness of Your Students' Needs   13

Proactive Search for Knowledge   15

Clarification of Values and Principles   15

Creative Synthesis of Ideas to Fit Your Classroom   16

Persistence and Problem Solving   17

Communication Skills   17

An Example of a Student Teacher Using the Reflective Action Model   18

References   24

CHAPTER 2   **PLANNING A HEALTHY, SAFE ENVIRONMENT FOR LEARNING   25**

A Good Beginning for the School Year   26

Organizing the Physical Environment   27

The First Day of School   30

Preventive Discipline Strategies   36

Teachers' Body Language   36

Withitness   37

Teachers' Leadership Styles   39

Establishing Rules and Consequences   40

The Consequence Called Time-Out   41

Using Positive Consequences and Rewards   42

Two-Way Communication with Parents   43

Discipline Systems That Build Character and Self-Esteem   46

Humor in the Classroom   47

Building Self-Esteem and Intrinsic Motivation   48

The Enhancing Effects of Success   48

Meeting Students' Affective Needs   49

Classrooms As Communities   50

Teaching Students How to Resolve Conflicts   51

Classroom Meetings   54

The Self-Fulfilling Prophecy   57

Scheduling Time for Active Learning   57

Daily and Weekly Schedules   57

Planning Time   58

References   60

CHAPTER 3   **PERCEIVING AND MEETING STUDENTS' NEEDS IN A DIVERSE SOCIETY   63**

Celebrating Diversity in Your Classroom   64

Perceiving the Needs of Bilingual and Bicultural Students   65

Assessing the Academic Needs of Your Students   68

Teachers' Conceptions of How Students Learn   68

Interpreting Data from Students' Cumulative Files   69

Interpreting Standardized Test Results   70

Perceiving Students' Learning Styles and Multiple Intelligences   72

Pretests and Student-Teacher Conferences   73

Placement and Grouping Decisions   74

Determining the Causes of Underachievement   75

Assessment to Meet the Needs of High-Achieving Students   76

Perceiving and Meeting Students' Affective Needs   77

Planning for Students with Special Needs   78

Perceiving the Needs of Urban Children   82

Perceiving the Needs of Rural Students   83

Identifying Students' Needs without Labeling   83

References   86

CHAPTER 4   HOW TEACHERS PLAN SCHOOL PROGRAMS   87

How School Curricula Are Planned   90

National Standards in the Planning Stage   90

State Curriculum Guidelines   91

How Curriculum Is Transformed in Practice   92

Evaluation and Use of Textbooks   93

Curriculum Orientations   94

Tyler's Basic Principles of Curriculum Planning   96

Bloom's Taxonomy of Educational Objectives   97

Clarifying Educational Goals and Outcomes   97

Writing Useful and Appropriate Outcome Statements   99

Examples of Long-Term Curriculum Planning   100

Designing a Common Core Curriculum   100

Redesigning the Curriculum to Reflect Multicultural Values   102

Redesigning the Curriculum Using Multidisciplinary Themes   103

Designing a Whole Language Curriculum   104

A Thematic Curriculum for a Multicultural, Bilingual Classroom   108

Long-Term Planning in Mathematics   110

Long-Term Planning in Science   111

Long-Term Planning in Social Studies   112

Creating Time Lines That Fit Your Goals and Outcome Statements   116

Collaborative Long-Term Planning   119

References   121

CHAPTER 5   PLANNING THEMATIC UNITS FOR AUTHENTIC LEARNING   123

How Teachers Plan Thematic Units   124

Deciding on Unit Topics   125

Creating a Curriculum Unit Using Reflective Actions   126

Using Perceptiveness   126

Constructing Knowledge on the Topic   126

Clarifying Values and Moral Principles   126

Creating the Unit   126

Being Persistent and Solving Problems   127

Using Good Communication Skills   127

Sequencing Learning Experiences in Unit Plans   128

Examples of Thematic units   130

Creating a Multidisciplinary Primary Unit   130

A Multidisciplinary, Multicultural Unit   131

Developing a Mathematics Unit   138

Creating a Language-Arts Unit   138

Two Colleagues Create a High School Science Unit   145

References   149

CHAPTER 6   LESSON PLANNING AND SEQUENCING   151

Writing Objectives to Fit Goals and Outcome Statements   152

Behavioral Objectives   153

Problem-Solving Objectives   153

Expressive Outcomes   154

Bloom's Taxonomy   155

Sequencing Objectives in School Subjects   157

Sequencing Objectives in Mathematics   157

Sequencing Objectives in Language Arts   159

Sequencing Objectives in Science   161

Sequencing Objectives in Social Studies   162

Sequencing Objectives in Interdisciplinary Units   163

Planning Assessments That Fit Your Objectives   164

Varying Objectives for Students with Special Needs   167

Writing a Well-Organized Lesson Plan   170

Sample Lesson Plan in Mathematics   171

Sample Lesson Plan in Language Arts/Social Studies   174

Sample Lesson Plan in Science   176

*Sample Primary Bilingual Lesson Plan Using Learning
  Centers*   177

References   182

CHAPTER 7   AUTHENTIC TEACHING AND LEARNING   **183**

The Cognitive-Mediational Conception of Learning   185

Schema Theory   186

Advance Organizers   187

Presentation Skills That Increase Clarity and Motivation   188

Getting Students' Attention   189

Enthusiasm   190

Clarity   190

Smooth Transitions   192

Timing   193

Variation   194

Interaction   194

Active, Authentic Learning Experiences   194

Closure   195

Systematic Classroom Instruction   195

Direct Instruction of New Knowledge and Skills   195

Teacher Modeling and Demonstration   198

Scaffolding   198

Structuring Tasks for Success   199

Matching Teaching and Learning Styles   200

Multiple Intelligences   201

References   203

CHAPTER 8   DISCUSSION AND QUESTIONING STRATEGIES THAT MAKE LEARNING MORE AUTHENTIC   **205**

Asking Questions That Stimulate Higher-Level Thinking   206

Knowledge Level   207

Comprehension Level   207

Application Level   208

Analysis Level   208

Synthesis Level   208

Evaluation Level   208

Strategies for Authentic Discussions   210

Problem-Solving Discussions   211

Group Investigations   213

Discussions That Promote Critical Thinking   214

Discussions That Improve Observation Skills   215

Discussions That Enhance Comparing Skills   215

Discussions That Guide Classification Skills   215

Discussions That Identify Assumptions   216

Socratic Dialogues   216

Discussions That Enhance Creative Thinking   217

Discussions That Encourage Imagination and Inventiveness   218

Prewriting Discussions   218

Discussions That Address Multiple Intelligences   219

The Role of the Teacher in Leading Discussions   220

References   226

CHAPTER 9   COOPERATIVE LEARNING STRATEGIES   227

Models of Cooperative Learning   228

Group Investigation   228

Jigsaw Model   231

Learning Teams   231

Peacemaking Groups   233

The Purpose of Cooperative Learning   233

Selecting and Adapting Models   234

How Cooperative Learning Is Used in Classrooms   235

Kindergarten Applications   235

First-Grade Applications   236

Second-Grade Applications   238

Third-Grade Applications   239

Fourth-Grade Applications   240

Fifth-Grade Applications   240

Sixth-Grade Applications   241

Middle School Applications   243

High School Applications   243

Classroom Conditions That Encourage Cooperation   244

The Effects of Cooperative Learning   246

References   249

CHAPTER 10   USING TECHNOLOGY AND OTHER TEACHING STRATEGIES TO INCREASE AUTHENTIC LEARNING   251

Technology Can Increase Authentic Learning   252

Word Processing Programs   253

Computer-Assisted Research Projects   254

Networking to Share Information   255

Mathematics and Problem-Solving Programs   255

Record Keeping and Grading   257

Calculators   258

Audio-Video Technology   258

Managing Technology in the Classroom   259

Teaching Strategies That Fit Bloom's Taxonomy   260

Teaching Strategies That Develop a Knowledge Base   260

Teaching Strategies That Promote Comprehension   261

Teaching Strategies That Allow Students to Apply What They Learn   263

Teaching Strategies That Require Analysis   264

Teaching Strategies That Encourage Synthesis   264

Teaching Strategies That Generate Evaluation   265

Classroom Examples of Teaching Strategies   266

Discovery Learning   266

Inquiry Training   267

Role Playing   268

Simulation   269

Mastery Learning   271

Contracts for Independent Learning   272

Group Rotations Using Learning Centers   274

Your Own Repertoire of Teaching Strategies   278

References   280

CHAPTER 11   AUTHENTIC ASSESSMENT   281

Assessment Terminology   282

Public Interest in Student Achievement   285

How Teachers Select and Use Assessment Methods   286

Informal Observations   288

Performance Tasks to Demonstrate Mastery of Outcomes   289

Criterion-Referenced Quizzes and Tests   290

Mastery Learning   292

Essays Evaluated with Rubric Guidelines   293

Oral Reports and Examinations   295

Designing Authentic Assessment Performance Tasks   296

Rubrics, Checklists, and Rating Scales   297

Learning Contracts   300

Portfolios of Student Products   303

Videotape Records   306

Cooperative Group Projects and Products   307

References   308

CHAPTER 12   RECORDING AND REPORTING STUDENT ACCOMPLISHMENTS   309

Varied Perspectives about the Purpose of Evaluation   311

Philosophies Underlying Various Evaluation Systems   314

How Curriculum Orientations Influence Evaluation   314

How Various Orientations Affect Teachers' Observations   315

How Curriculum Orientations Relate to Test Construction   315

How Curriculum Orientations Affect the Selection of Assessment Devices   316

Methods of Reporting Student Accomplishment   317

Combining Evaluation Data   318

An Authentic Grading System That Encourages Success   322

Using Performance Tasks to Create an Authentic Evaluation System   324

Computation of Grades   327

Writing Anecdotal Records   329

Organizing Portfolios to Document Accomplishments   330

Involving Students in Evaluation Procedures   332

References   335

CHAPTER 13   REFLECTIVE TEACHERS AND THE SCHOOL COMMUNITY   337

Two-Way Communication with Parents   338

Fall Open House   339

Parent-Teacher Conferences   340

Through the Eyes of Parents   345

Teaching and Learning in a Multicultural Community   348

Visits to Students' Homes   349

Newsletters and Notes   350

Parent Support of Educational Activities   351

Telephone Calls   351

Spring Open House and Other Special Events   352

Community Involvement in Classroom Activities   353

Parents As Volunteers   353

Community Resources   354

Character Education Programs   355

Collegial Relationships   356

Teacher Empowerment   356

Teachers Mentoring and Coaching One Another   357

References   360

NAME INDEX   363

SUBJECT INDEX   367

ABOUT THE AUTHOR   377

Reflective Action in Teaching

Walk into any classroom in any school building and you are likely to observe a teacher facing a stream of questions that need immediate responses, decisions that affect the well-being of students, value judgments that may conflict with other points of view, and complex problems that need elegant solutions. You are likely to observe the teacher fielding unexpected questions, often from children who speak a dozen different languages. In the midst of an important lesson, you will undoubtedly watch the teacher respond to a series of unplanned interruptions, including student behavior problems, intercom announcements, and unexpected visitors. As you evaluate the situation, you may think that the responsibilities teachers face are overwhelming and wonder if you have the stamina and resources necessary to become an effective teacher yourself. No one denies that teaching has its unique stresses, but for teachers who learn how to reflect on events and respond in creative, caring ways, no other career is as exciting and rewarding.

If you think that you might enjoy seeing a wide variety of innovative school projects around the globe, turn on your computer and surf the Internet to orient yourself to schools. Start searching with the key words *K–12 education*, and you are likely to be surprised and excited by the results. Many schools have their own web pages and use them to describe their communities and special programs and to highlight the contributions made by their faculty and students.

At *http://www.leap.yale.edu*, for instance, you can become acquainted with Project L.E.A.P., located in New Haven, Connecticut. L.E.A.P stands for Leadership, Education, and Athletics in Partnership. The developers have created an extracurricular educational model that pairs high school or college-age counselors with inner-city elementary school children. Each counselor is assigned four young students and is encouraged to create his or her own unique curriculum emphasizing reading, writing, math, science, and sports. Field trips are a primary emphasis of the program and may include camping trips in the wilderness as well as trips to nearby cities.

Surf over to *http://www.fred.net/nhhs/nhhs.html#* and you will meet the students and faculty at North Hagerstown High School in Maryland. As part of an interdisciplinary curriculum on the environment, the web site asks anyone who stops by to respond to the question "What environmental concerns are important in your region?" I responded to this question by describing the concerns about conserving water in the southwestern city where I live. That began a dialogue with George Cassutto, a social studies teacher at North Hagerstown High School. Although we have never met face to face or even spoken on the telephone, he e-mailed this message back to me:

We have received posts from all over the world. One post came from the Marshall Islands in the Pacific, but we get many comments from the Pacific Northwest, where the environment and the economy are in constant struggle. These data are not evenly distributed geographically, but they can be used to illustrate to the kids that some areas have more pressing concerns than others.

The web site contains a number of other on-going projects. The one that I am most involved with is an e-mail essay exchange project. This project is what started our web site. In this on-line effort, North Hagerstown students publish their essays on the web page and then receive feedback on their essays via e-mail. Internauts from all over the world can access the writings and send in their comments, and we discuss the comments in class. The students maintain folders of the reviews they receive, and they can even respond to their critics. In this way, they get independent comments from a variety of sources. One can surely take an inventory of writing and thinking skills when one receives comments saying the same thing from halfway across the globe!

Teachers' Many Roles and Responsibilities

As you begin to think about your roles and responsibilities as a teacher, you may compare them with the roles and responsibilities of your own teachers when you were in elementary school. It may occur to you that there are many differences between what you observed then and what you are seeing now. Until recently, teachers were responsible for managing their own classroom, but they rarely had any say in the decisions affecting the whole school. Ten to twenty years ago, schools provided classroom teachers with textbooks and curriculum guides prepared by other educational specialists. Now teachers are often asked to select the textbooks and other classroom materials they want to use and to take an active role in designing curriculum.

Until recently, the principal of an elementary school was likely to make most or all of the decisions regarding class scheduling, playground supervision, materials purchasing, school events planning, and hiring and evaluating new teachers. Now in many school districts, each school has a governance team made up of classroom teachers and administrators who work together to make these decisions.

As you observe and work in schools today, you are likely to hear a great deal about school reform, restructuring, systemic change, or site-based governance. These terms refer to the new emphasis on shared decision making about important and often controversial issues. In many schools, teachers are assigned to committees that must gather information, organize it, consider many alternatives, select priorities, and recommend them to the rest of their colleagues. New teachers are not exempt from this process. On the contrary, in many schools, new teachers are welcomed and given special attention because the rest of the faculty wants to hear their fresh ideas and insights into the school's complex problems.

As a new teacher, you may feel overwhelmed by the sheer number and seriousness of the decisions and choices you are asked to make. You may question your readiness for so many responsibilities so early in your career. As you observe other student teachers, interns, or first-year teachers, you may even hear a great deal of grumbling. These are some of the comments that I've heard recently:

> "I don't have time to be on another committee."
>
> "Don't they want me to have any time to work in my own classroom?"
>
> "I can't think about another thing. I've got enough to think about right now."
>
> "My husband (or wife) is really upset with the amount of time that I spend on schoolwork at home. Why don't they give us time during the day if they want us to do all this extra work?"

"I don't think I know enough to make good suggestions or recommendations about these big issues."

"How can I be expected to make so many decisions?"

For most beginning teachers, it isn't a lack of interest or caring that causes them such anguish about planning and decision making. It's just the opposite. They know that each decision they make has important consequences and thus requires a thoughtful response.

PROCESSING INFORMATION

To make thoughtful or reflective responses to new or unfamiliar questions and issues, teachers may want to familiarize themselves with the way in which the brain processes information. Cognitive psychologists argue that thinking is, first, a perceptual process. As Figure 1.1 shows, each new bit of knowledge from the environment enters the consciousness of an individual through one or more of the five senses. For example, a new fact stated by a teacher is taken in by an individual's sense of hearing. A new idea read in a book enters through the sense of sight, and a new skill such as operating the clutch and stick shift on an automobile enters the consciousness through the sense of touch. The senses register these new bits of knowledge in one-quarter of a second, and within that instant an executive function of the brain selects some bits of knowledge for retention in its *working memory* and discards other bits of knowledge entirely. This process, known as *selective perception,* is extremely important to the thinking and learning processes. We experience it simply as an initial awareness of a new fact, term, idea, or other sensation.

Why are some bits discarded while others are sent to the working memory? Psychologists have shown that we reject some stimuli when too many bombard us at one time. We can only listen to or observe so many items in a given time. When overloaded with new information, we simply disregard or don't perceive some of the data. Our brains reject other stimuli because they are so foreign to our experience that we think of them as unintelligible. When we have little or no experience with a subject, it is likely that we can consider only items that fit or match some other knowledge already stored in our brains. Finally, we all have prejudices—what cognitive psychologists call perceptual sieves. When we have made a firm judgment about a given subject, we are likely to allow into our sieves only those items or data that agree with the position we've taken.

A perceived idea, fact, or skill that is allowed to pass through our perceptual sieves reaches the working memory and stays there to be processed for less than 10 seconds. The obvious analogy with working memory is the computer. In fact, although the term *information processing* was originally coined in the field of computer technology, it is currently used to describe human thinking as well. Cognitive psychologists also use the term *cognitive processing* to describe the concept of the human mind's perceiving, sorting, organizing, storing, and recalling knowledge and information.

The stream of new information that is acted on in the working memory is again directed by an executive function of the brain into the *long-term memory* or is rejected and forgotten. A statement made by a teacher, a fact read in a book, or a process such as adding two numbers is selected either for retention into the long-term memory

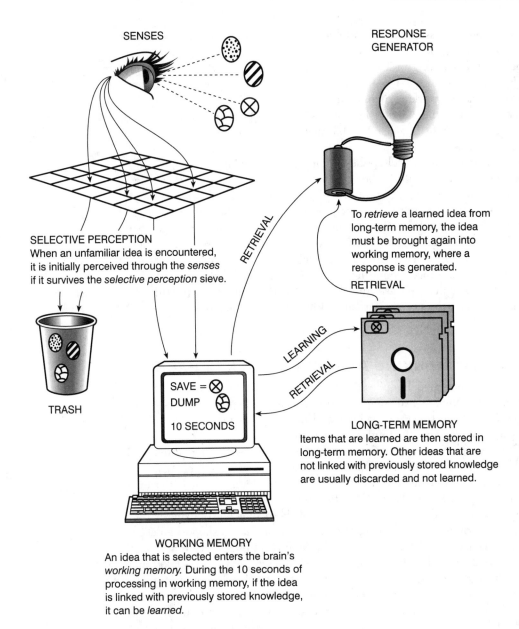

SENSES

RESPONSE
GENERATOR

SELECTIVE PERCEPTION
When an unfamiliar idea is encountered,
it is initially perceived through the *senses*
if it survives the *selective perception* sieve.

RETRIEVAL

To *retrieve* a learned idea from
long-term memory, the idea
must be brought again into
working memory, where a
response is generated.

RETRIEVAL

LEARNING

RETRIEVAL

SAVE = ⊗
DUMP ⊗
10 SECONDS

TRASH

LONG-TERM MEMORY
Items that are learned are then stored in
long-term memory. Other ideas that are
not linked with previously stored knowledge
are usually discarded and not learned.

WORKING MEMORY
An idea that is selected enters the brain's
working memory. During the 10 seconds of
processing in working memory, if the idea
is linked with previously stored knowledge,
it can be *learned.*

Figure 1.1   Information processing model.

because it is perceived as important, useful, and comprehensible or is discarded as
unimportant, useless, or incomprehensible. Another possibility is that the material is
discarded simply because the working memory has a small capacity and cannot process
many bits of knowledge at the same time.

What we call *learning* occurs after the information is processed. It refers to the
retention of knowledge in the long-term memory in such a way that it can be retrieved

at will. This retention process is analogous to storing the information on a computer disk using the "save" command.

Another part of the thinking process occurs during the *retrieval* of information stored in the long-term memory. When we call up a fact or an idea from the long-term memory, it moves back into working memory for further processing and then moves to a *response generator* where the individual considers an array of possible responses and selects the one that seems to be most suitable in the given situation. The selected response is then performed.

The information processing model applies to all kinds of thinking. Students use it when they learn new facts and skills in the classroom. Teachers use it when they assess their students' needs and consider how best to explain the new skill they are teaching.

Teachers who understand the process of acquiring and processing information can apply this knowledge in countless ways to the benefit of their students. They can reduce external stimuli so that the important bits of knowledge are perceived by their students' short-term memories. They can pace the delivery of new information to give students sufficient time to process one bit of knowledge in working memory before introducing another. They can phrase questions so that the questions provide the appropriate cue to retrieve the stored information from long-term memory.

HOW TEACHERS' THINKING AFFECTS STUDENT LEARNING

The information processing model implies that all human beings think alike—that one brain is as much like another as two computer terminals are. Of course, we know that this is not true. Human personalities, values, and philosophies must be taken into account if we want to understand the thinking process fully.

As a beginning teacher, you are undoubtedly interested in how teachers think, and you are probably even more interested in beginning to assess your own thinking attributes. Are you a rational, systematic thinker? A meditative ponderer? A quick, dynamic speculator? A moderate, calm calculator? A creative, original hypothesizer?

Before answering, you may want to know which of these styles of thinking is best suited to the teaching profession. But there is no research or data to support an accurate response to that question. I have observed successful and effective teachers who think in all of these styles and more. From my observations of dozens of schools and hundreds of teachers, the less successful and less effective teachers seem to be those who think very little, believe that very simple answers exist for every question, and think that they know it all and have all the answers. These teachers don't seem to improve their teaching over the years. They just repeat the same patterns over and over without questioning whether what they are doing or the curriculum they are teaching truly meets their students' needs. You've probably observed teachers like this, but you don't want to become one.

A growing body of knowledge supports the point of view expressed in this book: that successful, effective teachers tend to reflect actively and productively about the important things in their careers, their educational goals, the classroom environment, and their own professional abilities. They question everything, asking, "How can I do this better?" "Why isn't this working?" "Why aren't my students responding or learning more?" "What can I do to improve things in my classroom or my school?"

In classrooms that I observe, when teachers model this type of questioning—searching for knowledge and reflecting on their own performance—students often seem to behave in the same way. They ask more questions, suggest more alternatives, weigh the consequences of various options, and seem more honest in their evaluations of their own performance. Conventional wisdom has often stated that the teacher establishes the tone of the intellectual and emotional climate of a classroom. If you want your students to think critically and creatively, you must model these qualities yourself.

How will you recognize whether you are a reflective thinker with the potential of becoming a reflective teacher? This book is designed to assist you in making that assessment. You will face many dilemmas and ambiguous situations that will require you to use your thinking processes. You can monitor your own responses and processes to gain a better understanding of your capacity for reflection. You will also be provided with a model of reflective thinking that may aid you in developing your reflective thinking abilities.

The guiding assumption of this book is that reflective teachers deserve the opportunity to select from a repertoire of ideas rather than to accept and duplicate a single pattern. Therefore, this book provides you with a wide-ranging repertoire of curriculum planning ideas, teaching strategies, and evaluation methods that you can apply in the classroom.

That does not mean that all of the elements presented here agree with each other. Because this book emphasizes the right and the responsibility of the teacher to make informed decisions, it frequently presents conflicting and competing theories and ideas so you may reflect upon them and make your own judgments. Underlying the ideas presented in this text is the high value placed on encouraging you, the beginning teacher, to use reflective thinking as you consider the alternative modes and methods of teaching.

DEFINITIONS OF REFLECTIVE THINKING AND ACTION

In *How We Think: A Restatement of the Relation of Reflective Thinking to the Educative Process,* John Dewey (1933) defined reflective thinking as the "active, persistent and careful consideration of any belief or supposed form of knowledge in light of the grounds that support it" (p. 9). An analysis of this carefully worded statement evokes a powerful verbal image of the reflective thinker and correlates very well with the notion of a reflective teacher.

Dewey's first descriptive adjective, *active,* indicates a person who voluntarily and willingly takes responsibility for considering personal actions. The reflective teacher is one who actively engages in an energetic search for information and solutions to problems that arise in the classroom. In contrast, many passive teachers fail to consider issues that confront them and their students.

Dewey's use of the word *persistent* implies a commitment to thinking deeply through difficult issues, continuing to consider matters even though it may be uncomfortable or tiring to do so. Although some teachers may begin to seek knowledge and information, they may be satisfied with easy answers and simple solutions. The reflective teacher is rarely satisfied but continually and persistently seeks more knowledge and better ways to teach and manage the classroom.

The *careful* thinker is one who has concern for both self and others. Reflective teachers care deeply about ways to improve their own classroom performance and how to bring the greatest possible benefit to the lives of their students. Caring teachers create positive, nurturing classroom environments that promote high self-esteem and concern for each other among their students. Less careful teachers are likely to consider their own needs and feelings to be of greater importance than those of their students. Because they do not reason with care, they may make unreasonable demands on their students.

Dewey's phrase "belief or supposed form of knowledge" implies that little is known for sure in the teaching profession. The reflective thinker maintains a healthy skepticism about educational theories and practices. While a less reflective teacher might be persuaded that there is only one right way to teach, the reflective teacher observes that individual students may need different conditions for learning and a variety of incentives to be successful. A less reflective teacher might adopt each new educational fad without questioning its value; the reflective teacher greets each of these new ideas with an open but questioning mind, considering whether it is valuable and how it can be adapted to fit the needs of the class.

The final phrase in Dewey's definition, "in light of the grounds that support it," directly relates to the reflective thinker's practice of using evidence and criteria in making a judgment. While less reflective teachers may quickly jump to conclusions based on initial observations or prior cases, the reflective teacher gathers as much information as possible about any given problem, weighs the value of the evidence against suitable criteria, then draws a conclusion and makes a judgment. After making a decision, the less reflective teacher may stick to it rigidly, but the reflective teacher will reconsider decisions and judgments whenever new evidence or information becomes available.

But reflective thinking, even when it is persistent and careful, does not automatically lead to change and improvement. Dewey also acknowledged the importance of *translating thought into action* and specified that attitudes of open-mindedness, responsibility, and wholeheartedness are needed for teachers to translate their thoughts into reflective actions.

Schon (1987) concurs with Dewey's emphasis on action as an essential aspect of the reflective process. He defines the reflective practitioner as one who engages in "reflection-in-action," an interior observation and criticism of personal actions.

> Reflection gives rise to on-the-spot experiment. We think up and try out new actions, test our tentative understandings of them, or affirm the moves we have invented to change things for the better. On-the-spot experiment may work, or it may produce surprises that call for further reflection and experiment. (pp. 28–29)

Schon's definition endows the concept of reflectiveness with an aura of power, strength, imagination, and courage by linking it to the concept of action. He suggests that reflectivity in teaching leads to "professional artistry," a special type of competence some teachers display when they find themselves in situations full of surprise, ambiguity, or conflict. Schon believes that, just as physicians respond to each patient's unique array of symptoms by questioning, inventing, testing, and creating a new diagnosis, reflective teachers respond to the unexpected by asking questions such as "What are my students experiencing?" "What can I do to improve this situation?" "How does my students' performance relate to the way I am teaching this material?"

Often, during the process of reflection, individuals find that the new, surprising event contradicts something they already "knew." When this happens, reflective individuals can cope with paradoxes and dilemmas by reexamining what they already know, restructuring their strategies, or reframing the problem. They often invent on-the-spot experiments to put their new understandings to the test or to answer the puzzling questions that have arisen from the event.

Reflective thinking is made up of many elements and reflects an individual's willingness to explore, be curious, and be assertive to gain self-awareness, self-knowledge, and new understandings of the world. It is not something that occurs easily for most of us, and it takes time to develop.

REFLECTING ON YOUR ETHICS AND PRINCIPLES

Reflective thinking is a time-consuming practice that may involve a personal risk for the individual willing to engage in it. Personal examination of why you do something and how you can do something better and an honest look at the effects of your actions from others' points of view can result in feelings of discomfort. When you engage in reflective thinking about actions you have just taken or are about to take, you may become critical of your own behavior or your motives. Peters (1991) observed that reflective practice involves a personal risk because it requires practitioners to be open to an examination of sometimes very sensitive beliefs, values, and feelings.

When teachers are engaged in reflection about their decisions, actions, and behaviors, they are likely to begin asking themselves questions such as "Why do I have this rule?" "Why do I care so much about what happens in my classroom?" "How did I come to believe so strongly about this element of my teaching?"

When teachers ask themselves these searching questions, they may find themselves reexamining their beliefs and values. For example, if teachers have been raised and schooled in traditional settings where children were "seen but not heard" unless they were responding to a direct question from an adult, then they may expect the same type of behavior from their own students. Imagine such a teacher observing a classroom that allows students to interact, discuss their ideas with other students, and take part in very spirited discussions with the teacher. Because of past assumptions, some beginning teachers may feel very uncomfortable in a classroom with this noise level and consider the students to be rude. But if the teacher is willing and able to ask "Why am I uncomfortable with this noise level?" that self-examination may lead to further questions and hypotheses: "Is it because I was never allowed to speak up when I was a child? How did I feel about the rules when I was a child? How do I feel about them now? What are the differences in the way these children are learning and the way I learned? What do I want my future students to learn: how to be quiet and orderly or how to be curious and assertive?"

When teachers honestly confront such confusing, ambiguous questions, they are becoming "real." Honest self-reflection can improve your understanding of how your past experiences and beliefs influence your present choices and actions. Continued reflective thinking can help you clarify your philosophy of life and teaching, ethical standards, and moral code.

Do you think as a teacher you need to know what you stand for, believe, and value? Is it important that you be able to state clearly the ethical and philosophical basis for your decisions? Strike (1990) notes two important reasons why teachers ought to have a code of ethics: (1) they work with a particularly vulnerable clientele, and (2) the teaching profession has no clear set of ethical principles or standards. Strike believes the ethical concepts most central to teachers' activities are honesty, respect for diversity, fairness and due process in matters such as discipline and grading, and equity in the distribution of educational resources such as their time. Are these part of your personal code of ethics?

You probably believe your students ought to be honest, respect diversity, and be fair. If so, it is very important that you demonstrate these behaviors for them, for it is well known that teachers are important models of moral and ethical behavior for their students. As Ryan (1986) noted,

> research has now confirmed what humankind long ago recognized intuitively: People with power and prestige are imitated by those around them. And, although some teachers may not think of themselves as people with power and prestige, the children they teach certainly see them as such. Children watch their teachers to find out how grown-ups act. Therefore, teachers need to be constantly aware of the powerful influence that their actions in the classroom have on students. (p. 231)

Your students are your clients. They are quite vulnerable to the influence of their teachers' beliefs and ethics. Teachers are very important role models for behavior and character. In classrooms that I observe, the teacher's character and ethics set the standards and the tone or climate for the classroom. If the teacher is fair, students are influenced to treat others fairly. If the teacher is impulsive and selfish, students are likely to behave in the same way. When teachers demonstrate a willingness to listen openly and honestly to other points of view, students begin to respect the opinions of others as well. When teachers are closed and rigid in their approach to teaching and learning, students mold their behavior into a search for right answers and rote learning.

Kohlberg (1987) describes *moral judgments* as decisions that are based on what an individual values rather than on facts. In his studies of the development of moral reasoning, Kohlberg found that each individual has a set of beliefs about what people ought to do in various situations and what each of us considers to be right and wrong. The teacher who paddles a student may value compliance with authority over respect for students' feelings of self-esteem.

Kohlberg made the study of moral reasoning and development his life's work. His well-respected theory focuses on the concept of *justice*, which includes how people view rules, authority, fairness, and the social contract that binds individuals to society. A teacher who values justice and fairness as important moral values is likely to use these concepts as criteria when called upon to make a difficult choice. For example, imagine that a teacher promises to award the class with a pizza party if every member of the class is able to get 100 percent on a spelling test. The next week, everyone in the class appears to have achieved this goal. But the teacher discovers that one student changed the answers on the test of another classmate to gain the reward for the class. What is the teacher to do in this difficult situation? Withhold the pizza party from the test taker, the one who changed the score, or the entire class? Teachers who believe in being just and fair will struggle with this issue. There are no easy answers or solutions to the problem, but the teacher will endeavor to find the answer that is most fair or just under the circumstances.

Gilligan (1982) asserts that the feminine concepts of caring and responsibility are also essential elements of moral development. Teachers may express these qualities by show-ing respect for students' feelings and taking responsibility for meeting students' needs without shifting the blame for their low performance to other factors. Noddings (1984) emphasizes the need for ethical caring in schools because schools are places where human beings learn how to interact. She proposes that caring is the basis of the Golden Rule. Caring as a moral attribute is probably high on the list of most aspiring teachers. Many people choose a teaching career because they do care deeply about the needs of children in our society. They are also likely to feel responsible for meeting the needs of their students. Occasionally, you may observe teachers who seem to have lost the ability to care for others because they are overwhelmed with meeting their own needs. They tend to blame others when their students don't behave or achieve. Reflective, caring teachers accept that it is their responsibility to design a program that allows their stu-dents to succeed; they work every day to balance their own needs with their students'.

Other moral attributes that teachers cite as important in their personal lives and in their work with children are honesty, courage, friendliness, and firmness of purpose.

These are just a few of the many important principles and values that reflective teachers may hold. Because many are important, it is vital for you to clarify your stan-dards and then consider these priorities when you must make a choice about an issue that may bring more than one principle or value into conflict. For example, in the choice between academic excellence and developing a sense of community, you are likely to face many decision points on whether to push students toward accomplishing challenging academic tasks or to listen to their fears and frustrations about the task's level of difficulty. At this point, the reflective teacher considers which of these priorities is most important in this case and takes the appropriate action as a result.

Many textbooks reflect the principles and values of the author. This work is no exception. In it, you will find a strong emphasis on developing a sense of community in the classroom as well as planning, teaching, and evaluation strategies that promote suc-cess rather than failure among students of all achievement levels. These principles are the criteria that guided me in selecting the classroom management strategies, disci-pline models, teaching methods, examples of classroom materials, and experiences and methods of evaluation for this book.

Translated into action, this book presents a model of reflective planning, teaching, and evaluation based upon a set of clarified moral principles in the hope that education stu-dents and beginning teachers will view reflection and clarification of their moral princi-ples as one of the first and most important steps in becoming caring and effective teach-ers. Accepting this challenge will not be easy. It represents an enormous responsibility with very important consequences. As Schon (1987) suggests, many teaching actions lead to surprising outcomes, some successful and others with negative or unpleasant results. Reflective teachers are able to reflect on both positive and negative classroom experiences productively, consider what they can learn from each event, gather information to make better judgments, consider how their actions reflect their moral priorities, and then select and implement the best possible strategy under the circumstances.

Presented throughout this text are situations similar to those that teachers confront every day in their classrooms. You are asked to consider these situations and ask yourself how you would react and what you would decide or choose to do in each case. By writing journal entries regarding topics described in this book, you will examine your beliefs and defend your point of view. You are asked to observe and analyze classroom events, hypothesize cause-and-effect relationships, and look for evidence to test your hypotheses. You are asked to debate and argue educational issues with your classmates, take a stand on complex questions, and propose solutions to multifaceted problems. You are asked to make decisions and predict their consequences or to take actions and examine the consequences, looking for ways to improve the outcomes. By taking an active, persistent, open-minded, and intellectually responsible role in your present educational experiences, you can become a reflective teacher, a lifelong learner, and an agent for positive growth and change in your educational community.

A Model of Reflective Action in Teaching

Reflective thinking may occur spontaneously. Faced with a classroom dilemma, such as a student who refuses to turn in classwork or a class that challenges the teacher's grading of a test, most teachers are likely to reflect on the conditions that brought about this trouble and to consider possible actions that might improve the situation. Faced with a student who refuses to turn in classwork, the teacher may think that the contributing factors to this problem include the student's home environment, previous school experiences, or lack of readiness to learn the new material. The teacher may decide to talk to the student's parents about the problem or to have the student tested by the school psychologist.

Confronted by a class of angry students who disagree with the grades they received on a recent test, the teacher who values honest feedback is likely to reflect on the quality of teaching and the amount of preparation students had before the test. The teacher who values student success may also reconsider the suitability of the test items and the system used for determining grades. After thinking about these matters, the teacher may decide to allow students to retake the exam, rescore the present test, or stand firm on the grades as given.

In these examples, teachers are reflecting, making decisions, considering moral principles, and taking actions as a result. But is spontaneous reflection adequate in the face of the hundreds of important dilemmas and decisions teachers must make every day? Are the teacher's personal observations and insights adequate to make informed judgments, or is there a need to gather information from other informed sources?

Some current models suggest ways in which teachers can become more reflective in their practice. Some are made up of a series of strategies and practices that teachers can learn to use to improve their ability to use reflective thinking. Other proposed models are based on a systematic inquiry designed to help teachers gain more insight into their own beliefs and actions.

Schulman (1988) suggests that reflection is what a teacher does when he or she looks back at the teaching and learning that have occurred and reconstructs, reenacts, or recaptures the events, emotions, and accomplishments. Using this process, teachers can begin to develop their own capacity for reflection by systematically reviewing important teaching and learning events to recapture emotions felt by the teacher and the students and to compare the accomplishments made during this learning event with those made during other types of learning experiences.

Peters (1991) proposes a system of inquiry into teaching practices that he terms *DATA*: Describe, Analyze, Theorize, Act. Using this easy-to-remember model, teachers can learn to examine puzzling classroom events by describing them in writing or in a conversation with a colleague. Next comes a careful analysis of the event and its consequences, looking for cause and effect or patterns and relationships or trying to separate the important from the unimportant aspects of the event. After analysis, the teacher can propose theories about the event and listen to the theories of others who may have observed the event or have had similar experiences. With a theory in mind, the teacher can then consider future actions and begin to implement the one that most closely fits the analysis and theory.

As an active researcher myself, I have synthesized elements of these and other researchers with original theories that have resulted from my own experience and reflection on teaching and learning into a model of how caring and responsible teachers think and act. I use the term *reflective action* to describe this model because I believe it shows the synergistic relationship between interior thought processes and exterior actions. Teachers are actively choosing, deciding, acting, doing, and behaving every minute of the day. Figure 1.2 provides a graphic representation of the model of reflective action that I believe best illustrates the cyclical or spiraling process in which teachers continually monitor, evaluate, and revise their own practice.

PERCEPTIVENESS OF YOUR STUDENTS' NEEDS

If this model appears to be complex, that's because it *is*, just as most important elements of teaching and learning are complex. Like other types of cognitive processing (see Figure 1.1), reflective actions begin with our perceptual processes. To become a reflective teacher, you need to use all five senses plus a lively intuition to pick up cues about what is happening in your classroom and, at the same time, monitor your own feelings and be aware of the effects of your actions on your students.

This quality of being sensitive to subtle cues from students was first observed and described by Kounin (1977) when he analyzed and compared videotapes of teachers who were able to establish very smoothly functioning classrooms with those who were not. Kounin observed that the teachers whose classrooms functioned well were very perceptive of all types of cues from their students and responded to each cue in an efficient and appropriate manner. He labeled this type of perceptive behavior *withitness*. It is the first step in the cyclical pattern of reflective action in teaching. Withitness

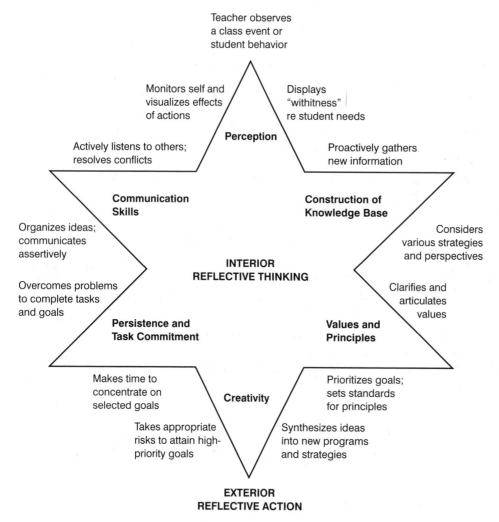

Figure 1.2   A model of reflective action in teaching.

allows teachers to perceive subtle hints of potential trouble from students in time to prevent a situation from getting too serious. Withitness also allows teachers to monitor their own behavior and actions and make changes in their own teaching strategies so that students become actively engaged in the learning process.

For example, a teacher may *see* a student behaving in an unusual or unacceptable way, *hear* softly spoken comments that hint at student needs, or *smell* an odor signaling that classroom materials are being mishandled. In these cases, the teacher can take action in a timely manner to prevent a classroom scuffle or accident. Some cues come from within. When reflective teachers experience the *taste* of bitterness or a dry mouth that accompanies fear, anger, or resentment, they can recognize their own need to step back or slow down and reflect on what is occurring to cause such strong emotions. Reflective teachers are able to *feel* many other body cues and use them to select new strategies that create a more comfortable learning environment for themselves and their students. For example, a stiff neck or a headache may signal the need to take a break from the present activity and approach the subject at another time in a new way.

Perceptive teachers can also sense the body cues of their students, picking up restlessness or other distress signals and dealing with them in ways that acknowledge their students' needs for physical movement rather than blaming them for being inattentive. Intuitive teachers are also often able to sense emotional states of their students, and are "withit" enough to be willing to select strategies that will resolve students' fears or conflicts to promote better learning.

PROACTIVE SEARCH FOR KNOWLEDGE

The next step in the cycle of reflective action is to respond to perceived cues and sensations by gathering information and building a knowledge base related to the issues or concerns. Reflective teachers are willing to be proactive in their search for information. Rather than wait passively for someone to pass on a tip that may assist them or meet their students' needs, teachers who use reflective action are continually searching for answers to questions raised by their students, new strategies to meet students' needs, and new sources of information about the subject matter they teach.

Once they have gathered a great deal of new knowledge and ideas from other teachers, books, journals, conferences, workshops, and other sources, teachers who use reflective action spend time sorting and filing the newly gathered information so they can retrieve and use it later. Beginning teachers often have to create a filing system that works for them. Gradually, their file cabinets and computer files begin to fill up with a wealth of knowledge that they can access at any time.

Gathering knowledge from outside sources is just the first half of the proactive process of development of a knowledge base. The next step in the reflective action model is for teachers to consider how to apply the new information in their own classrooms. Teachers must consider alternative strategies that they have learned about and select one or more to try out, on an experimental basis, to see how well they work. This process takes a great deal of *reflection-in-action,* thinking about how effective a strategy is while using it, and *reflection-on-action,* evaluating the effectiveness of the selected strategy after the lesson is completed and the results are in.

A reflective teacher's knowledge base, just like any good filing system, is continually updated, reorganized, and improved. Less reflective teachers may use the same strategies and the same facts and ideas over and over again, but reflective teachers are never satisfied with the status quo. They are always searching for new ways to improve their own knowledge and performance.

CLARIFICATION OF VALUES AND PRINCIPLES

Teachers using reflective action must establish criteria for which strategies to use and which to discard. They must make value decisions on a daily basis about what material to include in their lessons and what to delete. The most caring and reflective teachers are those who have clarified their own ethical standards and use them consistently as the basis for choosing what to do in their classrooms.

You have probably experienced teaching and learning situations in which teachers seem unaware of the reasons or motives for their actions. Perhaps you have been a student in a class where the rules seemed to change from day to day depending upon the teacher's mood or where students were able to bully or confuse the teacher into changing a rule or expectation because the teacher did not seem to know what he or she really believed or stood for.

Osterman (1993) observes that teachers who have never taken the time, energy, or personal risk needed to clarify what they believe and examine how well their actions fit their beliefs are often caught saying one thing and doing another. For example, you may have observed teachers who state that they expect students to respect the rights and feelings of others but then use sarcastic and hurtful remarks to "control" the class, demonstrating little respect for students' feelings.

If you want to avoid that type of situation in your classroom, then you must begin to clarify your values, assumptions, and beliefs during these early years of preparing to become a teacher. You must be willing to examine your actions and look for ways in which your small, everyday decisions reflect or do not reflect the ethical standards you have set for yourself. It is important also to realize that this process of self-examination never really ends for a reflective teacher. The best teachers I observe are still questioning their actions, searching for understanding of their motives, and gaining new insight into what they believe and value even after 20 or more years of teaching.

When teachers have taken the reflective action necessary to clarify their standards, they are often able to consider a new strategy by visualizing themselves putting it into action. Because they are so tuned-in to their students' needs and their own beliefs about what is important, they are often able to visualize the effects of the new strategy on their students and make a good judgment about how those effects match or clash with the values they want to develop. For example, when considering a new strategy for managing behavior, teachers who use reflective action can play out a scene in their minds of how their students would perceive this strategy and what their response is likely to be. This visualization, sifted through the perceptual sieve of the teacher's moral code, is likely to assist the teacher in deciding whether to try it out or not.

The goals and outcomes of the classroom are more easily written and delivered by teachers who use reflective action than by teachers who do not. While some teachers seem to be confused about what their goals should be, reflective teachers are confident that the goals they articulate for their students' learning are the "right" ones when they match the teacher's set of moral and ethical principles.

CREATIVE SYNTHESIS OF IDEAS TO FIT YOUR CLASSROOM

Reflective teachers do not rely on the library or the ideas of other teachers when they search for new knowledge and strategies to use in their classrooms. In many cases, they invent their own strategies and create their own knowledge. After considering all of the ideas they have seen, read, or heard about, teachers who use reflective action begin to adapt and change them to fit their own classrooms. In this highly creative process, teachers often invent original strategies and methods that they try out in their classrooms, refining and adapting in a very productive way.

One result of this creative process is that reflective teachers gradually begin to share their ideas with other teachers, extending the value and the power of their ideas to many more children than they will ever be able to teach in their own classrooms during their teaching careers. The sharing of creative ideas among teachers can take place quite informally over the lunch table or during a visit to another teacher's classroom. Gradually, many reflective teachers begin to develop the confidence to enjoy sharing their ideas at conferences or publishing the classroom materials they have created. They are willing to take appropriate risks to attain the goals they have set for themselves and to share what works for them with other teachers who are engaged in the same cyclical search for new knowledge and ideas.

PERSISTENCE AND PROBLEM SOLVING

Reflective teachers don't get bored easily and don't give up. Once they have identified a worthwhile goal for themselves or their students, they become committed to achieving it. With the limited time and resources they have available, teachers who use reflective actions are likely to focus on concerns they have identified as important and concentrate on those concerns until they consider them satisfactorily resolved.

As you begin to understand the different views on any classroom issue and to observe the different ways other teachers handle similar dilemmas, you are likely to encounter many problems and setbacks in achieving your goals. As a reflective teacher, you must be able to encourage yourself to keep up your interests and solve each problem as it occurs. You will gain great satisfaction as you begin to resolve problems that occur and make the gains you have visualized for yourself and your students.

One way to increase your success in problem solving and building your capacity to be persistent is to create a network of other teachers who share your values and goals. By supporting each other as you face each new dilemma, you will all grow in ways that will greatly benefit your students.

COMMUNICATION SKILLS

Even when teachers resolve an issue to their own satisfaction and select a strategy or create a plan that they are confident is a good fit for their students and their own standards and priorities, problems may arise outside of the teacher's domain. There may be conflicts within the school about how to tackle difficult problems. For example, teachers who have clarified an ethical standard of encouraging children to express their feelings and opinions and resolve conflicts through open discussion may allow this to occur in their classrooms. Other teachers, however, may disagree with this practice. A playground monitor may be angry when students from that teacher's class challenge their authority. The teacher may attend a faculty meeting where the administrators are suggesting the use of a discipline system that appears to reduce students' rights to due process and expression of their own opinions.

Teachers using reflective action must learn how to resist the strong temptation to argue aggressively or give in and accept the group's goals passively. Instead of overreacting or underreacting to outside stimuli, reflective teachers need to be able to state their case assertively, giving evidence from their own research or classroom experience to back up their claims. When they are able to organize their arguments effectively and communicate persuasively, they know that they are more likely to be successful in influencing the opinions of others who have decision-making power. They must learn to recognize that few of the issues they care most about have easy or black-and-white answers. They must be able to accept and listen to the ideas of others empathically and attempt to resolve the conflicts they encounter using negotiation skills.

When you are able to accomplish this among your own peers or with your supervisors, you will grow stronger and even more confident in your own reflective actions. As the cycle starts up again and you reflect on your own self-esteem, behavior, accomplishments, and other actions, you will be better equipped to begin the process of reflective action all over again. Your withitness skills pick up new cues that signal new areas of concern for your students. You will begin again to use reflective actions to cope with this new issue.

AN EXAMPLE OF A STUDENT TEACHER USING THE REFLECTIVE ACTION MODEL

The model of reflective action illustrated in Figure 1.2 is not something that you need to memorize to become a reflective teacher. It is meant to show my vision of how reflection and action occur cyclically among the teachers I most admire. If you ask practicing, professional teachers whether they use a model of reflective teaching to guide their thinking, they are likely to chuckle. They don't rely on patterns or models, and neither will you. However, a model can assist beginning teachers in understanding the types of processes likely to help them improve their teaching performance; that is why I present one.

Reflective teachers may not be familiar with models such as this one, but I believe that they do use the processes and elements in the reflective action model almost intuitively in their teaching and in their reflection about their teaching. To demonstrate this for myself, I interviewed Carleen Mullenix, a caring, careful, and creative student teacher whom I have had the pleasure of observing at San Diego State University. At the time of this interview she was doing her student teaching in Lori Curci's third-grade classroom at Valencia Park School in the San Diego Unified School District.

Before the interview, I had observed Carleen teach a hands-on science lesson about rocks and minerals using cooperative groups as investigative teams. She had planned the lesson to take 40 to 50 minutes, but at the end of that time, the class still had the major part of the investigation ahead of them. She had formed them into groups of four, assigned roles, reviewed what the class had already learned about rocks and minerals, discussed how to observe and record the properties of different rocks, and distributed the materials involved in testing rock samples for the mineral calcite. Suddenly it was time for recess. Carleen decided to continue the lesson after recess even though it meant putting off another subject until later.

At recess, Carleen and I talked about the lesson so far. She was not satisfied with the amount of time it had taken her to organize the cooperative groups and the material distribution. I had seen many strengths in the lesson that I pointed out to her. In my view, the time she had spent on organization of cooperative groups would pay off later because her students would have a clear understanding of that type of arrangement. I encouraged Carleen to go back and enjoy the rest of the lesson with her students. The students came back from recess refreshed and eager to resume their experiments. They tested rocks for calcite by measuring white vinegar into vials and observing four different rocks in their four vials. In cooperative groups, the students discussed and recorded their observations. The lesson ended with a class discussion on what they had observed and learned.

Afterward, Carleen and I talked at length about this lesson. We used the elements of the reflective action model as a guide for part of our discussion. In Case 1.1 she shares her thoughts and actions with you.

Case 1.1 ⊃ Reflective Action
A Teacher Thinks about Her Lesson

Carleen Mullenix, Student Teacher
San Diego State University

Perceptiveness

So many things were going on at the same time during this lesson. So much was happening. I was just trying to stay one step ahead of the game. I was feeling stressed out and thought the lesson wasn't going well. At times I thought there was no way to improve it. I try to be more animated. While I was doing the lesson I thought I was stressed and that I looked like I was stressed. I kept wondering, do I look relaxed? Do I look inviting? Do they feel free to ask me any questions that they have or are they intimidated? I hope they're not because I want them to be able to ask what's on their minds.

Proactive Search for Knowledge
(on Cooperative Learning in Science)

I need to find out how long science lessons like this are supposed to take. How long should it take to break into groups? What happens if someone spills the vinegar? I had no model for this lesson. We just started using the FOSS materials and my master teacher let me try it first. I talk to the other student teachers and they haven't used it either. I've read the resource manuals that come with the kit, but I want to see an experienced science teacher teach a lesson. A FOSS trainer did a lesson with us at a conference, but I'd like to see a teacher work with students. My master teacher was able to give me tips on managing the cooperative groups. It was her idea to use the cards to identify students' roles and responsibilities.

Clarification of Values and Principles

There are so many things I want to instill in my students that my job as a teacher often feels overwhelming. I'm not sure what I believe yet. One time I think of something as important, another time it's something else. I know that people need to be honest. I want my students to have a love of learning. That may be impossible to teach, but I try to make it happen by making my lessons interesting and guiding them to ask good questions. If they went home today and read more about rocks or brought in some rocks from their yards to test tomorrow, I'd know I had succeeded. This type of science lesson is a lot of work for me. If I were just thinking about myself, I wouldn't do it. But, I believe that it is what the students need, so I'll use it for their sakes. I believe that I have a responsibility to my students. They come first. If I keep an attitude that children come first, then the other important things will happen. Children will learn. They'll learn to respect the team atmosphere and feel a sense of security and respect themselves and each other.

Creative Synthesis of Ideas

I still shadow a lot of what my master teacher does. I use a lot of her materials and I think that's important for continuity. I have taken over the language arts and I adapt her ideas. For example, she told me to do a book about bats and I designed the book myself. With the next unit, I have free rein to come up with my own ideas. I'm willing to take risks if I believe in the payoff for students. It was a big risk to do the FOSS science unit, but I'm glad I did it.

Persistence and Problem Solving

At this point, I take things one day at a time. Except for the Native American unit, I do my planning the night before. I feel so much pressure right now from every direction. I'm still taking courses and they require work. I'm more stressed than at any other time in my life. But, I'm coping with it, and I work every night until I'm ready for the next day.

Communication Skills

I believe that I have good communication skills, especially with children. Sometimes I have to reword what I'm saying to students because I catch myself using words or phrases that are too difficult for them. I can tell by the puzzled expressions on their faces. I'm also very honest with them when I make a mistake or when I'm upset or sad. I think it's important for them to see that teachers are people too, and that they cry and laugh.

During the interview, Carleen and I analyzed how her daily thinking, decision making, and actions fit the model of reflective action. We both noticed that at the end of her reflection, when she discussed her communication skills, she noted that she "can tell by the puzzled expressions on their faces" when her students don't understand what she is saying. This reflection brought us right back to the top of the reflective action star, where she is using her perceptiveness to gather information from her students. That illustrates very well the cyclical nature of reflective actions. Each action brings about a reaction that creates a new opportunity for reflection.

Questions that enhance perceptiveness and withitness

What am I feeling about the present event? Why do I feel this way?
How do my feelings and needs govern my actions in class?
How do my students see me and perceive my actions?
What does my body language show to my students?
What are my students experiencing from this event?
What does this student need from me right now?
Why are students showing this behavior?
What do I expect from my students? Am I being realistic?

Questions that develop a proactive search for information

What information do I need right now?
What can I learn from my colleagues?
Which of my colleagues is likely to have information I need?
Who else can I ask about this?
What books or articles are available on this subject?
How could a reference librarian help me find what I need?
How could the school librarian help me?
What other teaching materials are available on this subject?
Where can I learn new teaching strategies to use?
What conferences are coming up on this topic?
How can I approach the principal to get support for my search?

Questions that help clarify your values and moral principles

What are the values and principles that guide my life?
Are these the same principles that guide my classroom decisions?
What do I believe children need to succeed in school and life?
Am I meeting those needs in my classroom?
What attitudes do I want my students to have at the end of the year?
What values do I model for my students with my own behavior?
Are those values consistent with the ones I believe in?
What is the most important goal I have for myself this year?
What is the most important goal I have for my students this year?

Figure 1.3   Questions teachers ask themselves using reflective actions.

Questions that encourage your creativity

How can I adapt the materials available to me to meet my goals?
How can I create new teaching materials to meet my goals?
How can I adapt the teaching strategies I've learned to fit me?
What risks are there in trying new strategies or materials?
Am I willing to take those risks?
What gains are possible if I try new strategies or materials?
Do the possible gains outweigh the risks in this instance?
What new challenge do I want to set for myself this year?

Questions that promote persistence and task commitment

What goals am I most interested in working on this year?
Am I motivated enough by this interest to complete the task?
How can I make time for myself to reach my goals this year?
What will I have to give up or put aside to reach my goals?
What can I do to recognize and deal with roadblocks on my path?
Who can assist me in reaching my goals? How can they help?
When I visualize reaching my goal, what are the rewards?
When I visualize my goal, what tasks do I still have to accomplish?
How can I organize those tasks to fit the time remaining?

Questions that improve your communication skills

How can I organize my ideas to make them comprehensible?
How can I learn whether my ideas are clearly understood?
To whom do I need to communicate my ideas to achieve my goal?
What data or evidence do I need to be more persuasive?
How can I learn to communicate better with parents?
What do I want to say to my colleagues about the goals I value?
Am I assertive in my communications?
When I am not assertive, do I tend toward passivity or aggression?
What can I do to become more consistently assertive?
How can I learn to resolve conflicts with students in my class?
How can I express my own needs and feelings to my class?

Figure 1.3 *continued*

Reflective teachers are responding to the needs of our society by considering them as opportunities for reflective action. They recognize the value of the service they perform in educating our nation's young people. Through continuing education, they increase their knowledge and skills in teaching and learning throughout their careers. They reflect upon the decisions they make and take responsibility for the consequences of their actions. They work with their teachers' associations or school committees to develop standards for professional competency and growth.

This is an exciting time to be a teacher. As a career, teaching offers individuals the opportunity to fulfill their own needs for achievement, recognition, and meaningful contribution as they meet the needs of the students they teach. Teaching is also among the most creative of all careers. Teachers create new learning experiences, materials, organizational systems, and interactions every day of the school year. This book is designed to assist you in developing your own reflectiveness and building a repertoire of teaching strategies to enhance your professional growth. In turn, I hope you will apply your reflective actions by taking an active, professional role in every aspect of your school community.

If you would like to ask yourself the types of questions reflective teachers ask themselves, you may refer to Figure 1.3.

⊃ Reflective Actions for Your Professional Portfolio
Your Philosophy of Teaching

Many beginning teachers create portfolios of their professional experiences and accomplishments in educational settings. At the end of each chapter, you will find ideas for recording your philosophy, describing your achievements, and demonstrating your reflective actions for a professional portfolio that communicates your unique talents and teaching style to prospective employers.

Perceptiveness: Classroom Environments

Visit a classroom and use all your senses to observe and describe how the teacher uses space and other resources. How are the students' desks arranged? Where is the teacher's desk? Does the room feel crowded or spacious? Are there activity spaces? If so, for what purpose are they used? Observe and describe the use of light, color, and decorations. What do you hear when you walk into this classroom? How does the room smell? Are there any tastes associated with your visit? Would you like to be a student in this room? Why or why not? Take photos or draw a sketch of this classroom and include them in your portfolio, along with your written reflections. Draw another sketch of how you would arrange this classroom to make it fit your preferences.

Construction of Knowledge Base: Gather Information

Ask yourself, "How does the classroom environment demonstrate one's philosophy of teaching?" Discuss your question with other colleagues. Read articles or books about the effects of various physical arrangements on students' sense of well-being and motivation. List the books and articles that you have found valuable in an appendix or bibliography in your portfolio.

Clarification of Values: Reflect on Your Moral and Ethical Code

Brainstorm with a colleague to create a list of moral and ethical attributes that are highly valued by humankind (examples: honesty, courage, fairness, and so on). Then select four to six of those attributes that represent the attributes that you value most. Describe how your classroom environment will represent these values.

Creativity: Designing Your Classroom Environment

Teaching is a very creative career. Some of the creative talents that teachers use include art, music, interior design, drama, photography, and cartooning. What are some creative talents that you use to create a unique and welcoming classroom environment for your students? Include photographs of the bulletin boards, centers, or class projects that you have designed to enhance your classroom environment.

Persistence and Communication: Articulate Your Philosophy of Teaching

Write a paragraph or two about why each value you identified is important to you and how you will attempt to model and teach those concepts to your students. Consider this paper a first draft. Revise and refine it as the year goes by. The final draft goes in your portfolio.

References

Bell, M. (1990). *Everyday mathematics first grade teachers' manual.* Evanston, IL: Everyday Learning.

Dewey, J. (1933). *How we think* (rev. ed.). Lexington, MA: D. C. Heath.

Gilligan, C. (1982). *In a different voice.* Cambridge, MA: Harvard University Press.

Kohlberg, L. (1987). *The measurement of moral judgment.* Vol. 1: *Theoretical foundations and research validation.* London: Cambridge University Press.

Kounin, J. (1977). *Discipline and group management in classrooms.* New York: Holt, Rinehart, & Winston.

Noddings, N. (1984). *Caring: A feminine approach to ethics and moral education.* Berkeley: University of California Press.

Osterman, K. (1993). *Reflective practice for educators: Improving schooling through professional development.* Newbury Park, CA: Corwin.

Peters, J. (1991). Strategies for reflective practice. *Professional and Continuing Education, 51,* 83–102.

Ryan, K. (1986). The new moral education. *Phi Delta Kappan, 67,* 228–233.

Schon, D. (1987). *Educating the reflective practitioner.* San Francisco: Jossey-Bass.

Schulman, L. (1988). Knowledge and teaching foundations of the new reform. *Harvard Educational Review, 57,* 1–22.

Strike, K. (1990). The legal and moral responsibility of teachers. In J. Goodlad, R. Soder, & K. Sirotnik (Eds.), *The moral dimensions of teaching* (pp. 188–223). San Francisco: Jossey-Bass.

Planning a Healthy, Safe Environment for Learning

When you walk into a classroom, you can sense a particular climate or environment within a few moments. A multitude of sensory images enters your consciousness—sights, sounds, and smells, for the most part. The way the room is arranged, its messiness or neatness, wall decorations, movements and noises made by the students, and the smell of chalk dust or an animal cage all combine to create a unique flavor or climate in the classroom. The behavior, body language, and facial expressions of the teacher and students give you the most important clues about what life is like in this classroom. You may sense healthy elements such as excitement, energy, joy, cooperation, and pride, or you may sense debilitating elements such as fear, aimlessness, frustration, and tension. These are all components of the classroom environment, which is largely established by the teacher during the first days and weeks of the school year.

This chapter describes in some detail what reflective teachers think about and how they make decisions to promote a healthy classroom climate that encourages student achievement and satisfaction. It also describes how reflective teachers think about the psychosocial environment of their classrooms and how they carefully structure classroom expectations and incentives to promote enduring patterns of achievement and interest in school.

A Good Beginning for the School Year

Studies show that it is the teacher who establishes the particular climate of each classroom. Given identical classrooms in the same school, identical materials and resources, and the same clientele, each teacher creates a unique learning environment based on a unique set of expectations, beliefs, attitudes, knowledge, effort, and repertoire of teaching strategies and skills. You have experienced the power of the teacher for many years as a student. It is likely that you still enter every classroom on the first day of a new course hoping that the teacher will be interesting, fair, knowledgeable, and caring.

Many people think that inner-city schools serving less affluent students are deadly and sterile, while suburban schools serving middle-class students are vital and stimulating. In reality, though, within each school a great variety of classroom environments exist. Talented, caring, and reflective teachers in inner-city schools can and do make learning a joyful experience, and their classrooms shine with goodwill, understanding, wit, and creativity. There are, however, just as many careless, nonreflective teachers in rural areas and in the suburbs as there are in the inner cities. In any environment, such teachers give little thought to their job or to their classrooms, which are dull with anxiety, disorder, anger, and despair.

Unfortunately, great social and economic disparities exist in the world. Children, who have not created these differences, are their victims. Historically, school has been the great equalizer, the means to rising out of poverty, the chance to make the most of one's potential. Reflective, caring, and creative teachers know they can make a significant difference in students' lives, and they work especially hard at creating a positive, healthy classroom environment to counteract the effects of poverty, discrimination, and neglect.

ORGANIZING THE PHYSICAL ENVIRONMENT

The classroom appearance makes a statement about the extent to which the teacher cares for the environment in which the class lives and works. It may be untidy, neat, colorful, drab; filled with objects, plants, animals, and children's art or left undecorated and unkempt. No two classrooms are alike; each has its unique environment. However, some classrooms (and their occupants) bloom with health, vitality, and strength, while others appear sickly, listless, and debilitated.

Studies of teacher planning show that during the days immediately preceding the school year, teachers are primarily concerned with setting up the physical environment of the classroom. Reflective teachers want to come to school several days before their contracts call for them to be there. They hang posters, decorate bulletin boards, and carefully consider ways to arrange the students' desks, tables, bookcases, and other furniture to fit their curriculum plans and the needs of their students. You know from the many years you have spent in classrooms as students that a bright, colorful, cheerful, and stimulating classroom leads you to expect that school will be interesting and that the teacher celebrates life and learning. You also know that drab, undecorated spaces lead to expectations of dullness and boredom.

How to arrange the desks is a complex issue. Often the room contains many more desks than it was designed to hold comfortably. The number of students in a classroom may vary from 15 to 35, and the precise number of students is not known until the last minute, making preplanning difficult. Generally, though, teachers know approximately how many students they will have in their classrooms, and they set about arranging the desks in a way that uses space economically and strategically. Their plans are governed by an image of themselves and their students in teaching and learning experiences.

While arranging the classroom, reflective teachers envision its "activity flow"—what it will be like when the classroom is filled with students. This imaging process helps reflective teachers decide how to arrange the furniture in the room. As with other important decisions, each option has both advantages and disadvantages. Desks can be arranged in rows, circles, semicircles, and small groups. Each arrangement influences how students work and how they perceive their environment. Rows of desks provide an advantage in keeping order but leave little space for activities (Figure 2.1). A large circle of desks can be used if the teacher envisions that teaching and learning experiences will take place in the center of the circle, but it will be difficult for all students to see the chalkboard (Figure 2.2).

Doyle (1986) reports that open (nonrow) arrangements result in students' spending more time working together, initiating their own tasks, and working without teacher attention when compared with students in traditional rooms. Teachers who value cooperative group learning experiences over teacher-centered learning experiences often use clusters of four to six desks (Figure 2.3).

Jones (1987) recommends organizing the classroom into shallow concentric circles, no more than three rows deep (Figure 2.4). In this setting, the teacher can maintain eye contact with all students and is able to move quickly to the side of any student who needs assistance or a reminder to pay attention. The increased physical proximity allows the teacher to circulate more easily to provide individual help.

Activity and work spaces can be arranged by using bookcases and room dividers or simply by arranging tables and chairs in the corners of the room. Some teachers bring in comfortable furniture and rugs to design a space just for quiet reading. Computer or lis-

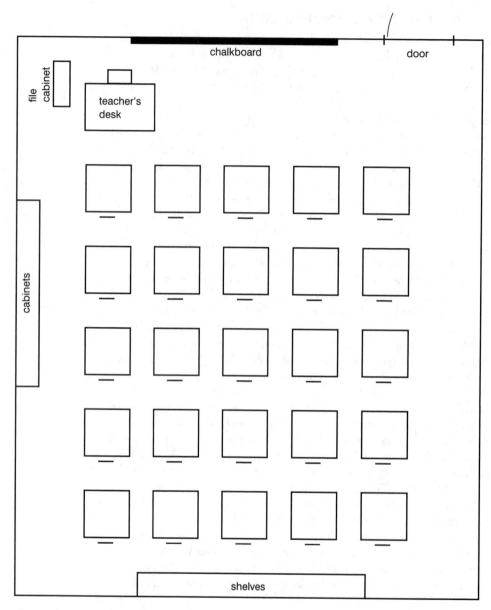

Figure 2.1 Classroom arrangement: Rows of desks.

tening stations must also be designated. Room arrangement and the use of space are highly individualized decisions. Teachers make these decisions to fit their personal image of what a classroom should be, by considering what they value most highly and how the room arrangement fits their values as well as the curriculum and grade level of the class.

Reflective teachers also consider the effects of the physical arrangement of the room on developing a healthy classroom environment. Rows of desks connote order and effi-

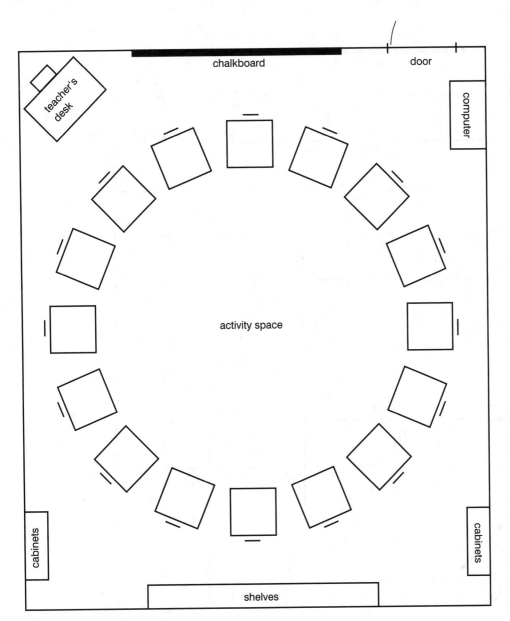

Figure 2.2   Classroom arrangement: Circle of desks.

ciency but do little to build a sense of community. Clusters of desks promote cooperation and communication among groups of students. Large circle or concentric circle
arrangements encourage communication and sharing among the entire class. Many
reflective teachers change their room arrangements depending on the goals of a particular learning experience and thus create a variety of classroom environments to fit a
variety of purposes.

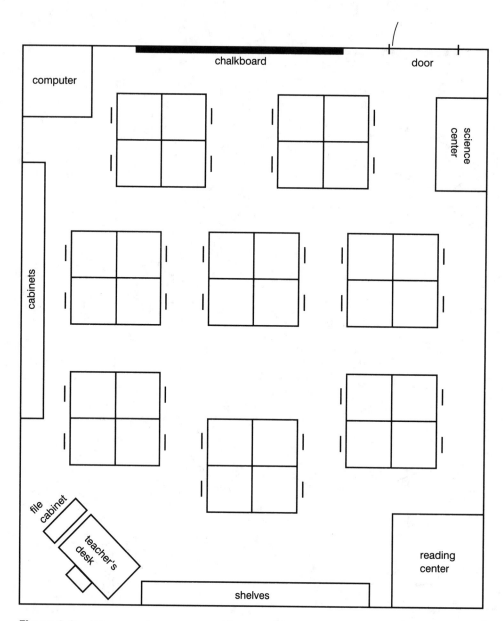

Figure 2.3   Classroom arrangement: Clusters of desks.

THE FIRST DAY OF SCHOOL

The physical environment and schedule of the classroom may lead students to expect certain things about the way teaching and learning will occur during the school year. These expectations are reinforced even more strongly during the first few minutes of the first day of school. For example, consider the students' experience on their first day of school in the following elementary and high school classroom scenarios.

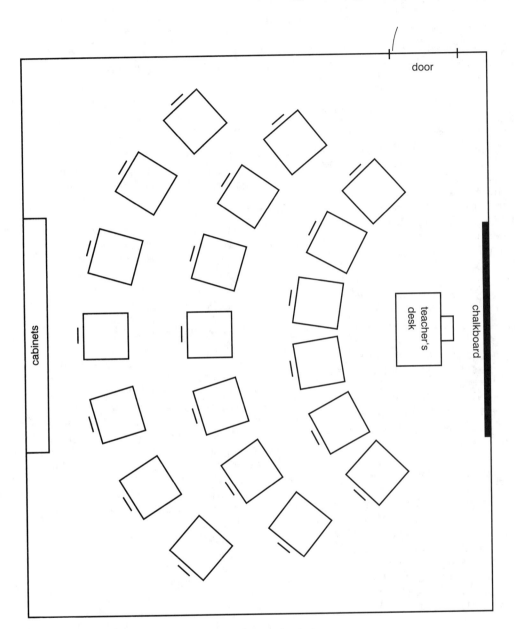

Figure 2.4   Classroom arrangement: Concentric circles.

   You can probably recognize the teachers in these opening day scenarios and can give them names and faces from your own experiences in school. You have been exposed to a variety of teaching styles, methods, attitudes, and philosophies as consumers of education. Now you will soon become teachers yourselves. What style will you have? How will your students perceive you? What values and principles will you model? How will your students feel when they walk into your classroom on the first day of school?

The scene is an elementary school. It is the first day of the new school year. In one corridor, several classroom doors are open. We see and hear four teachers greet the students in their classes.

Room 101

Miss Adams is standing at the doorway. As children walk in, she says, in a calm, even-toned voice, to each of them, "You'll find your name on a desk," as she gestures toward six clusters of desks. "Sit in that desk and wait quietly." The children obey and the room is quiet within. When all the children have entered, Miss Adams goes into her classroom and quietly shuts the door behind her. The beginning bell rings at precisely that moment.

Room 102

Mr. Baron is nowhere to be seen. Children enter the classroom looking for him, but when they don't see him, they begin to talk and walk around the room. The desks are arranged haphazardly in ragged rows. Two boys try to sit in the same desk, and a scuffle breaks out. The beginning bell rings. Suddenly Mr. Baron comes running down the hall, enters the room yelling, "All right, you guys, sit down and be quiet. What do you think this place is? A zoo?"

Room 103

Mr. Catlin is standing at the door wearing a big smile. As each child enters, he gives the child a sticker with his or her name on it. "Put this sticker on a desk that you like and sit in it," he says. The children enter and quickly claim desks, which are arranged in four concentric arcs facing the front of the room. They talk with each other in the classroom. When the bell rings, Mr. Catlin enters, leaving the door ajar for latecomers.

Room 104

Mrs. Destry is sitting at her desk when the children enter. Without standing up, she tells the children to line up along the side of the room. They comply. When the bell rings, she tells a student to shut the door.

If we were able to enter the classrooms with the students, this is what we might see, hear, and experience after the beginning bell ceased.

Room 101

Miss Adams stands in front of the class. She has excellent posture and a level gaze. As she waits quietly for the children to find their seats, she looks at each child eye to eye. They settle down quickly. When the classroom is perfectly quiet, she begins to talk.

"I see that you have all found your desks. Good. Now we can begin. I like the way you have quieted down. That tells me that you know how to behave in school. Let's review some of the important rules of our classroom."

Pointing to a chart entitled "Class Rules," she reads each aloud and tells the children its significance. "Rule 1: Students will pay attention when the teacher is speaking. This is important because we are here to learn and there can be no learning if you do not hear what the teacher is saying. Rule 2: Students will use quiet voices when talking in the classroom. This rule is important because a quiet, orderly classroom is conducive to learning. Rule 3: No fighting, arguing, or name calling is allowed."

The children listen attentively to all items. They do not ask questions or comment on the rules. After the rules are read, Miss Adams assigns helpers for class jobs. The newly appointed monitors pass out the reading books, and the children begin to read the first story in their books. Miss Adams walks quietly from desk to desk to see that each child is reading.

Figure 2.5 The first day of elementary school scenario.

Room 102

Mr. Baron rushes in and slams some books and papers on the desk. Some of them land on the floor nearby. Stooping to pick them up, he says, "Sit down, sit down, or I'll find cages for you instead of desks." The children sit down, but the noise level remains high.

"Enough! Do you want to begin the school year by going to the principal's office? Don't you care about school? Don't you want to learn something?" Gradually, the noise diminishes, but children's voices continue to interrupt from time to time with remarks to their teacher or to fellow classmates.

Mr. Baron calls roll from an attendance book. He does not even look up when a child says "Here" but stares intently at the book. He has several children pass out books at one time, resulting in more confusion about whether children received all the necessary books. Finally, he tells them to begin reading the first story in their reading books. Some do so, others do not. Mr. Baron begins looking through his file cabinet, ignoring the noise.

Room 103

Mr. Catlin walks throughout the room as he talks to the class. From time to time, he stops near a child and puts his hand on the child's shoulder, especially a child who appears restless or insecure. This action seems to help the child settle down and pay attention.

"Welcome back to school! This year should be a good one for all of us. I've got some great new ideas for our math and social studies programs, and we'll be using paperback novels to supplement our reading series. But first, let's establish the rules for our classroom. Why are we here?"

A student raises her hand. Mr. Catlin reads the name tag sticker on her desk and calls on her by name. "To learn," she says timidly.

"Exactly!" Mr. Catlin agrees. "And, what rules can help us to learn the most we've ever learned in a single year?"

Several children begin to call out responses at the same time.

"Wait a moment, class. Can we learn anything like this?"

A chorus of "No's" is heard.

"Then what rule do we need to solve this problem?"

A child raises his hand, is called on, and says, "We need to raise our hands before we talk."

"What a fine rule," Mr. Catlin says with a broad smile. "How many agree?" The hands of most children go up. Mr. Catlin spots one child whose hand is not raised. He walks over to that child, kneels next to the child's desk and says, "Do you agree that this rule will help you learn this year?" "Yes," says the child and his hand goes up.

After the class has established and agreed on several other class rules, Mr. Catlin talks about the reading program. He offers the children a choice among five paperback novels, distributes them, and tells the children to begin reading. As they read, he circulates around the room, stopping from time to time to ask questions or make comments about the stories to individual children.

Room 104

Mrs. Destry regards the children in their line with an unfriendly gaze. When a child moves or talks, she gives that child a withering stare. From a class list, she begins to read the students' names in alphabetical order, indicating which seat they are to take. The students sit down meekly. No one says a word or makes a sound.

"Now, class, you will find your books in your desks. Take out your reading books and turn to the first page." Going down the rows, each child reads a paragraph aloud while the other children sit silently and listlessly, following along in their books.

Figure 2.5 *Continued.*

The scene is a high school. It is the first day of the new school year. In one corridor, several classroom doors are open. We see and hear two teachers greet their classes.

Room 205

Mr. Evans is waiting at the front door, welcoming his students. The students enter the classroom and can be heard saying, "Hello, Mr. E." Mr. Evans says hello and that he's glad to have each student in class. He tells them to locate their seats by looking at the overhead in the front of the room. He has a seating chart shown on the overhead. Students begin to sit down and talk about their summer experiences.

After the bell rings, Mr. Evans walks to the center of the room and waits for quiet. The students look up and begin to prepare themselves for Mr. Evans's beginning remarks. One bulletin board in the front of the room is completed in the school colors and includes a picture of the school mascot, a pennant, and words from the fight song. The other bulletin board is filled with mathematical symbols and sayings by famous mathematicians. Along the top of the chalkboard is a set of very colorful geometric designs.

A set of rules is posted conspicuously on one of the walls of the room:

Rule 1: Respect each other.
Rule 2: Participate in class.
Rule 3: Help one another.
Rule 4: Everyone tries 100%.

Mr. Evans begins by saying, "Welcome to the best high school in the city. I hope each student has found his or her seat using the chart on the overhead. I believe that it is important that you know how to use such items as charts and graphs. I like to take every opportunity to use mathematics in my classroom. In addition, I would like to review the rules of this classroom. If you have any questions related to the rules, we should discuss them immediately. If you have suggestions for any additional rules, we may want to include them in the initial set of rules I've listed."

Room 206

Mr. Green leaves the teacher's lounge about 30 seconds before class starts. When he arrives at his classroom, the bell rings. Some students are still outside talking with friends. Mr. Green yells at the students to "get inside or I'll begin writing detention slips on the first day." The students begin to take seats or lean against the side shelves.

As you look around the classroom, there is nothing on any of the bulletin boards. Student books are stacked on the side shelves. They are obviously ready to be distributed to the class.

Mr. Green tells the students to "shut up" so that he can call the roll and tell students where their seats are going to be. He stands behind a podium and begins to call names and assign seats. As students go to their seats, they continue talking among themselves. Frequently, Mr. Green calls for silence, but the noise level does not diminish very much.

After the students are seated, Mr. Green complains that this is a bad beginning to the school year and warns the students again that he is not afraid to send them to detention if they don't know how to behave. He has used this tactic in the past, and he will use it with this class if necessary.

With no discussion of goals, rules, or expectations, Mr. Green appoints some of the boys to pass out the textbooks and writes, "Read Chapter 1" on the chalkboard. Some students begin to read, while others continue to talk with each other. Mr. Green gets out his detention slips and begins to write names on them.

Figure 2.6 The first day of high school scenario.

Each scenario depicts a variation of what is termed *teaching style*. A teaching style is a highly individualized and complex concept made up of personality, philosophy, values, physical and emotional health, past experiences, and current knowledge about the effects of a teacher's behavior on the classroom environment.

Perhaps you may be considering the important question, "Is it possible to control and decide on my teaching style, or is it simply a function of my personality?" The more information you can gather about how teachers create healthy climates for learning, the more power you have to gain self-understanding and control over this and other important matters pertaining to teaching and learning. Evertson (1989) has demonstrated that when teachers learn to examine their own practices and behaviors, they can learn to use the more productive and positive classroom practices and discontinue less effective methods.

To identify the most effective classroom management strategies, Emmer, Evertson, and Anderson (1980) conducted a study about how teachers begin the school year and establish their expectations with students. They were especially interested to learn how teachers who are effective classroom managers begin the school year. They hoped to discover some basic principles of effective classroom management that could be taught to beginning teachers. They selected 27 third-grade classrooms in eight elementary schools for their study. Observers were present in each of these classrooms during the first few weeks of school. Using criteria for effective management developed by the team of observers, the 27 teachers were classified into two categories: more effective and less effective classroom managers.

Both groups of teachers had rules and procedures planned for their classes. What distinguished the more effective managers from the others was that they spent a major part of the first day and much time during the next three weeks helping their students adjust to their classroom expectations and learn to understand the rules and procedures established for the class. Like Miss Adams and Mr. Catlin, the teachers began describing their carefully planned rules and procedures as soon as most students had arrived at the classroom. In some cases, but not always, students were asked to suggest rules for the class. The rules and procedures were explained clearly, with examples and reasons.

More effective managers did not rely simply on a discussion of the rules. They spent a considerable amount of time during the first week of school explaining and reminding students of the rules. One of the most effective way to communicate your expectations to your class is to lead them through a rehearsal on how to follow the procedures. Teachers take time to rehearse procedures such as how to line up for lunch or what to take out of their desks for math class. Many teachers teach students to respond to specific signals, such as a bell or a hand signal to call for attention. Emmer et al. (1980) observed, "In summary, the more effective managers clearly established themselves as the classroom leaders. They worked on rules and procedures until the students learned them. Teaching content was important for these teachers, but they stressed, initially, socialization into the classroom system. By the end of the first three weeks, these classes were ready for the rest of the year" (p. 225).

The reflective teacher, guided by moral principles, also recognizes that it is not simply a matter of establishing leadership that is important; the style of leadership counts as well. Miss Adams, Mr. Catlin, and Mr. Evans quickly established that they were the classroom leaders, but Mr. Catlin's style of leadership best exhibited the underlying moral principles of caring, consideration, and honesty as he interacted with his students. The result is that students in such an environment return the caring, consideration, and honesty to the teacher and exhibit it in their interactions with one another.

In contrast, less effective managers (exemplified by Mr. Baron and Mr. Green) did not have well-thought-out procedures. Although teachers like Mr. Baron always have rules, the rules are often vague and the teachers tend to tell the class the rules and procedures quickly without spending time discussing and rehearsing what they really mean. Others, like Mrs. Destry, try to move quickly to academic matters. They seem to expect the students to be able to comprehend and retain the rules from a single, brief statement. They do not teach the class routines and procedures. As a result, they are often found to waste many, many hours of class time during the year as they remind the students again and again to behave.

The way the two groups of teachers monitor the behavior of their students is also a critical factor in establishing a clear set of expectations for students. The Emmer study disclosed that less effective teacher-managers did not actively monitor students' behavior. Instead, they busied themselves with clerical tasks or worked with a single student on a task while ignoring the rest of the class. The consequence of vague and untaught rules and poor monitoring was that the children were frequently left without enough information or a good enough example to guide their behavior.

From this study, you can conclude that if you expect your students to obey the rules of your classroom, you must give them clear directions, allow them to rehearse the procedures until they get it right, and actively observe while your students work, showing them that you expect them to pay attention to the task and do their work.

Preventive Discipline Strategies

TEACHERS' BODY LANGUAGE

Jones (1987) found that effective classroom management and control of student behavior depend a great deal on the teacher's body language. Strong, effective teachers are able to communicate many important things with eye contact, physical proximity, bodily carriage, gestures, and facial expressions. These teachers do not have to be 6 feet, 5 inches tall and weigh 230 pounds. It is fascinating to observe teachers who are small in stature control classrooms with a glance by standing next to a student who is disturbing the classroom.

Consider the eye contact of the teachers in the first day of school scenario. Miss Adams had a level gaze and met the students' eyes as she looked at each of them at their first meeting. She communicated that she was aware and in control in a positive, nonthreatening manner. Mr. Evans made immediate eye contact with each student in a positive way and demonstrated enthusiasm for the school where he teaches and the students themselves. Mrs. Destry gave the students withering stares that probably caused them to feel anxious and fearful about the year ahead. Mr. Baron and Mr. Green never met the eyes of their students at all, communicating their lack of preparation and confidence to manage the classroom.

Mr. Catlin used *physical proximity* as well as eye contact to put his students at ease and to communicate that he was in charge. Jones (1987) recommends the concentric circle desk arrangement that Mr. Catlin used because it causes students to focus their attention on the teacher and enables the teacher to provide help efficiently by moving quickly to the side of any student who is having difficulty. By moving close to the restless student and placing a hand on the student's shoulders, he can help them allay their fears and turn the focus to the classroom activity. Room arrangement can help or hinder a teacher's ability to control children's behavior. To use physical proximity effectively, the teacher must be able to step quickly to the side of the misbehaving student, as Mr. Catlin did.

The strong, straight posture of Miss Adams reinforced the students' perception that she was an authority worthy of their respect. Good posture and confident *bodily carriage* convey strong leadership, while a drooping posture and lethargic movements convey weakness, resignation, or fearfulness (Jones, 1987).

Gestures are also a form of body language that can communicate positive expectations and prevent problems. Teachers can use gestures to mean "stop," "continue," or "quiet, please" without interrupting the verbal instruction. When used with positive eye contact, physical proximity, bodily carriage, or facial expression, gestures can prevent small disruptions from growing into major behavior problems.

Facial expressions vary greatly among teachers. They can show enthusiasm, seriousness, enjoyment, and appreciation, all of which encourage good behavior; or they can reveal boredom, annoyance, and resignation, which may tend to encourage misbehavior (Jones, 1987). Facial expressions that display warmth, joy, and a sense of humor are those that students themselves report to be the most meaningful. Candidates training to be teachers may even want to look in the mirror at their own expressions to discover how students see them when they are happy, angry, feeling good about themselves, or upset.

WITHITNESS

Kounin (1977) videotaped classrooms in action to discover the differences between well-managed, smoothly functioning classrooms and ill-managed, poorly functioning ones. Although he expected to find that smoothly functioning classrooms followed certain rules and discipline strategies, he found no such relationship. Instead, he found that the most smoothly functioning classrooms were those led by a teacher whose management style demonstrated a high degree of alertness and the ability to pay attention to two things at the same time.

Kounin labeled this teacher characteristic *withitness*. The good managers he observed knew what was going on in their classrooms at all times. They were aware of who was working and who was not. They were also able to *overlap* their instruction with their monitoring of student behavior. As a result, they were able to alter a presentation at the first sign of restlessness or boredom. If a minor disruption occurred between students, the teacher perceived it immediately and was likely to move a student or otherwise prevent the disruption from growing.

Withitness is expressed more through teacher perceptiveness and behavior than through words. Eye contact, facial expressions, proximity, gestures, and actions such as stopping an activity demonstrate teacher withitness to students. These teachers are able to continue teaching a lesson while gesturing to a group or standing next to an overactive student who needs to refocus on the lesson. These are examples of the concept of overlapping, in which the teacher is able to deal with both the behavior and the lesson at the same time.

Kounin also studied what he calls the *ripple effect*, a preventive discipline strategy that he found to be particularly useful in elementary classrooms. Kounin observed a student in his own college class reading a newspaper during the lecture. When Kounin reprimanded the student, he observed that his remarks caused changes in behavior among the other members of the class as well. "Side glances to others ceased, whispers stopped, eyes went from windows or the instructor to notebooks on the desk" (1977, p. 1). In subsequent observations in kindergarten classrooms, Kounin found that when teachers spoke firmly but kindly to a student, asking that student to desist from misbehavior, the other students in the class were also likely to desist from that behavior as well. When teachers spoke with roughness, however, the ripple effect was not as strong. "Children who witnessed a teacher desist another child with anger or punitiveness did not conform more nor misbehave less than those witnessing a teacher desist another without anger or punitiveness" (p. 10).

Teacher withitness is an essential attribute of reflective teaching. The model of reflective action in teaching presented in this book begins with it: observing conditions and gathering information to make good judgments. Withitness raises the quality and level of reflective thinking because it raises the accuracy of teachers' observations and results in more complete collection of information about classroom conditions. Reflective teachers are always monitoring students' reactions to classroom events, and they are ready to respond when students show confusion or boredom. Reflective teachers actively monitor students during group activities and independent seatwork, looking for signs that students need clarification of the task or the teacher's expectations.

Can withitness be learned? I believe so. If you are willing to examine the cause-and-effect relationships in your classroom honestly and search for reasons for students' misbehavior, you are likely to develop your withitness in the process. If you are willing to ask other adults to observe your interactions with students and give you feedback on how you respond to various situations, you will be able to make changes and improve the quality of your withitness radar and responses. If you are willing to discuss classroom problems openly and honestly with your students, in a problem-solving manner, you are likely to learn from them what their signals mean.

As an example, I once visited a second-grade classroom in which a teacher planned the morning activities to go from reading to math to science without a break. By the time the teacher asked the students to put away their math books and take out their science books, the grumbling and murmuring and shuffling feet had grown to intolerable proportions. With no trace of withitness, this teacher's voice went higher and higher as she scolded the children and told them to be quiet and listen, keep their hands and feet quiet, sit up and pay attention over and over again until lunchtime. A reflective, caring teacher using withitness as a tool would have perceived that the problem could be easily solved by allowing the children to move and stretch for a few minutes before starting another lesson.

Principals and supervising teachers often note that withitness grows with experience. Few first-year teachers exhibit consistent and accurate withitness. Teachers gradually develop it as they actively reflect on the effects of their actions and decisions on their students' behavior.

A beginning teacher may gradually become aware that lessons are too long for students' attention spans and, from that time on, can perceive when a lesson is moving too slowly or lasting too long. Another teacher may begin to notice that whenever a certain student is made to establish eye contact, the student ceases to misbehave; this teacher develops the active use of eye contact as a part of a repertoire of classroom management skills. The teacher may also become aware that members of certain cultures prefer to avoid eye contact as a sign of respect. A third teacher may notice that using a strong, confident voice causes students to pay attention, whereas using a tentative, meek voice causes their attention to wander. Active self-reflection is the first step toward developing withitness.

TEACHERS' LEADERSHIP STYLES

Leadership style is not a reflection of the teacher's ability to teach; teachers using any style may or may not be effective in teaching the academic subjects they are employed to teach. But leadership style does significantly affect the way students feel about school and, to a great extent, how students feel about themselves and one another.

Although all teachers have styles unique to their own personalities, behaviors, attitudes, and beliefs, Dreikurs and Cassel (1972) identified one type of leadership style that they labeled *autocratic*. Others have used the term *authoritarian* to denote a similar style. Authoritarian teachers believe they are responsible for planning furniture arrangements to maintain order in the classroom and to plan schedules that seldom vary. According to this view, it is the teacher's responsibility to make all class rules and establish consequences for misbehavior. Such teachers believe that they have the knowledge of subject matter and the responsibility to convey it to students through teacher-centered lectures, discussions, and assignments. It is the student's role to obey the rules and do all assigned work satisfactorily.

In the opening-day scenarios, Miss Adams represented a moderately authoritarian teacher, while Mrs. Destry and Mr. Green were quite autocratic. Teachers using these leadership styles are attempting to create a quiet, orderly classroom climate. There is little positive social interaction in the class. Individuals compete for grades and the teacher's attention. Some students attempt to please the teacher by any means possible, while others revolt and undermine the teacher's efforts to control students' behavior. A positive sense of community is rare in a classroom led by an autocratic teacher; the only sense of community that may develop among the students is a shared sense of resentment or even rebellion in extreme cases.

Dreikurs and Cassel label a second type of leadership *permissive,* although others have used the term *laissez-faire.* Teachers, such as Mr. Baron, who employ a permissive style appear tentative and powerless. They make few rules and are inconsistent in establishing or delivering the consequences for misbehavior. They accept excuses and seem unable to assert authority over academic work or student behavior. Confusion is the chief characteristic of the classroom climate created by such a permissive teacher. Students don't know what is expected or how they can succeed. Limits are fuzzy, leading to a constant testing of how much the students can get away with. Little sense of community can develop within a permissive classroom because students often learn to play one against the other to get their way.

The third type of leadership described by Dreikurs and Cassel is the *democratic* style. Democratic teachers, such as Mr. Catlin and Mr. Evans, are neither permissive nor autocratic. They are firm and reasonably consistent about their expectations for academic achievement and student behavior. They discuss the need for rules with their students and involve them in establishing the specific rules and consequences for the class. From time to time, they may initiate a reevaluation of certain rules to update them and make them more usable and meaningful. Democratic teachers assert their power to make decisions but are willing to listen to their students' reactions, needs, and desires. The result is that the sense of power and ownership is distributed among students and the teacher in the same way that it is distributed in a healthy community.

ESTABLISHING RULES AND CONSEQUENCES

In a healthy democratic community, the citizens understand and accept the laws that govern their behavior. They also understand and accept that if they break the laws, certain consequences will follow. Healthy democratic classrooms also have laws that govern behavior, although they are usually called *rules*. In the most smoothly managed classrooms, students also learn to understand and accept the consequences for breaking a rule from the very first week.

In the opening-day scenarios, each teacher established rules and consequences for the classroom differently. Miss Adams had established a set of rules beforehand. She read them to the class and explained why each was important. Mr. Baron, Mr. Green, and Mrs. Destry did not present a clear set of rules. Their actions indicated that they expected the students to discover the rules of the classroom. These are likely to be quite consistent in Mrs. Destry's classroom; but in the cases of Mr. Baron and Mr. Green, we suspect that the rules may change from day to day. Mr. Catlin had planned an entire process for establishing rules. His process involved the students in helping to establish the class rules based on shared expectations and consequences.

Two different types of consequences are used to guide or shape student behavior. *Natural consequences* are those that follow directly from a student's behavior or action. For example, if a student gets so frustrated while working on an assignment that he rips the paper in half, the natural consequence is that the work will have to be redone from the beginning. If another student wakes up late, the natural consequence is that she misses the bus and has to walk to school, arrives late, and suffers the embarrassment of coming to class tardy. In these cases, there was no adult intervention; the consequence grew directly from the student's behavior.

Logical consequences are those the teacher selects to fit students' actions; they are intended to cause students to change their behavior. For example, a teacher may decide that the logical consequence of not turning in a paper on time is that the student must stay in for recess or miss another activity period to finish the paper. When the paper is turned in, the logical consequence is that the student may go out to recess or take part in the activity period.

The difference between a punishment and a consequence is that a consequence is not arbitrary and is not dispensed with anger or any other strong emotion. To work effectively, logical consequences must be understood fully by the students. The teacher must describe them and explain the connections between the action and the consequence so that students understand the justification for the consequence. They must be applied consistently to all students who exhibit the behavior.

In many classrooms, teachers write a set of rules on a large piece of posterboard that is prominently displayed. Many teachers try to word the rules in positive ways, describing what they expect rather than what they forbid. Many teachers also write very specific consequences for each rule on the same poster for all students to see. For example, an elementary teacher may display these rules:

Class Rules	*Consequence If Rule Not Followed*
We wait in line courteously.	You will go to the end of the line.
We listen to the teacher.	You will lose 5 minutes of free time.
We turn in work on time.	You will finish during free time.
We work and talk quietly.	You will take a time-out.
We treat others with respect.	You will write a letter of apology.

At the middle or high school level, the posted rules and consequences may resemble these:

Class Rules	*Consequence If Rule Not Followed*
Work quietly in study hall.	Attend after-school study hall.
Use appropriate language.	Write an essay on swearing.
Maintain school property.	Clean and/or repaint property.
Turn in assignments on time.	Three late assignments equals a grade reduction.

THE CONSEQUENCE CALLED TIME-OUT

Teachers frequently use a discipline strategy known as *time-out* as a consequence for students whose behavior disrupts the classroom. It can be quite a powerful tool in your repertoire of behavior management strategies because most students want to be part of the group and will change their behavior to return to the group.

There are two types of time-outs. The fixed-interval time-out specifies a length of time, such as 5, 10, or 15 minutes, for first, second, and third offenses. Another form is conditioned upon changing behavior. Students may return to the class when they are able to convince the teacher that they will choose to cooperate with the rules.

To be effective, you must describe this entire procedure to the class so that every student knows what it represents. It is important to describe it as a consequence rather than as a punishment and to explain that a time-out is an opportunity for the student to go to a quiet area and get back the self-control that was temporarily lost.

When a student breaks the rule, quietly but firmly tell the student that the consequence for breaking the rule is to go to the time-out area and stay for the specified number of minutes or until he or she agrees to cooperate and obey the rule. The student is expected to stay in the time-out area (preferably out of sight of the rest of the class) without causing any noise or disruption. Rimm (1995) suggests that the teacher use a timer and set it only when the student has calmed down and is quietly sitting in the time-out area. When the buzzer signals that the time has elapsed, the student may quietly return to the group and resume working.

When used with caution and respect for the feelings of the student, this technique can be a powerful way to modify disruptive behavior. It is a strategy, however, that can be very difficult to apply fairly. If your voice or body language shows anger and vindictiveness when you tell the student to take the time-out, the student may feel embarrassed and lose rather than gain self-control.

USING POSITIVE CONSEQUENCES AND REWARDS

Jones (1987) focuses on preventing discipline problems by helping students to develop self-control. One way to assist students in developing self-control is through the use of positive consequences or incentives for learning and behaving cooperatively. To this end, Jones has examined familiar and widely used teacher practices and has recommended ways to refine these practices to make them more effective and to eliminate negative side effects. For example, he examined the familiar incentive systems of grades, gold stars, and being dismissed first and discovered that these systems appear to benefit only the top achievers; they are not genuine incentives for students who cannot realistically meet the established criteria.

Jones also noted that if teachers offer incentives that are not particularly attractive to many students, they will not positively affect student behavior or achievement. He uses the term *genuine incentives* to distinguish those that students perceive as both valuable and realistic for them to earn from those that students perceive to be of little benefit or impossible to achieve.

Jones uses the phrase *Grandma's Rule* to describe a familiar teaching practice: "First, eat your dinner; then you can have dessert." Applied to the classroom, this rule requires that students first do what the teacher expects; then they can do something that they genuinely want to do. Examples of genuine incentives that many students prize are computer activities, films, or free time in which students can choose and play games in small groups and learning experiences in art, drama, and music.

If students are to continue to perceive these favored activities as genuine incentives, they must be delivered as promised. Some teachers promise the incentive but run out of time and do not deliver on their promises. Another counterproductive practice is continually to threaten to reduce or eliminate the incentive if students do not cooperate. Still others deliver the reward even when the work is not done acceptably. When this occurs, the students learn that they can have dessert even if they do not eat their dinner—that is, they can get the reward without doing their work. This practice can destroy the balance of trust between student and teacher so that when the teacher establishes incentives, the students are skeptical that they will be delivered as promised.

When delivered as promised and as earned, genuine incentives can promote increased achievement among individuals and groups and can cause peer pressure to encourage good behavior. Caring, reflective teachers attempt to understand the real needs and desires of their students and to provide incentives that meet these needs.

Many schools have designed schoolwide systems of behavior management based on Canter and Canter's (1976) theory known as assertive discipline. According to this theory, teachers have the right to expect good behavior from their students. In these schools, the rules and consequences are the same in every classroom. A set of procedures is established for the first, second, and third infraction of each school rule. For example, the first offense causes the student's name to go on the board and serves as a warning. If students are disciplined for the second time, a check goes by their names, and they must write the rule 25 times. For a third offense, students lose recess or stay after school, and parents are notified of the student's behavior.

In assertive discipline systems, individuals or classrooms often can earn positive rewards for demonstrating their cooperation with the rules. For example, a school may establish a Friday afternoon movie with popcorn for students who have not received any citations for misbehavior during the week.

TWO-WAY COMMUNICATION WITH PARENTS

Discipline problems are less likely when teachers communicate their expectations to students and parents so that everyone is working with the same set of expectations. Communication with parents needs to occur early in the school year. Teachers should clearly explain the policies, procedures, and rules that govern the classroom and should establish procedures for parents to ask questions and voice their concerns.

Vernice Mallory teaches fifth grade in a neighborhood of small homes and apartments that houses a diverse population of African Americans, Caucasians, and recent immigrants from Asia, Mexico, and Central America. In the reflective action in Case 2.1, Vernice describes the ways she builds effective two-way communication with the parents. You will notice that as she reflects on the processes she uses in her classroom, the elements described in the model of reflective action do not appear in the order given in Figure 1.2. As you have no doubt observed, teachers do not reflect on events in any one set order or pattern. Still, it is evident that Vernice does exhibit all six of the reflective actions as she discusses how she establishes rapport and trust with her students' parents.

Case 2.1 ⊃ Reflective Action
Two-Way Communication with Parents

Vernice Mallory, Fifth-Grade Teacher
Edison Elementary School, San Diego

Perceptiveness

I have been teaching for many, many years, and I have found that one thing has-n't changed. To prevent discipline problems, it is absolutely necessary to estab-lish good quality two-way communication with parents early in the school year. This policy holds true for every ethnic group. What has changed is that there seems to be less and less supervision at home because so many parents are work-ing so hard to support their families these days. For example, at the beginning of this year, I noticed that many of my students were not turning in their homework on a regular basis. I knew I had to attack this problem right away before a pat-tern was established.

Constructing a Knowledge Base

What I want to tell beginning teachers is that when you graduate from college, it does not mean that you know everything but that you have the ability to learn. For me, teaching has been a learning process from day one until the day I retire. I've read many books about teaching and discipline systems in my career, and I've attended many workshops to learn new methods, but I know I still have a lot to learn. Each year, I have to learn what the parents of my students are thinking about. I don't wait for the fall open house. In the second week of school, I send home a notice inviting all the parents to come to my classroom for a kaffee klatsch or get-together. I don't make the note formal or threatening. It might look some-thing like this:

> Hi!
> I'm your child's teacher this year, and I want to get to know you. Let's all get together and discuss the plans for this year. In Africa, there is a saying that it takes a whole village to educate a child, and this goes for our neighborhood too. So come next Wednesday at 1:00 to meet your child's classmates and their parents. We'll discuss homework policies, attendance, parent involvement, and whatever else piques your interest.
> Signed, Vernice
> _____ Yes, I can attend.
> _____ No, I cannot attend. A more convenient time for me is
> _____.

Persistence and Problem Solving

The majority of parents come to the meeting, but for the ones who don't I follow up and ask them to come in at their convenience. I don't limit them to any time of day. I make time for them. I make myself available because I feel that getting my students' parents to work with me is one of the most important parts of my job.

When parents have had bad experiences with other teachers, and they have made up their minds that they don't trust schools or teachers, I have to build trust. I had a parent who was absolutely irate because the child's homework was too hard for him to understand and he couldn't help his child. I tried to convince him that the homework was not for him, it was for his child, but that if he really wanted to learn, he was welcome to come in while we were doing math. A few weeks later, he walked into my classroom, and I nodded him to an available seat. He sat very quietly. When the class was over, I went to him, and he said, "Math isn't the way it was when I was in school." He started coming in every day for about two months. I asked him if he wanted to sit by his son, and he did. He sat by his son, and they learned fractions together.

Clarification of Values and Principles

Parents are the child's first teachers, and I feel that children respond better when they know their parents are behind them. When I hear other teachers criticize parents and say that they won't come to conferences, I believe that it often occurs because teachers erect barriers between themselves and the parents. They don't try to understand how the parents feel. For example, many African American parents come from an old school: God first, preachers second, and teachers come right next to God and the preacher. So it isn't that they don't respect the school or the teacher. Something else comes between them and feeling comfortable visiting their children's classes. Some African American parents may believe that when they send their children to school, the teacher is the boss and has the right to do whatever it takes to make the child learn. But I'd rather work as partners with parents, so I build a partnership.

Communication Skills

When the parents come for my get-togethers, they may be skeptical at first, but when I greet them in a friendly way, they respond with enthusiasm. I always do a survey of my parents at the meeting. I ask the question, "What are your strengths and interests?" Then I try to make a place for them in my classroom, putting their strengths to work. By the way, this get-together includes the students, too. I want my students to see their parents at school and to have positive role models in their homes and neighborhood.

In the middle of the year, I call another meeting. We sit down and discuss anything the parents are concerned about or are not pleased with. We discuss class parties and schedules. I remind them of my expectations. When new parents move to the neighborhood, the meeting gives them a chance to meet the other parents. A feeling of community bonding develops.

At the end of the year, I invite parents to help us make class ribbons and autograph books. The culminating activity of the year is something I developed to celebrate the diversity of our classroom and to bring all of us together again. I have a potluck, and the parents make all of the food representing their cultures.

Creativity

Getting back to my problem with homework supervision: at the first parent get-together, with the students sitting there listening, I tell their parents to expect homework every day. I show them how I write the homework assignments on the board and then I tell them that they are expected to sign their names on the students' finished homework every day. In this way, we all understand each other, and I am confident that the parents know what I expect.

After the first meeting, I invite the parents to come be part of the program, based on their strengths and interests. For example, one parent loved math, so she led a math tutorial. Another parent wrote that her main interest was African American culture. She taught all the students to wrap material around their heads into authentic African crowns. Another parent volunteers to do physical education because his strength is physical fitness. One even teaches ballroom dancing. If the parent has to bring in a small child, I let her. I'd rather have her bring her child and do her good work for our classroom than stay at home. My classroom has a variety of dolls and games the young child can use to keep busy while the parent works with the students.

At the end of the year, during the potluck, every child in my classroom gets a special award, even if he just sharpened a pencil for me. And at the same time, I present awards for positive parenting to the parents. We all feel proud of our village of children that we have worked together to raise.

DISCIPLINE SYSTEMS THAT BUILD CHARACTER AND SELF-ESTEEM

Lickona (1992) confronts a very complex issue that teachers face today in his design of a system called moral discipline. He acknowledges that fewer students come to school with attitudes of respect for adults or schools; "many are astonishingly bold in their disrespect for teachers and other authority figures" (p. 109). He has observed student teachers and first-year teachers confront the harsh realities of working with students who bring their anger and resentment to school each day.

Lickona believes that the teacher is the central moral authority in the classroom and for many children the teacher functions as the primary moral mentor in their lives. "Exercising authority, however, doesn't mean being authoritarian. Authority works best when it's infused with respect and love" (p. 111).

To create a moral discipline system for your classroom, Lickona suggests involving your students in establishing the rules in a cooperative, mutually respectful manner. He describes how Kim McConnell, a sixth-grade teacher at Walt Disney Elementary School in San Ramon, California, develops rules with her students on the second day of school.

She arranges her classroom into groups of four students each because she believes it is important for students to have a support group. She asks each group to brainstorm rules that will help them do the following:

1. Get our work done.
2. Feel safe.
3. Be glad we're in school.

When they have written their rules on large pieces of paper, she shows them the list she has created. As a group, the class synthesizes the best elements into one list that serves as the class rules for that year.

Lickona compares the system of moral discipline with the system of assertive discipline and observes that assertive discipline is a fixed system that uses the same consequences for all types of behavior. Moral discipline, in contrast, focuses on the specific needs of each class and uses logical consequences that help students understand what they have done and what they must do to improve their moral conduct.

For example, with a rule such as "Use respectful language in this classroom," the consequences (designed by the students in cooperation with their teacher) might be:

First occasion: Take a time-out of 5 minutes and state or write the language you used that was disrespectful. Tell why it was disrespectful and to whom.

Second occasion: Write a letter of apology to the person or class to whom you were disrespectful.

Third occasion: Bring up your own behavior at a class meeting; ask for feedback on how you can stop using this type of language. Write a plan for improving your language and present it to the class.

HUMOR IN THE CLASSROOM

Csikszentmihalyi and McCormack (1986) recognized the importance of enjoyment in the learning process in a study they conducted on the influence of teachers on their students. When they asked students to tell them who or what influenced them to become the kinds of people they are, 58 percent mentioned one or more teachers, with descriptions such as these:

> Mrs. A. was influential because her class was a lot of fun. After all these years, I found out for the first time that I really liked English—it was really fun—and I've kept up my interest even though I'm not doing as well as other kids. (p. 419)

Csikszentmihalyi and McCormack believe that teacher enthusiasm, a sense of humor, and the ability to make learning enjoyable are vitally important in the classroom because they are connected with trust and meaningfulness. "How can young people believe that the information they are receiving is worth having, when their teachers seem bored, detached, or indifferent?" they ask (p. 419).

Pam Patterson, a student teacher in Mrs. Theresa Boone's fifth-grade classroom at Beasley School on Chicago's South Side, discovered that a humorous approach can frequently alleviate discipline problems. In class discussions, she was frustrated when many students tried to talk at the same time, calling out responses without being asked to speak. Although the students knew they were supposed to raise their hands and be called on before speaking, they would raise their hands and begin speaking at the same time. One day, during a disruptive discussion, Pam raised her hand and stood quietly in front of the noisy class. The noise subsided, and students asked Pam why her hand was raised. Pam told them she was raising her hand because she wanted to say something. A student responded, "Okay, Miss Patterson, we call on you!" Everyone laughed at the situation. From that time on, whenever the class got noisy during a discussion, Pam simply raised her hand, and the students would say, "We call on you," and settle down quietly.

Building Self-Esteem and Intrinsic Motivation
THE ENHANCING EFFECTS OF SUCCESS

All individuals want to win or succeed. Virtually all students who walk into a classroom on the first day of school hope that this year will be *the* year, that this grade will be *the* grade, and that this teacher will be *the* teacher who will make it possible for them to succeed. Some enter secure in the knowledge that they've succeeded before, but they are still anxious to determine whether they can duplicate that success in this new situation. Others enter with a history of failure and harbor no more than a dim, hidden hope that maybe they can succeed if only they can overcome their bad habits and learn how to succeed.

Winning and success are the most powerful motivations for future effort and achievement that we know of. Glasser (1969) noted:

> As a psychiatrist, I have worked many years with people who are failing. I have struggled with them as they try to find a way to a more successful life. From these struggles I have discovered an important fact: regardless of his background, his culture, his color, or his economic level, *he will not succeed in general until he can in some way first experience success in one important part of his life.* Given the first success to build upon, the negative factors . . . mean little. (p. 5)

It is possible to restate Glasser's message as a significant principle of teaching and learning: when an individual experiences success in one important part of life, that person can succeed in life regardless of background, culture, color, or economic level. Glasser's book *Schools Without Failure* has caused researchers and practitioners to reflect on the fundamental goals of education and to reexamine what students need from the school environment to succeed.

It is especially important for children who may have been raised in culturally different settings to experience success in their new school environments. Caring, reflective teachers are quick to perceive that children new to the school or the community need to experience success very quickly in order to adjust well to their new surroundings.

Assign new students a task that you are sure is well within their capability and then show your acceptance and satisfaction with the work they accomplish.

The same is true for students who may appear indifferent or even resentful of school and teachers. Try to understand that they may have a history of being unfairly treated by other, less caring teachers. Students who have faced failure over and over again often develop very negative attitudes toward schoolwork and frequently mask their need for approval with defensive and disruptive behaviors in an effort to hide their hurt and shame. You can be the teacher who helps them change their behavior by perceiving their need for success and structuring some tasks to fit their unique talents and abilities so that they can experience the true and lasting joy of succeeding and being productive.

MEETING STUDENTS' AFFECTIVE NEEDS

In *Motivation and Personality,* Abraham Maslow (1954) first described humans' *hierarchy of needs.* He recognized that people have basic physical and emotional needs that must be satisfied before the individual can attend to the higher need for achievement and recognition. If the lower needs are not satisfied, the individual is preoccupied by trying to meet them; and other, higher-level needs become nonexistent or are pushed into the background (p. 373). This explains why hungry or tired students cannot learn efficiently. All their capacities are focused on satisfying their need for food or sleep. To satisfy the real hunger needs experienced by many students, some schools provide breakfast, snacks, or milk so that students can pay attention to school tasks.

But what happens when the student has plenty of food and adequate shelter and is well rested? Then "at once other (and 'higher') needs emerge," and these become dominant (p. 375). The needs for safety and security follow basic physiological needs, and the needs for love and belonging follow safety needs. Imagine two classrooms, one led by an autocratic or permissive teacher in which students feel threatened, insecure, and isolated; the other led by a democratic teacher in which students feel safe, secure, cared for, and connected with other members of the class community. In the latter setting students are more likely to have their needs met and therefore be ready and able to achieve greater success in academic work.

Raths (1972) also identified eight emotional needs that people strive to satisfy. These include the need for love, achievement, belonging, self-respect, freedom from guilt, freedom from fear, economic security, and self-understanding. Raths believes that children whose needs are not satisfied exhibit negative, self-defeating behaviors such as aggressiveness, withdrawal, submissiveness, regressiveness, or psychosomatic illness.

Raths recognizes that teachers cannot expect to satisfy the many unmet needs experienced by all the students in their classrooms. However, he does believe that "children cannot check their emotions at the door and we should not expect them to. If unmet needs are getting in the way of a child's growth and development, his learning and his maturing, I insist that it is your obligation *to try* to meet his needs" (p. 141). Raths's book *Meeting the Needs of Children* contains many pages of specific suggestions about what teachers can do to help meet children's emotional needs so that they are free to learn.

Work by Glasser (1969, 1986), Raths (1972), and Maslow (1954) on recognizing and meeting children's needs has served, in many ways, as the basis for this chapter. It attempts to describe ways that classrooms can be organized and managed to satisfy students' basic needs for safety, security, love, and belonging. Only if these needs are satisfied can students concentrate a significant portion of their energy and drive on achieving success in school subjects. Maslow's work shows us that intrinsic motivation is something that can be set free and enhanced in school settings. The intrinsic motivation for achievement and recognition for achievement can be released and nurtured by teachers who carefully design a healthy, supportive sense of community in their classrooms.

CLASSROOMS AS COMMUNITIES

How does a class of strangers or competitive individuals develop into a community? As with all the other important classroom effects discussed in this chapter, the teacher has the power to create a positive, healthy, mutually supportive and productive classroom environment from the first day of school. Through furniture arrangement, schedules, the teacher's body language, words of welcome, rules, consequences, and interaction with the class, the teacher demonstrates a unique leadership or teaching style to the students. A sense of community is also achieved through honest, open communication of needs and feelings among students and their teachers.

Sandra Jackson, an African American woman who taught high school for several years in an urban school, recalls that "in order to create a community of learners in which the climate is open and conducive to dialogue and conversation, teachers must act in ways that students gain trust in them, and they in their students. This means that teachers must resist the urge to be in control and attempt to manage learning" (Jackson, 1995, p. 142). But Jackson also recognizes that students need and expect their teachers to demonstrate a sense of authority; otherwise, the students may doubt the value of the course and the teacher's knowledge . Reflective teachers explore this dilemma thoroughly, looking for ways to teach that strike a balance between demonstrating openness and acceptance of students' opinions and establishing a legitimate sense of authority and limits.

In the late twentieth century, business leaders have been looking for ways to establish the same type of balance in the corporate world. Glasser (1993) explored the way in which schools can emulate the principles of total quality management (TQM), a philosophy used in many business settings. TQM is designed to improve the quality of their products and build a sense of ownership among employees. This system is based on the theory of shared decision making by administrators and workers, who all examine the products or services they sell and try to improve them.

Glasser (1993) has adapted TQM to managing students' work and behavior in schools. He acknowledges the very difficult role that teachers have today in trying to manage and teach students from diverse backgrounds. Some students who come to school may not want to be there; they may have little or no interest in learning. To reach these students, you must be able to convince them that something new and important is happening in your classroom, that you are going to expect them to do quality schoolwork. Initially, they are likely to resist your efforts until you are able to convince them that this is *their* school, not yours, and that you are there to assist and support them to solve problems and create ways to do high-quality work.

Schools experimenting with TQM administrative systems have community building as one of their primary goals. One of the main tenets of TQM is that "everyone in the organization must be dedicated to continuous improvement, personally and collectively." Schools that have adopted TQM principles invest their resources to discover new and better ways to help realize the potential of every student. In Glenwood, Maryland, the middle school has created support teams (S-teams) of students who discuss how their work, collectively and individually, can be improved. They pledge specific efforts to make these improvements and monitor their own progress (Bonstingl, 1992).

The teacher's role in a TQM school is to provide a warm, supportive classroom environment. Students must be able to trust the teacher and believe that he or she has their welfare in mind. The next step is to renew the curriculum so that students perceive the work as meaningful and useful. Teachers must then communicate that they will expect students to do only high-quality work. Students are asked to help evaluate their own work and improve it until it reaches the standards of quality established by the teacher and students together.

Glasser believes that students need to feel safe, happy, and proud of themselves in a classroom if they are going to become convinced that schoolwork is worth the time and effort. To enlist their support, he recommends that you allow your students to know you as a human being, not just as an authority figure. Isn't it true that the better you know someone and the more you like them, the harder you will work for that person? Glasser asks you to use that same principle when establishing the expectations and procedures for your classroom. He suggests the following:

> During the first few months you are with your students, look for natural occasions to tell them:
>
> 1. Who you are.
> 2. What you stand for.
> 3. What you will ask them to do.
> 4. What you will not ask them to do.
> 5. What you will do for them.
> 6. What you will not do for them. (1993, p. 32)

TEACHING STUDENTS HOW TO RESOLVE CONFLICTS

In many schools, conflicts have escalated to violent confrontations. Students bicker, threaten, and harass one another. Conflicts among racial and ethnic groups are on the rise. Truancy is epidemic in some areas. Traditional discipline programs, involving scolding and suspensions, do not appear to improve this situation. What can we do? What will you do when you are confronted with these situations? In some learning communities, teachers are teaching students how to be peacemakers and resolve conflicts for themselves and their peers. Johnson and Johnson (1991) provide a curriculum for such programs in their book *Teaching Students to Be Peacemakers*. Through the use of role plays and other learning opportunities to practice conflict-resolution skills, students learn how to negotiate and mediate when conflicts arise.

Laurie Mednick, a fifth-grade teacher at Kellogg School in Chula Vista, California, teaches fourth-, fifth-, and sixth-grade students the communication skills they need to resolve conflicts peacefully. Basing her work on the belief that conflict is inevitable and can even be healthy if dealt with in an honest and caring manner, Laurie sponsors the Peace Patrol program at her school. She describes this program in Case 2.2.

Case 2.2 ⊃ Reflective Action
Teaching Students to Resolve Conflicts

Laurie Mednick, Fifth-Grade Teacher
Kellogg Elementary School, Chula Vista, California

Perceptiveness

I was very troubled by the apparent lack of concern my students felt for other people. Instead of treating one another with respect, many of my students were involved in behaviors such as fighting, tattling, putting each other down, and interrupting when others were talking.

Proactive Construction of Knowledge

As I observed these behaviors, I asked myself: "How can I help these children to understand that people are different and have different ideas and perceptions, but that they are still very important? How can I help them learn to resolve their own conflicts? How can I teach them to make better choices for themselves?"

I went to see mentor teachers in my district who were investigating a new Peace Education curriculum and asked them what programs or methods were helpful in building self-esteem. I gained an enormous amount of insight and information from these people as well as an enthusiasm to continue my search.

I did a literature search at a university library on the topic of Peace Education and found from the articles that I read that this topic is a major concern to teachers across the country and that a number of programs are designed to address this issue. This search took about two months. I became so interested in the topic that I wrote my master's thesis on the subject as well.

Making a Judgment Based on Values and Principles

I decided that instead of trying to solve this problem for my own classroom, that my whole school could really benefit from a conflict-management program. This decision was a direct reflection of my values because I believe that each individual is important and must be shown respect and value, even if you don't agree with them. I also believe that there are alternatives to violence and that we need to teach these alternatives to our students.

Creativity

I began my new effort by teaching my students to be more attentive listeners and how to solve problems among themselves without telling the teacher. We also began to practice sharing our feelings using "I" messages (e.g., "It hurts my feelings when you call me that name. I don't like it.")

Then I began to use role playing three to four times a week to involve my students in sharing feelings and practicing conflict resolution by listening to each other with respect. The students were very receptive to the curriculum. They loved being treated with respect by their peers. The class as a whole became very cohesive and helpful toward one another.

Persistence and Problem Solving

After implementing these strategies in my classroom, I selected 30 other fourth, fifth, and sixth graders from other classes to become part of a Peace Patrol program for the entire school. I taught them the same communication and conflict-management skills that I had used in my classroom. I meet with the Peace Patrol twice a month for continued training. Each day they wear their blue jackets out on the playground and assist other students to resolve their conflicts peacefully.

Communication Skills

Now, in our school, when a conflict occurs between students, a Conflict Manager takes the students involved in the conflict to a quiet corner or passageway to discuss the event. The patroller listens to each student and then asks them to suggest solutions. If a solution can be found by the children themselves, the Conflict Manager writes a brief report about the conflict and the solution. Copies of the report are given to the students, their teachers, and the principal. As a faculty, we have agreed that whenever we receive a Peace Patrol report, we show our respect for these successful conflict-management encounters by congratulating the students for resolving their conflicts peacefully. I feel very proud of the role I took in developing this program for my school community.

Effective communication between teacher and student is based on mutual trust that grows from the basic moral principles of caring, consideration, and honesty. Reflective teachers who are guided by these moral principles express them in the classroom by listening empathetically—or, as in the case of the Peace Patrol in Laurie's class, by teaching students to listen empathetically. Listening is one of the most important ways of gathering subjective information about students' needs to make informed judgments about why students behave the way they do.

Discussions between teacher and student must be guided by consideration for the child's feelings and fragile, developing self-concept. There is also a great need for honest, open exchanges of feelings and information among all members of a classroom. A sense of community and shared purpose grows from a realistic understanding of one another's perceptions and needs.

CLASSROOM MEETINGS

One method that democratic teachers often use to build mutual caring, consideration, and honest expression of opinions and perceptions is to hold classroom meetings to discuss problems confronting the class. The classroom meeting was first described by Glasser (1969) in *Schools Without Failure*. Some teachers hold regularly scheduled classroom meetings each week; others schedule them only when necessary. When I taught fifth grade, I scheduled mine just before lunch on Wednesdays so that it was in the middle of the week. One of the most important effects of a classroom meeting is the sense of community created when the students and teacher sit down to solve problems together.

For a detailed account of how to initiate and lead a class meeting, refer to Glasser's book. An abbreviated description is all that can be included in this chapter. The seating arrangement for a class meeting is a single circle of chairs, so that each member of the class can see the teacher and all other members of the class. The teacher has the responsibility for establishing rules and consequences for the meeting. These usually consist of a rule about one person speaking at a time and accepting the ideas and opinions of others without criticism or laughter. It is very important that as the leader of the meeting the teacher be nonjudgmental. When expressing anger or other feelings, class members are encouraged to use I-statements.

The meeting may be divided into several parts. For example, the teacher may choose to open with an unfinished statement such as "I sometimes wonder why" or "I am proud of" or "I am concerned about." Going once around the circle, every member of the class is encouraged to respond to this opening statement, which the teacher chooses to elicit communication from every member of the group. While members are encouraged to respond, the teacher makes it clear that any individual can simply say, "Pass." Opening the class meeting in this way has the advantage of allowing everyone to speak at least once during the meeting and may bring out important issues that need discussion.

The second part of the meeting can be devoted to students' concerns. The teacher opens this discussion by asking who has a concern. When a problem is expressed, the teacher moderates discussion on that issue alone until it is resolved. Issues are seldom resolved easily in one meeting; but class members can raise a problem, express different ideas and opinions, and then offer solutions. When a reasonable solution is worked out, the teacher's role is to restate the solution and suggest that the class try it for a week and discuss how it worked at the next classroom meeting. Other student concerns can then be expressed.

The third part of the class meeting can address the teacher's concerns. The teacher can bring up a problem by expressing personal feelings or stating expectations for future work. Students' responses can be brought out and discussed and solutions proposed. The sense of community that develops from expressing needs and opinions, hearing other perspectives, and solving problems together is translated into all aspects of life in the classroom. When an argument occurs during recess or when students perceive something as unfair, they know they can discuss it openly and freely in a class meeting. When the teacher needs more cooperation or wants higher-quality work, this issue can be brought up in a class meeting. Mutual understanding, tolerance for opposing views, and a way to resolve conflicts results in a strong sense of ownership and commitment to the academic, social, and emotional goals of the class as a whole.

The classroom meeting is a also a powerful vehicle for developing ownership of class rules, as Tim Curbo describes in Case 2.3. It satisfies a student's need for belonging, power, freedom, self-understanding, and self-respect and can diminish students' feelings of fear and guilt. Fun and enjoyment can also be planned so that students and teachers can celebrate and enjoy school life together.

Case 2.3 ⟲ Reflective Action
Classroom Meetings

Tim Curbo, First-Grade Teacher
Hawthorne School, San Francisco

Proactive Construction of Knowledge

Discipline begins even before the first child enters the classroom. Two weeks before school starts, I begin setting up my classroom. In the years that I have been teaching, I've found that the physical environment directly affects student behavior. I read about the physical arrangement of classrooms many years ago, but mostly I've gained my knowledge through experimentation based on the goals I have for my class. For example, I group children's desks into three large units because I want my students to interact. I believe that this interaction fosters cooperation, problem solving, and peer teaching and learning.

Creativity

On the first day of school, we begin with the first of our daily classroom meetings. I do not present a list of rules on the first day. Instead, most of our rules come from a class discussion of problems that arise in the classroom. A fight over a game generates a discussion about sharing, and we develop a common understanding of what we all expect of one another regarding the sharing of classroom materials. I do this because I believe that young children learn best from concrete personal experiences. Our meetings cause the children to generalize a shared value from a concrete example.

Perceptiveness

Whenever a problem is discussed, I also try to think about how I can modify the environment or my own teaching to facilitate more constructive behavior. In the example of the fight over a game, I may think about how I could place the game somewhere else to make it more accessible or could make a sign telling how many students can play this game. I may think about whether we need more games of this sort so that all the students can enjoy the participation.

Persistence and Problem Solving

Not all rules can be established in the first week of school. We hold our classroom meeting every day directly after lunch. The meeting serves as a forum for setting "public policies" (rules and procedures) and is a time to model and develop problem-solving skills. We place a chair at the front of the room. Each day six children are allowed to share something that they think is important. The number six is arbitrary, but it works out to about a 15-minute meeting, which is a realistic amount of time for first graders.

Communication Skills

When a student shares a problem, we discuss feelings about the problem. I try to draw in the whole class as much as possible, asking, for example, "How did you feel when you were excluded from the game?" or "How would the rest of you feel?" After dealing with feelings, we discuss solutions to the problem. Too often, our discussion of solutions degenerates into blaming and fault finding. I, as the teacher, try to stress that Billy is not the problem; *hitting* is. We need to decide how we feel about hitting so that our school will be a positive place. Billy is a friend who needs our help in learning another way to address his problems. In discussing our feelings, we establish that hitting is not a good solution to the conflict. Then we move on to what would be a good solution, one that is acceptable to all involved. Out of this process emerges our public policies—in other words, *our class rules*.

Clarifying Values and Principles

My philosophy about discipline is to accentuate the positive. I want to give lots of positive reinforcement to those kids who are modeling good discipline. Sometimes in our class meetings, a student will report a positive interaction. Then we discuss the good feelings that were experienced and heap appropriate praise on our friend who is helping make our school a better place.

As a teacher, I am in the position of enforcing the public policies that are established. Consistency is very important. If we generate a class rule, it must be fairly and evenly applied. We must all be aware of the rule, believe in it, and be committed to enforcing it. I've seen idle teacher threats and uneven application of rules erode classroom discipline.

Clarity is also very important. Many children seem to be crying out for help through their misbehavior. They need a caring adult to help them structure their chaotic lives. I've found that the best way to address the needs of these children is to provide them with clear and consistent limits, positive reinforcement, and an opportunity to discuss their feelings and learn new ways of handling their angry feelings.

THE SELF-FULFILLING PROPHECY

Children are extremely perceptive beings. They understand and react to subtle differences in adult expectations. As Good and Brophy (1987) have shown in their research, teachers' behaviors communicate to students what the teachers expect of themselves, of the class as a whole, and of individual students.

This effect has come to be known as the *self-fulfilling prophecy* (Brophy, 1983; Good & Brophy, 1987; Rosenthal & Jacobsen, 1968). The process appears to work like this: (1) the teacher makes a decision about the behavior and achievement to be expected from a certain student; (2) the teacher treats students differently depending on the expectations for each one; (3) this treatment communicates to the student what the teacher expects and affects the student's self-concept, achievement motivation, and aspirations either positively or negatively; (4) if the treatment is consistent over time, it may permanently shape the child's achievement and behavior. "High-expectation students will be led to achieve at higher levels, whereas the achievement of low-expectation students will decline" (Brophy, 1983, p. 54).

Many studies of how teachers' behaviors display their expectations have been done and replicated to confirm earlier findings. Brophy found that some teachers treat low achievers this way (1983, p. 55):

1. seat them far away from the teacher
2. call on them less often
3. wait less time for them to answer questions
4. criticize them more frequently
5. praise them less frequently
6. provide them with less detailed feedback
7. demand less work and effort from them

Scheduling Time for Active Learning

DAILY AND WEEKLY SCHEDULES

Teachers at all levels believe they cannot fit everything they want to teach into the school day. Charles (1983) cites "dealing with the trivial" as one of teachers' greatest time robbers (p. 243). When teachers simply try to fit everything into the day, they are as likely to include trivial matters as important ones. A reflective teacher weighs the relative importance of each element of the school program and allocates time accordingly. This may mean eliminating certain items entirely and carefully scheduling the minutes of the day to meet students' most important needs.

Schedules differ from grade to grade depending on the relative importance of the subject at that grade level and the way the school is structured and organized. The most frequently used structure in elementary schools is to place students into grade-level *self-contained classrooms* in which one teacher has the responsibility for teaching all the academic subjects. In other cases, students may have a homeroom but their academic subjects are *departmentalized*, meaning that teachers specialize in one academic area and students move from class to class during the day.

For example, the primary grades are usually structured as self-contained classrooms, and primary teachers often schedule reading and language-arts activities for up to one-half of the school day. The intermediate grades may be self-contained or departmentalized; but in either case, math, science, and social studies activities are usually given more time than they are at the primary grades. In junior high school, the schedules are likely to be departmentalized, meaning that each teacher specializes in one subject and teaches it to several classes of students during the day.

No two schedules are alike. Teachers in self-contained classrooms are usually allowed great discretion in how they allocate time. Typically, state requirements mandate how many minutes per week are to be allocated to each of several subjects, but teachers make varied plans within those prescriptions. For example, the state may require a minimum of 150 minutes of math per week. Teacher A may schedule 30 minutes per day; teacher B may schedule 40 minutes for four days; teacher C may schedule 45 minutes on Mondays, Wednesdays, and Fridays with brief review periods on other days.

Elementary class schedules may be rigid or flexible. They may be the same every day or vary greatly. They may be governed by bells or by the teacher's own inner clock. Charles (1983) recommends that, regardless of how it is determined, "the daily classroom schedule should be explained in such a manner that students know what activities are to occur at each part of the day and how they are to work and behave during those activities" (p. 10). When students know the schedule, they can learn to manage their own time more efficiently. A teacher who uses a consistent schedule may create a permanent display of the schedule on a bulletin board; a teacher who varies the schedule from day to day can write the current schedule on the chalkboard each morning.

The conventional wisdom of teachers is that the most difficult subjects should be scheduled early in the day when students are most likely to be attentive. Reading or language arts is frequently the first subject of the day in a self-contained classroom, followed by math. Science, social studies, art, and music compose the afternoons. This may be the preferred schedule, but often school constraints make it difficult to achieve. Physical education, art, and music may be taught by other teachers in separate classrooms. The schedule for these special classes may affect the classroom teacher's schedule. Some classes must be scheduled for special classes in the morning, causing classroom teachers to adjust their plans.

PLANNING TIME

Teachers may be annoyed when special classes interrupt their scheduled lessons, but they appreciate one important side effect: when the class leaves for art, music, or physical education, the classroom teacher has a planning period. Planning time is usually part of the teacher's contract and is designed to provide opportunities for individual or collegial planning. Teachers of self-contained classrooms have complete discretion over their planning time, but departmentalized teachers frequently hold meetings during their planning time to discuss how they will plan and deliver their shared curricula.

Teachers use planning time in various ways, some productive and others less so. Charles (1983) recommends that teachers use this time as efficiently as possible by "prioritizing tasks, giving attention to those that are absolutely necessary, such as planning, scoring papers, preparing for conferences, and preparing instructional materials and activities. Also high on the list should come those tasks that are difficult or boring, leaving for later those that are most enjoyable" (p. 244). Less efficient teachers may use the time for socializing, complaining, smoking, eating, reading magazines, or making personal telephone calls. Later they complain that the school day is too short and that they have too much work to do at home.

Charles (1983) recommends that routine tasks such as watering plants, cleaning the room, feeding animals, and distributing materials should not be done during planning time or by the teacher at all. The teacher who is an efficient time manager delegates as many of these routine tasks as possible to student helpers. This has two effects that contribute to a healthy classroom environment: (1) it reduces the stress teachers feel about time, and (2) it provides a sense of responsibility and meaningful accomplishment for the student helpers.

Most reflective teachers want to create a classroom in which students can meet their basic human needs for belonging and achievement. To accomplish this, they consider every aspect of the environment as it relates to children's needs. They arrange the furniture to meet students' needs for a sense of belonging; they create rules and schedule time to meet students' needs for security; they provide opportunities for students to write about and discuss their other feelings and needs. They do this because they want to create a nurturing sense of community in their classroom as a means of enhancing successful achievement.

➲ Reflective Actions for Your Professional Portfolio
A Sample of Your Classroom Management System

Perceptiveness: How Time Is Used in Classrooms

Observe and record how time is used in a classroom. Is a schedule posted? If so, is it followed rigidly or flexibly? If not, how is the schedule determined? Keep a record of how much time is spent on academic, nonacademic, and classroom-management concerns. Create a schedule that you would use if this were your classroom and you had control over the resource of time. Include a copy or photo of your schedule in your portfolio.

Construction of Knowledge:
Read about New Management Systems

Select a classroom-management strategy that you have observed or heard about and gather information about it. Perhaps you want to know more about class meetings, conflict resolution, or training students to be peacemakers. Read articles about the strategies you are interested in. Visit a teacher using them. Write your ideas of how you will incorporate these strategies into your classroom.

Clarification of Values and Principles: High-Priority Rules

What are the rules you consider most important to establish for your students? Write down the rules you believe are most effective. Write the consequences or incentives that fit each rule. Describe how you can explain these rules to your class and how you can incorporate students' suggestions into the class rules.

Creativity: Your Classroom as a Community

Consider a variety of strategies you could use to create a unique sense of community for your classroom. Synthesize your ideas and describe the theme of your community. How will your classroom environment reflect this theme? How will you articulate this theme to your students and engage their active participation in it?

Persistence and Problem Solving: Managing Class Time

You have previously created a sample daily or weekly time schedule that you would like to use. In reality, however, there are other demands on your students' time. Create a schedule that incorporates the best of your ideal use of time with the realities of your school environment. Write about the balance you try to achieve with this revised schedule.

Communication Skills: Conflict Resolution in Your Classroom

Carefully observe students in conflict with each other, and reflect on how you might assist them in becoming peacemakers and resolving their conflict. What can you say to them to motivate them to negotiate their differences? Do you model mediation and negotiation skills yourself? Write a plan for introducing and teaching conflict resolution skills to your students.

References

Bonstingl, J. (1992). The quality revolution in education. *Educational Leadership*, 50(3), 4–9.

Brophy, J. (1983). Classroom organization and management. In D. Smith (Ed.), *Essential knowledge for beginning educators* (pp. 42–59). Washington, DC: American Association of Colleges for Teacher Education.

Canter, L., & Canter, M. (1976). *Assertive discipline: A take charge approach for today's educator.* Santa Monica: Canter & Associates.

Charles, C. (1983). *Elementary classroom management.* New York: Longman.

Csikszentmihalyi, M., & McCormack, J. (1986). The influence of teachers. *Phi Delta Kappan*, 67(6), 415–419.

Doyle, W. (1986). Classroom organization and management. In M. Wittrock (Ed.), *Handbook of research on teaching* (3rd ed.) (pp. 392–431). Upper Saddle River, NJ: Merrill/Prentice Hall.

Dreikurs, R., & Cassel, P. (1972). *Discipline without tears.* New York: Hawthorn.

Emmer, E., Evertson, C., & Anderson, L. (1980). Effective classroom management at the beginning of the school year. *Elementary School Journal, 80*(5), 219–231.

Evertson, C. (1989). Improving elementary classroom management: A school-based training program for beginning the year. *Journal of Educational Research, 83*(2), 82–90.

Glasser, W. (1969). *Schools without failure.* New York: Harper & Row.

Glasser, W. (1986). *Control theory in the classroom.* New York: Harper & Row.

Glasser, W. (1993). *The quality school teacher.* New York: Harper Perennial.

Good, T., & Brophy, J. (1987). *Looking in classrooms* (4th ed). New York: Harper & Row.

Jackson, S. (1995). Negotiating self-defined standpoints. In S. Jackson & J. Solis (Eds.), *Beyond comfort zones in multiculturalism* (pp. 47–69). Westport, CT: Bergin & Garvey.

Johnson, D., & Johnson, R. (1991). *Teaching students to be peacemakers.* Edina, MN: Interaction.

Jones, F. (1987). *Positive classroom discipline.* New York: McGraw-Hill.

Kounin, J. (1977). *Discipline and group management in classrooms.* New York: Holt, Rinehart, & Winston.

Lickona, T. (1992). *Educating for character.* New York: Bantam.

Maslow, A. (1954). *Motivation and personality.* New York: Harper & Row.

Raths, L. (1972). *Meeting the needs of children.* Upper Saddle River, NJ: Merrill/Prentice Hall.

Rimm, S. (1995). *Why bright children get poor grades.* New York: Crown.

Rosenthal, R., & Jacobsen, L. (1968). *Pygmalion in the classroom.* New York: Holt, Rinehart, & Winston.

chapter

3

Perceiving and Meeting Students' Needs in a Diverse Society

As soon as they succeed in getting a teaching position, most teachers are eager to get into their new classrooms to arrange furniture, establish schedules, choose textbooks, consider rules and consequences, and outline major units of study before school begins. But surprises are usually inevitable when school begins and the classroom is filled with real, live students.

Students have a way of disrupting the most carefully considered plans. They walk in, and suddenly the teacher may see that the desks are much too close together or that some of the larger students don't even fit in their chairs. When books are distributed, it may become evident that some students will have great difficulty reading and understanding the texts at this grade level, especially those who have grown up speaking a language other than English. When the rules and consequences are discussed, it may become apparent that some of the rules must be spelled out in greater detail and that some of the consequences must be strengthened, at least for some students.

The first day of school can be a humbling and disheartening experience for teachers who have invested a great deal of energy and care in their initial plans. Reflective teachers who are using their withitness skills to perceive the needs of their new students can't help but be surprised by the contrasts and differences the students exhibit. Some may not show much interest in school. Others may appear to have very different values from the teacher's own. For experienced teachers who are teaching the same grade level they taught the year before, part of the jolt comes from their memories of how much more mature and able the class was last year. But when they consider this issue more fully, most teachers realize that their memories are based on what their students were able to accomplish at the end of the year, when they were nine months older and had become adjusted to life in that teacher's classroom.

There may be no adequate way to prevent this first-day letdown. It occurs primarily because a class is made up of unique individuals with widely varied backgrounds, personalities, and needs. Most schools today contain students with a rich diversity of racial, cultural, language, and religious affiliations. This diversity brings with it a wealth of opportunities for learning to view the world from different perspectives. But it also brings some of the most serious challenges we've faced as a nation.

Celebrating Diversity in Your Classroom

Cultural diversity and language differences among students can be viewed as a problem or as a great strength and a cause for celebration: the choice is yours. If you have been raised and gone to school yourself with students from many different cultures, you are probably well prepared to teach in a culturally diverse setting. You will recognize that Caucasian, middle-class students are no longer the majority in most school districts. Instead, a typical classroom in an urban setting now contains students representing a dozen or more nationalities, cultures, and languages.

New national and state social studies curriculum standards have been developed to ensure that multicultural education is a high priority in our schools. Banks (1994) urges teachers to transform the mainstream curriculum that had, until recently, attempted to coerce all citizens into a white, Anglo-Saxon mold.

This coerced assimilation does not work very well. An imposed unum is not authentic, is not perceived as legitimate by nonmainstream populations, does not have moral authority, and is inconsistent with democratic ideals. To create an authentic, democratic unum with moral authority and perceived legitimacy, the pluribus (diverse peoples) must negotiate and share power. (p. 4)

Your school will probably expect you to design and teach a multicultural, multilingual curriculum that is very different from what you experienced as an elementary school student yourself. This is very difficult for most people to do. We tend to believe that whatever type of educational experience we had was the "right" way, the standard to emulate. Without deep reflection, we tend to try to duplicate it when we become teachers. With reflection and a set of moral principles based on justice and caring for your students, however, you are likely to find that your own ideas have been transformed and that you are committed to meeting the diverse needs of your students with grace and goodwill.

Many students need a learning environment that encourages them to express their views and listen to the opinions of others in order to develop richer, more balanced views about life and learning. Most students also need a teacher who believes in them and expects them to do their very best work. Here's what Ylianna Romo, who teaches fifth grade at Washington School in downtown San Diego, believes:

My biggest goal is to have high expectations for my children. I think that when we expect the best, we get the best. As soon as a teacher starts to flounder and think, "Oh, they really can't do this work. It's too hard," is when the teacher loses her edge. I refuse to do that. I often struggle with this decision. Sometimes I feel pity for a child. His mother is not home very much or her dad is an alcoholic. But when I start to waver and expect less, I always try to think, "If this was my child, what would I expect?"

My first year of teaching was the hardest because at that time, my strongest value was not to hurt their self-esteem. Sometimes a student would turn in a paper I couldn't even read, and I really struggled with the conflict of which was more important: to expect high-quality work or not damage their self-esteem.

The turning point came for me when a boy turned in a very short writing assignment that I couldn't read. I thought about what this boy really needed from me, and I asked him to do it again. He took the paper away, and when he turned it in again, it was much better—neater, longer, more interesting. That's what made me realize that I need to do this for all my students—have high expectations for their work and require them to do it over until it meets those expectations.

PERCEIVING THE NEEDS OF BILINGUAL AND BICULTURAL STUDENTS

Until very recently, people describing students who came from homes that were culturally different from mainstream middle-class upbringings used terms such as *cultural deficiencies, disadvantaged,* or *socially deprived.* This language reveals a very ethnocentric view of the world and is no longer considered a valid or productive way to think about students whose culture, language, or economic circumstances differ from those of the prevailing culture. Indeed, in many cities, the prevailing culture may not be traditional, white, or middle class at all.

Teachers are not predominantly white or middle class these days either. African American teachers may be hired to teach in predominantly white locations; Hispanic teachers may be hired to teach in Asian American communities; Native American teachers may be placed in a classroom that has a diverse population of students from many different cultures. Studies show that when the parents' language, culture, and values match those of the teachers, students are likely to experience school as satisfying and supportive because they receive similar messages in each setting. When these important factors are different, the student may experience school as uncomfortable and threatening because the messages may conflict.

When you become a teacher, you can expect to teach a class made up of many different cultures and ethnic groups, particularly if you choose to teach in a large urban school district. In your own schooling, you have probably witnessed teachers who attempt to "remediate" and prod culturally different students into "adapting" to the majority culture. Reflective teachers, on the other hand, need to consider how to meet the academic, social, and emotional needs of students from cultures different from their own.

At least 10 percent of school-age children in the United States have grown up in homes in which English is the second language, and they need assistance in learning English to succeed in school. In urban areas, where the concentration of immigrants is highest, a school may have students who speak as many as 25 different languages (Anderson, 1989).

Most experts in bilingual education believe that students who are learning English require instruction in their primary language until they learn enough English to function in the regular classroom. Children with limited English proficiency (LEP) receive instruction in special classrooms designed to teach them English as a second language and academic skills in their own language. When students attain minimal proficiency in English, they are termed fluent English proficient and may be gradually mainstreamed into regular classrooms.

Diagnosing the needs of the culturally diverse student is very difficult for classroom teachers who do not share the same culture. In general, specialists in bilingual/bicultural education recommend that culturally diverse students need classroom experiences that are high in teacher involvement, have appropriate content for their ages, and allow them to work in heterogeneous groups. Many teacher education programs are now offering special diversity training for teachers. Some states are now providing special credentials such as the Culture, Language, and Academic Development (CLAD) teaching credential that is offered in California. These programs are designed to provide beginning teachers with special training and experience in working with students from a variety of language and cultural backgrounds. If you do not have the opportunity to take part in an organized program to prepare you to meet the needs of culturally diverse students, you would be wise to seek out opportunities to observe and participate in culturally diverse schools.

Schools that celebrate diversity no longer encourage students to forget their home languages or to speak and learn only in English. Many multicultural school programs support students as they learn to communicate in both their native language and English. In fact, in our multicultural society, it is becoming evident that knowing two or more languages is an asset in the career search. Opportunities are growing for fluent bilingual people in business, government, education, and the media. By acknowledging these strengths among their multilingual students, schools help enhance, rather than diminish, self-esteem for all students. Nowhere are the opportunities for fluent bilingual individuals more evident than in our elementary schools, where teachers who are bilingual are hired immediately upon graduation from a teacher education program.

Second language learning is most successful when teachers take a very active role in structuring learning experiences so that students can hear and practice the new language in a meaningful, purposeful way. To learn a new language, LEP students need time for linguistic input and feedback with the teacher. Other students are not necessarily good models for one another because they may also be learning the language. At first, the teacher must provide tasks that the student can respond to nonverbally. When the student does begin to attempt speaking English, the teacher must react as naturally as possible, talking in a way that models correct English rather than overtly correcting the student's pronunciation. In this way, the teacher provides a low-anxiety environment for LEP students, which will allow them to experiment with oral language without fear.

One technique of many reflective teachers is to create small heterogeneous groups for learning so that students have more opportunity to express their needs and opinions and teachers can learn more about each student in small group discussions. These are not the old-fashioned high, low, and average reading groups. Under the active-learning approach, students are randomly placed in the groups so that they can interact with others who are learning at different rates, speak different languages, and have different interests.

When students are grouped for learning, LEP students are more likely to learn English when they are grouped with English speakers in heterogeneous groups than if they are grouped with other LEP students. Washington School in San Diego offers such a specially designed biliteracy program. Every student learns in both English and Spanish. Ylianna Romo and her colleagues at the school have worked together to create a whole language program using three heterogeneous groups that rotate through various tasks.

During a 2-hour language-arts block, the groups move through four different half-hour classes: (1) literature discussion group, (2) writing at their desks in response to the reading, (3) art activities in response to their reading, and (4) working to publish their own individual books, using the writing process, at the author's table. Ylianna is especially pleased with the results of this grouping system because she can learn a great deal more about her students' needs and interests when she is able to interact with them in small groups. The system also allows her students to feel more comfortable about speaking in their new languages (for some Spanish and for others English) in a small group than in front of the entire class. Many reflective teachers recognize that the presence of bilingual/bicultural students in their classrooms offers exciting possibilities for developing curriculum that celebrates and informs all students in the class about the cultural diversity of our world. Culture fairs featuring the crafts, music, food, and language of the many students in the school are excellent ways to meet the needs of students of all cultures, including the needs of white, middle-class students, and help everyone become aware of the contributions and values of others.

At the high school level, reflective teachers look for teaching methods that encourage dialogues among students who have grown up with different experiences and points of view. They also encourage their students to think about, compare, and speak openly about their varied experiences. Within academic subject matter curricula, reflective teachers are able to recognize that "there is not one correct history; there are multiple histories. There are multiple and diverse literatures, mathematics and sciences (O'Connor, 1995, p. 204).

Reflective high school teachers look for opportunities to weave the contributions of culturally diverse populations to their subject matter into the curriculum. Math teachers may point out, for example, the unique properties of Colombian mathematical systems that allowed the Mayas to invent the concept of zero and the Mexicano mathematical systems that allowed that culture to develop a calendar system more accurate than the one commonly used today. Science teachers may include information about the engineering systems initiated by the Incas that resulted in the successful building of the first suspension bridges and the passive solar-energy use perfected by the Native American Anasazis. History teachers will be sure to describe how framers of the U.S. Constitution used agreements of the Iroquois Indians as one of their models (Churchill, 1995, p. 20).

Growing ethnic diversity has brought many new opportunities as well as challenges for reflective, caring teachers and their students. You may hear other, less reflective teachers discuss generalizations such as how unmotivated a certain ethnic group of students is. That comes from a conception of learning that is badly out of date and out of sync with the changes in our multidimensional and multicultural world.

Assessing the Academic Needs of Your Students
TEACHERS' CONCEPTIONS OF HOW STUDENTS LEARN

How teachers diagnose their students' needs depends heavily on their conception of how students learn. Through experience and research, teachers construct personal theories of learning that then affect their perceptions and reasoning about what students are able to do and what they need. Anderson (1989) has identified two basic conceptions of learning that she terms the *receptive-accrual* (R-A) view and the *cognitive-mediational* (C-M) view (p. 86). These are difficult terms to recall, so I shall take the liberty of renaming them the *receptive learning* and the *active learning* views.

The receptive learning conception is a view that many teachers have held over the years. It is based on the assumption that some students have greater ability than others and that those with greater ability are able to receive and accumulate knowledge better and faster than those with less ability. Teachers with this point of view often diagnose students by categorizing them into groups according to what the teacher perceives as variations in ability: highs, middles, and lows.

A growing number of reflective teachers are questioning the receptive learning view of teaching and learning. Because they believe that all children can learn and that all children are capable of performing well and producing high-quality work, they prefer the active learning point of view. Their philosophy is based on an assumption that learning is a function of processing information and that some students have learned from experience how to process information more quickly and accurately than others. Teachers who hold this view do not diagnose students as having a fixed amount of ability. They refuse to group students according to their present or past abilities and to teach lower-level skills to some of their students. Instead, they reflect on the background experiences of each student they meet and seek information to help them discover what the student needs from the school environment to process information more skillfully.

INTERPRETING DATA FROM STUDENTS' CUMULATIVE FILES

A record of information called the *cumulative file* (often referred to as a *cume file*) is kept on each student in a school. Each year, the classroom teacher records in the students' files data such as information about the student's family, standardized test scores, reading levels, samples of written work, grades, and notes on parent-teacher conferences. At the end of a school year, the cume files are stored in the school or district office until the next year, when they are redistributed to the students' new teachers.

Obviously, these files contain much useful information for teachers to use in preliminary planning. By studying them, the teacher can make judgments about placement in reading, math, or other study groups before meeting the students. Alert teachers may discover information about a student's home environment, such as a recent divorce or remarriage, that can help them communicate with the student. Some files may reveal little about the students; others may be overflowing with records of conferences and staffings indicating that the student has exhibited a special need or difficulty.

Yet many teachers resist looking at their students' cume files before meeting the class. Tracy Kidder's (1989) *Among Schoolchildren* provides a realistic look at the entire school year of a fifth-grade class in upstate New York. In the opening chapter, which describes the beginning of the school year, the teacher, Chris Zajac, reflects on the value of cumulative files as she ponders what to do with a student named Clarence, whose negative attitudes toward school have become apparent on the first day.

> Chris had received the students' "cumulative" records which were stuffed inside salmon-colored folders known as "cumes." For now she checked only addresses and phone numbers, and resisted looking into histories. It was usually better at first to let her own opinions form. But she couldn't help noticing the thickness of some cumes. "The thicker the cume, the more trouble," she told Miss Hunt. "If it looks like *War and Peace* . . . " Clarence's cume was about as thick as the Boston phone book. And Chris couldn't help having heard what some colleagues had insisted on telling her about Clarence. One teacher whom Chris trusted had described him as probably the most difficult child in all of last year's fourth-grade class. Chris wished she hadn't heard that. (pp. 8–9)

While data and observations about students from former teachers may be valuable resources for planning, many reflective teachers, like Chris Zajac, are aware of the power of the self-fulfilling prophecy, in which their own expectations may influence the way their students behave or achieve in school. Good and Brophy (1987) define *teachers' expectations* as "inferences that teachers make about the future behavior or academic achievement of their students" and show that the self-fulfilling prophecy occurs when "an originally erroneous expectation leads to behavior that causes the expectation to become true" (p. 116).

When cume files contain data and descriptions of low academic achievement or misbehavior, nonreflective teachers may assume that the students are unteachable or unmanageable. On the first day of school, the teacher may place them at desks set apart from the rest of the class or hand them textbooks from a lower grade. Such actions tell the students how the teacher expects them to behave and perform in this class. If consistent over time, these expectations are likely to affect the students' self-concepts and motivations in such a way that they achieve poorly and behave badly. Conversely, consider the possible effects of warm, encouraging behavior from a teacher. If the teacher builds rapport with the students, includes them in all classroom activities from the first day, and works with them to establish their achievement levels and needs, their behavior and achievement are likely to improve during the year.

Reflective teachers who understand the great influence of their expectations on their students prefer to assess the strengths and needs of each student independently in the first few weeks of class. They may read the cume folders at the end of September to see how their assessments fit with those of the students' previous teachers.

A good case can be made for either strategy: using cume folders for preliminary planning or waiting to read them until you know the students better. You will need to consider and decide this issue for yourself. Perhaps if you understand the power of teacher expectations, you can find a way to use the information in the files to establish positive expectations and resist the tendency to establish negative ones.

INTERPRETING STANDARDIZED TEST RESULTS

In many ways the teacher's role in diagnosing students' needs is quite similar to the role of the physician in diagnosing disease. Doctors get information from observing and talking with patients about their medical histories. Similarly, teachers observe and talk with their students to assess their learning histories. But some important information needed for an accurate diagnosis cannot be observed or discussed. Just as doctors may find that laboratory tests provide them with valuable information about the patient, so teachers may find that achievement tests and other assessment procedures can provide them with valuable data about their students.

Some tests, known as *criterion-referenced tests*, are created by teachers themselves. They are designed to fit the subject being taught. Questions and problems on the tests directly reflect the teacher's lessons, and the teacher establishes the criteria for success. For example, after a week of geometry lessons, the teacher presents the students with a test consisting of 20 geometry problems that are similar to those studied during the week. As criteria for success, the teacher establishes a grading system of A = 90 percent correct, B = 80 percent correct, C = 70 percent correct, and so forth. Tests like these allow teachers to diagnose which students have learned the previous lessons and which students need reteaching.

A second type of test that teachers frequently use as a diagnostic tool is the *norm-referenced* achievement test battery given to all students in a school district once a year. These test batteries consist of reading, spelling, English, mathematics, science, and social studies exams given over several days. The teacher neither writes the questions nor establishes the criteria to fit a particular classroom. Instead, nationally recognized testing companies create the tests, writing the items to approximate what is taught across the nation in each subject area at each grade level.

Statistical calculations of test scores provide information about a student's performance. The score may be translated into a percentile or a grade-equivalent score. These interpretations are done by comparing the student's raw score with the raw scores of the sample population. A *percentile rank* tells you what percentage of the people tested scored below a given score. For example, if Joe receives a percentile rank of 78, this means that 78 percent of the students at Joe's grade level scored lower than he did.

Grade-equivalent scores were created by test publishers especially for use in schools. The results are reported as a function of grade level. For example, if Sally receives a grade-equivalent score of 4.2, this means that her performance is similar to students who are in the second month of fourth grade. If Sally is in the fourth grade, her score tells the teacher that she is doing about as well as she is supposed to be doing. If Sally is in the second grade, the score tells the teacher that she is capable of functioning like students two years above her present grade level. But if Sally is in sixth grade, her score alerts the teacher that she is functioning like students who are two years below her present grade level.

The use of standardized tests varies widely from district to district. Some schools use them to diagnose learning difficulties of individuals so that corrective measures can be taken. Some systems publish the test results in local newspapers to show how well students from different schools are doing in the basic skills. This practice is a controversial issue among educators. The tests were not designed to be used as a measure of excellence among schools, but the public or the press have come to believe that they can be used that way.

For example, in elementary schools, the average test scores on standardized reading achievement tests for each school in a district may be compared. Educators know that these conclusions are misleading because there are many other contributing factors, such as the socioeconomic conditions of the families whose children attend each school and the degree to which the items on the test match the school's curriculum.

Achievement tests were not designed to show aptitude for learning or to predict the achievement of any student. Reflective, caring teachers recognize that the teacher's interpretation of a student's low achievement test results could contribute to a negative self-fulfilling prophecy. To avoid that problem, the reflective, caring teacher interprets the information gained on standardized achievement tests with great caution and uses the scores as only one of a number of items contributing to a diagnosis of a student's needs.

Achievement tests were designed to help you make a general diagnosis of the current achievement level of your class so you can plan lessons to begin at that level. These tests can help you pinpoint the students in your class who have low achievement in a certain subject so that you can prescribe a special course of action for them. These tests help you to identify the students who have mastered the basic skills in one or more subjects so that you can provide them with more challenging learning experiences.

Another form of standardized test that your school district may give is the *aptitude* or *ability* test. Some test publishers have created short, timed, paper-and-pencil tests that purport to test the student's innate ability, which is quite a different construct from achievement in school. The scores are reported in the same format as IQ tests, with 100 as the mean and a standard deviation of approximately 15. These scores look like IQ scores; but because of their brevity and mass-production scoring, many educators are reluctant to give them much credence.

> Achievement tests have been defined as measuring what the student *has* learned up to the moment of testing. Aptitude tests, on the other had, were said to measure the student's *ability* to learn in the future. Achievement and aptitude tests are not all that different. A study of the actual test would show that in format and content they are quite similar. (Wick, 1973, p. 152)

PERCEIVING STUDENTS' LEARNING STYLES AND MULTIPLE INTELLIGENCES

Fast replacing the idea of a single IQ is the concept of *multiple intelligences,* described in *Frames of Mind* by Howard Gardner (1983). Gardner asserts that the concept of a single IQ is much too simple to explain all of the many talents and gifts human beings display. Instead, he has identified seven different intelligences, each one very different from the others. They include linguistic, logical-mathematical, musical, visual-spatial, interpersonal, and intrapersonal talents as well as the bodily-kinesthetic skills of the athlete. When you observe your students, you may be able to identify which of these talents each student displays in his or her interests and performance.

Many schools are experimenting with designing new educational programs designed to enhance each of the seven intelligences and to better recognize and address the varied gifts of all students. For example, Laura Ellison, a fifth-grade teacher at Clara Barton School in Minneapolis, meets with each student in her classroom at the beginning of the year to set personal goals for each of the seven intelligences. Midway through the year, she has a second round of conferences to determine with all students how they are doing in accomplishing their goals and whether they want to revise any of them. She encourages her students to record their accomplishments in their journals.

By observing students at work and listening to them explain how they came to understand something, teachers can also perceive the varying learning styles of their students. Learning styles are believed to be derived in part from biological and physical characteristics, as in a preference for learning visually, auditorially, or kinesthetically. A student's preference, in these three cases, may depend in large part on the relative strength of the student's vision, hearing, and motor coordination.

But learning styles also strongly reflect developmental, cultural, and other experiential factors. For example, students have different preferences for working alone or working with a group. Given a complex problem to solve and a project to create, some students prefer the challenge of working alone while others prefer the experience of working with a group. This may be the result of familiar cultural tendencies to work alone or with a group.

Grant and Sleeter (1989) suggest that teachers need to observe the learning styles of each student and describe the patterns they see on a learning-style record sheet that can be used in planning for teaching. The record sheet might describe whether the student prefers to work alone or with other people, and whether the student needs a great deal of structure or very little. Then observe and take notes on whether the student appears to learn best while watching, reading, listening, discussing, touching, moving, or writing.

One element of learning style is the need of some individuals for physical activity. This need can be easily misdiagnosed as a behavior disorder. For example, Fadley and Hosler (1979) found that teachers frequently refer students to psychologists for hyperactivity or attention deficit disorder (ADD). The teachers complained that the students were unable to sit quietly and pay attention during lessons. The psychologists in the study reported that most of the referred students were not clinically hyperactive at all; they were normal students in need of movement.

Other studies have found that when previously restless youngsters were reassigned to classes that did not require passivity, their behaviors were rarely noticed. Teachers report that certain students thrive in activity-oriented classrooms, while others remain stationary, despite frequent attempts by teachers to coax them to move. This demonstrates the variation among students in learning-style preferences. Reflective teachers are willing and able to use their withitness to detect when children who have short attention spans display a need for physical movement. They respond to the cues of restlessness among their students not with anger and resentment but with opportunities for active learning that involve physical movement.

Learning styles are like fingerprints. No two are alike. Teachers cannot identify all aspects of their students' learning styles, nor can they meet the many diverse needs these styles represent. It would be frustrating in the extreme to attempt to diagnose each student's learning style and provide a unique set of experiences for every student in the class. But what reflective, caring teachers can do is to respect the fact that variations in learning styles exist and be flexible enough to allow students to work in the ways they find most comfortable and productive.

Learning-style diagnosis and treatment is probably best accomplished by allowing students to make choices. Through self-selection, students can choose to work on a project alone or with a group, read at a desk or in a bean-bag chair, view a filmstrip or listen to an audiotape, do a measuring project involving movement or one that can be accomplished quietly in one spot. "No learning style is better or worse than another. Since each style has similar intelligence ranges, a students cannot be labeled or stigmatized by having any type of style. Most students can master the same content; how they master it is determined by their individual styles" (Dunn, Beaudry, & Klavas, 1989, p. 56).

PRETESTS AND STUDENT-TEACHER CONFERENCES

Interactive goal setting by teachers and students is probably the wave of the future in elementary education. When students are involved in planning and setting goals for their own learning, they are likely to be more highly motivated to achieve their goals. Individual goal setting leads quite naturally to journal writing and collecting evidence of student accomplishments for their individual portfolios. These systems also honor individual differences and allow teachers to plan for a wide range of diverse needs in a way that tests rarely do.

Other assessment devices such as pretests, however, provide teachers and students with useful information to plan what students need to learn and what teachers need to teach. At the beginning of a term or a unit of study, teachers often use pretests to determine what skills and knowledge pertaining to the subject students already have mastered. Pretests, also known as *readiness tests,* are designed to determine whether students have the skills and knowledge that will allow them to succeed in the new unit of study.

Some elementary subject-matter textbooks provide pretests and readiness tests. Others are available separately through test publishers. Kindergarten and first-grade teachers frequently use reading readiness tests at the beginning of the year to determine which students are capable of succeeding at the complex task of learning to read. Certain skills, especially visual and auditory discrimination, have been shown to be essential prerequisites for learning to discriminate between letter shapes and sounds. Students who score very low on a reading readiness test may be provided with a curriculum designed to improve their visual and auditory discrimination skills before they even attempt to learn to read. Readiness tests, then, are designed to prevent students from failing by identifying those who need preliminary experiences to help prepare them for the academic curriculum.

Many textbooks provide pretests matched to the content of the books themselves. Math textbooks may provide an initial pretest to be used at the beginning of the school year. English textbooks often provide pretests for each unit of study in the book, such as grammar, punctuation, sentences, and organization of paragraphs.

When textbook publishers do not provide pretests, the teacher can create them to fit virtually any unit of study. For example, before introducing a teacher-made unit on molecules and atoms, the teacher may write a brief pretest to determine what the students already know about this subject. Pretests can be designed to show the specific skills that a student lacks, leading to an individual diagnosis and a corrective plan of action. The teacher, an aide, a classroom volunteer, or a more capable peer can then provide the student with feedback on deficiencies and show the student how to master those skills. After mastering the skills, the student is then ready to join the class in the regular curriculum.

Students and teachers both need to reflect on the information gained from a pretest. The best use of pretests occurs when the teacher and the student discuss the results together and share their insights into what the student needs to do next. For example, a pretest may reveal a pattern of correctable mistakes in a mathematics operation. The teacher may be able to reteach the process quickly, and the student will then be able to proceed successfully. In another instance, a pretest may reveal that the student has mastered the material already, and the conference may then focus on an enriched or accelerated learning opportunity for that child while the other students are learning the material.

PLACEMENT AND GROUPING DECISIONS

Standardized tests and pretests are occasionally used to place students in special programs, tracks, or ability groups. Did your own educational experiences include being placed in a high, low, or average reading group? Were you placed in a gifted and talented program or did you miss the cutoff score? If so, what effects did your placement have on what you learned and how you felt about it?

Many elementary schools have used ability groups in the teaching of reading and mathematics. Three reading groups are typically identified in this way, and students are then taught the skills they have not yet mastered at a pace that appears to fit the group of similar or homogeneous students. Although teachers who use this approach may believe the groups are temporary, expedient devices to allow them to teach more efficiently, research shows that the groups are likely to have a permanent effect on students' achievement. Studies show that the achievement gap between the low and high groups widens each year.

Teachers may use data from pretests or standardized tests when creating cooperative teams or pairs for peer tutoring. To strengthen student motivation and interaction, many teachers employ the cooperative team concept. Cooperative groups typically consist of three to five students who are assigned a set of tasks to complete by cooperating with and assisting one another. In some classrooms, teachers use pretest data to decide which students to assign to each team. Often, teachers use cooperative groups to promote peer coaching and interactive assistance among their students. In this case, a team of four students may consist of one student with very strong performance, two with moderate performance, and one with relatively weak performance in the subject area. Similarly, peer tutoring dyads may consist of one skilled and one less skilled student. These are simply two examples; other types of cooperative group placement decisions, for different purposes, are also possible.

DETERMINING THE CAUSES OF UNDERACHIEVEMENT

Teachers who carefully structure their classroom lessons to ensure success are frequently baffled by the tendency of some students to fail to succeed even under optimal conditions. Rimm (1995) observes that there is no single cause for underachievement, nor is there a single cure. Also, no consistent characteristics are associated with underachievement. Some underachievers are bossy and aggressive; others are lonely and withdrawn. Some are slow and perfectionistic; others are hurried and disorganized. A few have adopted a behavior pattern of *learned helplessness* because of previous experiences in school, unusually high expectations at home, or a combination of both. These students perceive that they are certain to fail at whatever they try, so they have learned not to try.

Students from culturally diverse backgrounds or those raised in poverty may underachieve because of low self-esteem. Marc Elrich, a sixth-grade teacher in Washington, DC, was frustrated to find that even though he and his colleagues had created a curriculum celebrating diversity and talking about it as a source of strength, he was unable to change his students' own preconceptions about their self-worth. One year 27 members of his class of 29 students were either African American or Hispanic and had been raised in economically disadvantaged neighborhoods. Marc observed that even at age 10 or 11, most showed very low self-esteem and had low expectations for their future. He enriched his curriculum with many examples of African American and Hispanic literature and other contributions to art and music. Still, the stereotype within the students didn't seem to change.

In a discussion with his students exploring the issues of race, Marc heard his African American students attribute negative racial stereotypes to themselves. "Blacks are poor and stay poor because they're dumber than whites (and Asians)," they said. "Black people don't like to work hard. White people are smart and have money. Hispanics are poor and don't try hard because, like blacks, they know it doesn't matter."

Teachers like Marc are not willing to accept the status quo. They keep trying to create a therapeutic classroom environment that will encourage their culturally diverse students to raise their own hopes and expectations to appropriate levels. He reflected on how to teach them to like themselves. He considered the frequently used strategy of setting aside a month for studying black history but decided that this is not an adequate remedy. "These students aren't naïve. What are the other seven months? White history months?"

Marc hasn't solved this problem yet. Neither has our society. But you as teachers will have an opportunity to confront this difficult issue and create new educational opportunities to improve your students' view of themselves and encourage the people of our nation to grow together rather than apart. Chapter 13 offers another discussion of underachievement, focusing on the interaction between teachers and parents in understanding and correcting patterns of underachievement in students.

ASSESSMENT TO MEET THE NEEDS OF HIGH-ACHIEVING STUDENTS

Each school year, teachers discover one or more students in their classrooms who learn extremely easily and rapidly. Some of these students may excel in only one subject area. One student may perform brilliantly in math computation and problem solving; another may write long and complex stories, poems, and essays that express ideas far more mature than those of other students at the same age or grade level; still another may show a strong sense of leadership and understanding of social interactions among classmates and adults.

To serve the needs of these students, many school systems have established *gifted programs.* The assumption inherent in most gifted programs is that the regular class-room curriculum cannot meet the needs of students with unusually strong ability and achievement. Educators who are specialists in gifted education have designed a num-ber of alternative programs to serve the needs of such students.

Some gifted programs stress accelerated curricula in a subject area such as math. Stu-dents with standardized math test scores in the 95 to 99 percentile range are often placed in special programs that allow them to learn advanced mathematical concepts at a rapid pace. Other students may be placed in special enrichment classes focusing on lit-erature and writing. Others may be placed in special programs that allow them to work with a mentor in a field such as science or government (Cox, Daniel, & Boston, 1985).

In some schools, the gifted programs are not subject-specific. They are pull-out pro-grams (meaning that students are pulled out of the regular classroom) that allow stu-dents to work on independent studies or group projects that stress higher-level think-ing, research skills, and creativity.

As a classroom teacher, you may be asked to help identify students for the school's gifted programs. You may be asked to nominate students you believe need the services the program has to offer. In many cases, gifted program coordinators provide a form on which you rate the recommended student's behaviors and characteristics.

Conflicts occasionally arise over the selection of students for gifted programs. Par-ents may perceive their child to be gifted or may simply want their children to be included in these enriched programs for the educational value they represent. Teachers have varied values and expectations about student behavior and achievement that lead to inconsistent recommendations. One teacher may see a student as clearly gifted because of his creative and independent behavior, and another teacher may think that the same student is just an obnoxious troublemaker.

Careful reflection is needed in recommending students for special gifted programs and services. Consider the consequences of labeling some students gifted. Eby and Smutny (1990) examined the effects of gifted programs on children and concluded that "one effect of labeling a small minority of students 'gifted' is that we are also unwittingly labeling the remaining children in the family or school 'nongifted'" (p. viii). We advocate the elimination of the term *gifted student* in schools because of its negative effects.

In *A Thoughtful Overview of Gifted Education* (Eby & Smutny, 1990), we sought methods of teaching that provide for the needs of the high-achieving and talented students in the classroom without setting them apart from their peers. Although many teachers choose the conventional ability groups described previously, reflective, caring teachers can use other alternatives to meet the needs of high-achieving students. You can provide enriched materials and activities for any students who finish their regular work. If the materials are interesting and the activities motivating, this strategy has the added advantage of serving as a genuine incentive for completing assignments.

Teachers can have students with very advanced skills work at an accelerated pace on suitably challenging material from higher grade levels by providing them with texts and worksheets from the upper grades and supervising their work on an individual basis. This strategy is known as *mastery learning* because when students master a certain skill, they are allowed to proceed at their own pace to the next level.

You can team up with your colleagues and allow high-achieving students to take their math or reading from teachers in the upper grades. This is sometimes called *walking reading* or *walking math* because the students walk to the classroom for that one subject. It works best when the school has a uniform time for math and reading. Some schools use a system called *curriculum compacting* to modify the amount of repetitive work that high-achieving students must do. Students who demonstrate mastery of a subject or skill on a pretest are allowed to skip the classwork and homework on that topic. In their place, the teacher and student design an individual investigation using skills that meet the student's needs for appropriately challenging schoolwork in the regular classroom.

Another strategy teachers use to avoid boredom and provide stimulating challenges appropriate for high-achieving students is to form students into cooperative groups to assist one another in learning. This strategy does not allow for acceleration but does enrich the experiences of high-achieving students by allowing them to develop their communication and leadership skills as they assist other students in academic areas. See Chapter 9 for a more complete description of cooperative group strategies.

Perceiving and Meeting Students' Affective Needs

Maslow's (1954) theory of motivation proposed that humans have unconscious physical and emotional needs that must be met or satisfied before the person is able to pay attention to outside stimuli. Translated into everyday classroom situations, a hungry student's need for food must be met before the multiplication facts can be learned; a frightened student must be comforted before full attention can be given to phonics; a lonely student must have a friend before learning to show concern for the environment.

If you have a concern about a student who is not performing well in school, you will want to make a very careful, thoughtful diagnosis about whether the student's basic needs for food, shelter, safety, security, and love are being met. To make this type of diagnosis, most reflective teachers rely on informal assessment strategies such as observation and conferences with the student, the parents, and the student's previous teachers.

Informal assessment and diagnostic strategies are quite different from formal testing procedures. To be effective, the teacher must handle the informal assessment with genuine caring and interest. Taking a student into the hall and asking, with teeth clenched and finger pointed, "What makes you act like this?" will elicit few illuminating responses. The student is likely to withdraw, lie, or rebel in this situation.

If a conference with a student or with parents is to succeed in helping a teacher discover the student's underlying needs and motivations, the teacher must be willing and able to listen empathetically to the student's (and the family's) fears and hopes. Sometimes a conference in the school setting is not sufficient to encourage students to talk about themselves. American teachers rarely visit students' homes, but such a visit may reveal much more about the student's needs than can be learned in a classroom. I have used, as a neutral ground, a lunchtime or after-school visit with a troubled student to a nearby hamburger stand to find out more about what makes the student behave as he or she does.

Whatever the setting, the informal assessment conference also needs some careful planning to be successful. Jot down ideas that you want to discuss, questions that you want to ask, and encouraging remarks that you want to make before you meet with the student or the parents. The conference may reveal some very surprising information, but you will need to follow the lead of the student and the family concerning how much of their private lives they want to reveal to you.

On occasion, you may find that students and families want to reveal more than you can comfortably assimilate. Difficult issues of poverty, divorce, abandonment, and other damaging social conditions may cause you to feel overwhelmed and helpless to serve the best interests of this student. In cases of severe social and emotional problems, it is recommended that you refer the student to the school psychologist and other school personnel who can assist in making a diagnosis and recommending a treatment plan.

PLANNING FOR STUDENTS WITH SPECIAL NEEDS

Students in most classrooms present a range of differences in abilities, experiences, motivations, and needs. No class is made up entirely of homogeneous, average, well-behaved students who learn easily. Recent studies show that "teaching and learning proceed nicely for about half of the students in our schools. For the other half, there are difficulties" (Anderson, 1989, p. 129). These students have many varied needs. Some have been identified as physically, mentally, or emotionally challenged; they may receive special services or classes from special education resource teachers who have received special training to address their needs. Others may be thought of as economically disadvantaged but have never been formally diagnosed or serviced by special education. Still others may have come from homes in which English is not spoken or from migrant families who move frequently, resulting in educational disruption.

Can a single teacher, in a single school year, fill all these needs, combat all these inequities, and right all these wrongs? No. But can a reflective, caring teacher fill some of these needs, combat some of these inequities, and right some of these wrongs for some students? Yes. Teachers who are willing to diagnose needs and search for solutions to difficult problems can assist some students in getting their needs met and can make significant, positive differences in the lives of some of the students placed in their classrooms. Moreover, if teachers are able to work with the special education teachers and other professionals in the school system or the community, they can help students and their families meet their needs more effectively.

Today, most students are screened for special needs in preschool or when they register for kindergarten. These needs may stem from physical challenges, emotional difficulties in the family, or social and economic circumstances that have prevented the child from having early learning experiences. Students who are identified as having special needs are believed to be at greater risk of failure in school than other children are. Educators refer to these children as *students at risk*.

Occasionally preschool screenings do not identify such students, and they enter school without the benefit of special services. In this case, it takes an alert teacher to spot the difficulties and refer the student for special testing and assessment. This is an important responsibility for teachers to consider when they examine the test scores of students in their classes and observe a pattern of learning difficulties that no one else has noted in the student's cume file.

Until recently, students at risk were often placed in special education programs, and many were categorized and labeled as being handicapped or learning disabled. Federal laws (in particular, Public Law 94-142) and the Americans with Disabilities Act (ADA) require that all states provide "a continuum of alternative placements" to meet the needs of at-risk students but also stipulate that they should be educated in "the least restrictive environment compatible with his or her educational needs." To meet these requirements, many schools are encouraging special education teachers to collaborate with regular classroom teachers in planning how to meet the needs of the at-risk students in each classroom. In many districts, at-risk students receive instruction from special education teachers and regular classroom teachers who coteach in the same classroom.

A learning disabilities specialist, Rick Bailey, who teaches at West Elementary School in Crystal Lake, Illinois, describes in Case 3.1 how he interacts with classroom teachers on these important decisions.

Case 3.1 ⟳ Reflective Action
How Special Education Teachers and Classroom Teachers Coteach to Meet the Needs of Students at Risk

Rick Bailey, Special Education Teacher
West Elementary School, Crystal Lake, Illinois

Perceptiveness

Until recently, special education teachers worked with students who had been referred to them because of special needs. Typically, the children were pulled out of the regular classroom, and the special education teacher provided an individualized program designed to meet the child's unique needs. However, research showed that the performance of those children did not significantly improve and, particularly as the children got older, there were social disadvantages because the children believed that there was a stigma attached to being required to go to the special education classroom.

Proactive Construction of Knowledge

The question I had to address was "How am I going to serve these children in the areas where they have identified needs and still let them remain in the regular classroom?" Initially, I believed that my pull-out program did make a difference for my students and that it was effective in meeting their needs. Larry Glowacki, the director of special education in my district, announced that we were going to move toward a new way of delivering special education services. The special education teacher would now go into the regular classroom where special education students were assigned and coteach with the regular classroom teacher. The goal was that through this coteaching partnership the needs of the special education student and the needs of the regular students would be met.

The primary source of information about this new type of programming was provided by consultants who came to our district to explain to all the special education teachers how we could implement a coteaching model. We saw videotapes of classes using this method, and we read a collection of articles describing a variety of ways that special education teachers could share responsibilities with the regular teachers.

Clarifying Values and Principles

As we learned about the new coteaching model, we recognized that there could be many pitfalls to success. We didn't want the special education teacher to be treated as an aide in the regular classroom or to be seen as the person who sat by the special education student as the classroom teacher taught the whole class. In order to make this coteaching successful, it was imperative for the classroom teacher and the special education teacher to discuss their roles thoroughly so that there was an understanding of each teacher's responsibilities.

Coteaching is based on the principle of inclusion, which means that children with special needs deserve to be included in the full range of school activities without being segregated because of their particular disability. We wanted our plan to exhibit this inclusive policy.

Communication Skills

I met with all the classroom teachers who had special education students in their classrooms. We discussed the numbers and the types of children who were going to be assigned to classrooms the following year. I believed that the classroom teachers deserved to have input into how the students were assigned and how the coteaching would be implemented. The strategies suggested by classroom teachers became very important in defining the new program.

Creativity

The whole language program provided the model that allowed me to see how I could teach effectively in the regular classroom. It allows the classroom teacher and me to provide instruction that is relevant for both children with learning difficulties and their peers. It is based on the whole language principle of demonstration, which means that instruction in specific skills is modeled by the teacher as children are involved with literature and writing experiences.

In the fall, I began coteaching in five classrooms in three grade levels. The scheduling was difficult and required a lot of negotiation with the classroom teachers. I made sure that I established myself as a coteacher in each classroom by doing a series of demonstration lessons from the Frameworks program to the entire class. Then I worked in small groups with children who needed additional teaching or extra practice. In these small groups were the children identified with learning difficulties who were assigned to that class. In these small group sessions, I made sure that the needs of my special education students were met.

Persistence and Problem Solving

In the classes in which I am coteaching, because there are two teachers, we act as role models for each other, giving each other support, guidance, ideas, and feedback. I have had classroom teachers say to me that they have learned so much by watching me teach, and I feel the same way about watching them. To a great extent, this model is helping many of the teachers in our building develop a new spirit of collaboration.

One of the things that has been so surprising and gratifying to me is to see how well the special education students are doing in the regular classroom. I'm seeing them have a more positive attitude about themselves and about learning than I saw in the pull-out program. I'm seeing greater academic success as well. Other children in the classroom who have needs that haven't been identified are also being served by this model. Another benefit for me is that by seeing and working with children in the regular classroom, I have a clearer understanding of how all children learn than I had by working only with special education students.

Teachers should not assume that all students in the regular classroom have been properly diagnosed. A fourth-grade teacher may be the first one to observe a student's learning disability; a sixth-grade teacher may be the first one to suspect a student of having a disabling emotional disturbance. When this occurs, the teacher's role is to refer the student to the school psychologist or other special education personnel for further testing and assessment. When the testing is completed, the classroom teacher will be part of a group of teachers and parents who recommend special educational opportunities for this particular student.

The beginning teacher should be aware that the process of referring, assessing, and identifying special needs is an imperfect system. Tests and their results may be invalidated by some condition in the testing situation, or the tests themselves may be limited in their ability to predict or measure complex human needs and traits. The size and budget of the school system may limit services to only a small percentage of those who could benefit from the services. Many teachers experience great frustration when they refer a student for special programs or services and the student is placed on a long waiting list for such services. Reduced budgets and resources in most school districts have caused cutbacks in services just at the time when more services seem to be needed. Classroom teachers must reflect on how they can provide an environment for learning for all their students, and they must be resourceful in getting assistance for the growing number of students who have special needs.

PERCEIVING THE NEEDS OF URBAN CHILDREN

Urban schools have many more immigrant families than do suburban or rural schools. This results in classrooms of greater diversity in language and culture when compared with other areas. Cities also have more than their share of poverty, violence, and drugs. What can a caring, reflective teacher do to perceive and meet the needs of students who live in an often chaotic, unsafe environment? One thing you can do is to choose to teach in the toughest, most difficult schools, where you are needed the most. Suburban school districts have many applications for a few teaching positions, while cities are often searching for teachers to fill their openings. Once inside the district, become one of the agents for change and school improvement.

Often, the initiatives that meet students' needs are started by teachers rather than by more distant school administrators or school boards. For example, in Chicago, a group of teachers proposed that schools be downsized in response to a study showing that small schools make school improvement more likely. Two years later, there are now 50 small schools in the city. Small schools fulfill students' need for a sense of belonging and the feeling that they know and are known by their classmates, teachers, and administrators. The need for a sense of community is difficult to meet in a large city, but it is possible when teachers have the moral courage to make it happen.

Urban areas have their strengths as well as their deficiencies for students and teachers. Many new curriculum initiatives bring students to work and learn in the great museums, libraries, and corporate and public offices of our urban centers.

PERCEIVING THE NEEDS OF RURAL STUDENTS

Rural schools also have a difficult time creating a sense of community for their students. Chris Roberts, another courageous teacher in the rural community of Spanish Fork, Utah, attended a workshop given by William Glasser on the total quality school. Wanting to know more and to construct his knowledge from the best source possible, he initiated a telephone dialogue with Dr. Glasser and invited him to visit Rees School, where Chris taught. As a result of this visit, Rees became one of the first six schools in Glasser's Quality School Consortium (Harris & Harris, 1992). This behavior epitomizes the heart of the reflective action model. Chris perceived a need for higher-quality educational experiences for himself and his students. He wanted to build his knowledge base, so he attended workshops on total quality schools and then took the risk of telephoning Dr. Glasser. Their communication about shared values and innovative strategies led to many changes in his school.

One of the innovations recommended by Chris Roberts and several other classroom teachers was the formation of "big friendly groups" and "little friendly groups," designed to encourage interaction among students who may live far away from each other in their far-flung community. They also designed a thematic, integrated curriculum based on six rotating themes: power, communities, change, interactions, form, and systems. Roberts's special education students are included in the study of these themes as part of a multi-age grouping system.

Displayed in every classroom at Rees School is this statement: "All problems will be solved by the staff and students talking with each other without anyone threatening or hurting anyone else." As teachers supervise or confer with students about their work, they ask each child to answer the question, "Is this high-quality work?" In this friendly environment, rural special education students are thriving and performing well along with their classmates in the regular program (Harris & Harris, 1992).

IDENTIFYING STUDENTS' NEEDS WITHOUT LABELING

Diagnosing students' needs certainly requires teachers to reflect as they consider the many causes of low achievement and plan appropriate school programs for students. It also requires a great deal of caring. Sometimes noncaring teachers view diagnosis as equivalent to labeling. For example, a quick perusal of a cume file, a glance at a standardized test score, and a few days of classroom observation can lead a teacher to label a student a "slow learner," "behavior-disordered," or and "underachiever." When communicated to the student and his or her parents, such labels can have disabling effects all by themselves. The implication of these labels—that the student is deficient in some important way—can lead to a self-fulfilling prophecy as further erosion of self-concept and self-confidence causes even more severe learning difficulties.

Students with excellent school performance can also suffer from labeling. Some teachers refer to their most capable and willing students as "overachievers." This pseudo-scientific term is attached to students whose standardized test scores are only moderate but whose grades and work habits are excellent. The implication is that these students are working beyond their capacity, and this is somehow seen as a negative characteristic by some teachers.

Students with high test scores on standardized tests, especially on IQ tests, are frequently labeled gifted students. This label may appear to be a very positive one; certainly, many parents seek it for their children. But careful reflection reveals that this label may be as damaging as any other. Rimm (1995) notes: "Any label that unrealistically narrows prospects for performance by a student may be damaging" (p. 84). Being labeled a gifted student tends to narrow the expectations for performance for that student to a constant state of excellence; any performance less than excellent can be interpreted by the student (and the parents) as unacceptable.

The label "gifted" has many other negative implications. When a small percentage of students (usually 2–5 percent) in a school are labeled "gifted," the other 95 percent of students are unwittingly labeled "not gifted." This has extremely negative consequences for those students who are siblings of "gifted students" and also for those who are excluded because their test scores are a few points below the cutoff score (Eby & Smutny, 1990).

While special programs are essential for the academic success and emotional well-being of many students in schools today, we must find ways of diagnosing students' needs and deciding on appropriate services without using damaging labels.

Broader labels can be just as damaging. "The term minority itself carries with it a connotation of being less than other groups with respect to power, status, and treatment. Even in situations where a minority group outnumbers other ethnic groups in population size, it may still be relegated to minority status due to the socioeconomic and power structure of the community" (Chinn, 1982, p. 25).

Terms such as *culturally disadvantaged, culturally deprived,* and *economically underprivileged* do not serve any useful purpose and can cause unknown effects when used without regard for the feelings of students and their parents from cultures other than the white middle class. Furthermore, these terms do not recognize the intrinsic value and unique contributions of individuals or groups.

Diagnosing students' needs can take place without reference to stereotypes and labels. Children who need assistance in learning English can be released from the classroom to work with an ESL teacher or tutor. Children who need a fast-paced math course can travel to another class for math. Children who need practice in visual discrimination and organizing for learning can have this service. But they can all be welcomed back to the regular classroom for most of the day, where they can share their cultural diversity and talents with each other in a community for learning and growing.

⊃ Reflective Actions for Your Professional Portfolio
An Example of Your Student Needs Assessment Plan

Perceptiveness: Assessing Learning Styles

Arrange to interview one student. Ask questions to learn about his or her preferred learning style. Sample questions are provided here, but you may want to make up your own as well.

> Do you learn easily by reading about something?
>
> Do you learn well by listening to a teacher explain something?
>
> Do you need the teacher to write examples on the board?
>
> Do you learn best by having somebody show you something or by working alone?
>
> Do you need a quiet room, or can you work when others are talking or when the TV is on?
>
> Does it bother you when there is movement around you?

Add to your information by calling the student's parents to find out what they have observed about how their child learns best. From your interview, write your diagnosis of this student's learning style. Then recommend the classroom conditions that you believe to be important for this student to learn effectively.

Construction of Knowledge Base: Students with Special Needs

Students come into your classroom with a variety of cognitive, affective, and social needs. How do you learn how to meet the special needs of students with physical handicaps, learning difficulties, and cultural or language differences? What strategies do you use to meet their needs and provide them with opportunities to experience pride and success?

Clarification of Values and Principles: Multiple Intelligences

Assess your own strengths and talents according to Gardner's seven intelligences: verbal, mathematical reasoning, musical, visual arts, physical/kinesthetic, interpersonal, and intrapersonal. Which are your greatest strengths or weaknesses? Do you wish to strengthen your talents or your weaknesses in your own life? Do you believe it is more important to strengthen your students' talents or develop the areas in which they are weak?

Creativity: Multiple Intelligence Curriculum

Select a topic for a learning experience that you would like to teach. Consider the needs of students with various learning styles or types of intelligence. Write a description of what you will do and what you will allow the students to do so that your students can use each type of intelligence to accomplish something of value.

Persistence and Problem Solving: Learning from Experience

Teach the multiple intelligence learning experience you designed. Assess the effects on your students. What did they gain from it? What were the troublesome areas? Did they expand their strengths or weaknesses? How can you improve this type of lesson?

Communication Skills: Building a Cultural Bridge

Select a student whose culture is very different from yours. Talk with the student about what is important and valued in his or her family. Share your own memories of growing up with that student. Look for common experiences and discuss your differences. If possible, try to meet the student's family and learn what the parents' hopes and expectations are for their child. Write in your journal what you have to teach this child and what the child can teach you.

References

Anderson, L. (1989). Learners and learning. In M. Reynolds, *Knowledge base for the beginning teacher* (pp. 85–104). New York: Pergamon.

Banks, J. (1994). Transforming the mainstream curriculum. *Educational Leadership, 51*(8), 4–8.

Chinn, P. (1982). Curriculum development for culturally different exceptional children. In C. Thomas & J. Thomas (Eds.), *Bilingual special education resource guide* (pp. 22–37). Phoenix: Oryx.

Churchill, W. (1995). White studies. In S. Jackson & J. Solis (Eds.), *Beyond comfort zones in multiculturalism* (pp. 47–69). Westport, CT: Bergin & Garvey.

Cox, J., Daniel, N., & Boston, B. (1985). *Educating able learners.* Austin: University of Texas Press.

Dunn, R., Beaudry, J., & Klavas, A. (1989). Survey of research on learning styles. *Educational Leadership, 46*(6), 50–57.

Eby, J., & Smutny, J. (1990). *A thoughtful overview of gifted education.* White Plains, NY: Longman.

Fadley, J., & Hosler, V. (1979). *Understanding the alpha child at home and at school.* Springfield, IL: Thomas.

Gardner, H. (1983). *Frames of mind.* New York: Basic Books.

Good, T., & Brophy, J. (1987). *Looking in classrooms.* New York: Harper & Row.

Grant, C. & Sleeter, C. (1989). *Turning on learning.* Upper Saddle River, NJ: Merrill/Prentice Hall.

Harris, M., & Harris, R. (1992). Glasser comes to a rural school. *Educational Leadership, 50*(3), 18–21.

Kidder, T. (1989). *Among schoolchildren.* Boston: Houghton Mifflin.

Maslow, A. (1954). *Motivation and personality.* New York: Harper & Row.

O'Connor, T. (1995) Education in community: The role of multicultural education. In S. Jackson & J. Solis (Eds.), *Beyond comfort zones in multiculturalism* (pp. 70–84). Westport, CT: Bergin & Garvey.

Rimm, S. (1995). *Why smart kids get poor grades.* New York: Crown. Wick, J. (1973). *Educational measurement: Where are we going and how will we know when we get there?* Upper Saddle River, NJ: Merrill/Prentice Hall.

4

How Teachers Plan School Programs

One of classroom teachers' most important responsibilities is to plan the *curriculum*, the course of events and learning experiences for their students. To illustrate the complexity of the planning process, here is a brief account of some of the issues that Lori Shoults faced during her first three months at Seth Paine Elementary School in Lake Zurich, Illinois.

When I first walked into my empty classroom in August, I was greeted by a big box of textbooks. I had been hired by this school district because of my interest in and enthusiasm for the whole language approach to teaching reading and writing. So I had the freedom to create my own curriculum rather than rely on the texts. With that freedom came a lot of hard work.

It was very hard to plan before knowing my students, especially the first year, when I didn't even know what second graders were like. I wanted the curriculum in my classroom to be fully integrated. I wanted science and social studies to be a part of reading and writing. What I did was examine all the textbooks in great detail. I made lists of skills that were taught in the English, phonics, and spelling books. From the science, social studies, and reading basals, I looked for topics. I divided the year into two- or three-week integrated units on topics such as plants, weather, light, magnets, dinosaurs, animals, and safety.

Within these units, I taught my reading and English skills every morning in a new poem that was related to the unit's theme. I distributed a poem to the students, and they glued it into their folders. We read the poem once just to enjoy its ideas and sounds. Then each day, I asked the students to look for examples of phonics rules, word structures, types of sentences, and punctuation. I focused on two or three new skills each day.

Because I used the whole language approach, the students chose their own reading materials from the books in our room or in the library. To encourage them to read, I decided to use a reading incentive program, which gave credit or rewards for the number of books each student read. But when I considered this idea, it had a lot of drawbacks. Children who read short, easy books would appear to get more credit than those who read long, challenging books. I talked to other teachers to find out what they had tried. One teacher told me about a system of having students keep track of the number of minutes they read rather than the number of books. When I considered this approach, I concluded that it was more productive than focusing on the number of books read because my goal was for the students to read longer stories and books rather than just counting books. It also seemed more fair because students at different achievement levels read books of different lengths. This system gave equivalent credit to each student for time spent reading at every reading level.

The social studies textbook focused on the concepts of community and geography. I decided to have an overall theme of community, which I implemented by establishing a simulated community in the classroom. We had a teacher, a sheriff, a mayor, a meteorologist, a banker, and a gardener. Students signed up for the jobs they wanted and rotated every week. The learning stations in the class were community sites such as a post office (letter-writing center), a greenhouse (science center), a newspaper stand (writing center), a telephone company (listening center), a library (reading center), a toy store (learning games), and a computer lab.

My organizational problems were growing more difficult each day. At the beginning of the year, I tried to do it all at once. In addition to my regular reading, writing, and math programs, I set up five rotating math enrichment stations, the community stations, a geography program, and literature circles in which students discussed books they were reading on their own. I wasn't able to get to all of these things as I had planned. I kept running out of time during the day. The students were confused. They were always asking me when we were going to do different things.

So I sat down and planned for one special activity each day. On Tuesdays we would do community stations, on Wednesdays we had our literature circles, and on Fridays we had math enrichment stations. I thought it would be better to have a consistent schedule. The students wanted to know what to expect, and I felt better knowing when to plan for each activity.

For mathematics, I examined the basal text and believed that I could cover the skills in more interesting ways. I wanted to teach with more hands-on activities and use fewer math pages. I decided to use the Everyday Mathematics *program (Bell, 1990) for teaching concepts and use the textbook for practice and review. I also gave the tests from the math book. After using this approach for several months, I found that the students were able to do the textbook tests successfully. More important to me, they were enthusiastic about math. Even my lowest-achieving students felt confident participating in math activities.*

After three months of teaching, I believed that I was beginning to think like a teacher. At the beginning of the year, my schema for teaching and learning was rudimentary, leading me to make most decisions by trial and error. But later I felt I had expanded my knowledge and experience base to the point that when I reflected on a decision, I had a much better understanding of the consequences of my actions.

As Lori's account shows, teachers face a multitude of complex issues and judgments in their own classrooms. As a teacher, Lori has a great deal of freedom to decide what to teach and when to teach it, but behind the scenes, her decisions are influenced by many forces, both past and present. For one thing, history and tradition exert powerful influences over what is taught in schools. The three Rs have served as the basis for planning in U.S. schools for more than a century, and there are active and vocal groups of citizens who believe that the primary goal of K–12 schools should be to instill these basic skills in their students.

Some groups believe that schools are the custodians of the culture and that the primary goal of education should be to develop good citizenship and understanding of the great ideas and literature produced by Western civilization. Others believe strongly that the primary goal of a modern education is to teach students how to use reasoning, problem-solving, and communication skills as a means of learning how to learn so that they are able to gather the information they will need in their lives.

Still others believe that the new wave of computer technology available to future generations makes older forms of learning obsolete. They call for an emphasis on the use of technology in K–12 schools to prepare students for a future that will be vastly different from the present. There is also a growing trend toward creating school programs that are multidisciplinary and multicultural by design, with a new emphasis on investigation, inquiry, research, experimentation, and conflict resolution.

Lori discovered how difficult it is to plan so many different types of school programs all at once. Like many beginning teachers, she wanted to incorporate the best ideas from all of the influential groups she had read about in her teacher education program. At times the responsibility seemed so overwhelming that she might have wished that there was just one standard curriculum for all teachers to follow.

How School Curricula Are Planned
NATIONAL STANDARDS IN THE PLANNING STAGE

Many nations have uniform standards for school curricula. When these standards exist, individual teachers plan their daily programs to coincide precisely with national expectations. In some countries, if you were able to visit several schools in various cities at the same time of the school year, you would find the students using the same textbooks and working on the same chapter as students in other cities and rural areas of that country. Periodically, all children attending the schools take national examinations as a means of testing whether they have learned the requisite material and, at the same time, whether schools are accomplishing their mission of teaching the national curriculum.

Other countries, including the United States, have no such tradition of a uniform mandated curriculum. Historically, the regulation and supervision of K–12 curriculum has resided with the states; and although many states have established curriculum guidelines and examinations, there has also been a strong public sense that the best curriculum is the one planned at the local level based upon local interests, values, resources, and the needs of a particular group of students in each school district.

Recently, however, some school districts have been criticized by the media or by citizen watchdog groups because their students have performed badly on a variety of tests and measurements of academic progress. As a result of the public's perception that some school districts prepare students for the world much better than other school districts do, a debate is growing over the value of establishing national standards for student performance. Concurrently, there are movements to establish national standards for the preparation of teachers and for teaching effectiveness.

In response to the public's desire to be able to measure and compare the progress of students across the nation, Congress mandated the Department of Education to provide a set of assessment tools to measure K–12 students' subject-matter knowledge in five areas. They produced a document known as the National Assessment of Educational Progress (NAEP), which is commonly referred to as the nation's report card. NAEP provides benchmarks for each subject area. A *benchmark* is a statement describing what students should be able to do or demonstrate at various grade levels.

As is often the case in a vigorous, multicultural democracy such as the United States, there is little agreement about the form that educational standards should take or how they should be used. Subject-area specialists, for example, argue that their disciplines are so different from each other that standardizing performance expectations across the disciplines would be impossible (Viadero, 1993).

Many other philosophical debates concern the purpose of national standards in education. Before establishing one set of universally accepted standards, educators will need to agree on issues such as whether the national standards and benchmarks ought to describe basic or minimal competency in each subject area or whether they ought to describe how experts perform. A national debate remains over the value of emphasizing content or process knowledge in most subject areas, and this causes the authors of standards and benchmarks to disagree about whether to assess content knowledge or performance standards.

National councils of various subject-matter specialties have led the debate by proposing their own standards, and these standards have gained wide respect among educators in many school districts across the country. The National Council of Teachers of Mathematics (NCTM), for example, contributed a set of guidelines for curriculum planning based upon what the NCTM believes every student needs to understand about mathematics (NCTM, 1989). These standards are described in more detail later in this chapter in the section entitled "Long-Term Planning in Mathematics."

In science, three national committees on science have each published a set of content standards for K–12 students as well as performance standards for teachers. The National Committee on Science Education Standards and Assessment (NCSESA) has issued a comprehensive set of standards and benchmarks in its document *National Science Education Standards* (1994). As you will read in the section "Long-Term Planning in Science," the NCSESA has provided content and process standards for grades K–4 and 5–8.

The National Council for the Social Studies (1994), has published *Expectations of Excellence: Curriculum Standards for Social Studies,* which organizes the social studies curriculum into 10 thematic strands. The National Center for History in the Schools (NCHS) has also published a document outlining its expectations of students' history knowledge.

A variety of language-arts standards are also available from the National Council of Teachers of English (NCTE) and other organizations. They attempt to describe the knowledge and skills important to learning to speak, read, write, and listen. Other standards have been created for the arts, health education, physical education, and foreign languages. Kendall and Marzano (1995) collected and synthesized the content standards and benchmarks in 11 different categories. As a teacher, you may be interested in reviewing a document such as this to help you begin to comprehend the scope and breadth of the debate about the value of implementing national curriculum standards.

STATE CURRICULUM GUIDELINES

In the United States, each state has a department of education that has traditionally taken responsibility for establishing guidelines for curriculum development. Many states are revising their curriculum guidelines by inviting representative teachers and administrators from all areas of the state to form a committee responsible for reviewing the standards and benchmarks created by national subject-matter councils and considering ways to incorporate these standards into the state's curricular goals for each major subject area. State departments of education publish and distribute the resulting documents to all of the school districts they serve.

The California State Department of Education, for example, provides teachers with two documents for each major academic subject area. The *Curriculum Framework* communicates the state committee's basic goals and expectations for each subject area, and the *Model Curriculum Guide* provides details for how the frameworks can be translated into classroom experiences.

In California school districts, teachers use the frameworks and curriculum guides to establish their own patterns of teaching and learning. Recommended textbooks and core literature have been identified in the model curriculum guides. These are made available to teachers in county- or district-run media centers throughout the state.

Maine, in contrast, provides a very different set of guidelines for its teachers. In place of reading, 'riting, and 'rithmetic, *Maine's Common Core of Learning* organizes the curriculum into four transdisciplinary categories of learning: The Human Record, Reasoning and Problem Solving, Communication, and Personal and Global Steward-ship (Gaidimas & Walters, 1993). School districts have the responsibility to interpret these broad categories and create learning experiences that develop students' compre-hension and application of these areas of knowledge.

How Curriculum Is Transformed in Practice

In response to state mandates or guidelines, school districts usually form committees of teachers, administrators, and curriculum consultants to write or revise their curriculum documents that specify goals and expectations for their students. Often these local school district curriculum guides specify textbooks and tests that teachers may use. While some people may believe that these documents are the one and only curriculum in that district, reflective teachers recognize that four different curricula exist in any school.

The *intended curriculum* is the explicit and approved one; usually it takes the form of curriculum guides or lesson plans. However, close observation reveals an implicit or *hidden curriculum* that is not written anywhere but is pervasive nonetheless. It varies from teacher to teacher, depending on individual values and interests. In practice, teachers can all use the same lesson plan but teach strikingly different lessons depend-ing on their values, knowledge about the subject, interests, and the time they have allotted to the lesson.

Another type is the *null curriculum*. In this context, the word *null* means "vacant" or "omitted." It consists of whatever the teacher deletes or omits because of lack of time, interest, or knowledge. This is an important issue that can't be ignored. Teachers send messages to their students in subtle ways. The elementary teacher who has science scheduled for the last period of the day and never seems to get to it is telling the stu-dents that science is something to be ignored, put off, or not liked. Or the method of teaching may nullify some important elements of the intended curriculum. When a teacher teaches science by reading aloud from the textbook and answering the ques-tions at the end of the chapter, he or she is clearly not meeting the intent of state frame-works to get students involved in the process of doing science.

Even when teachers follow the curriculum guides, the actual *delivered curriculum* may differ markedly from the intended, planned curriculum. This is because each teacher plans different lessons and delivers the intended curriculum in a unique way. Another transformation occurs as students receive the lessons taught by their teachers. Because each student has different aptitude, interests, and preexisting knowledge and schema, the *experienced curriculum* differs for every student.

In this chapter, practicing teachers discuss their role and share their experiences about how they reflect upon and synthesize the expectations of the state, the district, and their own perceptiveness of what their students need to plan and deliver the curriculum for their grade levels.

EVALUATION AND USE OF TEXTBOOKS

School textbooks have enormous impact on the curriculum. Elementary school textbooks are undergoing major revisions to meet the demand for updated, student-centered, active learning rather than the older emphasis on receptive, rote learning. Many of these changes are controversial, reflecting the often divisive issues that are hot topics among adults in our society.

One of the greatest controversies regarding textbooks today is the rewriting of social studies textbooks to include multiple perspectives on history. Critics of traditional textbooks suggest that they are written solely from the perspective of the white European male. They believe students should learn history from multiple perspectives. Traditionalists believe that eliminating or ignoring content in the traditional textbooks will misrepresent history and that the subject will become diluted in an effort to please every ethnic group. Reflective teachers attempt to clarify their own values and their own curriculum orientations and beliefs as they make decisions about the curriculum they teach.

When first-year teachers move into their classrooms, the textbooks are already there, in formidable rows or piled in cumbersome stacks. Novice teachers have been told about the importance of individualizing education and meeting the needs of all students in their professional preparation programs. When reality sets in, they realize that many of the materials they need to plan a highly creative program that meets the students' individual needs are not in the classroom. A less reflective teacher will, without thinking, distribute the textbooks and begin teaching on page 1, perhaps emulating former teachers, with the intent of plowing through the entire book by the end of the year.

Reflective teachers, however, are more inquisitive and more independent in their use of textbooks. They ask questions of other teachers: "How long have you been using these textbooks? How were they chosen? Which parts match the school or district curriculum guides? Which parts are most interesting to the students? What other resources are available? Where do you go to get your ideas to supplement the textbook? In your first year of teaching, how did you meet the individual needs of your students when you had only textbooks available to you?"

Connie Muther, director of the Textbook Adoption Advisory Service, advises teachers to examine critically the textbooks they use for redundancy of information. Textbooks are usually formatted to present information in a spiraling sequence of increasing difficulty at each grade level. She finds, however, that most publishers include repetitive material year after year:

> This mindless repetition exists primarily because every teacher at every grade wants to teach, or have available to teach, everything. Therefore, publishers, who usually produce what customers want, include almost everything in every book.

> What happens to sequencing and spiraling when several teachers within a district begin each year on page one and proceed sequentially through the book, completing only one-half to two-thirds by June? (Muther, 1987, p. 78)

What does happen? Less reflective teachers tend to think or rationalize that the "approved" or "correct" curriculum is the one found in textbooks because it is written by "experts." They attempt to deliver the curriculum as written, without questioning its effects or adapting it to the students' needs.

More reflective teachers consider decisions about curriculum planning to be within their jurisdiction, their domain of decision making. They consult with others, but they take responsibility for deciding which parts of a textbook to use to meet the needs of their own particular class and to match the goals and learning outcomes their state and local curriculum committees establish.

CURRICULUM ORIENTATIONS

Curriculum decisions depend heavily on the values of those making the choices. When educators discuss what to include in a course or how to teach a certain subject, several different viewpoints are usually expressed, depending on each individual's values. For example, should the subject of mathematics emphasize memorization of math facts and formulas, or should it emphasize the reasoning processes or problem-solving strategies that students can use to discover and apply mathematical relationships? Should schools teach the religious or the scientific theories of the development of the universe? What types of reading materials are suitable for students to read at various grade levels? The reason that curriculum questions such as these cause very heated debates is because each individual has a unique curriculum orientation.

Eisner (1985) describes five curriculum orientations to provide educators with an awareness of how their personal orientations may compare with others. He believes that by knowing all five, teachers may be able to expand their options in curriculum planning. An individual's personal values, experiences, and beliefs about what is important in the world contribute greatly to the type of orientation held. In many ways, one's curriculum orientation is related to one's philosophy of education because both are concerned with the goals of education, the relative importance of subject matter, and how teachers and students ought to interact.

Eisner (1985) labels one of the oldest and most basic orientations to curriculum *academic rationalism*. Educators with this orientation argue that the goal of education is to teach the basic fields of study and academic disciplines that have traditionally been known as a liberal education. These academic disciplines include mathematics, literature, science, and history. Within these disciplines, academic rationalists believe that the curriculum should consist of "the very best, the most powerful, the most profound, the grandest of man's intellectual works" (Eisner, 1985, p. 68). The role of the teacher is to help students acquire the content, concepts, and ideas of these classic academic disciplines.

An academic rationalist is likely to believe that the traditional subjects are important and to teach them through lecture, reading, and discussion. Tests and essays are employed to measure what students have learned.

A contrasting curriculum orientation is one that values developing students' *cognitive processes.* Teachers with this orientation do not concur with academic rationalists that there is one established content for courses. Instead, their major goal is to help students "learn how to learn" (Eisner, 1985, p. 62). The content of the curriculum is selected for its potential in causing students to use their problem-solving and information-gathering abilities. The role of the teacher is to generate problematic situations for students to investigate and solve.

Teachers with a cognitive-processes orientation would be likely to combine traditional courses into thematic units, where the major goal is not to teach content but to teach students processes such as the scientific method, research, problem solving, and communication skills. This teacher might employ methods such as experimentation, independent research, and group investigations. Although tests might be employed to measure student achievement, these teachers are likely to require students to turn in and report on projects that show what they have learned.

A third orientation is one that emphasizes *personal relevance,* meaning that the curriculum builds on the students' interests. Educators who hold this view believe that learning is a developmental process and that students will learn best from the "inside out" (Eisner, 1985, p. 70). The teacher's role is to construct educational situations that are based on students' present experiences, interests, and needs.

Teachers who are oriented toward personal relevance are likely to provide their students with many opportunities for free choice. They encourage students to select their own reading materials based on their interests. Students may negotiate with teachers about what they want to study and how they will do it. A method of evaluation that is used in this orientation is to have students work on contracts that specify what they are going to do. A completed contract is viewed as a successful school experience.

A *social perspective* in curriculum is an orientation that attempts to help students develop a critical consciousness of the major issues of society. This type of curriculum focuses on controversial social issues and is designed to encourage students to take an active role in improving the society in which they live. The teacher using this orientation tries to make students aware of important social issues and to prompt them to debate alternatives, make informed judgments, and act on them.

Although this orientation is rarely employed for the entire school curriculum, many teachers with this orientation find ways to incorporate social issues into the conventional curriculum. The teacher with this orientation is likely to select reading materials for their social relevance and use discussion, class meetings, role playing, and simulation activities. Evaluation is likely to center on the degree to which students show that they have developed mature understanding of social problems and are taking an active role in solving them.

A fifth orientation toward curriculum planning is concerned not with the values and content of the curriculum but with the way curriculum is constructed. A *technological orientation* stresses a scientific approach using measurable goals and objectives. The teacher plans the curriculum in a sequential, orderly manner by specifying a list of sequential objectives with tests that demonstrate the students' mastery of each objective.

Teachers with a technological orientation are likely to emphasize sequential learning of the basic skills in mathematics, reading, grammar, and other curriculum areas. Carefully planned lessons teach new information and skills in small steps, with much opportunity for practice. Pretests and posttests are likely to be used to show how much students have gained from each learning experience.

Teachers are unlikely to follow only one of these curriculum orientations. Instead, each teacher may have one orientation that is most preferred or dominant but can see value in some of the others as well. By recognizing and clarifying your own preferences, you can understand why you make the decisions that you do about what to teach and how to teach it. A teacher must also assume the responsibility to address students' various learning styles by using an orientation that may vary from the one he or she prefers. In addition, if you understand that other teachers may have different orientations, you will be more likely to have productive discussions with them even when you don't agree with their values and orientations.

TYLER'S BASIC PRINCIPLES OF CURRICULUM PLANNING

Tyler (1949) observed that in planning educational goals, teachers should first consider the needs of the learners, then the needs of society or what he termed "contemporary life," and finally the suggestions or recommendations of subject-matter specialists. Since 1949, there has been consistent support for Tyler's elegant (simple but not simplistic) curriculum planning method. He proposed four fundamental questions that should be considered in planning any curriculum (1949, p. 1):

1. What educational purposes should the school seek to attain?
2. What educational experiences can be provided that are likely to attain these purposes?
3. How can these educational experiences be effectively organized?
4. How can we determine whether these purposes are being attained?

Reflective educators are likely to use Tyler's basic principles in planning, organizing, and evaluating their programs because they are remarkably similar to the process of reflective thinking. Essentially, he suggests that teachers begin curriculum planning by perceiving the needs of students, gathering information, making a judgment about an educational purpose, selecting and organizing the strategies to be used, and then evaluating the effectiveness of their curriculum plan by perceiving its effects on their students. These are very similar processes to those outlined in the model of reflective action presented in Chapter 1.

Although reflective teachers are not likely to memorize Tyler's four questions word for word, they are likely to carry with them the fundamental notion of each:

1. What shall we teach?
2. How shall we teach it?
3. How can we organize it?
4. How can we evaluate it?

Reflective teachers ask themselves these questions each year because they have probably noticed subtle or dramatic changes in their communities, subject-matter materials, students, or themselves from year to year that cause them to reexamine their curricula.

On reexamination, they may confirm that they want to continue to teach the same curriculum in the same way or that they want to modify some aspects of the curriculum. As teachers grow in experience and skills, most greet each new year as an opportunity to improve on what they accomplished the previous year. Rather than continue to teach the same subjects in the same ways year after year, reflective teachers often experiment with new ways of teaching and organizing the curriculum.

An obvious contrast between more reflective and less reflective teachers is that after teaching for 20 years, a reflective teacher has accumulated 20 years of experience, while a less reflective teacher is likely to have repeated one year of experience 20 times. Reflective teachers want to have an active role in the decision-making processes in their schools, and curricular decisions are the ones that count the most. They also display a strong sense of responsibility for making good curriculum choices and decisions, ones that will ultimately result in valuable growth and learning for their students.

BLOOM'S TAXONOMY OF EDUCATIONAL OBJECTIVES

Benjamin Bloom, a student of Ralph Tyler's, extended Tyler's basic principles in a most useful way. Bloom and his colleagues Max Engelhart, Edward Furst, Walker Hill, and David Krathwohl (1956) attempted to respond to the first of Tyler's questions as completely as possible. In meetings with other teachers, they brainstormed and listed all the possible purposes of education, all the possible educational objectives that they could think of or had observed during many years of classroom experience. Then they attempted to organize and classify all of these possible objectives into what is now known as the *Taxonomy of Educational Objectives*. Their intent was to provide teachers with a ready source of possible objectives so that they could select ones that fit the needs of their own students and circumstances. They also intended to help teachers clarify for themselves how to achieve their educational goals. A third purpose for the taxonomy was to help teachers communicate more precisely with one another.

The taxonomy first subdivides educational purposes into three domains of learning: cognitive, affective, and psychomotor. The *cognitive domain* deals with "the recall or recognition of knowledge and the development of intellectual abilities and skills"; the *affective domain* deals with "interests, attitudes, and values"; and the *psychomotor domain* concerns the development of manipulative and motor skills (Bloom et al., 1956, p. 7).

CLARIFYING EDUCATIONAL GOALS AND OUTCOMES

All three domains are considered to be important in the curriculum because together they support the growth and development of the whole student. Educators used to begin writing curriculum documents by carefully wording their educational goals. An educational *goal* is a general long-term statement of an important aim or purpose of an educational program. For example, most schools have a goal of teaching students how to read and write, another to ensure that they understand the cultural heritage of the United States, and another to help them develop attitudes and habits of good citizenship.

To translate goals into operational plans, however, most educators today prefer to specify what *outcomes* are expected as a consequence of being in school and taking part in the planned curriculum. Eisner (1985) alerts educators to be aware that goals express intentions but that other factors may occur that alter the intentions in the educational process. According to Eisner, "outcomes are essentially what one ends up with, intended or not, after some form of engagement" (p. 120).

Outcomes are statements that describe what students will demonstrate as a culmination of their learning. Spady (1994) proposes that outcomes must specify "high quality, culminating demonstrations of significant learning in context" (p. 18). A high-quality demonstration means one that is thorough and complete, showing the important new learning the student has gained or demonstrating the mastery of a new skill or process. Outcomes are designed to be assessed at or near the end of a learning period.

Written outcome statements are used to translate goals into actions. They describe what students will be able do as a result of their educational program. If educators can envision what they want students to be able to do or know after a series of learning experiences, they can plan with that outcome in mind. Learning outcomes generally describe actions, processes, and products that the student will accomplish in a given period.

Cognitive outcomes are expressed in terms of students' mastery of content or subject-matter knowledge. For example, kindergartners are expected to master the alphabet, third graders are expected to master multiplication facts, and sixth graders are expected to show mastery of the history of ancient civilizations.

Educators also write many psychomotor outcomes, including strategies, processes, and skills that involve both the mind and the body in the psychomotor domain. For example, elementary students are expected to learn how to decode symbols to read, write, calculate, solve problems, observe, experiment, research, interpret, make maps, and create works of art, music, and other crafts.

Most teachers view affective outcome statements as being related to the development of character. Typically, schools highlight the affective outcomes emphasizing good citizenship, self-esteem, respect for individual and racial differences, and an appreciation of art, music, and other aspects of our cultural heritage.

Individual teachers may write outcome statements for their own classes, but when they work collectively to clarify a set of schoolwide outcome statements, the effect on students is likely to be much more powerful and result in greater growth and change. This enhanced growth is a result of the consistency of experiences that students have in every classroom and with every adult in the school. Many school districts have statements of philosophy (often called mission statements) and outcome statements written in policy documents, but they may or may not be articulated and applied in the schools themselves. For effective change to take place, the school faculty must consider its educational purposes each year, articulate them together, and communicate them to the students through words and deeds.

In a classroom, each teacher has the right and the responsibility to articulate a set of educational outcomes for their own students. Working alone or with teammates at the same grade level or subject area, the classroom teacher may want to articulate approximately two to four yearly outcome statements in each of the three domains. Tyler encourages teachers to select a small number of highly important goals "since time is required to change the behavior patterns of human beings. An educational program is not effective if so much is attempted that little is accomplished" (1949, p. 33).

WRITING USEFUL AND APPROPRIATE OUTCOME STATEMENTS

The wording of outcome statements must be general but not vague. This is a subtle but important distinction. Some school documents contain goals such as "to develop the full potential of each individual." What does this mean to you? Can you interpret it in a meaningful way in your classroom? Can you translate it into programs? Probably not. This goal statement is so general and vague that it cannot be put into operation, and it would be very difficult to determine whether it is being attained.

An outcome statement should be general, in keeping with its long-term effects. It should also describe, clearly and precisely, how you want your students to change and what you want them to be able to do at the end of the term of study.

Here are some examples of useful *cognitive* outcome statements:

> Kindergarten students will be able to recognize and name all the counting numbers from 1 to 20.
>
> Fifth-grade students will demonstrate that they understand how technology has changed the world by creating a time line, graph, chart, or set of models to show the effects of technology on human experience.

Here are some examples of *psychomotor* (sometimes referred to as skill or process) outcome statements:

> Third-grade students will be able to measure and compare a variety of common objects using metric units of measurement of length, weight, and volume.
>
> Sixth-grade students will be able to compose and edit written works using a word-processing program on a computer.

Here are some examples of *affective* outcome statements:

> Second-grade students will demonstrate that they enjoy reading by selecting books and other reading materials and spending time reading in class and at home.
>
> Students at all grade levels will demonstrate that they tolerate, accept, and prize cultural, ethnic, and other individual differences in human beings by working cooperatively and productively with students of various ethnic groups.

In many school programs, outcome statements are intended to be accomplished over the course of a school year. Yearly outcome statements can be written for one subject or across several disciplines. Outcome statements can also be written for a shorter period such as a term or a month. They are used as guides for planning curriculum and learning experiences for that length of time. At the end of a given time, the teacher assesses whether students have successfully demonstrated the outcome. If not, the teacher may need to repeat or restate the outcome statement to ensure that it can be met.

Some outcome statements may need to be modified because they are too vague. In the following example, compare the first vague statement with the improved second statement:

Original outcome statement: Students will be able to demonstrate that they understand the U.S. Constitution.

Improved outcome statement: Students will be able to describe the key concepts in the articles of the U.S. Constitution and give examples of how they are applied in American life today.

Other outcome statements may need to be modified because they are too difficult for the students. Compare these:

Original outcome statement: Fourth-grade students will demonstrate that they know the key concepts of the Bill of Rights by creating a time line showing how each has evolved over the past 200 years.

Improved outcome statement: Fourth-grade students will be able to create an illustrated mural showing pictorial representations of each of the articles in the Bill of Rights.

Some outcome statements may need to be improved by adding learning opportunities that will stimulate student interest and motivation to learn the material. Consider the following:

Original outcome statement: Students will be able to recite the Bill of Rights.

Improved outcome statement: Students will work in cooperative groups to plan and perform skits comparing how life in the United States would differ with and without the constitutional amendments known as the Bill of Rights.

Outcome statements are useful guides for educational planning but must be adapted to fit the needs of a particular teacher and class. For this reason, curriculum planning is an evolving process. A curriculum is never a finished product; it is constantly being changed and improved from day to day and year to year.

Examples of Long-Term Curriculum Planning
DESIGNING A COMMON CORE CURRICULUM

At the Ogunquit Village School in Ogunquit, Maine, Linda Gaidimas is the teaching principal. When *Maine's Common Core of Learning* was published and distributed to school districts in the state, Linda took a leadership role in designing a plan to implement the new ideas in her school. The state department had combined the traditional three Rs into four integrated categories of learning: The Human Record, Reasoning and Problem Solving, Communication, and Personal and Global Stewardship.

Many of Linda's staff were very apprehensive about the magnitude of the changes being asked of them, while others were excited by the potential for innovation. Linda began to lead her staff through the process of translating the four new categories into outcomes that fit the needs of the students in their community. Then they began to develop new performance-based authentic assessment measures to fit the outcomes they had written. Next, they have started to examine their teaching strategies and the organizational routines of the school that would need to be changed in order to allow the new design to be successfully implemented.

Linda has involved teachers in all aspects of the decision-making process to create these changes. She has also formed partnerships with other professional and industrial entities. For example, Pratt and Whitney, a division of United Technologies, agreed to provide her staff with training in team-building and problem-solving skills as they worked through the process of redesigning their curriculum. David Silvernail of the University of Southern Maine helped them define the new and unfamiliar terms that would become the basis for the written structure of the new curriculum document. It includes the following elements:

> *Student outcome:* a statement describing what students are expected to know and be able to do upon graduation from the school
>
> *Assessment criteria:* the highly valued qualities, skills, attributes, and habits that are going to be assessed
>
> *Assessment standards:* values assigned to different levels of these qualities
>
> *Benchmarks:* level of a student outcome that students are expected to achieve at certain points in their K—12 career
>
> *Authentic assessment:* tasks given to students so that they can demonstrate achievement of the outcome

For example, within the "communication" core category of learning, here is the way Linda's faculty used this structure to redesign their curriculum.

Core Category: Communication

> *Student outcome:* Graduates will be able to use language to communicate in order to understand themselves and others in the process of making sense of their world.
>
> *Assessment criteria:* Students will develop the ability to express personal feelings in writing.
>
> *Assessment standards:*
>
> Level 6: Students can use a variety of media to identify a social problem or issue in their own town, country, or the world and analyze their connection with the problem.
>
> Level 5: Students can identify a social problem or issue and explain how it affects them.

Level 4: Students can use a variety of media to explain how they solved a personal problem or dilemma.

Level 3: Students can use a variety of media to describe a personal problem or dilemma.

Level 2: Students can use a variety of media to communicate a story about themselves and others.

Level 1: Students can use a variety of media to tell a story about themselves.

Benchmarks: All fourth graders can use a variety of media to communicate a story about themselves and others.

Authentic assessment: Fourth graders will create a storybook about their family.

The process of creating this new curriculum document has been very challenging for the faculty at the Ogunquit Village School. Trained in the past to write behavioral objectives, many teachers struggled to understand how an outcome was different from an objective. They decided to limit themselves to only five to eight outcomes for the entire curriculum so that the ones they wrote would be sufficiently broad and crossdisciplinary.

REDESIGNING THE CURRICULUM TO REFLECT MULTICULTURAL VALUES

The trend in curriculum development is changing to encourage teachers to create new curricula that teach the basics and, at the same time, encourage students to see the world from points of view different from their own. James Banks, director of the Center for Multicultural Education at the University of Washington, defines multicultural education as "education for freedom" and recommends that curriculum planners redesign existing curricula to promote "cultural excellence" as well as academic excellence (Banks, 1991–1992).

Banks believes that the redesigned curriculum should describe the needs and contributions of all Americans, all their struggles, hopes, and dreams. It should not be an add-on to the existing curriculum but should become an integral part of every subject we teach. He recommends that we ask students to reflect, discuss, and write about questions such as "Who am I?" "Where have I been?" "What do I hope for?" Banks believes that when students can answer these questions, they will be better equipped to function in their own world as well as in the larger community that may be populated by people who answer the same questions very differently.

To develop a multicultural curriculum for your classroom, no matter what subject you teach, plan learning experiences that reflect the concerns of the diverse cultural groups that make up the class, the school, and the community. Encourage your students to share their different perspectives and opinions and show that you value the different ways that they solve problems and view the world around them.

Reissman (1994) recommends that, as you assign learning tasks, you should consider how each assignment can be used to strengthen intergroup understandings and respect for each other's cultures as well as develop skills that will later be needed for community, national, and global citizenship. Her book *The Evolving Multicultural Classroom* may be a valuable resource for you in your curriculum planning. It is available from the Association of Supervision and Curriculum Planning, which also publishes the journal *Educational Leadership,* the publication that I favor for keeping myself up to date on new curriculum initiatives and examples of how teachers create wonderful new answers to the questions "What should we teach?" "How should we teach it?" and "How will we know that we've succeeded?"

REDESIGNING THE CURRICULUM USING MULTIDISCIPLINARY THEMES

Students "develop knowledge by interacting mentally and to some extent physically with people and objects around them. This interaction requires active involvement. Knowledge that is poured into a passive mind is quickly forgotten" (Sleeter & Grant, 1994, p. 218).

One side benefit of the multidisciplinary curriculum is that it has led teachers to share what they are doing and work together to plan learning experiences. Teachers who come to school, close the doors of their classrooms, and teach in isolation are becoming a thing of the past. For example, in curriculum planning, many districts team beginning teachers with experienced teachers to develop and share curriculum materials.

This new trend has created an environment in which teachers do not structure their curricula into separate blocks of time. As Beane (1991) points out, when confronted with a problem, individuals do not say, "Now which part of this is science and which part of this is language arts?" Instead, people address problems with a multidisciplinary approach and use whatever resources and content they need to resolve them.

In his analysis of subject-matter teaching, Brophy (1992) emphasizes the importance of teaching fewer topics with more depth. This practice allows students to have a greater understanding of the topics and lets teachers emphasize higher-order applications. Brophy indicates that state curriculum guides and textbooks should be modified in order to accomplish this task, and in many cases they are being revised to include a greater emphasis on integrated curricula such as whole language programs.

In middle school, much energy is being focused on restructuring the curriculum. In many cases, middle school faculty are reflecting on whether to continue with the concept of the middle school as a mini high school, where students take subject-specific courses, or whether to consider alternative structures that combine subject matter into integrated curricula. Beane (1991) proposes a vision of the curriculum centered around themes rather than abstract or artificial subject areas. He suggests that middle school curricula could be focused on themes such as "living in the future," "wellness," or "cultural diversity."

When this integrated thematic approach is used in a middle school, the faculty plans together to design curricula that include literature, writing, mathematics, history, science, and health instruction within the selected theme. The result is often a highly motivating set of learning experiences designed specifically for the special needs of young adolescent students. Faculty members also report increased satisfaction with their own careers when they are involved in actively restructuring the curriculum to meet the needs of their students and celebrate their own special interests and talents.

At the middle school and high school levels, where teachers are usually responsible for teaching only one major subject area at a time, it may be more difficult to design a multidisciplinary curriculum than it is in elementary schools. It requires that several teachers agree to try this approach and collaborate to plan common goals and themes so that students can experience an integrated, multidisciplinary curriculum even though they still go to math, social studies, and English classes during different class periods.

If a team of secondary teachers decides to plan a multidisciplinary curriculum, it might, for example, choose a common theme such as "change." Individual science, mathematics, language arts, and English teachers then design learning experiences that allow students to identify how things change and to relate these changes to their own experiences. The mathematics teacher might choose to do the unit on renaming fractions during this period to illustrate how number concepts need to be changed in order to carry out mathematical operations. The social studies teacher may choose to focus on the changes in a community over a period of time. The English teacher will look for a novel or a series of other readings that fit the theme of change and carry out discussions of how change affects the characters' lives and beliefs.

To extend this example of the multidisciplinary curriculum to include a multicultural approach as well, the same teachers can highlight various cultural aspects within the theme. The mathematics teacher can describe the contributions made by various cultures to change the way in which mathematics is done. The social studies teacher can ask students to explore the way the changes in the community have affected various cultures and encourage students to express how these changes are experienced today by their own families. The English teacher can select a variety of readings on the theme of change, each one expressing the point of view of a different cultural or ethnic group.

We can also find examples of high schools that are using the integrated curriculum. One is the Humanitas Program in the Los Angeles Unified School District. This program integrates English, social studies, and art; some teams also include philosophy, mathematics, science, studio art, or dance. The Humanitas Programs are built around themes such as "women, race, and social protest"; "the Protestant ethic"; and "the spirit of capitalism." Students take core classes in these thematic programs that may include literature, writing, artistic expression, and discussion of social issues. They attend regular subject-matter classes for mathematics, science, and physical education. Teachers who work with the Humanitas Program are responsible for planning the program together; and as a result, they report that they believe a spirit of renewal and empowerment was missing when they worked alone.

DESIGNING A WHOLE LANGUAGE CURRICULUM

Until recently, the elementary curriculum contained separate subjects called *reading, English, spelling,* and *creative writing.* It was believed that if students learned how to read, spell, and use grammar and punctuation correctly, they would be literate and able to communicate effectively. However, research on the developmental learning of language has led to major philosophical and practical changes in this subject area.

Chomsky (1969) demonstrated that students learn to speak as they engage in talk with others around them, gradually comprehending the rule systems in the process. An investigation by Sulzby and Teale (1987) of children's early writing revealed it to be a developmental process similar to learning how to speak. Teachers apply the findings of these research studies by encouraging the natural development of both speaking and writing in their classrooms.

Educators have termed this type of educational experience the *whole language curriculum* because it encourages natural processes in the development of the whole child. The whole language curriculum places roughly equal emphasis on cognitive, affective, and psychomotor outcomes. Teachers who use this model of teaching are likely to have considered how these methods reflect their own values and moral principles. Often they base their acceptance of the whole language approach on their well-clarified belief that children need to learn at their own pace and have their interests and choices honored. They believe that the best environment for learning is one that enhances a child's love of reading, writing, speaking, listening, and being creative.

Graves (1983) and Murray (1984) have provided models of teaching for young students that treat writing as a continuous process rather than as a product. The process includes stimulating prewriting experiences, first drafts, editing conferences, revising, and sharing or publishing. Teachers who use these methods report that students show increased confidence in their ability to communicate in writing. Moreover, they like to write and see it as an opportunity to express their ideas.

Many schools are in the process of restructuring their curricula away from the separate rule-dependent subjects of reading, spelling, grammar, and writing toward a holistic, process-oriented approach. In schools with a whole language curriculum, students listen to or read literary works, write in journals, participate in editing groups, and speak for a variety of purposes. They gradually assimilate the proper grammar, punctuation, spelling, and other conventions of the English language.

As a first-grade teacher in Carpentersville, Illinois, Ginny Bailey experimented with using the whole language approach to teach reading and writing. Rather than relying on basal readers and workbooks, she used real students' literature, in the form of library materials and paperback books, as her texts. Judy Yount and Sandy Krakow, the other first-grade teachers on Ginny's team, worked with her to translate the State of Illinois Outcome Statements and the school district's written curriculum objectives into a form that would fit their philosophy and the particular needs of the students in their building. Ginny explains:

We began our plan by deciding that we would use thematic units to accomplish the state outcomes. We quickly discovered that language arts cannot be separated from science, social studies, and mathematics when you use a unit approach, so we incorporated those areas into our planning. All of us had attended numerous classes and workshops on using thematic units and had read every book we could find on the subject of using whole language in the classroom. But now it was time to sit down and make our plan for the coming school year. We began by going through the science, mathematics, and social studies curriculum guides to familiarize ourselves with what had to be covered in those areas. We then studied the Language Arts Outcome Statements. Our plan was to teach one or two thematic units a month depending on the length of the units.

Box 4.1 presents a year-long plan that provides a model of a whole language integrated curriculum.

MODEL LESSON PLANNING

Box 4.1 Year-Long Integrated Curriculum Plan for First Grade

by Ginny Bailey, Judy Yount, and Sandra Krakow, Woodland School, Carpentersville, Illinois,
Barrington Community Unified School District

These three teachers like to use a multidisciplinary approach for curriculum planning. They use themes that may be related to social studies, literature, or science, but all of them incorporate and emphasize language arts activities. In each unit, students read, write, speak, and otherwise investigate the topic. The themes change from year to year, but this is a typical example.

Author Study: Norman Bridwell (Clifford Books)

The purpose of this unit is to make the children feel comfortable in school. Young children relate to these familiar books. For the first week of school, we read the Clifford books and do many art and music activities related to the stories. The students discover that they can learn to read through singing and express themselves through art.

Changes

This unit emphasizes the patterns of cause and effect in life and encourages students to notice that things in the world change and evolve over time. Subtopics include

1. Butterflies and moths
2. Frogs
3. Colors
4. Apples
5. Seasons
6. Self

Zoo Animals

The purpose of this unit is to learn the characteristics of animals and to classify them as mammals, amphibians, reptiles, or birds. It is primarily a mathematics and science theme, but we integrate literature and writing activities in it and culminate the unit with a trip to the zoo.

1. Mammals
2. Amphibians
3. Reptiles
4. Birds

Human Bodies

In this unit, we help students understand their physical and emotional selves. Subtopics include

1. Inside the human body
2. Nutrition
3. Five senses
4. Feelings

Families

In this unit, we emphasize the importance of families and how each family is alike and different. Subtopics include

1. Family members
2. Different types of families
3. Families from different cultures
4. Family homes

Astronomy

The purpose of this unit is to understand that we are part of the universe and how the laws of science govern our lives. Subtopics include

1. Day and night
2. The sun and the nine planets
3. The force of gravity

The Earth

In this springtime unit, we examine earth science concepts and how they relate to our everyday lives. We emphasize the new beginnings that occur in the spring in each of the following subtopics:

1. Rocks and minerals
2. Farm animals
3. Insects
4. Plants

Community Helpers

The purpose of this unit is to acquaint students with the variety of jobs that people in the community do and how interconnected our lives are. Subtopics include

continued

1. Police
2. Fire protectors
3. Postal workers
4. Nurses and doctors

Transportation

The purpose of this unit is to study geography and learn where things are in the world by studying how we travel from place to place. Subtopics include

1. Trains
2. Airplanes
3. Automobiles
4. Ships and boats

As you undoubtedly noticed when you read Box 4.1, the whole language curriculum is often a multidisciplinary approach as well. The three teachers at Woodland School use themes that are related to social studies, literature, or science, but all of these themes incorporate and emphasize language arts activities. In each unit, students read, write, speak, and otherwise investigate the topic. The themes change from year to year, but this is a typical example of a year-long whole language program.

A THEMATIC CURRICULUM FOR A MULTICULTURAL, BILINGUAL CLASSROOM

Ruth Reyes teaches sixth grade at Washington School in downtown San Diego. This school follows a special policy of developing biliteracy among all its students. All classes are taught in both Spanish and English. In her class, Ruth teaches one day in Spanish and the next day in English. Her curriculum is designed to allow students to move from one language to another very flexibly. When she designs a unit of study, she selects resources in both English and Spanish. The students use both or select the ones that fit their own level of language development.

Ruth has chosen to use a year-long theme that she calls "environment/survival." This theme grows out of her own special interest in biology. It also ties in with the social studies curriculum and extends from her belief that sixth-grade students need to be aware of the concept of environment and the relationship between humans and their environment. She wants her students to leave her class with a commitment to saving our natural environment. She also wants them to begin to develop survival skills and strategies to improve their own environment.

I asked Ruth to describe how she translates this important goal into daily learning experiences that cover the state- and district-mandated curricula for math, science, social studies, and language arts. She describes the process in this way:

I looked through the course of study provided by the school district and the curriculum guides from the state and the school district. Then I opened up all the teacher's manuals for the textbooks we use in sixth grade. As I looked for a way to organize all this material into meaningful chunks, it was clear to me that I should use the social studies curriculum as the basis for planning. In sixth grade, we focus on the study of world history and geography. That's a perfect fit with my interest in the environment and its relationship to mankind. I can teach the historic material and at the same time bring in contemporary issues and show how they relate to each other.

But before I plunge into the year-long thematic curriculum, I spend the first week of school assessing students' interests and needs. My goals are to get to know my students and learn their strengths and interests. For that week, I use a short literature book that really interests me. This year, I used Kurusa's (1981) The Streets Are Free *and the Spanish edition* Las calles son libras. *This book about the rain forests fits my theme and allows me to introduce the major ideas we'll be studying all year long. The students do a lot of reading, writing, discussion, and group assignments so that I can observe them as they work together. I spend most of my time during that week observing and taking notes on students as they are working in various groupings. I try to identify what each student enjoys, what is easy, and what is a challenge for each of them. As I walk around with my clipboard, I take notes on computer labels (one label per student), which I can then transfer to their portfolios without rewriting. I look for as many positives as possible and also jot down what appears to be challenging for each student. Everyone in my class is learning a new language, so I have to be alert when I hear them speak in the unfamiliar language so that I can encourage them and plan activities that will allow them to be successful.*

During the second week of school, we begin our study of the first social studies/literature unit for the year. The topics that are covered in the social studies curriculum include "early man," "the beginning of civilization," "ancient Hebrews and Greeks," "India," "China," and "Rome." For language arts, I locate several literature books that are related in some way to each of these topics. We spend about three weeks on each novel. For example, with the study of early man, I use a book about a girl who lived during the Ice Age who has to help her family survive by moving to a winter cave. See, it fits my theme in every way. For math and science, we study the time lines and the ages of prehistoric earth. We also write word problems for math involving the characters in the novel.

I am not rigid in my organization of the whole year, but we spend about three weeks per book. For some historical eras, we read two or three books. I try to get each book in Spanish and in English. When this isn't possible, then I get similar books on the topic so that my students can choose to read in English for one book, Spanish for another.

We begin a new unit by brainstorming what we already know about rain forests. We make a chart of what we know and put it up in the classroom. Then we make another chart of what we want to learn about rain forests. Based on what we want to know, I create five categories and divide the class up into five groups. Each group focuses on researching one of the categories, such as animals or trees. The group researches its topic for about three days and then begins to organize the material into a book. Students use the computer to write, edit, and illustrate their books. When they are completed, they teach what they have learned to the rest of their classmates. The books they write become part of the school library's collection for the rest of the year.

When I think of what my students experience during the entire year, I want them to see that every subject is related to each other. When they see the connections between subject matter, I feel that I have been successful. Some children come to school believing that in order to do math, they have to use a math book. I want them to learn that we do math every day of our lives. I also want them to see the relationships between different authors and their style. We concentrate a lot on comparing and analyzing in my room. Whenever we read a new book, we are constantly looking for ways that this book compares to other books we've read or to the social studies book or to some idea in math or science. When I hear my students making these analyses, I feel that my methods of teaching are validated.

LONG-TERM PLANNING IN MATHEMATICS

As Ruth described, the teaching of mathematics is changing at every grade level. No longer a time for drill and practice, mathematics is often one of the most highly interactive parts of the elementary school curriculum. Manipulatives that primary children use to demonstrate their understanding of number concepts include beans, beads, and number lines. But many teachers also use motivating materials such as pretzels, fish-shaped crackers, jelly beans, or coated chocolate candies. In one school recently, a little girl was asked how she knew it was math time. She answered, "That's easy! Math is when we have our snacks."

Kendall and Marzano (1995) provide a summary of recommendations made by the National Council of Teachers of Mathematics (NCTM) and the Mathematics Assessment Framework of the NAEP. These groups stress the importance of teaching mathematics in the context of real-life situations, and they recommend that school curricula should be designed so that the student

1. effectively uses a variety of strategies in the problem solving process
2. understands and applies properties of the concept of number
3. uses a variety of procedures while performing computation
4. understands and applies the concept of measurement
5. understands and applies the concept of geometry
6. understands and applies concepts of data analysis and distributions
7. understands and applies concepts of probability and statistics
8. understands and applies properties of functions and algebra
9. understands the relationship between mathematics and other disciplines, particularly science and computer technology. (Kendall & Marzano, pp. 88–89)

With this emphasis on problem solving and application of mathematical concepts to real-life situations, the curriculum in many elementary schools has changed dramatically from drill and practice to mathematical explorations and investigations. Teachers who try to incorporate these recommendations into their mathematics curricula find that the best way to do it is through the use of projects and multidisciplinary units. A year-long plan in mathematics will be divided into several strands or concepts with opportunities for reviewing previously learned material from time to time. It may resemble the plan illustrated in Box 4.2. Its author derived the plan from the California Mathematics Framework guidelines, which emphasize the development of a sense of mathematical power.

LONG-TERM PLANNING IN SCIENCE

As a subject in the curriculum, science consists of a survey of the basic ideas in the academic disciplines of earth and space, life sciences, physical sciences, and environmental studies and the relationship between science and technology. When most of you were in elementary school, you may have learned about science as a collection of facts, laws, principles, and theories that have been found to be important in each of the science disciplines. When this content-oriented approach is used as the basis for curriculum planning in science, students are expected to read, comprehend, discuss, and take tests to demonstrate their mastery of the subject matter. This academic orientation toward science assumes that content is what students must learn to be able to understand science in later schooling.

Project 2061 (an educational study group of the American Association for the Advancement of Science) and the National Committee on Science Education Standards and Assessment (NCSESA) are among several national study groups recommending that we change that approach significantly. The new recommendations stress the need for students to have realistic, hands-on opportunities to experience the methods and processes scientists use to imagine possibilities, speculate on causes, hypothesize effects, gather and weigh evidence, and reach conclusions.

Reflective teachers who believe in teaching science processes use fewer textbooks and more laboratory experiences. Rather than teach *about* science, they believe that students must learn how to *do* science in order to understand it. They are likely to create a science curriculum that consists of a series of laboratory and experimental situations in which students observe, hypothesize, experiment, and evaluate their results in each topic of science. They may test rocks or create a model of plate tectonics for earth science. They may observe the moon or simulate an eclipse for astronomy or collect and classify plants and engage in microscopic examinations of pond water for biology. They may build and test simple machines for physics.

Reflective teachers recognize that the process approach provides students with many more opportunities for developing their critical and creative thinking about science than the textbook-centered, content-oriented approach does. Jim Hicks and Chris Chiaverina, two high school science teachers in Illinois, have created a curriculum that involves their students in active explorations designed to stimulate their curiosity, make them aware of the wonders that surround them, and equip them with skills to help them function effectively in the world. As you can see in their year-long plan for physics (Box 4.3), they build toward a culminating activity in which students do physics at a Great America theme park. In Chapter 5, you will find one of their units described in greater detail, and one of their lesson plans is included in Chapter 6.

The year-long plan in science may be planned in a wide variety of sequences. Teachers may decide to offer an earth and space science unit for the first six weeks, followed

MODEL LESSON PLANNING

Box 4.2 Long-Term Plan in Mathematics
MIDDLE SCHOOL GENERAL MATHEMATICS COURSE

by Pam Knight, Twin Peaks Middle School, Poway, California

From the California Mathematics Frameworks (1992), the goal of mathematics education is to develop mathematically powerful students who can think and communicate drawing on mathematical ideas and using mathematical tools and techniques.

Teachers are expected to plan their mathematics curricula to include the following strands: number, measurement, geometry, patterns and functions, statistics and probability, logic and language, and algebra and discrete mathematics.

At Twin Peaks Middle School the mathematics department has developed a core curriculum. In addition, Pam Knight has synthesized the state's frameworks, textbooks, and other resources into the following year-long plan.

Measurement (Three Days)

This involves hands-on activities in cooperative groups. Students measure classroom contents using standard English units and metric units. They create charts showing the various units of measurement.

Number (Four Weeks)

Students review the operations of whole numbers, fractions, and decimals and use calculators.

by units on life science, then science and technology, and ending with physical sciences. This order may easily be changed; many elementary teachers choose to coordinate their science units with other academic subjects. For example, at the same time as a unit on measurement is presented in mathematics, the science unit may emphasize measurement tools and strategies. When the social studies curriculum focuses on themes of exploration of new worlds, the science unit may be coordinated to emphasize scientific frontiers in technology.

LONG-TERM PLANNING IN SOCIAL STUDIES

As in science, development of the social studies curriculum can follow a content-oriented approach or a process-oriented approach. Educators committed to an academic or content-oriented view of social studies believe that students need to know and

Integers and Integer Operations (Five Weeks)

Using a time line from 500 B.C. to the present, students explore the concept of positive and negative numbers. They then learn how to express these concepts in operational terms and how to apply them in operations.

Equations (Six Weeks)

We begin by examining the order of operations, exponential operations, one- and two-step equations, and integers. Students learn to evaluate expressions, do ratios, and solve equations.

Geometry (Four Weeks)

We begin by learning the vocabulary of geometry and then explore area, perimeter, surface area, and volume and learn to measure and construct angles. We then do Euclidean drawing experiences using compass and straight-edge constructions such as tessellations.

Probability and Statistics (Three Weeks)

We begin with an experiment using colored candies. Students tally the colors and then predict the probability of getting each color. They learn to write probabilities as fractions and ratios. They conduct their own surveys and display their results graphically and then make an oral presentation to communicate their findings.

Scale Drawing (End-of-the-Year Activity)

Each student brings in a postcard. They divide up their postcards into square inches. They then transfer their postcard drawings to 12 inch by 18 inch paper using colored pens.

understand the important facts, persons, events, and sequences in the history of our country and the world. Also important to the academic orientation toward social studies are the important concepts that distinguish various cultures and the basic facts about world geography. Recent critics of U.S. schools have decried the lack of knowledge of history and geography among young people. Televised tests and magazine quizzes have demonstrated that many young people lack knowledge about geography. Content-oriented curriculum planners seek to improve this condition by providing history and geography courses that emphasize knowledge and comprehension objectives to teach facts and concepts.

Process-oriented curriculum planners believe that instead of memorizing facts, names, places, and dates, learners should experience the processes of acquiring information on their own. The National Center for History in the Schools (NCHS, 1994) provided benchmarks for teaching students how to think historically by learning to do

MODEL LESSON PLANNING

Box 4.3 Year-Long Plan in Science

by Jim Hicks, Barrington High School, Barrington, Illinois
and Chris Chiaverina, New Trier High School, Winnetka, Illinois

Planning as a team, Jim and Chris have incorporated these basic guidelines into their plan for their physics course.

Measurement Techniques (Four Weeks)

Focusing on the question "What is time?" this unit is designed to enrich students' concepts of time. Students learn how to measure short time intervals using stroboscopic photography and a cathode ray oscilloscope (CRO) and how to measure long time intervals using time-lapse photography and motion pictures. Students create motion picture machines called *xeroscopes*. Measurement of length is also covered. To investigate probability, estimation, and errors in measurement, students throw paper snowballs into a hidden trash can to estimate how large the trash can opening is. The probability nature of the second law of thermodynamics is also investigated.

Wave Phenomena in Light and Sound (10 Weeks)

In this unit we deal with reflection of light, refraction of light, and properties of waves associated with light and acoustics. The unit culminates in a field trip to the University of Wisconsin at Whitewater, where students learn the theory of holograms and then make and develop their own.

Forces, Vectors, and Equilibrium (Seven Weeks)

In this unit, students learn that forces come in pairs: action and reaction. We examine the forces of nature—gravitational, electromagnetic, nuclear, and the weak force.

In our exploration of vectors, students learn how to add forces. We examine the directions of forces and how they relate to each other. We construct graphs to demonstrate the effects of various forces and vectors.

their own research in social studies and learning how to use tools such as maps, globes, atlases, charts, graphs, and other resources to enable them to find information when the occasion demands it. The credo of this orientation toward curriculum development can be summed up in the adage "Give a man a fish, and he will be hungry the next day; teach him to fish, and he'll never go hungry again."

Decision making is also a key focus in the process-oriented approach to teaching social studies. Harlan Cleveland defined social studies as "the study of how citizens in a

Our study of equilibrium demonstrates how to combine forces to make a net force of zero. We examine Newton's first law of motion (an object at rest tends to remain at rest).

Acceleration (Two Weeks)

Using Newton's second law of motion (force equals mass times acceleration), we explore acceleration with ordinary objects. Students design and build a hovercraft and also spend a day measuring the mass of a car by applying a net force and measuring the resulting acceleration.

Kinematics (Five Weeks)

Kinematics is the study of motion. Our students investigate the properties of motion and its relationship to time, velocity, and acceleration through racetrack games. We also study projectile motion and circular motion, which extends the study of motion to two dimensions.

Work and Energy (Three Weeks)

We discuss all the types of energy that can be observed and learn to classify them into kinetic and potential energy.

Momentum (Two Weeks)

We explore practical applications of the concept of momentum by focusing on automobile safety, especially the use of seatbelts and air bags. We explore forces in collisions. This unit culminates in a field trip to an amusement park to explore energy conservation and circular motion. We have created a guidebook for physics experiences in an amusement park.

Electricity (Two Weeks)

We explore electrostatic forces between stationary charges and charges in motion or current electricity and emphasize their uses in the home and the workplace.

society make personal and public decisions on issues that affect their destiny" (Bragaw & Hartoonian, 1988, p. 9). To accomplish this, Bragaw and Hartoonian suggest that the curriculum planner must make sure that students do the following:

1. Develop an information base in the social sciences
2. Think using the logic and patterns of history and the social sciences
3. Communicate with others about social science data

4. Make enlightened personal and policy decisions and participate in civic activities

To illustrate the process of creating a year-long plan in social studies, I asked an education student taking a teaching methods course much like the one you are taking to create a year-long plan in social studies. The student began by consulting the California State Frameworks for History and Social Science. He also used a textbook approved by the state as one of his major resources. From these resources he decided on several unit topics that would cover the most important aspects of the curriculum. The units were then ordered chronologically as shown in Box 4.4. The student had to estimate the amount of time that would be needed to cover each unit topic, but he plans to revise those time allotments in his first year of teaching when he will be able to assess how much time each unit actually takes.

CREATING TIME LINES THAT FIT YOUR GOALS AND OUTCOME STATEMENTS

Time is the scarcest resource in school. Reflective teachers who organize time wisely are more successful in delivering the curriculum they have planned than are teachers who fail to consider it. Teachers who simply start each subject on page 1 of every textbook and hope to finish the text by June are frequently surprised by the lack of time. In some cases, they finish a text early in the year, but more often the school year ends and students never get to the subjects at the back of the textbook. In mathematics, some classes never get to geometry year after year. In social studies, history after the Civil War is often crammed into a few short lessons at the end of the year.

Will you be satisfied if this happens in your classroom? If not, you can prevent it by preplanning the time you will give to each element or subtopic of each subject area you are going to teach. This may seem like an overwhelming task at first, but it can be less threatening if you understand that you are not required to plan every outcome and objective for every subject before the year begins. You need to give the entire curriculum an overview and determine the number of days or weeks you will allot to each element.

Begin by examining the textbooks in your classroom, looking at the way in which they are organized. Most books are divided into units, each covering a single topic or collection of related topics within the academic subject. Mathematics books are likely to contain units such as "place value," "operations," "measuring," and "geometry." History books are divided into units on "exploration," "settling the new frontier," "creating government," and others. English books contain units such as "listening," "writing," and "speaking."

Curriculum units are excellent planning devices because they show students how facts, skills, concepts, and application of ideas are all related. The alternative to planning with units is planning a single, continuous, year-long sequence of experiences or planning unconnected and unrelated daily experiences. Units will be used as the basis for planning throughout the rest of this book.

Decide if the units in your school's textbooks are valuable and important as well as whether you agree with the way in which they are organized and the quality of learning experiences they contain. Consider whether using the textbook will result in achieving

MODEL LESSON PLANNING

Box 4.4 An Education Student's Plan for Sixth-Grade Social Studies

Although this year-long plan emphasizes history and social science, it is multidisciplinary wherever practical and beneficial. I plan to integrate language arts (readings from the period of history, speaking, and writing activities), mathematics and science (learning about the development of mathematics and science in the various cultures), visual and performing arts (exposing students to art and drama from the cultures), and physical education (reenacting the activities and competitions of ancient civilizations).

Overview and Sequence of Social Studies Units

INTRODUCTION: WHAT IT MEANS TO BE HUMAN
    What it means to be human
    Overview of year
    Introduction of terms and vocabulary
    Procedures used to discover the story of peoples of the past

EARLY HUMANKIND AND THE DEVELOPMENT OF HUMAN SOCIETIES
    Prehistoric humans
    Life and world of prehistoric humans
    Family, tribes, and society

THE BEGINNINGS OF CIVILIZATION IN THE NEAR EAST AND AFRICA
    Fertile Crescent
    Sumerians
    Ancient empires
    Ancient Egypt
    Kingdom of Kush

THE FOUNDATION OF WESTERN IDEAS: ANCIENT HEBREWS AND GREEKS
    Ancient Israelites
    Old Testament

continued

Ancient Greeks

Greek life

Greek ideals

Alexander the Great

WEST MEETS EAST: THE EARLY CIVILIZATIONS OF INDIA AND CHINA

Indus Valley

Buddhism

Hinduism

China

Confucius

EAST MEETS WEST: ROME

All roads lead to Rome

The Roman Empire

Roman life

Christianity

Life of Jesus

Decline of Rome

the outcomes in your school curriculum guide. Will it result in achieving the goals and outcomes you have for your class? If the textbook learning experiences match your outcomes, you can plan the year to coincide with the sequence of units in the book. If the textbook does not coincide with your planned outcomes or if you disagree with the quality or the organizational pattern of the book, you have several options. You can plan to use the book but present the units in a different order. You can delete units, or you can use some units in the book as they are written but supplement with other materials for additional units not covered or inadequately covered in the book. The most adventuresome and creative teachers may even decide to use the textbook only as a resource and plan original teaching units for the subject.

In any case, you should carefully consider the amount of time you want to allot to each unit you plan to teach. Create a time line, chart, or calendar for each subject and use it as you judge how much time to spend on each subtopic. For time-line planning, you can divide the school year into weeks, months, or quarters. For a subject such as mathematics, you may think about the year as a total of 36 weeks and allot varying numbers of weeks to each math topic you want to cover during the year. For a subject such as language arts, you might think of the school year as eight months long and create eight different units that involve students in listening, speaking, writing, and reading activities. You may divide the year into four quarters for subjects such as science or social studies with four major units planned for the year. These examples are only suggestions. Each subject can be subdivided into any time segment, or you may combine subjects into interdisciplinary units that involve students in mathematics, science, and language arts activities under one combined topic for a time.

Making reasonable and professional judgments about time-line planning depends on having information about your students' prior knowledge and their history of success or failure before the year begins. The pace of your curriculum depends to some degree on the skills and knowledge your students have acquired before you meet them. But your own expectation for their success is also important. You want to avoid the trap many teachers fall into of reviewing basic skills all year because a majority of your students have been unsuccessful in the past. If you expect them to succeed in your curriculum and be ready to move on to new challenges, then you should provide them with new challenges. They are likely to respond to your positive expectations.

The time lines you create at the beginning of the year need not be rigid and unchanging. They are guidelines based on the best knowledge you have at the time. As the year progresses, you will undoubtedly have reasons to change your original time line. Students' needs, interests, and success will cause you to alter the pace of the original plan. Current events in the country, your classroom, or your local community may cause you to add a new unit to your plan. Interaction with other faculty members may bring you fresh insights about how you want to organize the way you allocate time in your classroom.

COLLABORATIVE LONG-TERM PLANNING

Long-term planning, either individually or collectively, is an important job for teachers. If you are teaching in a self-contained classroom, you have the freedom to write your own outcomes as long as they relate to the district and state guidelines. If you are working in a team-teaching school, you will need to articulate your vision of student outcomes to your teammates and adjust yours to include their ideas as well as your own. In either case, the outcome statements you create will improve with experience. As you see the effects of your original outcome statements, you will reflect on them and find ways to improve them with each succeeding year.

When you begin teaching, you may be assigned to a curriculum task force or planning committee. In discussions with your colleagues, you are likely to gain new insights and information, but you may also experience frustration with points of view that differ from your own. When this occurs, remember the five different curriculum orientations of teachers. That may help you see things from a different perspective. Be prepared to speak assertively about your own ideas and beliefs. You may be the one to suggest innovative ways of dividing the curriculum into units. Although your ideas may meet skepticism or resistance from some teachers, it is quite appropriate for you to articulate them because schools rely on fresh ideas from faculty members with the most recent college or university training to enhance the curriculum and create positive innovations and change.

⟳ Reflective Actions for Your Professional Portfolio
A Sample of Your Long-Term Planning

Perceptiveness: Observe Goals and Long-Term Plans

Observe a classroom in action for a few hours and try to infer what the goals are from what you see taking place. Write what you perceive to be the major affective, cognitive, and psychomotor goals in effect. Write a brief description of the hidden and null curriculum that you observed.

Construction of Knowledge: School Mission Statements

Visit a school and ask to see the mission statement and curriculum goals or outcomes for that site. Ask a classroom teacher to describe his or her goals and show you the long-range plans. Talk with the teacher about how the school's mission statement and goals have affected the class curriculum.

Clarification of Values and Principles: Articulate Your Goals

Based on your perception of students' needs, what are your highest-priority educational goals? Write at least one cognitive, affective, and psychomotor outcome statement that you consider to be extremely important in the elementary curriculum.

Creativity: Plan a Series of Multidisciplinary Themes

Imagine that you have been hired to teach in the school that you are currently visiting. Create a series of themes for the grade level you'd most like to teach. Describe how you would integrate the subject areas into each theme.

Persistence and Problem Solving: A Year-Long Plan

Using the themes you selected for your grade level, sketch out a brief year-long plan using months or quarters of the year as units of planning. What would be the major outcomes in language arts, social studies, math, and science for each month or quarter? How do they relate to the theme?

Communication Skills: Collaborative Feedback

Describe your most important educational goals and the theme you have created to your classmates or the teacher you are visiting. Speak as assertively as possible about the importance you attach to your choices. Listen to their reactions and use the feedback to enrich your own plan.

References

Banks, J. (1991–1992). Multicultural education: For freedom's sake. *Educational Leadership, 49,* 4.

Beane, J. (1991). Middle school: The natural home of the integrated curriculum. *Educational Leadership, 49*(2), 9–13.

Bell, M. (1990). *Everyday mathematics: First grade teachers' manual.* Evanston, IL: Everyday Learning.

Bloom, B., Engelhart, M., Furst, E., Hill, W., & Krathwohl, D. (1956). *Taxonomy of educational objectives: Cognitive domain.* New York: Longman.

Bragaw, D., & Hartoonian, M. (1988). Social studies: The study of people in society. In R. Brandt (Ed.), *Content of the curriculum* (pp. 9–29). Alexandria, VA: Association for Supervision and Curriculum Development.

Brophy, J. (1992). Probing the subtleties of subject-matter teaching. *Educational Leadership, 49*(7), 4–8.

California State Department of Education. (1992). *Mathematics framework.* Sacramento Board of Publications Sales, P.O. Box 271, Sacramento, CA 95802-0271.

Chomsky, C. (1969). *The acquisition of syntax from 5 to 10.* Cambridge, MA: MIT Press.

Eisner, E. (1985). *Educational imagination* (2nd ed). Upper Saddle River, NJ: Merrill/Prentice Hall.

Gaidimas, L., & Walters, S. (1993). Maine's common core of learning moves forward. *Educational Leadership, 50*(8), 31–34.

Graves, D. (1983). *Writing: Teachers and children at work.* Exeter, NH: Heinemann.

Kendall, J., & Marzano, R. (1995). *The systematic identification and articulation of content standards and benchmarks.* Aurora, CO: Mid-Continent Regional Educational Laboratory.

Kurusa. (1981). *The streets are free (Las calles son libras).* Caracas: Ekare-Banco del Libro (Spanish version); New York: Annick Firefly Books (English version).

Murray, D. (1984). *Write to learn.* New York: Holt.

Muther, C. (1987). What do we teach and when do we teach it? *Educational Leadership, 45*(1), 77–80.

National Center for History in the Schools. (1994). *National standards for United States history: Exploring paths to the present.* Los Angeles: Author.

National Committee on Science Education Standards and Assessment. (1994). *National science education standards.* Washington, DC: National Academy Press.

National Council for Social Studies. (1994). *Expectations of excellence: Curriculum standards for social studies.* Washington, DC: Author.

National Council of Teachers of Mathematics. (1989). *Curriculum and evaluation standards for school mathematics.* Reston, VA: Author.

Reissman, R. (1994). *The evolving multicultural classroom.* Alexandria, VA: Association for Supervision and Curriculum Development.

Sleeter, C., & Grant, C. (1994). *Making choices for multicultural education.* Upper Saddle River, NJ: Merrill/Prentice Hall.

Spady, W. (1994). Choosing outcomes of significance. *Educational Leadership, 51*(6), 18–22.

Sulzby, E., & Teale, W. (1987). *Emergent literacy: Writing and reading.* Norwood, NJ: Ablex.

Tyler, R. (1949). *Basic principles of curriculum and instruction.* Chicago: University of Chicago Press.

Viadero, D. (1993, June 16). Standards deviation: Benchmark-setting is marked by diversity. *Education Week,* pp. 14–17.

Planning Thematic Units
for Authentic Learning

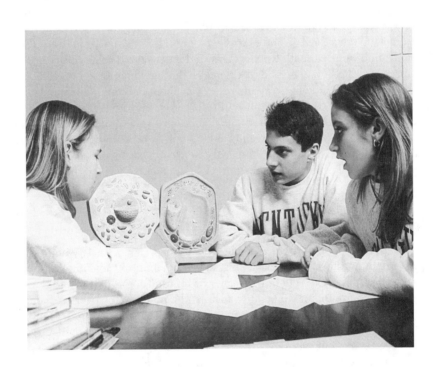

Do you have a vision of yourself teaching a roomful of students who are excitedly investigating, experimenting, discussing, and reporting on what they are learning? Beginning teachers and student teachers often report that what they want to do most is create a learning environment that motivates their students to want to come to school and want to learn as much as they can about important matters.

Current national standards and state curriculum guides are also the products of the vision of experienced teachers, working in collaboration to provide beginning teachers with guidelines for what to teach and how to teach it. These documents encourage teachers to create programs that develop students' deeper understandings of a few important subjects rather than provide them with superficial surveys of data. At the local school district level, teachers are responsible for translating the curricular visions described at the national or state level into practical classroom learning experiences. The word *vision* is carefully chosen in this discussion because at the local level teachers and principals are asked to develop a common vision and create a mental image of what they want to accomplish with students.

One of the most natural and authentic ways to translate a vision of core curriculum goals into practical classroom experiences is to plan thematic units of study that engage students in actively seeking information on a topic that has meaning in their lives. Many teachers, like Ruth Reyes and Ginny Bailey, described in Chapter 4, use a series of thematic units for their long-term planning. There is something refreshing and inherently motivating for both teachers and students who are using this plan. A unit of study lasts a specified number of days or weeks, during which time everyone is motivated to investigate and find out everything they can about the topic. Then, during an exciting culmination, the students proudly display what they've learned. After a brief period devoted to assessment, the unit ends, and a new one begins. When this rhythm is established in a classroom, complaints of boredom or repetition are rare from students or the teacher. The pace is quick, the goals are clear, and the expectations are high when everyone is involved in a thematic unit on an interesting, challenging topic.

How Teachers Plan Thematic Units

No other model of curriculum development involves teachers in a more active and professional capacity than do the planning, teaching, and evaluation of thematic curriculum units. They appeal greatly to reflective teachers who want to be part of the decision-making process and use their own creative ideas and methods. However, planning thematic curriculum units also adds greatly to the responsibility of classroom teachers. To create a successful unit, teachers must be willing to gather information and create an excellent knowledge base about the topics they've chosen so that the learning experiences they plan will be based on accurate information. They must also be willing to work with their colleagues to make sure that their curriculum units do not repeat or skip important material in the elementary curriculum. They must take care to articulate their units with what was covered in earlier grades and what their students will learn in subsequent years.

Even when teachers decide that they want to create their own thematic curriculum units to translate curricular visions into actual classroom experiences, many are not certain how to begin to create a unit or what can or should be covered in each one. In this chapter, we examine how teachers decide what units to teach and how they organize the learning experiences in a curriculum unit to ensure that students learn the knowledge, skills, and processes that are intended when a unit is planned.

DECIDING ON UNIT TOPICS

A single teacher can work alone or with colleagues to translate state and local curriculum outcomes into units of study. Working alone, a single teacher analyzes state and local outcome statements to be implemented at that grade level in math, science, social studies, language arts, and fine arts. The teacher also examines the curriculum materials supplied by the school district, looking for themes or topics. The teacher may choose to look for topics within a subject, such as a math unit on fractions, a science unit on magnets and electricity, or a social studies unit on the electoral process. Other units may be interdisciplinary—that is, designed to include information and material from several subjects at one time. For example, a theme of "change" may include learning experiences in science, math, social studies, and literature.

Although many teachers choose to work alone, other teachers at the same grade level frequently work together to create units of study. When this occurs, their combined knowledge and ideas are likely to result in a much more comprehensive set of units and a greater variety of learning experiences. Whether a teacher works alone or with a team, the first step is to decide on a series of curriculum units that correspond to the major educational goals in a subject or several subjects for that grade level.

Unit topics may be suggested or recommended by the district curriculum guide and the textbooks purchased for the subject area. Teachers can decide to use the suggested topics in either the order presented or a different order. Teachers may choose to delete or add units to those recommended to fulfill the needs of their students.

Teachers may decide not to use units for every subject throughout the year. Instead, they may choose to teach a subject as an unconnected series of lessons. They may use units occasionally to highlight a particular topic in the curriculum. Sometimes teachers are able to plan units that combine more than one subject area, such as language arts and social studies or math and science. No two teachers will use the same units in the same order. Teachers have much discretion in planning units that fit their own strengths and the students' needs.

When a series of units is planned for a subject, each unit within the series is then developed in planning sessions that may begin in the summer before school begins or take place in after-school meetings during the year. Often teachers plan the first unit during the summer so that it is ready for the fall. Later units are then planned during the school year. Once a unit has been planned, it can be reused in subsequent years, although reflective teachers usually review their older units and revise and update them before teaching them a second or third time.

CREATING A CURRICULUM UNIT USING REFLECTIVE ACTIONS

When reflective teachers approach the development of a curriculum unit in a subject area, they first consider their long-term goals for that subject. They may begin with the question "What are my major social studies goals this year, and what should I include in each unit of study to accomplish these goals?" Or they may begin by considering the core outcomes they are expected to achieve during the year and plan curriculum units that will encourage their students to learn the content and enhance the skills that make up those outcomes.

USING PERCEPTIVENESS

Teachers who think and plan using the reflective actions described in Chapter 1 are also likely to consider the cues they perceive from their students' interests and talents when planning thematic units. As they plan curriculum, they tend to ask themselves, "What do my students need to learn? How do they enjoy working? What learning experiences will motivate them to become actively engaged in the learning process?"

CONSTRUCTING KNOWLEDGE ON THE TOPIC

When they have decided on a topic, teachers who use reflective actions then begin an energetic search for information on the subject matter and on interesting ways to teach it. At this stage, they are likely to consider questions such as "What information do I need? Where can I get it? What can I learn from my colleagues? What can I learn from a library? How could a reference librarian help me? What is available from the district's resources for teachers?"

CLARIFYING VALUES AND MORAL PRINCIPLES

As they begin to search through available resources, teachers who use reflective actions establish some criteria for selecting certain content or methods while omitting others. These decisions are likely to be made on the basis of the teacher's values and moral principles or a philosophy of teaching. As reflective teachers consider what to include and what to exclude, they are likely to ask themselves, "What do I believe that my students need most to succeed in school or in life? How can this curriculum assist them in developing what they need most? What attitudes do I want to instill among my students? How can this unit help them to attain those attitudes? What values do I want to model for my students during this curriculum unit? How can I best model those values for them?"

CREATING THE UNIT

Now the fun part begins. Teachers who use reflective actions tend to enjoy the process of combining all the content materials and methods they've learned during planning into an original set of learning experiences that fit their own teaching style and the needs of their students. No two thematic units are ever alike. Even when teachers plan together up to this point, they are likely to interpret the materials they have gathered differently and add their own unique spin to the way they teach the unit.

Throughout the process of planning and teaching the unit, teachers who use reflective actions are likely to ask themselves, "How can I adapt these materials to meet my goals? What new instructional materials shall I create to teach this material effectively? What risks are possible if I try to teach this unit in my own way? Which risks am I willing to take? What gains are possible if I take these risks? Do the possible gains outweigh the risks?"

During a thematic unit, teachers create original bulletin boards, group activities, work or activity sheets, processes for promoting student interaction, methods to assess student accomplishments, and ways to allow their students to perform or display what they have learned. For many reflective teachers, these opportunities for creativity are among their most important sources of pride and are often cited as some of the most significant perks of their careers.

BEING PERSISTENT AND SOLVING PROBLEMS

All teachers encounter problems in teaching and managing their classrooms. But teachers who use reflective actions are able to bounce back a little more easily than most. This may be due to their expectations that problems are inevitable. You are likely to find that if you solve one problem, a new one may develop. For example, if you introduce some innovative learning materials to motivate students to want to learn more about a subject, you may find that a behavior management problem develops. You must then reflect on new ways to gain students' cooperation when they use the new materials. Redesigning the curriculum for your classroom or school may eliminate redundancy but may also cause articulation problems among grade levels. For example, when teachers are allowed to select the reading materials for their classes based on students' interests, they may find that teachers at other grade levels have used or plan to use the same book.

Teachers who use reflective actions in their thinking and planning expect these kinds of difficulties. When they occur, the teachers simply work them out with their colleagues or students until they reach the best possible solution under the circumstances. Reflective teachers are also able to laugh at their own mistakes and learn from their errors in judgment without an overwhelming fear of the consequences or feelings of guilt. As they plan their thematic units, they are likely to encounter difficulties in locating suitable materials. When this happens, they become very good at scrounging for the materials they need; or they substitute and go on anyway.

When teachers begin to teach their units, some of the lessons they planned are likely to turn out very different from what they expected; but they simply assess, regroup, and reteach as needed. As the unit nears completion, they may discover that, due to their students' choices and actions, some unplanned effects occur. These are simply accounted for and evaluated along with the outcomes that were planned.

USING GOOD COMMUNICATION SKILLS

Throughout the process of planning, organizing, teaching, and evaluating a thematic unit, good communication skills are necessary. Reflective teachers must often convince or persuade their colleagues or administrators to allow them to take the time, spend money, take certain risks, and establish certain priorities necessary to teach their thematic units the way they want. Assertiveness is an important trait in curriculum development, especially considering the very different curriculum orientations that various members of the faculty adopt.

Conflicts are likely to arise with students as well. When reflective teachers introduce a creative new way to learn a difficult subject, students are likely to react by stating their own preferences. When this occurs, teachers who use reflective actions simply begin the cyclical process anew by perceiving what student needs have not been sufficiently addressed in the plan so far and accommodating those needs in a revised version of the unit plan.

SEQUENCING LEARNING EXPERIENCES IN UNIT PLANS

Practically speaking, the process of developing a curriculum unit also includes the following steps:

1. Defining the topics and subject matter to be covered in the unit
2. Defining the cognitive, process, and affective goals or outcomes that tell what students will gain and be able to do as a result
3. Outlining the major concepts that will be covered
4. Gathering resources that can be used in planning and teaching
5. Brainstorming learning activities and experiences that can be used in the unit
6. Organizing the ideas and activities into a meaningful sequence
7. Planning lesson plans that follow the sequence
8. Planning evaluation processes that will be used to measure student achievement and satisfaction

Analysis will reveal that these statements correspond to Tyler's four questions. Items 1, 2, and 3 pertain to Tyler's (1949) question "What shall we teach?" Items 4 and 5 relate to the question "How shall we teach it?" Items 6 and 7 respond to the question "How shall we organize it?" Item 8 answers the question "How will we know if we are successful?"

When seen in print, as they are here, these steps appear to depict an orderly process, but curriculum planning is rarely such a linear activity. Instead, teachers find themselves starting at various points in this process. They skip or go back and forth among these steps as ideas occur to them. For example, a team member may begin a discussion by showing a resource book with a particular learning activity that could be taught as part of the new unit. Discussions may skip from activities to goals to concepts to evaluation to organization. Nothing is wrong with this nonlinear process as long as teachers are responsible enough to reflect on the overall plan to determine if all of Tyler's questions have been addressed fully and adequately. When the plan is complete, it is important to review it and ask yourself: "What are the outcomes I expect from this unit? Are the learning experiences directly related to the outcomes? Is my organization of activities going to make it possible for my students to achieve my outcomes? Are the assessment systems I've established going to measure the extent to which the students have accomplished the outcomes?"

Thematic units vary in types of learning experiences and in organization. Some subjects, such as math, are organized very sequentially; others are not. The type of learning experiences also vary greatly depending on the subject, the resources available, and the creativity or risk taking of the teacher.

Most teachers use the textbook or a district curriculum guide as the basis for planning and as an important resource. *Do not limit yourself, however, to a single textbook as the source of all information in planning your unit or in teaching it.* A good textbook can be a valuable resource for you as you plan and for your students as they learn about the topic, but a rich and motivating unit plan will contain many other elements.

Supplemental reading materials from libraries or bookstores might include biographies, histories, novels, short stories, plays, poems, newspapers, magazines, how-to books, and a myriad of other printed materials. Other resources to consider are films, videotapes, audiotapes, and computer programs on topics that relate to your unit. Many interesting student-centered computer programs allow your students to have simulated experiences, solve problems, and make decisions as if they were involved in the event themselves. A good example is the computer game called *Oregon Trail*, distributed by the Minnesota Educational Computer Consortium (MECC), in which the student travels along the Oregon Trail, making decisions about what supplies to buy, when and where to stop along the way, and how to handle emergencies. This program can enrich a unit on westward expansion by providing more problem-solving and critical-thinking experiences than reading and discussion can ever yield.

Many educational games also provide students with simulated experiences. Some are board games that can be purchased in a good toy store or bookstore. Others are more specialized learning games sold by educational publishers or distributors. Your school district probably receives hundreds of catalogs from educational publishers. Locate them and find out about the many manipulative and simulation games available on your topic.

Consider field trips that will provide your students with experiences beyond the four walls of the classroom. Which museums have exhibits related to your topic? A simple walk through a neighborhood to look for evidence of pollution or to view variations in architecture can add depth to your unit. If you cannot travel, consider inviting a guest to speak to your students about the topic. Sometimes parents are excellent resources and are willing to talk about their careers or other interests.

In thinking about how to organize a unit, many reflective teachers prefer to begin with a highly motivating activity such as a field trip, a guest speaker, a simulation game, a hands-on experiment, or a film. They know that when the students' initial experience with a topic is stimulating and involving, interest and curiosity are aroused. The next several lessons in the unit are frequently planned at the knowledge and comprehension levels of Bloom's taxonomy to provide students with basic facts and concepts so that they can build a substantial knowledge base and understanding of the topic. After establishing the knowledge base, teachers can design further learning experiences at the application, analysis, synthesis, and evaluation levels to ensure that the students are able to think critically and creatively about the subject. This model of unit planning is not universal, nor is it the only logical sequence, but it can be adapted to fit many topics and subjects with excellent results.

Examples of Thematic Units

The following sections illustrate the processes that teachers use as they select, order, and create unit plans in several subjects from the elementary curriculum. Because each teacher has a personal curriculum orientation and philosophy, the process of decision making is more complex when teachers plan together than it is when they plan alone. The following examples demonstrate how teachers create their own curriculum units and what they put down on paper to record their plans for teaching. You will notice many variations in the way in which units are created and what they contain, depending on their purposes and the philosophies and values of the teachers who create them.

CREATING A MULTIDISCIPLINARY PRIMARY UNIT

Some units of study cross the boundaries among subjects or disciplines such as math, science, language arts, and social studies. For example, a unit on ancient Rome may incorporate many communication and language-arts skills in what is primarily a social studies unit.

Curriculum plans that include learning experiences from more than one subject area are called *multidisciplinary* or *interdisciplinary* units. To create such units, teachers frequently choose themes or topics and plan learning experiences that involve students in reading, writing, speaking, science investigations, mathematical problem solving, music, and art. A single teacher can certainly plan and teach a multidisciplinary unit, but we've found that the units planned by two to four teachers are often more exciting because they incorporate each teacher's different perspectives and strengths. For example, at Woodland School in Carpentersville, Illinois, three first-grade teachers often plan their whole language thematic units together. Ginny Bailey, Judy Yount, and Sandra Krakow recently planned an interdisciplinary unit on "change," highlighting the changes of butterflies and moths.

Bailey, Yount, and Krakow know that teachers often have difficulty fitting in all the subjects of their busy curricula. They find that by using a thematic unit, they can teach several subjects simultaneously. To plan a unit, these teachers use a graphic organizer known as a planning web. They sit down with a large piece of paper and write the thematic topic in the middle of the page. They write the various disciplines they want to cover at different positions on the paper and then brainstorm learning experiences that fit the topic under the appropriate subject areas. An example of one of their planning webs is shown in Figure 5.1.

Through their observations of the students they teach, the three teachers learned that, in the minds of first-grade students, reading and writing are very closely related. Their interdisciplinary thematic units allow students to read, write, and investigate interesting topics such as caterpillars, cookies, and planets. In each unit they select appropriate topic-specific children's books of fiction, nonfiction, and poetry. They locate songs on the topics when possible. Skill teaching is embedded in the unit, within the context of the literature, poetry, or music. The science and social studies facts and concepts are easily mastered by students when they are presented in the context of hands-

Figure 5.1 Planning web for a thematic unit.

Source: Ginny Bailey, Judy Yount, and Sandra Krakow, Woodland School, Carpentersville, Illinois

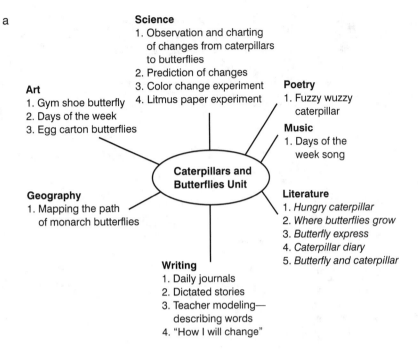

Science
1. Observation and charting of changes from caterpillars to butterflies
2. Prediction of changes
3. Color change experiment
4. Litmus paper experiment

Art
1. Gym shoe butterfly
2. Days of the week
3. Egg carton butterflies

Poetry
1. Fuzzy wuzzy caterpillar

Music
1. Days of the week song

Caterpillars and Butterflies Unit

Geography
1. Mapping the path of monarch butterflies

Literature
1. *Hungry caterpillar*
2. *Where butterflies grow*
3. *Butterfly express*
4. *Caterpillar diary*
5. *Butterfly and caterpillar*

Writing
1. Daily journals
2. Dictated stories
3. Teacher modeling—describing words
4. "How I will change"

on experiments and are reinforced by illustrated stories, poems, and songs. Math concepts are introduced by counting, measuring, sequencing, and patterning games and activities appropriate to each unit. Box 5.1 shows a written plan for the unit "changes," describing some of the specific learning experiences and how the unit is evaluated.

A MULTIDISCIPLINARY, MULTICULTURAL UNIT

Frequently, when teachers want to create multidisciplinary thematic units, they choose to begin with their social studies curriculum. Social studies already combines several academic disciplines, including geography, history, economics, political science, anthropology, sociology, and psychology. By adding learning experiences in literature and the arts, a teacher can fairly easily create a high-quality multidisciplinary thematic unit. If your goal is also to infuse the unit with multicultural learning experiences, then social studies is a very appropriate subject. Typically, the social studies curriculum is designed as an ever-widening circle of ideas, in keeping with the developmental stages of students. In the early grades, the curriculum centers on the home and the community; the middle grades focus on the states and the United States; concepts related to nations and the world are dealt with in the later grades. At each level, teachers can find many interesting ways to address the issues and contributions of various cultures.

Primary teachers often create units on the community, including maps of the school neighborhood, history of the community, roles of community helpers, economic activities related to stores in the community, and other similar experiences. To make this unit

MODEL LESSON PLANNING

Box 5.1 Unit Theme: Changes
Subtopic: Butterflies and Moths
A FIRST-GRADE UNIT PLAN

by Virginia Bailey, Judy Yount, and Sandra Krakow, Woodland School, Carpentersville, Illinois

Description

This primary learning unit was planned to provide students with a set of varied learning experiences to understand the concept of change, with an emphasis on changes in the life cycle of living things.

Cognitive goal: Students will understand that all living things change over time.

Affective goal: Students will accept change as a natural part of their own lives and environment.

Psychomotor goals: Students will use observation skills to identify changes. They will use writing and speaking skills to report what they have learned through observation.

Nature Walk

Before the nature walk, students are asked to imagine what they might find out about caterpillars and butterflies on their walk. During the walk, they look especially for cocoons. When they return to the classroom, they discuss their findings. They predict whether the cocoons they found will become butterflies or moths. Then they write about what they saw on their nature walk.

Observing Caterpillars

Caterpillars ordered from a science supply dealer arrive in plastic jars. Students observe them climb to the top of the jar preparing to form a chrysalis. In just a few days, they begin to spin their chrysalis. They remain in this form for three or four days and then emerge as butterflies or moths.

As a follow-up activity, students are asked to illustrate the various changes they observe. A strip of 18-inch by 6-inch paper is prepared for each child. Children fold the paper into fourths and draw each stage of a butterfly's development: (1) egg on a leaf, (2) caterpillar, (3) chrysalis or cocoon, and (4) butterfly or moth.

In groups of four, children evaluate their products and check the proper sequence. Each child can then tell the other children a story about his or her butterfly.

Color Changes

In a learning center, students experiment to discover how colors change. Working with diluted red, blue, and yellow food color, the children use an empty cup and an eye dropper to mix colors and experiment on their own to create new colors from the original primary colors.

Children's Literature

The teacher collects a variety of picture books related to change. Some books will be read aloud by the teacher and used as a focus for discussion. Others will be selected by the children to read on their own.

Caterpillar/Butterfly Art Activity

Students create a wiggly caterpillar by cutting 12 cups from an egg carton. They make a small hole in the bottom of each cup, tie a knot at one end of a piece of yarn, and string the 12 cups together. Then they add paper eyes and decorate the caterpillars with crayons or paint.

They create a butterfly by cutting out 3 of the 12 cups from an egg carton for the body. Then they add wings and pipe-cleaner antennae.

Gym Shoe Butterfly

Each child places his or her gym shoes on a large piece of pastel paper (arches facing out) and traces the shoes into a butterfly shape. The child then cuts out the shape and adds antennae. The child can write a poem inside the butterfly shape.

Days of the Week

Students create a caterpillar with seven circles cut from construction paper. They then copy one name of each day of the week on each circle and glue them onto a background paper in the correct order. Afterward, they added a face, legs, and antennae. Students learn a song about the days of the week.

How People Change

Students bring in pictures of themselves as babies and put them on a bulletin board. Current school pictures are also arranged on the bulletin board. Students have to try to match the baby pictures with the current pictures of their classmates. Discussions focus on how people change (observing differences in size, hair, and other physical features) and what people are able to do at different ages. As a follow-up, students write in their journals about how they have changed.

continued

Growth Charts

Charts on the students' current heights and weights are initiated during this unit. Each student measures and weighs a partner. These data are recorded on a wall graph. The charts are updated three times during the year.

Poetry about Change

Poems about caterpillars and butterflies, seasons, and other changes are distributed frequently during the unit. Students read them, memorize and recite them, discuss them, and illustrate them. The poems are also used to teach language structure and vocabulary skills. A poem is projected onto a screen using an overhead projector. Students also have copies of the poem on their desks. We teach skills such as these:

1. Reading from left to right
2. Finding and reading individual words
3. Using the context of the poem to decode words
4. Learning specific phonics skills (such as beginning sounds, endings, rhyming words)

Art/Nutrition

Create a caterpillar out of fruit, vegetables, and peanut butter. Eat it for a snack and discuss its nutritional value.

Unit Evaluation Activity

Provide students with a paper that has the beginning of three paragraphs (shown later in this box). Use a copy on the overhead projector and clarify for students how to begin and what is expected.

Because primary students are unable to write all that they know and have observed, this evaluation can be extended by asking children from an upper elementary grade to interview the primary children and write the younger students' responses for them.

This week, I learned about butterflies and moths. First, I learned _____

_____ .

Next, I learned. _____ .
Finally, I learned. _____ .

a valid multicultural experience, primary teachers invite family members of the students to participate by sharing their cultural heritage with the rest of the class.

Middle-grade teachers frequently create units on the life experiences and cultural beliefs of the first citizens of North America, the Native Americans. They also bring in the wide variety of contributions made by the people who immigrated from Asia, Europe, Africa, and Central and South America. Upper-grade teachers may offer units comparing nations of the world in terms of culture, geography, politics, economics, and history.

High school teachers also focus on U.S. history or world history and are able to infuse their units with many references and investigations of the differences and similarities among the peoples of the world.

Consider Box 5.2, an example of how a multicultural and multidisciplinary unit may be developed. This world history teacher began with the history of ancient Rome and wove in learning experiences comparing Roman culture with other cultures around the world.

MODEL LESSON PLANNING

Box 5.2 When in Rome, Do As the Romans Do
A SIXTH-GRADE SOCIAL STUDIES UNIT

Description

This unit provides students with knowledge about an important ancient culture and civilization in a way that allows them to compare and contrast their own culture with that of the ancient Romans. It involves students' attaining and using skills in research, using primary sources, thinking critically, writing, and doing oral presentations in order to communicate what they've learned to others.

Cognitive Goals

Students will know why primary sources are important for understanding an ancient culture and will be able to describe a primary source.

Students will be able to describe Roman culture as it relates to class; housing; slavery; family life; roles and status of men, women, and children; educational processes and values; social life; entertainment; economy and occupations; religion; art; ideals; and values.

Students will compare and contrast the culture of their own families with that of the ancient Romans.

Affective Goals

Students will develop an interest in Roman history and culture and see how it is related to their own lives and cultures.

Psychomotor Goals

Students will act out aspects of Roman life in order to gain an understanding of Roman customs, ceremonies, and rituals.

Students will improve their critical thinking and communication skills by writing and speaking about the lives of Roman citizens in comparison to their own.

continued

Time Line of Learning Events

WEEK 1: ALL ROADS LEAD TO ROME

The legendary beginning of Rome

Romulus and Remus

Etruscans

Latium

Development of the Roman republic

Expansion of power, conquering Greece

WEEKS 2 AND 3: FRIENDS, ROMANS, COUNTRYMEN, LEND ME YOUR EARS

The Roman Empire

Julius Caesar

Augustus Caesar

Pax Romana

Government

Justice

Military

Highways

Architecture

Technology

Aqueducts

WEEKS 4 AND 5: WHEN IN ROME, DO AS THE ROMANS DO

Roman life

Class

Housing

Slaves

Family life

Men's roles and responsibilities

Women's roles and responsibilities

Children's roles

Education

Social life

Entertainment

continued

Economy

Occupations

Religion

Art

Ideals and values

WEEKS 6 AND 7: CROSSROADS

Students will investigate their own cultural heritage and compare and contrast their lives with those of the ancient Romans. In their personal investigations, each student will focus on the differences and similarities in terms of the following:

Class

Housing

Slaves

Family life

Men's roles and responsibilities

Women's roles and responsibilities

Children's roles

Education

Social life

Entertainment

Economy

Occupations

Religion

Art

Ideals and values

WEEK 8: STUDENT PERFORMANCES DEPICTING THE COMPARISONS BETWEEN THEIR OWN LIVES AND THE LIVES OF ANCIENT ROMANS

Working individually or with classmates, students will demonstrate the differences they have discovered between their own culture and that of the ancient Romans by delivering original essays, stories, plays, poems, songs, arts, or crafts.

EVALUATION PROCESS FOR THIS UNIT

Students will keep individual portfolios of their work, which will contain copies of their personal investigations, reflective writings, and other class work and homework assigned during the unit.

A videotape will be made of each student's original work during the final week of performances.

DEVELOPING A MATHEMATICS UNIT

Mathematics is generally thought of as a subject that does not lend itself to multidisciplinary planning, but recently many teachers have begun experimenting with ways to connect mathematics to other subject areas and life experiences. As Piaget demonstrated, mathematics is a subject that requires early experiences with concrete examples and hands-on experiences allowing students to manipulate materials to understand mathematical relationships. Only in the upper intermediate grades can students be expected to understand these same relationships at an abstract level without the need to "see" them in a concrete way. Many teachers like to plan their mathematics curriculum using thematic units so that students have many opportunities to experience and investigate the mathematical relationships they are learning.

Mathematics is also a subject that requires lateral thinking, reasoning, and problem-solving strategies that cannot be taught in a sequential series of lessons. Current mathematics units encourage students to explore mathematical relationships and select from a variety of strategies to set up and solve problems. Skillful computation is no longer sufficient as an outcome or performance expectation; it is also important that students be able to apply mathematical operations to real-life problems and tasks.

Based on these organizational principles, an effective curriculum unit in math is likely to (1) present new skills and concepts in order of difficulty; (2) initiate new learning with concrete, manipulative experiences so that students can understand the concepts involved; (3) teach students a variety of problem-solving strategies; and (4) provide examples, tasks, and problems that call on students to apply their newly learned skills and strategies in lifelike situations to problems they can relate to and want to solve.

Mathematics is an example of a *spiral curriculum.* This means that certain concepts and skills are taught every year but in an upward spiral of difficulty. Each year begins with a review of skills from previous years, then introduces new skills and concepts. For this reason, the topics of mathematics units are likely to be similar from year to year, but the way in which these topics are addressed and the complexity of the concepts vary greatly. Mathematics education now emphasizes problem solving and investigation as a means of developing mathematical power. Whenever possible, real situations and problems are becoming the basis for the curriculum.

A good example of a mathematics unit that involves students in realistic investigations and problem solving is presented in Box 5.3. Pam Knight created this unit, entitled "Television Viewing Habits," for her sixth-grade students. She uses it during the first week of school to engage her students' interest in mathematics, help to develop a sense of confidence in their mathematical power, and show them how useful and important mathematics can be in their everyday lives.

CREATING A LANGUAGE-ARTS UNIT

Units created for the language-arts curriculum are likely to be very different from math units. Because language arts is a composite of the skills and creative abilities related to reading, writing, speaking, and listening, a language-arts unit is likely to include a great variety of learning experiences. Expected outcomes are likely to call on students to apply basic skills in some form of creative product.

MODEL LESSON PLANNING

Box 5.3 Television Viewing Habits
A MIDDLE SCHOOL MATHEMATICS UNIT

by Pam Knight, Poway School District, Poway, California

Description
This unit functions both as a personal exploration of how students use their free time and as a mathematics investigation. Students keep a log of all the time they spend watching TV every day for a week. With parental permission, students may also log the TV viewing habits of their parents. After a week of data gathering, students carry out a variety of mathematical calculations and interpret the data they collected.

Cognitive and Skill Outcome Statements
- Students will be able to collect and record data accurately and efficiently.
- Students will be able to calculate percentages of time spent watching television and compare those with percentages of time spent doing other activities.
- Students will be able to create bar and circle graphs based on the data they collected and the percentages they calculated.
- Individually, students will interpret the data they collected about their own television-viewing habits.
- As a class, students will combine their data with that collected by other members of the class to make interpretations and generalizations regarding TV-viewing habits of their age group.
- Individually, students will write articles describing the conclusions and generalizations they reached from this study.
- In small groups, students will make oral presentations on the findings of their group.

Affective Outcome Statement
Students will become aware of the amount of time they and their classmates spend watching television and will make value judgments about whether they want to continue spending their time in this way.

continued

Calendar of Events

I plan this investigation for the first week of school. It gives me insight into the students' incoming work habits and mathematical power.

FIRST WEEK OF SCHOOL

Friday: Introduce unit and distribute data collection materials. Assign students the task of collecting data, beginning Sunday, on the amount of time they watch television. Because video games are played on a TV screen, my students also decided to count the time spent playing video games. I ask students to be as honest as possible and to keep track to the nearest quarter of an hour.

SECOND WEEK OF SCHOOL

Monday–Friday: Data collection continues. Discussions in class focus on data collection problems and techniques.

THIRD WEEK OF SCHOOL

Monday: BAR GRAPHS   Individually, students create bar graphs demonstrating the amount of time they watched TV each day of the preceding week.

Tuesday: CALCULATING PERCENTAGES AND CIRCLE GRAPHS   Individually, students calculate the amount and percentage of time they spent sleeping, in school, in after-school or weekend activities, and watching television, as well as extra time not spent watching television. They create circle graphs showing these percentages.

Wednesday–Friday: DATA INTERPRETATION   Cooperative groups combine class data in order to answer these questions:

For an example of a language-arts unit, let us consider the thinking and planning processes used by a fourth-grade teacher as she created a unit called "friendship in fiction" (Box 5.4). She decided on the topic because she observed that friendship is a very important element in the lives of her fourth-grade students. She noticed that the students in her classroom who had a number of good friends seemed to enjoy and succeed in school activities better than students with few friends. She knew that it would not be possible to order students to be friendlier to isolated students, but she believed she could influence the students in her class to become more sensitive to the friendship needs of their classmates.

This teacher's understanding of student development led her to believe that her students would have a strong interest in the topic of friendship and that they would be more than willing to spend class time reading, writing, speaking, and listening on a topic of such vital social interest to fourth graders. Therefore, she decided to blend her goals of meeting the social needs of her students with her goal of teaching students to

1. Which grade level watches more television? Explain how you came to this conclusion.
2. Which day of the week do people watch the most television? Explain how you came to this conclusion.
3. Who watches more television in general: boys or girls? Does any particular age group watch more television? How did you come to your conclusions?
4. By using data about parent viewing habits, have you discovered any relationship between the television-viewing habits of a parent and the habits of a child?

FOURTH WEEK OF SCHOOL

Monday: WRITING ARTICLES   Individuals are assigned to write an article about their conclusions about the television-viewing habits of middle school students. They must answer the questions "Who? What? When? Where? and Why?" in the articles.

Tuesday–Wednesday: ORAL PRESENTATION PLANNING   Cooperative groups plan presentations on the findings of their groups. They create visual displays to show the data they collected.

Thursday: ORAL PRESENTATIONS   Cooperative groups present their findings to the rest of the class.

Friday: UNIT EVALUATION   Students evaluate their accomplishments in this unit. Individuals participate in a teacher-student conference to discuss the points each student earned in the unit. Cooperative groups discuss the processes they used in their group planning sessions, the visual displays they made, and the effectiveness of their oral presentations.

listen, think, and read critically and to express their ideas effectively in writing and speaking. The goals and purposes for the unit plan began to take shape in her mind.

Next, she went to the school learning center and made a list of students' books with friendship as a theme. She also asked the learning center teacher to recommend her favorites. She purposely chose books with reading levels at, below, and above the fourth-grade level to accommodate the students in her class with varying reading levels. She found that the books themselves suggested learning experiences and activities that used reading, writing, listening, and speaking skills.

She created a list of possible activities and began to envision the unit's taking place. In her mind's eye, she could see the students role-playing scenes from the books they read and writing in journals about their own views of friendship. She tried to envision the class meetings she would hold on the topic of friendship and how she would introduce the subject to the students to gain their interest and willingness to learn and grow. She silently rehearsed the words she would use to ensure that they understood what

MODEL LESSON PLANNING

Box 5.4 What Are Friends For?

A FOURTH-GRADE LANGUAGE-ARTS UNIT

Description

In this unit students will read books on the theme of friendship. Discussions, writing, speeches, dramatizations, and other events are planned to allow students to express their views on what they have read.

Outcome Statements

OUTCOME 1

Students will read at least six books on friendship and demonstrate comprehension of and critical and creative thinking about the books by interacting with classmates to create an original product related to each book.

Related Projects and Performance Objectives   Students will do the following:

Read: Choose and read at least six books (at a reading level appropriate for the student) from the list provided.

Listen: In cooperative groups of students who have read the same book, each student will listen to the opinions and ideas of others in discussions about the book's content and meaning and to the ideas and suggestions of others about the creation of an original product related to the book.

Speak: Each student will take part in a group project to create an original product related to each book and perform or describe it to the class.

OUTCOME 2

Students will express their opinions, ideas, and suggestions to others in the classroom with clarity, creativity, and supportive evidence for their opinions.

Related Projects and Performance Expectations   Students will do the following:

Speak: In cooperative groups, students will create an "advertisement" to sell others on reading the book.

Write: Students will choose to write an original story, poem, play, or essay in response to at least one book

OUTCOME 3

Students will demonstrate that they recognize, accept, and understand that the need for friendship is important to each member of the class and that each student has a responsibility to offer support and friendship to other students in the classroom community.

Related Projects and Performance Expectations   Students will do the following:

Read: Students will look for examples of the importance and value of friendship as they read the books they select for this unit.

Speak: During classroom meetings, students will contribute opinions about what friendship means.

Listen: Students will listen to and paraphrase opinions stated by others about what friendship means to them.

Write: Students will choose one classmate and write in a journal about the experience of offering friendship to that person.

Organizational Plan

BOOK SELECTION

Each week for six weeks, students will select a book from a list of four titles, each with a different reading level. Students are encouraged to select titles at their own personal reading level but are allowed to select titles above or below this level if they have a strong interest in reading that book.

SUSTAINED SILENT READING (SSR)

Each day, students will spend 45 minutes in sustained silent reading of the books they have selected.

LITERATURE CIRCLES

During (or immediately following) SSR, the teacher may call on four students to form a literature circle. The students bring their books and discuss interesting passages from them with others in the circle. The teacher shares a book in the same way.

continued

COOPERATIVE GROUPS

Each week cooperative groups are formed by those who have selected a particular book. They must discuss the book, create a plan for advertising the book to the rest of the class, and perform their advertisement on Fridays.

ENRICHMENT PLAN

Individual students may select additional titles to read from the list in response to student advertisements. Individuals may work alone or with partners to create original projects in response to the book.

CLASSROOM MEETINGS

Weekly classroom meetings on the topic of friendship will be led by the teacher. In these meetings, students will relate the stories they are reading to their own lives and friendships. Suggested topics for the classroom meetings include the following:

Week 1:   What are friends for? What are some of the reasons to have friends? What can friends do together that a person cannot do alone?

Week 2:   What does it feel like to move away from friends or to lose a good friend?

Week 3:   Is it good to have one best friend or many friends? What happens if your best friend chooses another best friend?

Week 4:   What happens when friends fight or disagree? How can you make up with a friend after a quarrel? How can you deal with conflict?

Week 5:   How can you make more friends or better friends?

Week 6:   What can you do if you notice that someone needs a friend? How can you include them in your activities? How can a class of children make sure that everyone is included and no one is left out? Do we want to do that after all that we've learned about friendship? If so, what will we do differently?

Evaluation Plan

Outcome 1 will be evaluated by recording the books each child reads in a cooperative group or independently. Descriptions of the original products are also kept on the checklist. At the end of the unit, the checklist can serve as a means of communicating with the parents about what the student has accomplished.

Outcome 2 will be documented by keeping a portfolio of each student's written responses to books read in the unit.

Outcome 3 will be individually recorded by having students write in their journals following each weekly classroom meeting. They will write their own views on the questions raised in the class meeting. The teacher will write at the same time on the same topic.

she expected of them as they read and discussed their books in cooperative groups and planned their creative products together.

She believed that, if her unit was successful, she would be able to detect an affective change or growth in her students in at least two ways: (1) they would show a greater degree of friendliness toward classmates, and (2) individuals would express in their journals or in discussions that they felt more accepted and better liked by their classmates. She also believed that, if her unit was successful, notable changes would occur in the ways in which students used language in her classroom, including the following: (1) students would choose to read more fiction, (2) they would listen with greater accuracy and empathy, and (3) they would be able to express more clearly their ideas in writing and speaking.

During a long weekend, the teacher organized her materials, ideas, and learning experiences into a sequence of events that she could envision taking place in her classroom with her students. That sequence of events is presented in Box 5.4 as an example of a language-arts unit plan initiated and created by a single teacher.

TWO COLLEAGUES CREATE A HIGH SCHOOL SCIENCE UNIT

Chris Chiaverina and Jim Hicks are high school science teachers who believe that the world is a richer and more interesting place when people are aware of the principles of physics that operate around us. They plan their physics units to replace students' misconceptions about science as a dull and abstruse body of knowledge with a new view that science consists of exciting opportunities to satisfy their curiosity about how things work.

Working as colleagues, Jim and Chris have created a number of science units that begin with concrete explorations that encourage students to explore and investigate science phenomena. When they begin to create a new unit, they think about spectacular opening demonstrations to pique the students' interest in the topic. Jim and Chris report that they work very hard to plan and teach science units that are full of active exploration, real-life applications, and opportunities for students to experience the wonders of science. The say that the payoffs for them and their students are worth the effort. When a student looks at Jim with a light in her eyes and says, "Hey, that's neat!" he knows that all the work that went into the lesson was well spent. Their unit on wave phenomena is shown in Box 5.5.

The curriculum of any subject or of a combination of subjects may be subdivided into thematic units of study that are often highly motivating to students and a source of pride for the teachers who create them. Teacher-crafted curriculum units are often very creative and original products. For teachers who choose to create them rather than rely on textbook lessons and content, units are a way of individualizing the curriculum to capitalize on the interests and talents of the teacher and the students.

MODEL LESSON PLANNING

Box 5.5 Wave Phenomena
A HIGH SCHOOL PHYSICS UNIT

by Chris Chiaverina, New Trier High School, Winnetka, Illinois
and Jim Hicks, Barrington High School, Barrington, Illinois

Description

In this unit about wave phenomena, we study both sound and light waves. As with all our units, we begin with dramatic and puzzling demonstrations by the teacher to generate students' interest in the topic. Students then explore waves in a qualitative laboratory experience in order to observe them in action. This enables students to construct their own meaning and understanding of the properties of waves. During class discussions, we probe students' preconceived ideas about the phenomena and help them unlearn their preconceptions in order to construct more accurate understandings. Only after students have experienced the phenomena in action do we introduce mathematical relationships. At this point, students do a quantitative laboratory experiment in which they learn to express their new understandings in a formula or mathematical expression.

Outcome Statements

COGNITIVE OUTCOMES

- Students will investigate wave phenomena and identify key features of light and sound waves.
- Students will distinguish between energy transfer by waves and particles.

SKILL AND PROCESS OUTCOMES

- Through kinesthetic learning experiences, students will derive the relationship among wave speed, wave length, and frequency.
- Students will investigate constructive and destructive interference of waves and apply the principle of superposition.
- Students will demonstrate how sound is produced and transmitted.

AFFECTIVE OUTCOME

Students unlearn their preconceived notions of physical phenomena and replace them with scientifically accurate observations and understandings.

Time Line and Calendar of Events

SLINKIES AND HUMAN SLINKIES

Students create and observe waves in the hallways using Slinkies. They explore their views, preconceptions, and observations of wave phenomena and examine different types of waves. Mathematical relationships are derived from students' observations. Students learn to communicate what they have observed about the speed of waves, what happens when waves meet and interfere with each other, and other basic properties of waves using mathematical expressions.

SOUND WAVES

We explore what happens when sound waves meet and interfere with each other. We discuss acoustics and how sound is produced and perceived. We look at the sources of sound, including musical instruments, and how sound is recorded and reproduced. We make Edison record players so that students can experience the reproduction of sound.

LIGHT AND ITS PROPERTIES

Using mirrors and lenses, students look at how light interacts with matter. As a culminating activity, we go to the University of Wisconsin, where the students attend college classes and create their own holograms. They keep a journal of their observations on this trip.

SOUND AND LIGHT SHOW

In the school auditorium, we use loudspeakers connected to a signal generator. Students line up in the regions in the auditorium that have no sound because of wave interference. We also explore how the walls act as acoustical mirrors. Using primary colors, we produce all the other colors of the spectrum by mixing light.

Evaluation Plan

Students complete both quantitative and qualitative laboratory explorations, worksheets, and paper and pencil tests. They take notes and write reports on holograms and the sound and light show. They create acoustical and optical devices.

Tests and quizzes: 50 percent

Laboratory experiments: 25 percent

Homework: 20 percent

Special projects: 5 percent

continued

Resources

Edmund scientific catalogue. 101 E. Gloucester Pike, Barrington, NJ 08007; (609) 547-3488.

Exploratorium science snackbook. San Francisco: Exploratorium Museum Store; (800) 359-9899.

Edge, R. (1981). *String and sticky tape experiments.* College Park, MD: American Association of Physics Teachers.

Freier, G., & Anderson, F. (1981). *A demonstration handbook for physics.* College Park, MD: American Association of Physics Teachers.

Hewitt, P. (1987). *Conceptual physics.* Palo Alto: Scott, Foresman.

Liem, T. (1981a) *Invitations to scientific inquiry.* El Cajon, CA: Science Inquiry Enterprises.

Liem, T. (1981b). *A potpourri of physics teaching ideas.* College Park, MD: American Association of Physics Teachers.

The physics teacher. American Association of Physics Teachers (AAPT), 5112 Berwyn Rd., College Park, MD 20740.

The science teacher. National Science Teachers Association (NSTA),

1742 Connecticut Ave., NW, Washington, DC 20009.

⟳ Reflective Actions for Your Professional Portfolio
A Sample Thematic Unit Plan

Perceptiveness: Search for a Unit Topic

Examine your curriculum guides and consider the needs and interests of your students. List several unit topics or themes that interest you and fit the needs of your students.

Construction of Knowledge: Use School Resources

Visit a school library or media center. Locate resources that you could use in the thematic units you are considering. Interview the librarian to ask for suggestions for other resources on that topic. Include these materials in your unit resource list.

Values and Principles: Your Curriculum Priorities

Select one unit theme and brainstorm ideas for the cognitive, affective, and psychomotor outcomes that are possible for your students. Select another interesting theme and do the same thing. Now compare the outcomes possible with each theme and decide which one best fits the values and principles that guide your teaching philosophy.

Creativity: Design a Thematic Unit Plan

Give your thematic unit an interesting, motivating title. Then, using your cognitive, affective, and psychomotor outcomes as a place to begin, allow yourself to envision your students accomplishing these outcomes. Sketch out a planning web as you brainstorm learning experiences that will allow your students to achieve these outcomes. Use a calendar to plan the sequence of learning events for your unit. Plan a way to assess the outcomes for your unit.

Persistence and Problem Solving: Prepare for Implementation

What are the sources of difficulty standing in the way of your implementing your unit plan? What materials do you need to gather or create? What modifications to your schedule are needed? Create a time line of events for your students and a complementary one for yourself so that your planning coincides with the events in the unit.

Communication Skills: Letter to Parents

Who do you need to communicate with regarding your thematic unit? Write a letter to the parents of your students describing the purpose and the goals of the unit. Describe the types of support you would like them to provide to their children during the learning process. Inform them about the culminating events of the unit.

In addition, create a plan for communicating with your students about what you expect from them during the unit. Explain and rehearse any special procedures that will be used during the unit. Give them a clear understanding of how their work will be evaluated. Allow them to offer suggestions and be ready to modify your plans to accommodate their ideas.

Reference

Tyler, R. (1949). *Basic principles of curriculum and instruction.* Chicago: University of Chicago Press.

Lesson Planning and Sequencing

Educational goals, learning outcomes, and unit plans are important elements used in planning curricula to educate our young people. But they are meaningless words on paper unless they are translated into a practical set of logically ordered day-to-day learning events. Goals, outcome statements, and unit plans are only guides for the real-life classroom encounters between teacher and students. For your unit plans to succeed, you will need a systematic plan for what to teach on each day of the unit.

Reflecting on goals and outcomes is a particularly difficult task for teachers with limited experience in the classroom. To establish goals and outcomes with some degree of confidence, you must be able to envision your students' accomplishing what you have planned for them to do. Experienced teachers are able to recall from previous years how their students' behavior and achievements changed over time; they use these memories as a guide in planning realistic goals for the future. For your first years of teaching, allow yourself to imagine the very finest behavior and the highest accomplishments possible as you plan your initial goals and outcomes. Not every goal you set may come true, but it is far better to have high expectations for yourself and your students than to have minimal ones.

Once you have imagined the outcomes you wish your students to achieve, then you can begin to use your reflective actions to create a sequence of day-to-day learning events, usually referred to as *lesson plans,* that will allow your students to progress toward the outcomes you envision. Each lesson plan represents a small vision in itself. As you plan a lesson, you are likely to find yourself picturing the lesson taking place. This visualization is very useful, allowing you to consider the consequences of each action you take. As you gain experience, you will find yourself picturing the possible pitfalls and challenges that may occur with each step of the lesson, and you will be able to consider ahead of time what to do for students who have insufficient skills to master the planned objectives or for those who have already mastered the content or skill you are planning to teach.

Writing Objectives to Fit Goals and Outcome Statements

Goals and outcome statements are the broad, long-term descriptions of how you want your students to grow and develop and what you want them to know, understand, and be able to do during a given time. As you try to visualize students' accomplishing these goals and outcomes, it is useful also to envision a sequence of events that will lead to successful accomplishment of these goals. Teachers often find it useful to write down these sequential steps as a series of objectives that work together to enable your students to show that they are achieving the intended outcomes.

Educational *objectives* are short-term, specific descriptions of what teachers are expected to teach or what students are expected to learn. As described by Bloom and colleagues in the *Taxonomy of Educational Objectives* (1956), they are intended to be used as an organizational framework for selecting and sequencing learning experiences. Embedded in the goal of teaching children how to read are hundreds of possible specific objectives. One teacher may have an objective of teaching students how to decode an unfamiliar word using phonics and another objective of teaching students how to decode an unfamiliar word using context clues. Another teacher may select and emphasize the objectives of decoding unfamiliar words by using syllabification or linguistic patterns.

Objectives are used to describe the sequence of learning events necessary to realize an outcome statement. Objectives also allow teachers to chart the group's or an individual's progress. Teachers can diagnose students' needs and deficiencies accurately if they have available a guideline or chart of normal progress with which to compare each student's achievement.

BEHAVIORAL OBJECTIVES

During the past several decades, many educators have searched for ways to apply scientific principles of controlling for conditions and measuring outcomes of educational planning. Many reflective teachers find that when they state precisely what the learner will be able to do after successfully completing a learning experience, their lesson plans are more likely to be successful. The most precise method of stating an objective is by stating the actual behavior the teacher expects from the student at the conclusion of the lesson.

Behavioral objectives are distinguished from other types of objectives in that they describe observable, measurable behavior. They are written in a form that specifies the *conditions* under which the learning will take place, the *action or behavior,* and the *criteria for success.* Here is an example of a behavioral objective:

> After practice-writing the spelling words five times each, the student will write the words when dictated by the teacher, spelling 18 of the 20 words correctly.

This statement includes a description of the conditions for learning ("after practice-writing the spelling words five times each"), the behavior ("write the words when dictated by the teacher"), and the criteria for success ("spelling 18 of the 20 words correctly").

Behavioral objectives can have a very positive effect on teaching effectiveness; teachers who use them become better organized and more efficient in teaching and measuring the growth of students' basic skills. When following a planned sequence of behavioral objectives, the teacher knows exactly what to do and how to judge the students' success. This system of planning also allows the teacher to explain better to students exactly what is expected and how to succeed.

As with any educational practice, however, overreliance on specific objectives can have a negative result. Critics of behavioral objectives believe that when curriculum planning is reduced to a rigid behavioral form, it can trivialize much of what is worth teaching and knowing. Like many things in life, the use of objectives can be destructive if used in excess.

PROBLEM-SOLVING OBJECTIVES

Eliott Eisner (1985) observes that when specific skills or competencies are being taught, behavioral objectives can serve as a useful way of visualizing and organizing the appropriate learning experiences. "One must be able to swim four lengths of the pool to be able to swim in the deep end," he writes, but "one should not feel compelled to abandon educational aims that cannot be reduced to measurable forms of predictable performance" (p. 114).

Eisner (1985) suggests the *problem-solving objective* as an alternative form for learning that cannot be predicted and calibrated:

> In a problem-solving objective, the students formulate or are given a problem to solve—say, to find out how deterrents to smoking might be made more effective, how to design a paper structure that will hold two bricks 16 inches above a table, or how the variety and quality of food served in the school cafeteria could be increased within the existing budget.
>
> In each of these examples, the problem is posed and the criteria necessary to resolve the problem are clear. But the forms of its solution are virtually infinite. (pp. 117–118)

Eisner points out that behavioral objectives have "both the form and the content defined in advance. There is, after all, only one way to spell aardvark" (p. 119). The teacher using behavioral objectives is successful if all of the children display the identical behavior at the end of the instructional period. "This is not the case with problem-solving objectives. The solutions individual students or groups of students reach may be just as much a surprise for the teacher as they are for the students who created them" (p. 119). Here is an example of a problem-solving objective:

> When given a battery, a light bulb, and a piece of copper wire, the student will figure out how to make the bulb light.

This objective describes the conditions and the problem that is to be solved but does not specify the actual behaviors the student is to use. The criterion for success is straightforward but not quantifiable; in fact, some of the most important results of this experience are only implied. The teacher's primary aim is to cause the student to experiment, hypothesize, and test methods of solving the problem. This cannot be quantified and reported as a percentage. Problem-solving objectives, then, are appropriate when teachers are planning learning events that allow and encourage students to think, make decisions, and create solutions. For that reason they are frequently employed when teachers plan lessons that are designed to develop critical, creative thinking. They are especially valuable when teachers are planning learning events at the higher levels of Bloom's taxonomy (1956).

EXPRESSIVE OUTCOMES

Some lessons are purposely designed to be quite open-ended experiences. In any of the fine arts, for example, lessons may be designed that have no preplanned or explicit objectives. An example of an expressive outcome lesson is for students to listen to a symphony and draw or paint a response to the music. To expose children to new ideas and experiences, a lesson may consist of a field trip to a museum or through a forest.

The teacher may have no prespecified objectives for either event except to allow the students to discuss their observations afterward. For lessons such as these, Eisner (1985) suggests that the appropriate planning device is the *expressive outcome*, which is intended to "provide a fertile field for personal purposing and experience" (p. 120).

Expressive outcomes are also valuable for including the affective domain in lesson plans. If an affective goal of the unit is to encourage independent thought and action, lesson plans must include outcome statements that allow room for exploration and original ideas. If you have an affective goal to increase cooperation among students, lessons must be planned to allow students to work together. If you hope to encourage any form of creative expression, your lesson plans can reflect and acknowledge the importance of such creative pursuits through the use of expressive outcome statements.

BLOOM'S TAXONOMY

Many teachers use Bloom's *Taxonomy of Educational Objectives* (1956) as the basis for organizing instructional objectives into coherent, connected learning experiences. The term *Bloom's taxonomy* (as commonly used by teachers) refers to the six levels of the cognitive domain described here. Any curriculum project—a year-long plan, a unit, or a lesson plan—can be enriched by the conscious planning of learning events at all six levels of the taxonomy:

Higher-level objectives

> Level 6:   evaluation
>
> Level 5:   synthesis
>
> Level 4:   analysis
>
> Level 3:   application

Lower-level objectives

> Level 2:   comprehension
>
> Level 1:   knowledge

Knowledge-level objectives can be planned to ensure that students have a knowledge base of facts, concepts, and other important data on any topic or subject. *Comprehension-level objectives* cause students to clarify and articulate the main idea of what they are learning. Behavioral objectives are very useful and appropriate at the knowledge and comprehension levels.

At the *application level*, problem-solving objectives or expressive outcomes can be written that ask students to apply what they've learned to other cases or to their own lives, thereby causing them to transfer what they've learned in the classroom to other arenas. *Analysis-level* objectives and outcomes call on students to look for motives, assumptions, and relationships such as cause and effect, differences and similarities, hypotheses, and conclusions. When analysis outcomes are planned, the students are likely to be engaged in critical thinking about the subject matter. Because the *synthesis level* implies an original response, expressive outcomes are very appropriate. They offer students opportunities to use creative thinking as they combine elements in new ways, plan original experiments, and create original solutions to problems. At the *evaluation level,* students engage again in critical thinking as they make judgments using internal or external criteria and evidence. For these levels, problem-solving objectives or expressive outcomes are likely to be the most appropriate planning devices.

For example, in planning a series of learning events on metric measurement, the teacher may formulate the following objectives and outcome statements:

Knowledge-level behavioral objective: When given a meter stick, students will point to the length of a meter, a decimeter, and a centimeter with no errors.

Comprehension-level behavioral objective: When asked to state a purpose or use for each of the following units of measure, the student will write a short response for meter, centimeter, liter, milliliter, gram, and kilogram, with no more than one error.

Application-level problem-solving objective: Using a unit of measure of their choice, students will measure the length and width of the classroom and compute the area.

Analysis-level problem-solving objective: Students will create a chart showing five logical uses or purposes for each measuring unit in the metric family.

Synthesis-level expressive outcome: A group of four students will hide a "treasure" on the playground and create a set of instructions using metric measures that will enable another group to locate the treasure.

Evaluation-level expressive outcome: Students will debate their preference for metric or nonmetric measurement as a standard form of measurement.

When we review the six objectives and outcomes for metric measurement, we see clearly that the first two differ from the others in that they specify exactly what students will do or write to get a correct answer. In addition, the criteria for success are not ambiguous. These two qualities are useful to ensure successful teaching and learning at the knowledge and comprehension levels. After successfully completing these first two objectives, students will have developed a knowledge base for metric measurement that they will need to do the higher-level activities. In the problem-solving objectives, students are given greater discretion in determining the methods they use and the form of their final product. In the expressive outcome statements, discretionary power is necessary if students are to be empowered to think critically and creatively to solve problems for themselves.

Although the taxonomy was originally envisioned as a hierarchy, and although it was believed that students should be introduced to a topic beginning with level 1 and working upward through level 6, most educators have found that the objectives and learning experiences can be successfully taught in any order. For example, a teacher may introduce the topic of nutrition and health by asking students to discuss their opinions or attitudes about smoking (an evaluation-level objective). The teacher may then provide the students with knowledge-level data about the contents of tobacco smoke and work back up to the evaluation level. When students are asked their opinions again, at the end of the lesson, their judgments are likely to be stronger and better informed.

As in the example about smoking and health, it is often desirable to begin with objectives that call on students to do, think, find, question, or create something and thereby instill in them a desire to know more about the topic. Knowledge- and comprehension-level objectives can then be designed to provide the students with the facts, data, and main ideas they need to know to further apply, analyze, synthesize, and evaluate the ideas that interest them. Figure 6.1 shows a planning device offering teachers ideas for learning events that correspond to each level of the taxonomy.

Sequencing Objectives in School Subjects
SEQUENCING OBJECTIVES IN MATHEMATICS

Some subjects are very sequential in nature. Mathematics is the best example in the elementary curriculum because its concepts and operations can be readily ordered from simple to complex. Teachers can organize effectively the teaching of computational skills in the basic operations of addition, subtraction, multiplication, and division very easily. For example, outcome statement 1 describes a possible sequence for teaching an essential understanding about the concept of numbers:

> *Mathematics outcome statement 1:*   Primary students will be able to show how addition and subtraction are related to one another.

To accomplish this outcome, primary teachers will introduce the students to the concept of numbers and give them concrete, manipulative experiences in adding and subtracting one-digit numbers. Students may act out stories in which children are added and subtracted from a group. They may make up stories about animals or objects that are taken away and then brought back to demonstrate subtraction and addition.

Math textbooks offer a sequence of learning activities and practice of math facts, but reflective teachers find that the math textbook must be used flexibly and supplemented with other learning experiences. Before planning math lessons for a particular group of students, the teacher must pretest their entry-level knowledge and skills. Pretests will reveal that some children have already mastered some of the skills in the sequence and do not need to spend valuable time redoing what they already know. They need enriched math activities to allow them to progress. Other children may not have the conceptual understanding of number relationships to succeed on the first step. For them, preliminary concrete experiences with manipulative materials are essential for success.

Sample Math Objectives to Fit Outcome Statement 1

Students will be able to
   1. Use blocks to show addition of two single-digit integers
   2. Use blocks to show subtraction of two single-digit integers

Learning objectives can be planned at all levels of Bloom's Taxonomy. Behavioral objectives are best suited for knowledge and comprehension levels; problem solving and expressive objectives are best suited for application, analysis, synthesis, and evaluation levels.

Examples of Objectives	Appropriate Action Verbs
Knowledge Level	**Knowledge Level**
Can recognize and recall specific terms, facts, and symbols	Find, locate, identify, list, recite, memorize, recognize, name, repeat, point to, match, pick, choose, state, select, record, spell, say, show, circle, underline.
Comprehension Level	**Comprehension Level**
Can understand the main idea of material heard, viewed, or read. Is able to interpret or summarize the ideas in their own words.	Explain, define, translate, relate, demonstrate, calculate, discuss, express in own words, write, review, report, paraphrase, summarize.
Application Level	**Application Level**
Is able to apply an abstract idea in a concrete situation, to solve a problem or relate it to prior experiences.	Change, adapt, employ, use, make, construct, demonstrate, compute, calculate, illustrate, modify, prepare, put into action, solve, do.
Analysis Level	**Analysis Level**
Can break down a concept or idea into its constituent parts. Is able to identify relationships among elements, cause and effect, similarities and differences.	Classify, distinguish, categorize, deduce, dissect, examine, compare, contrast, divide, catalog, inventory, question, outline, chart, survey.
Synthesis Level	**Synthesis Level**
Is able to put together elements in new and original ways. Creates patterns or structures that were not there before.	Combine, create, develop, design, construct, build, arrange, assemble, collect, concoct, connect, devise, hypothesize, invent, imagine, plan, generate, revise, organize, produce.
Evaluation Level	**Evaluation Level**
Makes informed judgments about the value of ideas or materials. Uses standards and criteria to support opinions and views.	Appraise, critique, consider, decide, judge, editorialize, give opinion, grade, rank, prioritize, value.

Figure 6.1   Curriculum planning using Bloom's taxonomy.

Source: From TAXONOMY OF EDUCATIONAL OBJECTIVES: The Classification of Educational Goals: HANDBOOK I: COGNITIVE DOMAIN. By Benjamin S. Bloom et al. Copyright 1956. By Longman Publishing Group. Reprinted by permission of Longman Publishing Group.

3. Use pennies and dimes to show place value of 1s and 10s
4. Subtract pennies without regrouping
5. Add pennies and exchange 10 pennies for a dime
6. Subtract pennies by making change for a dime to show regrouping
7. Tell how subtraction is related to addition using coins as an example

These sample objectives are representative of the basic knowledge- and comprehension-level skills needed to accomplish the outcome statement. They can be written in the behavioral objective form, specifying what percentage of correct answers must be attained to demonstrate mastery.

These objectives emphasize basic computational skills that all students need to learn. However, in keeping with the National Council of Teachers of Mathematics' recommendations to emphasize problem solving over computation, reflective teachers are likely to plan lessons that allow students to explore the relationships between addition and subtraction. They are also likely to include many additional math outcomes and objectives at the higher levels of Bloom's taxonomy (1956) to teach students how to apply the math facts and computation skills they are learning to actual problem-solving situations. However, this example does illustrate the importance of matching objectives to outcome statements in a logical sequence. Each of the objectives builds on the one before it. As students master each objective, they are continually progressing toward mastering the outcome statement.

SEQUENCING OBJECTIVES IN LANGUAGE ARTS

Not all subjects in the elementary curriculum are as sequential as mathematics. Language arts consists of knowledge, skills, and abilities that develop children's understanding and use of language. Reading, writing, speaking, and listening are all part of the language-arts curriculum, and each one can and should have its own outcome statement(s). Outcome statement 2 suggests one illustration of how the language arts curriculum is designed:

> *Language-arts outcome statement 2:*   Students will be able to write standard English with correct spelling, accurate grammar, and well-organized meaning and form.

Again, this outcome statement will take years to accomplish, but teachers at every grade level are responsible for providing learning experiences that build toward the ultimate goal. The objectives to reach this goal may be similar each year for several years but written in increasing levels of difficulty. This is known as a *spiral curriculum.*

Sample Language-Arts Objectives to Fit Outcome Statement 2

By the end of grade 2, students will be able to

1. Write a sentence containing a subject and a verb
2. Use a capital letter at the beginning of a sentence
3. Use a period or question mark at the end of a sentence
4. Review and edit sentences for complete meaning

By the end of grade 4, students will be able to

1. Write a paragraph that focuses on one central idea
2. Spell common words correctly in writing samples
3. Use capitalization and sentence-end punctuation correctly
4. Review and edit a paragraph to improve the organization of ideas

By the end of grade 6, students will be able to

1. Write several paragraphs that explain one concept or theme
2. Use a dictionary to spell all words in a paper correctly
3. Use correct punctuation, including end marks, comma, apostrophe, quotation marks, and colon
4. Review and edit papers to correct spelling, punctuation, grammar, and organization of ideas

By the end of grade 8, students will be able to

1. Write papers with introductory paragraph, logical reasons, data to support the main idea, and a closing statement
2. Use a dictionary to spell all words in a paper correctly; use a thesaurus to add to vocabulary of the paper
3. Eliminate fragments and run-on sentences
4. Review and edit papers to correct spelling, punctuation, grammar, organization of ideas, and appropriateness for the purpose

By the end of grade 12, students will be able to

1. Write compositions that demonstrate effective use of descriptive language that clarifies and enhances the ideas expressed in the paper
2. Write compositions that have no significant errors in the proper use of punctuation, grammar, and spelling
3. Write compositions that synthesize and cite a variety of resources used for information gathering
4. Write compositions that exhibit a clear personal style and voice

When teachers have curriculum guidelines such as these, they must still translate the outcome statements and objectives into actual learning experiences that are appropriate and motivating for their students. To pretest how well your students can use written language when they enter your classroom, plan a writing experience in the first week. Analyzing these writing samples will allow you to plan suitably challenging activities for your students. In this example, the second-grade teacher must decide what topics to have students write about and when to limit students to copying teacher-made examples or allow them to begin to write their own sentences. The fourth-grade teacher knows that students will not learn all of these skills in just one writing lesson. It is necessary to provide many interesting classroom experiences so that students will have ideas to express in their writing. The sixth-grade teacher has to plan a series of research and writing experiences so that students will have ample opportunities to synthesize all of the skills required at that grade level.

Curriculum planning of subjects such as language arts is a complex undertaking because it contains so many varied outcomes and objectives. The previous example illustrates only a single outcome for teaching students how to write. Teachers must also plan outcome statements and objectives for reading, listening, and speaking.

SEQUENCING OBJECTIVES IN SCIENCE

As discussed in chapter 4, the science curriculum should inform students of the basic facts and concepts of science topics but should also allow students opportunities to experience how scientists work. These dual goals of the science curriculum are often expressed as *teaching both content and process*. Here is an example of an outcome statement in science that covers both content and process:

> *Science outcome statement 3:*   Students will demonstrate how sound is produced and transmitted.

The following learning objectives show a sequence of learning experiences that allow students to discover some important properties of waves:

Sample Science Objectives to Fit Outcome Statement 3

By the end of the unit on wave phenomena, students will
1. Investigate wave phenomena using Slinkies
2. Investigate waves using water in plastic containers
3. Write observations, analysis, and hypothesis of how waves behave
4. Investigate waves using films of waves in slow motion and computer simulations of waves to discover whether their hypotheses are accurate
5. Discuss observations and theories of wave phenomena as a class with an emphasis on students' articulating their own ideas
6. Identify key features of waves, define wave terminology, and derive the wave equations through a kinesthetic learning experience (Under the direction of the teacher, students line up in the hall and simulate the motion of a Slinky. Wave terminology is introduced by the teacher during the experience.)

This set of learning experiences, designed by Jim Hicks and Chris Chiaverina, begins with hands-on investigations allowing students to observe the wave phenomena. They are involved in the process of science during these learning experiences because they are behaving like scientists investigating unknown phenomena. Content (wave properties and terminology) is introduced by the teachers after students are immersed in the process. Because of its emphasis on exploration, discovery, and communication of findings, the sequence of lessons in science is rarely linear but more often circular or even a figure-eight pattern.

Chris Chiaverina and Jim Hicks find that, rather than lecture about scientific phenomena, they first must use a smorgasbord of concrete experiences in which students interact with the scientific materials and literally begin to see the world in a new and more scientifically principled way. The concrete experiences are followed by class discussions that allow time to deal with the students' initial misconceptions about the phenomenon they are exploring. The discussions are very important as students describe their experiences and gradually begin to construct new schemata to fit what they've observed. Jim and Chris organize a series of lessons to include qualitative demonstrations and explorations followed by homework. The next day, there are discussions to get rid of prior misconceptions and build new scientific schemata. During quantitative laboratory experiences, Chris and Jim rarely give formulas. Instead, they present open-ended challenges that cause students to translate what they've learned into mathematical language. Following the quantitative labs, they spend time on discussion of practical applications of what they have learned in the unit. Figure 6.2 shows the figure-eight sequence of events that Jim and Chris have developed for the science courses they teach.

SEQUENCING OBJECTIVES IN SOCIAL STUDIES

Reflective elementary teachers can also see the need for both content and process in their social studies curriculum. They attempt to help their students build a knowledge base in history and geography, but they also give attention and time to teaching students how to acquire information on their own.

Here is an example of an outcome statement in social studies that covers both content and process:

Social studies outcome statement 4:   Students will be able to use a map and a globe to find place names and locations. They will then create a chart listing the countries, major cities, rivers, and mountain ranges in each continent.

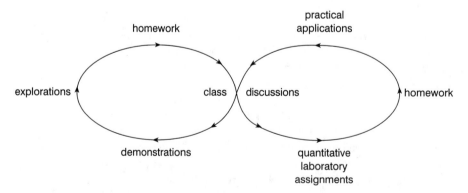

Figure 6.2   Planning sequence for science lessons.
Source: Jim Hicks and Chris Chiaverina

Sample Social Studies Objectives to Meet Outcome Statement 4

At the end of the map and globe unit, students will be able to

1. Identify the seven continents on a world map and a globe
2. Interpret the country boundaries with a map legend
3. List the countries in each continent
4. Interpret the symbol for rivers on the map legend
5. List the major rivers in each continent
6. Interpret the symbol for mountain ranges on the map legend
7. List the mountain ranges in each continent
8. Create a chart showing the countries, cities, rivers, and mountain ranges in each continent

In this example, the teacher has planned a set of learning activities that will add to the students' knowledge base about world geography. This set of activities also equips the student to be able to find and interpret information on maps and globes. This social studies curriculum demonstrates that by employing hands-on learning experiences, students are able to learn both content and processes simultaneously and that they are active rather than passive learners throughout the entire set of activities. An oral or written pretest might consist of having students name or point to certain geographical locations and read and interpret a map legend. The information from the pretest is valuable in planning lessons that use students' existing knowledge and add to it.

SEQUENCING OBJECTIVES IN INTERDISCIPLINARY UNITS

Whenever possible, many teachers enjoy enriching the curriculum units they plan by incorporating fine-arts experiences into the academic subjects. Primary children are often asked to illustrate math examples by drawing one pumpkin plus two pumpkins or to create 10 different pictures using a rectangle. Songs and rhymes frequently accompany learning about historical events and people. Many such events are dramatized as well. Stories and films are often used to augment many aspects of the curriculum.

In later years, emphasis on the fine arts may decline except in special art and music classes or on special occasions and holidays. This is due, in part, to the crowded curriculum that teachers are required to deliver. Given the prevailing culture of the late 20th century, the fine arts often take a back seat to academic and social subjects. But each teacher must consider the place of fine arts in the curriculum. Reflective teachers are likely to consider the importance of the arts in enhancing the joy of living and to make them an integral part of every learning experience. This has the effect of increasing children's active involvement, creative thinking, and inventiveness.

Here is an example of an outcome statement that includes fine arts with an academic subject:

> *Fine arts/social studies outcome statement 5:* Students will be able to distinguish the important contributions made by various world cultures in sports, art, music, literature, and drama.

Sample Objectives to Meet Outcome Statement 5

Each learning team of students will be able to
1. Select one country of the world to study
2. Locate at least three sources of information about that country
3. Draw a map of the country's geographical boundaries and features
4. Describe the country's contributions to sports
5. Play or sing an example of the country's music
6. Draw examples of the country's art and architecture treasures
7. Read aloud a story or a poem from that country
8. Work with other learning teams to create a dramatic event featuring the stories, poems, art, and music of all the countries

This ambitious set of learning experiences demonstrates how well the fine arts can be incorporated into an academic subject. Cognitively, children who take part in this series of experiences will learn a knowledge base of facts, ideas, and concepts about the world. They will also gain understanding and use of such processes as communication and problem-solving skills. Affectively, they will learn to appreciate and understand differences and similarities among people by sharing the cultural arts of each country.

Planning Assessments That Fit Your Objectives

How does a teacher measure success? Chapters 11 and 12 cover in detail the topic of assessing students' needs and accomplishments, with a focus on creating authentic assessment systems that describe students' progress over time. In designing lesson plans, however, it is useful to consider some options for assessing students' accomplishments on a single lesson.

Traditionally, the methods used to assess individual achievement are written or oral quizzes, tests, and essays. When elementary teachers want to determine whether the class as a whole has understood what was taught in a lesson, they frequently use oral responses to questions that usually begin with "Who can tell me?" These are useful and efficient ways to assess student achievement at the knowledge and comprehension levels of Bloom's taxonomy, but reflective teachers are seldom satisfied with these measures alone. They seek out other methods that are less frequently used but more appropriate in evaluating learning at the higher levels.

Knowledge-level objectives are tested by determining if the student can remember or recognize accurate statements or facts. Bloom et al. (1956) observed: "Probably the art of testing has been developed to the greatest extent in the measurement of knowledge. This type of behavior can be measured with great efficiency and economy" (p. 78). Multiple-choice and matching tests are the most frequently used measuring devices.

Comprehension-level objectives are often tested by asking students to define terms in their own words. (Only knowledge would be tested if the students were asked to write a definition from memory.) Another frequently used testing device is a question requiring a short-answer response, either oral or written, showing that the student understands the main idea. Essays that ask students to summarize or interpret are also appropriate. Multiple-choice tests are also used as a test of comprehension, but the questions call on the students to do more than recall a fact from memory; they ask students to read a selection and choose the best response from among several choices.

Knowledge- and comprehension-level objectives are frequently written as behavioral objectives that specify the criteria for success in a measurable form. If the observable behavior is writing an essay, the teacher may need to describe the length, form, and content of a paper that is acceptable. For example, the criteria may be specified as follows:

> . . . with a minimum of five paragraphs, each describing a geographical feature of the country being studied. . . .

At the *application level,* students are usually asked to apply what was learned in a classroom to a new situation. For that reason, application-level objectives are usually assessed by presenting an unfamiliar problem that requires the student to transfer what has been learned to the unfamiliar situation. Assessment of student success cannot be quantified into minimums, maximums, or percentages. Instead, success is measured by the extent to which the problem is solved and the means employed to solve it.

To assess application, then, teachers must provide students with challenging problems to solve and a format for tendering their solutions. Essays in which the students describe what they would do to solve an unfamiliar problem can be used. In classrooms where students are encouraged to use manipulative materials and experiment with methods to solve problems, teachers assess the processes used by the student and the end product such as a hand-drawn or computer-generated design of a new device, a written plan for solving a problem, or a model of a new product. These products may or may not be graded, depending on the teacher's need to quantify or qualify students' success.

Analysis-level objectives may also require that the teacher present unfamiliar material and ask the student to analyze it according to some specified criteria. "The material given for analysis in a test may be a literary passage, a description of a scientific experiment or a social situation, a set of data, an argument, a picture, or a musical selection" (Bloom et al., 1956, p. 149). In these situations, students may be asked to analyze various elements, relationships, or organizational principles, such as the way in which elements are categorized, differences and similarities, cause and effect, logical conclusions, or relevant and irrelevant data.

Again, essays may be used to assess analytical behavior, but the essays must do more than tell the main idea (comprehension) and describe how the student would apply previously learned knowledge. Analytical essays must clarify relationships, compare and contrast, show cause and effect, and provide evidence for conclusions. Other student products that are appropriate for assessing analysis are time lines; charts that compare, contrast, or categorize data; and a variety of graphs that show relationships.

Bloom et al. (1956) noted that there were special problems in the assessment of *synthesis-level* objectives:

> A major problem in testing for synthesis objectives is that of providing conditions favorable to creative work. Perhaps the most important condition is that of

freedom. This should include freedom from excessive tension and from pressures to adopt a particular viewpoint. The student should be made to believe that the product of his efforts need not conform to the views of the instructor. Time is another important condition. Many synthesis tasks require far more time than an hour or two; the product is likely to emerge only after the student spends considerable time familiarizing himself with the task, exploring different approaches, interpreting and analyzing relevant materials, and trying out various schemes of organization. (p. 173)

The types of student products that demonstrate synthesis are infinitely variable. Written work such as creative essays, stories, poems, plays, books, and articles are certainly appropriate for assessing language-arts objectives. Performances are just as useful, including original speeches, drama, poems, and musical compositions. Student-created products may include original plans, blueprints, artwork, computer programs, and models of proposed inventions. Student work may be collected in portfolios to demonstrate growth and achievement in a subject area.

Evaluating the relative success of synthesis products is very difficult. No objective criteria may exist for judging the value or worth of a student's original product. When student products are entered in a contest or submitted for publication, outside judges with expertise in the subject area provide feedback and may even make judgments that the classroom teacher cannot make. "Checklists and rating scales should be especially useful here, but the examiner ought to insure that they do not emphasize elements of the product to the neglect of *global* qualities which, after all, may be more fundamental in any synthesis" (Bloom et al., 1956, p. 174). Many elementary teachers simply record whether a finished product was turned in by the student rather than attempt to evaluate or grade it.

Bloom and his colleagues describe two quite different forms of *evaluation-level* objectives. One type calls on students to make a judgment based on internal evidence. In this case, all of the facts and data needed to make the judgment are provided in the test situation, and the student simply selects and applies them. To test a student's ability to make this type of judgment, the teacher must provide all of the needed data, perhaps in the form of charts or graphs, and ask the student to draw certain conclusions from these data.

Another form of evaluation is to make judgments based on external criteria, such as rules and standards by which such works are generally judged—in this case, assessment strategies in which the student is given a situation, makes a judgment, and justifies that judgment by applying the appropriate criteria. For example, students may be asked to make and justify aesthetic judgments of a work of art or to judge the validity of a political theory, stating the appropriate criteria used in making the evaluation. The types of products that students create at this level are critical essays, discussions, speeches, letters to the editor, debates, drama, videotapes, and other forms that allow them to express their points of view.

Like synthesis outcomes, evaluation outcomes and objectives are difficult to grade. A teacher who offers students an opportunity to express their own views usually places high value on independent thinking and freedom of expression. Therefore, the teacher cannot grade a student response as right or wrong. But the teacher can assess whether the student has used accurate, sufficient, and appropriate criteria in defending a personal opinion. Student work that has cited inaccurate, insufficient, or inappropriate evidence should probably be returned to the student with suggestions for revision.

Affective outcomes may be assessed by teacher observation as students work on various projects. It is also useful to involve students in self-evaluation to monitor their own affective growth in areas such as self-confidence, independence, cooperation, or creativity.

In summary, evaluation of student accomplishment should be directly linked to the lesson's objectives. To assess basic knowledge and skills, behavioral objectives are useful because they state exactly what the student will be able to do and specify the criteria for success. For higher-level objectives, problem-solving objectives may be less precise but still should describe the type of student behavior or product expected and give some general criteria for success. To assess the growth in the affective domain, expressive outcomes are planned, and students can state orally or in writing what they have gained from a certain experience.

When teachers plan by writing clear behavioral, problem-solving, and expressive objectives for their lessons, they are, in effect, clarifying their expectations regarding what students will gain from the lesson and their criteria for success. The evaluation section of a lesson plan is then usually a restatement of the criteria expressed in the objectives. You will see an example of this in the sample lesson plans in this chapter.

VARYING OBJECTIVES FOR STUDENTS WITH SPECIAL NEEDS

Often teachers plan their lessons with a set of objectives for the students in their class whose knowledge and skills are at grade level. The term *at grade level* means the average or typical level of understanding or skill that most children are able to achieve at that age and in that grade. As teachers gain experience teaching at a grade level, they are able to describe what the typical learner at that grade level can accomplish. Because most children in the class will have skills and knowledge near the average, it makes sense for teachers to plan lessons with difficulty levels conforming to that average.

But reflective teachers also observe that within each classroom, there are likely to be children whose skills and knowledge levels are quite different than the norm or average. *Criterion-referenced pretests* are essential tools in determining what students know and what they are ready to learn. Pretests may reveal that some students do not have the prerequisite skills and knowledge that will allow them to achieve the planned objectives. They are not likely to succeed unless the teacher modifies the initial lesson plans of the new unit to provide them with individual or small-group lessons to reteach the skills they lack. For some children to achieve successful growth of skills and understanding, the teacher must be willing to alter the pace of the lessons, the difficulty of the material, and the criteria for success.

For students who learn more slowly, one modification that is needed is to reduce the volume of material in a lesson. If the grade-level lesson calls for the students to complete 20 problems in one class period, the teacher may reduce this requirement to 10 or 15 problems for a student who works slowly. If 20 were expected of this child, there would be little chance for success, resulting in frustration for both teacher and student. When the pace is lowered, the student has an opportunity to succeed and is likely to show the increase in motivation that accompanies success.

A child may have missed or not learned some important basic skills in previous grades for a variety of reasons. Illness, family problems, emotional difficulties, inferior teaching, or frequent moves may have prevented a child from learning the skills that most students his or her age have attained. In the children's novel *Roosevelt Grady* (Shotwell, 1963), a child from a migrant family moves so often that he never learns what "putting into" means.

> This was his question: When you put something into something else and it does-n't come out even, what do you do with what's left over?
>
> What happened yesterday was exactly what had happened at the school where he'd first heard about putting into. The teacher came to where it seemed she must explain it the very next day. And then what? That time it was the beans that ran out. This time it was celery. And same as yesterday, Roosevelt never got back to school to hear what the teacher had to say. (pp. 19–20)

For students like Roosevelt Grady, who through no fault of their own have not attained the basic skills necessary for a grade-level task, the modification needed is to teach the prerequisite skills before introducing the new material. When these prerequisite skills have been successfully mastered, the student may proceed at the pace of the rest of the class.

Some children in your classroom may have been identified as having *learning disabilities*. This label may mean that a child has one or more of a variety of learning disorders, some physical and others social or emotional in origin. When a student has been labeled learning disabled, a teacher who specializes in working with such students will be called on to create an individualized educational plan (known as an IEP) for that student. The classroom teacher will receive some guidance from the IEP on how to modify lessons for that student.

In some schools, many students come from backgrounds where the primary language of the home is not English. This has implications for instruction and lesson planning. Although these students may be able to understand the content of the lessons, they may not be able to understand the teacher's delivery of the content because of their language differences.

These students are frequently served by English as a second language (ESL) or sheltered English programs. When this is the case, the ESL teacher can assist teachers in assigning appropriate materials and helping students acquire language skills that will help them to succeed. For students learning the language, it is necessary to offer learning experiences that provide context clues using props, visuals, graphs, and real objects. Teachers may need to encourage their classmates to speak more slowly and enunciate more clearly.

Children with hearing impairments need lessons that are modified to provide directions and instruction using visual aids. Similarly, sight-impaired children may require extra auditory learning aids. Less obviously, some children in your classroom may have strong auditory, visual, or kinesthetic learning style preferences. To meet the needs of these children, teachers must modify their lessons to accommodate all three types of learning styles. This is usually accomplished by providing instructions and examples using visual aids to learn such as the chalkboard, books, and written handouts. For auditory learners, the teacher may allow students to use tape recorders to record the instructions and examples given in class. Kinesthetic learners require manipulative materials and hands-on experience to make sense of unfamiliar material. When a teacher provides visual, auditory, and kinesthetic learning aids and experiences, students may modify their own lessons by taking in the needed information in the form that fits their own learning style preferences.

For students who work unusually rapidly and accurately on grade-level material, the task is to provide appropriately challenging learning experiences so that these students are able to continue to make gains even though they have mastered the grade-level requirements. Two standard methods serve the needs of highly able learners: *acceleration* and *enrichment*. Although both strategies are valuable modifications, acceleration is appropriate for sequential subjects such as math, and enrichment is appropriate for other subject areas. An *inappropriate* modification is to give the child more work at the same level. For example, if 20 math problems are required of the students working at grade level, an inappropriate modification is to require the highly able learner to do 40. This practice is common but does not serve the student's real need to be challenged to gain new skills and understanding.

Some acceleration strategies that teachers can choose from include ability grouping, curriculum compacting, and mastery learning. *Ability grouping* requires the teacher to modify the curriculum to correspond to three different groups in the classroom. High, middle, and low groups are created, with variations in material and expectations for success. Reflective teachers must consider the possible negative consequences of lowered self-esteem and the possible positive benefits of academic fit and organizational efficiency when deciding whether or how to use ability grouping in the classroom.

In some schools, ability grouping may be organized across several grade levels. Subjects such as math and language arts may be scheduled at the same time of day, allowing students who work above or below grade level to leave their own classrooms and travel to other classrooms where the instruction is geared to their learning level.

Curriculum compacting can occur in a single classroom. This strategy requires the teacher to pretest students in various subject areas. Those children who demonstrate mastery at the time of the pretest are allowed to skip the subsequent lessons altogether. This strategy compacts the grade-level curriculum for them. Teachers then provide materials at a higher level of difficulty for these students, who typically work on their own through the more difficult material with little assistance from the teacher, who is busy instructing the students at grade level.

Mastery learning is a highly individualized teaching strategy designed to allow students to work at their own pace on material at their own difficulty level. Pretests are used to place students at the appropriate difficulty level. As each new skill is learned, a posttest demonstrates mastery. This technique is described in more detail in Chapter 10.

Enrichment strategies vary according to the imagination of the teacher who creates them. The teacher provides students who demonstrate mastery of a basic skill with a challenging application of that skill. Objectives and learning experiences at the higher levels of Bloom's taxonomy are often used as the basis for enrichment activities. A child who easily masters grade-level material is frequently allowed to investigate or research the topic in greater depth. For outcomes of enriched activities, students typically create an original product, perform an original skit, or teach the class something that they have learned from research.

Modification of lessons is a continual challenge to teachers. It is not easy to decide whether a student needs a modified lesson. Reflective teachers struggle with this decision because they know that when they lower their expectations for a student, one of the effects may be lower self-esteem, creating the conditions for a self-fulfilling prophecy that the student cannot achieve at grade level. But they also know that when adult expectations are too high, students experience little or no success, leading to a similar downward spiral. For beginning teachers, it is wise to consult with other teachers in the school, especially teachers who specialize in working with learning-disabled, gifted, or handicapped youngsters. Talk over your concerns with these specialists and make informed decisions about lesson modifications.

Writing a Well-Organized Lesson Plan

When teachers plan for day-to-day learning experiences, they are creating lesson plans. Usually a lesson plan is created for a single subject or topic for one day, although some experiential, hands-on lessons may be continued for several days in a row. Teachers in self-contained classrooms must devise several different lesson plans each day, one for each subject they teach, unless they choose to use multidisciplinary units. Teachers in the upper grades who work in departmentalized settings where students travel from class to class for various subjects must still create different lesson plans for each grade or group of students they teach.

In the university or college courses designed to prepare teachers, the lesson plan is an important teaching/learning device. The professor and experienced classroom teachers can provide the aspiring teacher with models of good lesson plans. As students create their own, they are able to demonstrate the extent to which they understand and can apply the theories and principles they have learned about reflective thinking and planning.

For that reason, many university and college programs require students to create a number of precise and detailed lesson plans. Sometimes students observe that the classroom teachers they know do not write such extensive plans for every lesson. Instead, these teachers write their lesson plans in large weekly planning books, and a single lesson plan may consist of "Math: p. 108," or "Social Studies: Review Ch. 7," or "Science: Continue Nutrition." Although experienced teachers may record their lesson plans with brief notes, novice teachers need to write lessons in great detail to know which resources to gather for a lesson. Writing detailed lesson plans also enables novice teachers to communicate their plans to the professor or mentor teacher, who can provide feedback on the plan before the lesson is taught.

Well-written lesson plans have additional value: they can be shared. A teacher's shorthand notes that serve as a personal reminder can rarely be interpreted by an outsider. If a substitute teacher is called to replace a classroom teacher for a day or longer, the substitute needs to understand the daily plans in language he or she can use. Teams of teachers often write lesson plans together or for one another. In this case, they need to have a common understanding of the lesson objectives, procedures, evaluation, and resources.

The form may vary, but most lesson plans share a number of common elements. Three essential features of a complete, well-organized lesson plan are objectives, procedures, and evaluation. These correspond to the four questions of curriculum planning formulated by Tyler (1949). Lesson *objectives* specify the "educational purposes" of the lesson. The *procedures* section describes both "what educational experiences can be provided" and the way in which they can be "effectively organized." The *evaluation* section describes the way in which the teacher has planned in advance to determine "whether these purposes are being attained" (Tyler, 1949, p. 1).

The *description,* another feature in a lesson plan, is used to identify it and give the reader a quick overview of its purpose or description. In addition, a lesson plan often contains information about the resources teachers need as background preparation for teaching the lesson as well as any materials necessary for actual execution of the lesson.

A suggestion for teachers in this age of computers is to create a basic outline of a lesson plan on a word processor and save it on a disk. Then, whenever you wish to write a lesson plan, you can put the outline on the screen and fill in the spaces. The outline for a lesson plan should contain elements such as those given in Figure 6.3. Not all of these elements, especially in the procedures section, may be needed for every lesson; but this outline gives you a framework for thinking about what to include as you begin to plan your own lessons. This outline can be copied onto your computer disk for use in college and the rest of your teaching career.

On rare occasions, a teacher may create a single lesson on a topic such as fire safety, a holiday, or a news item. Usually, however, a single lesson plan does not stand alone in a classroom. It is part of a unit or a year-long plan for a subject in the curriculum. As shown earlier in this chapter, learning events are planned in a logical sequence of lessons designed gradually to increase student understanding and skill in the subject area. The next four sections describe sample lesson plans for four subjects in the elementary curriculum, showing the lesson itself and how it fits into the long-term plan for that subject.

SAMPLE LESSON PLAN IN MATHEMATICS

Students like to explore their own world. A large portion of time in the middle school student's world is devoted to watching television. Box 6.1 shows a lesson plan from Pam Knight's unit on television-viewing habits (see Chapter 5). On the surface, this appears to be a mathematics lesson. However, after analyzing the objectives and activities in it, you will see that it involves the social sciences and language arts as well.

This lesson plan requires more than one class period. One day is needed to prepare for data collection; a week is needed to collect and record the data; and a day or two are required for constructing the bar graphs and describing the findings.

Pam's lesson demonstrates how students can use mathematics in their lives. They become researchers who collect and organize data. For the data to be relevant, they must be able to analyze them and explain what they found. Finally, the students are expected to make inferences and evaluate an important factor in their lives.

Title of Lesson:

Subject Area:

Grade Level:

Description or Outcome Statement:

Objectives:

1.

2.

3.

Materials and Resources:

Procedures (What will you be doing? What will students be doing?):

1. Motivation:

2. Statement of purpose:

3. Teacher modeling or demonstration:

4. Check for understanding:

5. Guided practice or activity:

6. Independent practice or activity:

Assessment Plan:

Figure 6.3   Lesson plan model (which may be entered and saved in your word processor).

MODEL LESSON PLANNING

Box 6.1 Mathematics/Social Studies Lesson Plan

Pam Knight, Twin Peaks Middle School, Poway, California

Title of lesson: Television-Viewing Habits of Students
Subject area: mathematics/social sciences
Grade level: middle school

Description

Students will keep records of the amount of television they watch and present this information using graphs.

Objectives

1. *Application level:*   Students will construct bar graphs using data collected on television-viewing habits.
2. *Analysis level:*   Students will interpret and make inferences based on the analysis of the data gathered by writing a statement that describes the data on the graph.
3. *Evaluation level:*   Students will evaluate their television-viewing habits and the television-viewing habits of the class as a whole.

Materials Needed

Graph paper, rulers, and pencils

Procedures

1. *Motivation:*   The lesson begins with a discussion of the observations students have made about their own television-viewing habits. This is an open-ended discussion, and students may talk about types of shows seen (MTV, movies, sports contests, etc.). Ask students: "Do students watch too much television and play too many video games? How much TV do students really watch? Are there methods by which students can gather data on their television-viewing habits?"
2. *Statement of purpose:*   We will learn how to gather information and data to make informed decisions about important matters in our lives.

continued

3. *Teacher modeling and demonstration:*   Teacher models data collection by surveying students on their favorite TV show. Teacher tallies these data and, with class participation, creates a bar graph of the data at the chalkboard.
4. *Guided practice:*   Students duplicate the teacher's tally and bar graph at their desks.
5. *Check for understanding:*   Ask questions to determine whether the students know the processes of recording data and constructing a bar graph.
6. *Independent study/activity:*   Students gather data on their television-viewing habits for one week.
7. *Class discussion:*   At the end of the week, students choose ways to display their data using bar graphs. Examples of displaying the data could be the amount of television boys watched compared with the amount girls watched, the amount of television watched on different days of the week, or the types of programs watched. After looking at the different ways the data could be displayed, the class is divided into groups of three.
8. *Group activity:*   In groups of three, students construct the graph and identify an inference they could make based on their graph. They share their graph and inference and display them on a bulletin board.
9. *Closure:*   Students discuss what they have learned about their television-viewing habits. They discuss what the results mean to them. For example, do they think they watch too much television? Do they watch more or less television than they expected? Is the bar graph an effective way to display the data they gathered?

Assessment Plan

Students write in their journals about the activity completed. Students graphs are examined to see if the data have been correctly graphed. The inferences made by students are checked against the constructed bar graphs. The graphs become part of the students' mathematics and social studies portfolios.

SAMPLE LESSON PLAN IN LANGUAGE ARTS/SOCIAL STUDIES

Many times a single unit contains learning events in more than one subject, and a single lesson can accomplish objectives in two or more areas at the same time. For example, students can use language skills in a social studies unit or discuss and write about social studies topics in a language-arts unit.

The example of the lesson on epitaphs in Box 6.2 is such a lesson. The focus of this lesson is to show how history can be studied by looking at gravestones in cemeteries. But as a language-arts lesson, it demonstrates an important aspect of the writing process. It allows students to be creative but does not require them to write long essays. All students can be successful at such a task, regardless of previous language and writing experiences.

This lesson also makes history come alive. The characters from other times and places literally speak to the students about concerns and issues important to their lives. Discussions will naturally occur that cause students to compare their lives to the writers of the epitaphs.

MODEL LESSON PLANNING

Box 6.2 Sample Elementary Social Studies Lesson Plan

Title of lesson: Epitaphs
Subject area(s):   social studies and language arts
Grade level: elementary

Description

Students will learn what an epitaph is and how to write one.

Objectives

1. *Comprehension level:*   After a discussion of epitaphs and the teacher's reading of samples, the students will be able to describe an epitaph and write one.
2. *Analysis level:*   After learning about epitaphs from the discussion and the exercise of writing one, the students will read Roman epitaphs and analyze their value and their problems as sources of information about a culture.

Materials and Resources Needed

- *California State Framework for History-Social Sciences*
- *A Message of Ancient Days* (Houghton Mifflin)
- Epitaph sheets for everyone in class

Procedures

1. *Motivation:*   Ask students, "Have you have ever visited a cemetery? What would you find there? What kind of literature would you find in a cemetery? Why would it be there? Who would have written it? What would the literature be like? Serious? Funny?"
2. *Purpose:*   Students will learn what an epitaph is and be able to write one.
3. *Connection with previous learning:*   Students are studying history. One method of tracing history is to observe what people have written about themselves and others. Students may have read excerpts from journals, letters, and notes people have written. They may also read an epitaph.
4. *Model/demonstration:*   Explain what an epitaph is. Use an overhead or pass out a sheet of real epitaphs. Review these with the students. Some examples follow:

continued

Elizabeth Cupper:

Sharp was her wit, mild her nature

A tender wife and a good humored creature

George Warmington:

'Tis my request

My bones may rest

Within my chest

without molest

Anne Jennings:

Some have children

Some have none

Here lies the mother

of twenty-one

George Morgan:

Say more I need not, and say less who can

Here lies the generous, humane, honest man

Ask students which example they liked best and why. Have them write the definition of an epitaph in their own words.

5. *Guided practice:*   The class will write an epitaph for a fictional or cartoon character: for example, Mickey Mouse or Indiana Jones.
6. *Independent activity:*   Students will choose someone who is dead or some fictional character and write an epitaph for that person. If there is time, students will read their epitaphs to the class.
7. *Closure:*   Students will review how history can be examined through an individual's epitaph.

Assessment Plan

Students' epitaphs will be read and written comments made on them. Students will be asked how an epitaph can be used to study history. Students will be asked to write in their own words what an epitaph is.

SAMPLE LESSON PLAN IN SCIENCE

The lesson plan for science is taken from the unit developed by Chris Chiaverina and Jim Hicks described in Chapter 5. Their plan is exciting because they are constantly trying to find ways to make science interesting, practical, and fun. In their words, "if there isn't a common understanding of the application of a concept in science, then it isn't worth teaching." As you read their lesson plan, remember that the philosophy of their approach to science is to use a smorgasbord of examples and demonstrations as well as a hands-on approach by their students. Their lessons clearly meet the expectations of the new science frameworks that require teachers to take an active and exploratory approach to the learning of science.

SAMPLE PRIMARY BILINGUAL LESSON PLAN USING LEARNING CENTERS

Conchita Encinas teaches in a bilingual first-grade classroom in Chula Vista, California. To encourage her students to interact and use oral language in small groups, she likes to plan many of her lessons using learning centers. For each topic that she wants to teach, she designs four different activities that students can do independently or in a small group. For example, her spring curriculum includes a unit on plants and growing things. For the lesson on plants and seeds, she designs four different learning center activities.

She begins the lesson with all of the children sitting in a circle, where she provides students with some general information in both Spanish and English about plants and seeds. She encourages her students to learn and use new English words related to the topic being studied. Then she introduces the four different activities they will be able to explore in the centers. She divides the class into four groups, and each group travels from one center to another for 20-minute intervals. At the end of the morning, the students gather in a circle to share what they have done and learned about seeds and plants. Conchita reads aloud the stories the children have written at the first center. Box 6.4 shows Conchita's lesson plan for the exploration of seeds and plants.

Lesson plans are scripts that teachers write so that they can present a well-organized set of learning experiences for their students. The objectives of the lesson specify the teacher's expectations for what the students will learn or be able to do as a result of the lesson. When teachers plan objectives that specify the criteria for success, they are clarifying for themselves what the students must be able to do to demonstrate mastery of the skill or understanding of the lesson's concepts.

To plan the procedures of a lesson in advance, many reflective teachers visualize themselves teaching the lesson. They write what they must do to teach the lesson successfully and what the students must do to learn the material. Teachers who can visualize the entire process of teaching and learning can write richly detailed lesson plans. When they begin to teach the lesson, they have a supportive script to follow.

As teachers become more proficient and experienced at planning and teaching, their written lesson plans are likely to become less detailed. But for beginning teachers, a thorough, richly detailed plan is an essential element for a successful lesson.

MODEL LESSON PLANNING

Box 6.3 Sample High School Science Lesson Plan

Chris Chiaverina and Jim Hicks

> *Title of the lesson:*   Wave Phenomena
> *Subject area:*   science
> *Grade level:*   high school physics

Description

Using a variety of items that vibrate and produce sounds, students investigate wave phenomena.

Objectives

1. *Comprehension:*   Students will become aware of their naïve ideas about sound and be able to describe how sound is produced.
2. *Application:*   Students will make their own source of sound through a device called the hummer.
4. *Knowledge:*   Students will develop their science vocabulary by being able to define and use wave terminology appropriately.

Materials Needed

> Tuning fork, guitar, carpet tubing, music box, 78 RPM record, needle, pencil, "talking strip," Fisher burner, aluminum rod, resin, "sound wagon" toy, rubber bands, file cards, tongue depressors, string

Procedures

1. *Motivation/modeling/demonstration:* The teacher demonstrates a variety of common vibrating systems that produce audible sounds. For example, strike a tuning fork and have the students observe if there is a noticeable visible vibration on the fork. Strike the tuning fork and place it in a glass of water and observe what happens. The water will be stirred. The teacher plucks a guitar string and the students listen to the sound.

   The teacher then demonstrates some unusual sources of sound. An old record is played with a straight pin. A carpet tube is placed over a Fisher burner, which makes a sound like a fog horn. A talking plastic strip is pulled across a fingernail and delivers a message. An aluminum rod is stroked with rosin and produces a high-pitched tone.

2. *Statement of purpose:* Students will learn how sound is produced by vibrations.

3. *Connect to previous learning:* Students have done laboratory work, seen demonstrations, and watched a movie on waves. They have also done labs using Slinkies and a ripple tank. After students have observed the demonstration of sounds in the motivation activity, they are asked to relate their observations to the concepts learned in the previous lessons on wave phenomena, including reflection and transmission. They are also asked to relate this to the terminology of wave speed and amplitude.

4. *Independent activity:* Students produce their own hummer. (a) A rubber band is stretched around a tongue depressor and acts as a vibrating object. (b) A file card is stapled to the tongue depressor and used to amplify the vibrations. (c) A string is attached to an end of the device. (d) The hummer is spun around in a circle by the string, and a sound is produced.

5. *Guided practice:* Students are assigned problems on the sources and transmission of sound. These problems relate to the earlier examples as well as the hummer.

6. *Closure:* Students interpret this phrase: "Sound equals vibrations." They demonstrate their hummers.

Assessment Plan

Students create hummers and describe in their own words how the hummer produces sound, using correct wave terminology.

MODEL LESSON PLANNING

Box 6.4 Primary Bilingual Lesson Plan on Seeds and Plants
A HANDS-ON SCIENCE LESSON DESIGNED FOR LEARNING CENTERS

Conchita Encinas, First-Grade Bilingual Class, Chula Vista, California

Description
Students will explore how seeds grow into plants.

Objectives
- Students will observe that seeds are different sizes, shapes, and colors.
- Students will be able to describe how seeds grow into plants.

  Students will increase their English vocabulary and oral speaking and listening skills by learning and using new words related to the topic

- Students will analyze the variation in number and type of seeds among several different types of plants.

Procedures
1. Begin in a circle. Review concepts students have already learned about plants. Have students give a thumbs-up signal if they agree, a thumbs-down signal if they disagree

⬆ Reflective Actions for Your Professional Portfolio
Three Sample Lesson Plans

Perceptiveness: Examine Other Lesson Plans
Ask the cooperating teacher to show you his or her lesson plans. How do these plans differ from the ones in this chapter? Observe a lesson and try to perceive the teacher's objectives, procedures, and assessment strategies.

Construction of Knowledge: Write Objectives and Outcomes
Choose a subject or thematic unit topic and write objectives for each of the levels of Bloom's taxonomy:

with statements such as "Flowers are plants. Plants need water to grow. Plants need milk to grow."

2. Teach children the English words for *plants, seeds, garden, grow,* and *food.* Have children repeat these words in the circle and use them while working in the centers.

3. Review with the whole group directions for the activities at the four centers. Divide the class into four groups. Assign a rotation schedule so that each group goes to all four centers.

4. *Center 1:* Students cut out parts of a plant, glue them on a piece of paper, and write a story about it.

5. *Center 2:* Students examine and count a variety of vegetable and fruit seeds, including an apple, cantaloupe, pea pod, and green pepper. They graph the number of seeds in each vegetable.

6. *Center 3:* Students plant rye seeds in a paper cup and discuss what happens to seeds under the ground.

7. *Center 4:* Students identify various vegetables, cut them up, and taste them. They list words about the way each vegetable tastes.

Assessment

Story boards and stories from Center 1 are read aloud at the closing circle. Graphs from Center 2 are displayed on the bulletin board. Seeds in cups from Center 3 are placed near a window to grow. Students discuss the tastes of different vegetables during the closing circle.

Knowledge (behavioral objective)

Comprehension (behavioral objective)

Application (problem-solving objective)

Analysis (problem-solving objective)

Synthesis (expressive outcome)

Evaluation (expressive outcome)

At the knowledge and comprehension levels, use behavioral objectives. Evaluate them to be sure that you have included a clear and accurate description of the behavior, the conditions, and the criteria for success.

Values and Principles: Adapt Lessons to Students' Needs

What are your views on meeting the individual needs of students in your classroom? With mainstreaming and full inclusion becoming more prevalent, you are likely to have a number of students with special needs in your classroom every year. How will you provide them with appropriate learning experiences and criteria for success that they can achieve? How will you cope with the fairness issue if other children complain that they have to do more work than a student with special needs?

Creativity: Design Your Own Lesson Plans

Write three sample lesson plans to fit the unit plan you have created. You may wish to use very different types of lessons to demonstrate your flexibility and creativity.

Persistence, Problem Solving, and Communication: Revise Your Lessons Based on Feedback

Show your lesson plans to a knowledgeable teacher and get feedback that will help you to improve them. Make the revisions that you agree with and explain your rationale for elements that you retain. If possible, teach the lessons and then make further revisions. Describe the changes that you made as a result of teaching the lessons.

References

Bloom, B., Engelhart, M., Furst, E., Hill, W., & Krathwohl, D. (1956). *Taxonomy of educational objectives: Cognitive domain.* New York: Longman.

Eisner, E. (1985). *Educational imagination* (2nd ed). Upper Saddle River, NJ: Merrill/Prentice Hall.

Shotwell, L. (1963). *Roosevelt Grady.* New York: Grosset & Dunlap.

Tyler, R. (1949). *Basic principles of curriculum and instruction.* Chicago: University of Chicago Press.

7

Authentic Teaching and Learning

Your lessons and unit plans are ready to go. You've taken the time and effort to create a safe, encouraging, and stimulating classroom environment. You've clarified your expectations for student behavior and involved your students in the process of creating classroom rules. You've rehearsed the procedures for coming in and going out of the classroom, and you know the names of each student and something about their background and needs. Now you can begin to focus on developing instructional strategies that will promote authentic learning.

The term *authentic learning* is used to distinguish between the achievement of significant, meaningful, and useful knowledge and skills from that which is trivial and unrelated to students' lives. The Wisconsin Center on Organizing and Restructuring of Schools has concentrated on defining standards of authentic instruction. Its studies have led it to conclude that many conventional instructional methods do not allow students to use their minds well and result in learning that has little or no intrinsic meaning or value to them beyond achieving success in school.

These studies recommend establishing standards for teachers to use as guidelines in selecting and learning to use teaching strategies that promote authentic learning. According to their research, the standards for authentic instructional methods should emphasize higher-order thinking, depth of knowledge, connectedness to the world, and substantive conversation and should provide social support for student achievement (Newman & Wehlage, 1993).

As a learner, you may have had teachers who used teaching strategies that stimulated you to use your higher-level thinking and problem-solving skills. You may recall learning experiences that encouraged you to delve deeply into a subject that had real meaning to your life. You may recall class discussions that sparkled with enthusiastic exchanges of ideas and opinions within a social system that encouraged you to challenge yourself to make more and more meaningful accomplishments. If you recall school experiences such as these, you have experienced authentic learning.

Unfortunately, it is likely that you had other teachers who relied on very conventional methods that required rote memorization of meaningless material. You may recall learning a lot about little and boring recitations in which students were expected to parrot what they had memorized. You may recall competitive social systems that encouraged only those students who were able to memorize and recite quickly and those who were able to figure out what the teacher wanted to hear. If you recall school experiences such as these, you will need to overcome the natural tendency to repeat learned patterns and challenge yourself to learn to use many new and exciting instructional strategies.

Your personal conception of the teaching-learning process is drawn from your own experiences as a learner, but for reflective teachers it is also drawn from the values and beliefs they hold about what students need to know and how students ought to behave and from perceptions and reflections about the theories and practices of other classroom teachers they observe. To become a reflective teacher, you must make yourself aware of the emerging research and knowledge base about teaching and learning. Gathering information from research is an important attribute of a reflective thinker and teacher.

The Cognitive-Mediational Conception of Learning

Anderson (1989b) describes two conceptions of learning that clarify and support the argument for authentic teaching and learning. One conception of learning is termed the *receptive-accrual (R-A)* view and the other the *cognitive-mediational (C-M)* view.

Teachers who hold the R-A view believe that each student has innate, immutable individual differences in the ability to learn. Learning itself is defined as a relatively passive act of receiving information and storing it in memory without modification. To demonstrate achievement, the student is expected to recall information from memory and demonstrate that it was retained accurately. One implication of this view is that, although teaching may be a very active process, learning is passive.

Because R-A teachers view learning as the gaining and storing of information, they believe that the best method to assess how much a student has learned is through tests of memorized data and skills. An important derivative of this view is that success in school results from a combination of a student's innate ability and the effort to accrue and retain knowledge. This view leads teachers to explain student failure as a result of inherent inadequacies or lack of effort. When failure occurs, teachers who have this view comfort themselves with the conviction that some students are able to learn and achieve success in school while others can't or won't learn (Anderson, 1989b).

In contrast, teachers who hold the C-M view believe that learning depends on the student's cognitive activity. Learning is defined as the act of processing new information through active, selective perception, relating the new information to prior knowledge, and storing it in an organized way until it is called for again.

In this view, which you can readily see has many common attributes with the concept of authentic learning, teachers view success in school not as dependent on ability or effort but on the student's background knowledge and on knowing how to select and apply cognitive strategies appropriately. Teachers with this view explain student failure as most likely a result of the student's having inadequate prior knowledge or a need for more training in selecting and using the cognitive strategies appropriate for the task.

Which view do you hold? Your many years as a student in conventional classrooms will strongly influence your belief in the R-A theory. For many years, you were led to believe that students are smart, average, or stupid. Because you are now in a teacher education program, it is likely that you were one of the smart ones. You may have observed long-suffering teachers struggling with students in the low reading group or the low tracks in high school and you may be convinced, as your former teachers were, that these students can't or won't learn.

The C-M viewpoint, then, will be difficult for you to accept. From experience, you can expect some of your students to be skillful, accurate, and quick in processing new information and others to be clumsy, erroneous, and slow. As a teacher, it is your task to diagnose the reasons for students' failure to process information efficiently and accurately. You then must plan a set of learning experiences that assist students in activating their existing knowledge so that they can comprehend the new information or skill you are teaching.

In practice, the teaching methods selected by teachers with these two contrasting conceptions of learning are likely to be quite different. The teacher with the R-A view is likely to assign a reading or a page of problems and then monitor students by responding to questions but doing little else to deliberately stimulate the cognitive processes necessary for students to actively construct meaning. From this perspective, the teacher's role is simply to provide tasks and information, then to offer incentives in the form of grades or gold stars for students to perform these tasks. Unfortunately, the R-A teacher may believe that actual learning of the material is "out of the teacher's power" (Anderson, 1989b, p. 87).

In contrast, a C-M teacher believes in the power to mediate in the learning process. This power is not automatic and is not easily won; but by using the reflective teaching model, the C-M teacher observes students carefully, gathering information about what prior knowledge they possess and what they lack. This teacher observes students as they work on a problem and listens to them as they read or respond to a question. From this process of gathering information, the C-M teacher plans lessons and selects teaching strategies that will fill in the gaps in students' knowledge, then helps them to organize what they know into useful patterns and structures so they are able to activate the appropriate knowledge and bring it to bear on new learning situations. In the process, they create an environment for authentic learning.

Teachers who understand the cognitive process of acquiring and processing information can apply their power in countless ways to the benefit of their students. They can reduce external stimuli so that the important bits of knowledge are perceived by their students' short-term memories. They can pace the delivery of new information to give students sufficient time to process one bit of knowledge in working memory before introducing another. They can phrase questions in such a way that they provide the appropriate cue to retrieve the stored information from long-term memory.

SCHEMA THEORY

The retrieval process is obviously a critical factor in being able to use stored information. Knowledge, concepts, and skills that are learned must be stored in the brain until they are needed. According to the *schema theory,* each subset of knowledge is stored in a *schema,* an outline or organized network of knowledge about a single concept or subject. It is believed that young children develop *schemata* (the plural form of schema) made up of visual or other sensory images and, as language increases, verbal imagery replaces the sensory images (Anderson 1989b; Anderson & Pearson, 1984; Bransford, 1983).

For example, an infant stores sensual images in the schemata for mother, bottle, bed, and bath. Later the verbal labels are added. A schema grows, expands, or otherwise changes due to new experiences. If the infant sees and touches a large, round, blue ball, he or she can store sensory images of its size, color, rubbery feel, and softness. At a later encounter, the infant may experience it bounce, and he or she can store these images in the same schema. A year later, when the child learns to say the word *ball,* the label is acted on in working memory and stored in long-term memory within the schema for ball.

Students come to school with varied schema. Some students who have had many experiences at home, in parks, at zoos, in museums, and in other circumstances may enter kindergarten with complex schemata for hundreds of topics and experiences. Other students, whose experiences have been severely limited by poverty or other circumstances, are likely to have very different schemata, and some of these may not match the prevailing culture's values or verbal labels. Similarly, if students come from highly verbal homes where parents talk with them frequently, their schemata are likely to contain accurate verbal labels for stored sensory experiences and phenomena. But students who are raised in less verbal homes will have fewer verbal components to their schemata. This theory complements Piaget's observations of stages of development and helps us to understand how a child's vocabulary develops.

Schemata also vary according to their organizational patterns. As children mature, each schema expands to include many more facts, ideas, and examples. In cases of healthy development, the schemata are frequently clarified and reorganized. Learning new information or observing unfamiliar examples often causes a schema to be renamed or otherwise altered. For example, very young children have a schema labeled *doggy* that includes all four-legged, furry creatures. As they see new examples of animals and hear the appropriate labels for each type, the original schema of doggy is reorganized to become simply a subset of the schema *animal*. New patterns and relationships among schemata are forming every day of a child's life when the environment is full of unfamiliar concepts and experiences.

The importance of schema theory in the C-M conception of learning is that it helps to explain why some students are able to retrieve knowledge better than others. Students who have many accurately labeled schemata are more likely to have the background knowledge needed to learn an unfamiliar concept. Students whose schemata are richly detailed and well organized into patterns and hierarchies are much more likely to be able to retrieve useful information on request than are students whose schemata are vague and sparse.

Several other important connections link schema theory and the C-M view of learning. Teachers who believe that it is in their power to help their students improve their cognitive processing recognize that one of the best ways to do this is to stimulate students to actively create more well-developed, accurately labeled, and better-organized schemata.

At the elementary grade levels, teachers recognize that one of their most important responsibilities is to aid students in schema development with accurate verbal labels. At the earliest grades (especially kindergarten), teachers emphasize spoken labels, teaching students to recognize and be able to name objects and concepts such as numbers, letters of the alphabet, and colors. At the primary grades, teachers emphasize the recognition and decoding of written labels as an integral part of the reading program. When students exhibit difficulties in learning to read, the C-M teacher is likely to plan learning experiences that assist the student in developing schemata that are prerequisites for reading.

Students who have been raised in environments characterized by few experiences with books are likely to have an underdeveloped schema for reading and books. Reflective teachers who consider the needs of the whole individual are likely to provide their students with many opportunities to hear stories read aloud, to choose from a tempting array of books, and to write their own stories as a means of developing a rich and positive schema for the concept of reading.

ADVANCE ORGANIZERS

When teachers want to assist students in retrieving information from their schemata, they provide verbal cues that help the students access the appropriate information efficiently.

Teachers can also provide cues to assist students in accurately and efficiently processing and storing what they read, see, or hear. Ausubel (1960) proposed that learners can comprehend new material better when, in advance of the lesson, the teacher provides a clear statement about the purpose of the lesson and the type of information that learners should look or listen for. This introductory statement is known as an *advance organizer.*

When we relate this theory to information processing theory, it is apparent that the advance organizer provides the learner with an important cue as to which schema will incorporate this new knowledge. The learner can be more efficient in processing the information in working memory and transferring it to the appropriate schema in long-term memory than if no advance information was presented.

For example, consider what is likely to happen when a third-grade teacher introduces a lesson on long division with no advance organizer. Some students will simply reject the new knowledge as incomprehensible. But say the teacher tells students to listen for how division is similar to subtraction and how it is the opposite of multiplication. The teacher is providing students with the cues they need to retrieve their subtraction and multiplication schema in advance of the new learning. In the second case, students are more likely to route the new facts into working memory, where they can be processed using the subtraction and multiplication schemata as a framework.

In follow-up studies of Ausubel's hypothesis, many educational researchers designed experiments that showed the same effects. Therefore, this knowledge has been added to our growing common knowledge base about teaching and learning. In fact, this particular study demonstrates the way in which the knowledge base grows. The original hypothesis and study conducted by Ausubel (1960) led others to apply the principle to different types of students and environments. As the hypothesis was confirmed in subsequent studies, the knowledge was gradually accepted as a reliable principle of effective teaching. You probably experience the beneficial effects of advance organizers when your teachers tell you in advance what to listen for in a lecture or what to study for an exam. Now you can learn how to use this principle in your teaching career for the benefit of your students.

Presentation Skills That Increase Clarity and Motivation

Teaching is more than telling. You have been on the receiving end of teachers' lectures, discussions, and other forms of lessons for many years. You know from your own experience that the way that teachers teach or present material has an effect on student interest and motivation, which are both integral aspects of the classroom climate. You may have been unable to understand the beginning of a lesson taught by a teacher who failed to get the full attention of a class before speaking. You have probably experienced sinking feelings when a teacher droned on in a monotonous voice during a lecture. You may have experienced frustration when a teacher explained a concept once and hurried on, ignoring questions or comments from the class. Reflective teachers are not likely to be satisfied with a dull, repetitive, or unresponsive presentation style. Most of them are anxious to improve their presentation skills to stimulate interest and motivate student achievement.

GETTING STUDENTS' ATTENTION

To consider systematically the way in which you present a lesson, think about the beginning. The introduction to a lesson is very important, whether it is the first lesson of the day or a transition from one lesson to another. As Kounin (1977) found in his study of well-functioning classrooms, transitions and lesson beginnings start with a clear, straightforward message or cue signaling that the teacher is ready to begin teaching and stating exactly what students should do to prepare themselves for the lesson. To accomplish this when you teach, you need to tell your students to get ready for a certain lesson and to give you their full attention. Some teachers use a visual cue for this purpose, such as a finger on the lips or a raised arm. Others may strike a chime or turn off the lights to cue the students that it is time to listen.

It is unlikely that students will become quiet instantly. It will probably take a few moments to get the attention of every student in the class. While you are waiting, stand up straight and direct eye contact with those who are slow to respond. Watch quietly as the students get their desks, pencils, books, and other needed materials ready for the lesson. The waiting may seem uncomfortable at first. You will be tempted to begin before they are ready because you will think that time is being wasted. Don't give in to this feeling. Wait until every voice is quiet, every chair stops scraping, every desk top stops banging, and every pencil stops tapping. Wait for a moment of pure, undisturbed silence. Then quietly begin your lesson. You will have the attention of every student.

Some teachers use a bit of drama to begin a lesson. They may pose a question or describe a condition that will interest their students. Richard Klein, a teacher at the Ericson School on Chicago's West Side, begins teaching a unit on aviation by asking students what they know about the Wright brothers. The students' replies are seldom very enthusiastic, so he unexpectedly asks them, "Then what do you know about the Wrong brothers?" They show a bit more interest but are still unable to provide many informed responses. So Mr. Klein turns off the lights and turns on a videotape of the Three Stooges in a skit called "The Wrong Brothers." Afterward, partly in appreciation of Mr. Klein's humor, the students show a greater willingness to learn about the real historical events.

Often teachers begin with a statement of purpose, describing how this particular lesson will help their students to make an important gain in skills or knowledge. Still others begin by doing a demonstration or distributing some interesting manipulative materials. Madeline Hunter (1982) calls this technique providing an *anticipatory set* both to gain attention and to motivate students to be interested in the lesson. She encourages teachers to use a variety of anticipatory sets appropriate to the lesson content and objective.

In contrast, less reflective teachers begin almost every lesson with: "Open your books to page _____. David, read the first paragraph aloud." This example employs no presentation skills. This nonmethod relies on the material itself to whet the students' interest in the topic. Although some materials may be stimulating and appealing, most are not. The message the teacher gives to the students is "I don't care much about anything; let's just get through this." The students' motivation to learn drops to the same level as this message and can best be expressed as "Why bother?"

Teachers often display a greater degree of excitement and interest for material they themselves enjoyed learning, and they pass that excitement about learning on to the students. A teacher who reads aloud with enthusiasm conveys the message that reading is fun. A teacher who plunges into a science investigation with delight causes students to look forward to science.

After you gain your students' attention and inspire them to want to know more, you move on to the lesson itself. Presentation skills that you can learn to use systematically in your lessons include the following:

Enthusiasm

Clarity

Smooth transitions

Timing

Variation

Interaction

Active learning

Closure

ENTHUSIASM

Animation is the outward sign of a teacher's interest in the students and the subject. Enthusiasm is the inner experience. "There are at least two major aspects of enthusiasm. The first is conveying sincere interest in the subject. The other aspect is vigor and dynamics," and both are related to getting and maintaining student attention (Good & Brophy, 1987, p. 479). Outwardly, the teacher displays enthusiasm by using a bright, lively voice; open, expansive gestures; and facial expressions that show interest and pleasure. Salespeople who use animated, enthusiastic behavior could sell beach umbrellas in the Yukon in January. Why shouldn't teachers employ these techniques as well? You can "sell" long division better with an enthusiastic voice. You can convince your students that recycling is important with a look of commitment on your own face. You can encourage students' participation in a discussion with welcoming gestures and a warm smile.

Is animation something you can control? Absolutely. You can practice presenting information on a topic with your classmates, using an animated voice and gestures. They can give you feedback, which you can use to improve your presentation. Have yourself videotaped as you make a presentation. When you view yourself, you can be your own best teacher. Redo your presentation with new gestures and a different voice. Repeat this procedure several times, if necessary. Gradually, you will notice a change in your presentation style. You will add these techniques to your growing repertoire of effective presentation skills.

CLARITY

The clarity of the teacher's presentation of lesson directions and content is a critical factor in student success. Brophy and Good (1986) listed the importance of teacher clarity as a consistent finding in studies of teacher effectiveness. Their review of research on teacher clarity describes negative teacher behaviors that detract from clarity. These include using vagueness terms, mazes, and discontinuity and saying "uh" repeatedly.

As an example of *vagueness terms,* Brophy and Good (1986) present the following, with ambiguous language in italics:

> This mathematics lesson *might* enable you to understand *a little more* about *some of the things* we *usually* call number patterns. *Maybe* before we get to *probably* the main idea of the lesson, you should review *a few* prerequisite concepts. (p. 355)

The vague terms in this example have the effect of making the teacher sound tentative and unsure of the content. As an introduction to a lesson, it is not likely to capture students' attention or interest. Clarity can be improved, in this example, by exchanging the vague terms for specific ones, resulting in a simple, straightforward statement: "This mathematics lesson will enable you to understand the concept of number patterns. Before we get to the main idea of the lesson, we will review three prerequisite concepts."

Clarity also suffers from what Brophy and Good call *mazes:* false starts or halts in the teacher's speech, redundancy, and tangled words. For example:

> This mathematics lesson *will enab*—will get you to understand *number, uh,* number patterns. Before we get to the *main idea of the,* main idea of the lesson, you need to review *four conc*—four prerequisite concepts. (Brophy & Good, 1986, p. 355)

Even when students attempt to pay attention, they may be unable to decipher the meaning of the teachers' words if the presentation is characterized by the false starts in this example. It is obvious that the way to improve this statement is to eliminate the redundant words. This example is a very simple one. Clarity is also reduced when the teacher has begun to present a lesson, is interrupted by a student's misbehavior or a knock at the door, then begins the lesson again. Kounin (1977) observed that the most effective teachers are able to *overlap* teaching with other classroom management actions. That is, they are able to continue with the primary task, presenting the lesson to the class, while at the same time opening the classroom door or stopping misbehavior with a glance or a touch on the shoulder. When teachers can overlap their presentations, the clarity of their lessons is greatly enhanced.

The third teacher behavior that detracts from clarity is *discontinuity,* "in which the teacher interrupts the flow of the lesson by interjecting irrelevant content" (Brophy & Good, 1986, p. 355). This is why lesson planning is so important. Without a plan, teachers may simply begin a lesson by reading from a textbook. As they or the students are reading, the teacher (or a student) may be reminded of something they find interesting. They may discuss the related topic for quite some time before returning to the original lesson. This side discussion may or may not be interesting or important, but it is likely to detract from the clarity of the original lesson.

The fourth detractor from teacher clarity noted by Brophy and Good (1986) is repeatedly saying "uh." It is also likely that other repetitive speech patterns are just as annoying, such as "you know." For the beginning teacher, it is likely that some of these teacher behaviors will occur simply as a result of nervousness or unfamiliarity with the content being taught. It would be interesting to study the hypothesis that these four detracting behaviors decrease as a result of teaching experience—in other words, as a teacher gains experience, the four detracting behaviors subside and clarity increases. Two teacher behaviors found to enhance clarity were an "emphasis on key aspects of the content to be learned and clear signaling of transitions between parts of lessons" (Brophy & Good, 1986, p. 355).

SMOOTH TRANSITIONS

Just as lesson introductions are important to gain students' attention, smooth transitions are essential to maintaining that attention and making the classroom a productive working environment. Transitions occur within a lesson as the teacher guides students from one activity to another. They also occur between lessons as students put away what they were working on in one lesson and get ready for a different subject.

Good and Brophy note that knowing when to terminate a lesson is an important element of teacher withitness.

> When the group is having difficulty maintaining attention, it is better to end the lesson early than to doggedly continue. This is especially important for younger students, whose attention span for even the best lesson is limited. When lessons go on after the point where they should have been terminated, more of the teacher's time is spent compelling attention and less of the students' time is spent thinking about the material. (Good & Brophy, 1987, p. 245)

In addition to moving students to another classroom, transitions between activities and lessons may require that students move from place to place in the room, such as having one group come to the reading circle while another group returns to their seats. Usually students are required to exchange one set of books and materials for another. These movements and exchanges have high potential for noise in the form of banging desk tops, scraping chairs, dropped equipment, and students' voices as they move from lesson to lesson.

Jerky, chaotic transitions are often caused by incomplete directions or vague expectations about student behavior from the teacher. "Take out your math books" is incomplete in that the teacher does not first specify that the students should put away other materials they have been working with. The result may be that the students begin to work on desks cluttered with unnecessary materials.

Often, inexperienced teachers begin to give directions for a transition, and the students start to get up and move around while the teacher is speaking. When this happens, teachers may attempt to talk louder so that they can be heard over the din. A way to prevent this from occurring is to inform students clearly that they are to wait until all directions have been given before they begin to move.

Smooth transitions are characterized by clear directions from the teacher about what is to be put away and what is to be taken out, who is to move and where they are to go. Clear statements of behavioral expectations are also important. The same techniques for getting attention that were described previously apply to the beginning of each new lesson. After a noisy transition between lessons, it is essential for the teacher to have the students' complete attention before beginning the new lesson. The teacher should wait until all students move into their new positions and get all their materials ready before trying to introduce the lesson.

The teacher can use a signal to indicate that the new lesson is about to begin. A raised hand, lights turned off and on, or a simple verbal statement such as "I am ready to begin" will signal to the students that they should be ready for the next lesson. After giving the signal, the teacher should wait until the students have all complied and are silent before beginning the new lesson.

In considering strategies that result in smooth transitions, teachers do well to reflect on the students' needs for physical activity. In a junior high or high school, students can move between periods. At the elementary school or in a block period of time in the middle school, it is unrealistic to expect students to be able to sit still through one lesson after another. Some teachers take 5 to 10 minutes to lead students in singing or movement games between two working periods. Other teachers allow students to have a few moments of free time in which they may talk to friends, go to the washroom, or get a drink of water. Some transitions are good opportunities for teachers to read aloud from a story book or challenge students to solve a brain teaser or puzzling mathematics problem. Reflective teachers find that when they allow students a respite and a change of pace during a brief transition period, the work periods are more productive and motivation to learn is enhanced.

TIMING

Actors, speakers, and comedians give considerable attention to improving the timing of their presentations. Good use of timing engages the attention of an audience, emphasizes major points, and sometimes creates a laugh. Teachers also work in front of an audience, and class presentations can be improved by considering timing and pacing as a means of getting attention and keeping it. Pausing for a moment of complete silence before you begin teaching is a good example of a way to incorporate timing into your presentation.

In most instances, students respond best to teachers who use a brisk pace of delivering information and instructions. Kounin's (1977) research on the most effective classroom managers demonstrated that students are best able to focus on the subject when the lesson has continuity and momentum. Interruptions result in confusion. When teachers forget to bring a prop, pause to consult a teacher's manual, or backtrack to present material that should have been presented earlier, inattention and disruptive behavior are likely to occur (Kounin, 1977). Jones (1987) found that students' attention improved when teachers gave them efficient help, allocating 20 seconds or less to each request for individual help or reteaching. When this time was lengthened, the result was restlessness and dependency on the part of students.

However, there are times when a pause in instruction can improve your presentation. Researchers have found that it is important to present new information in small steps, with a pause after the initial explanation to check for understanding. Students may not respond immediately during this pause because they need a moment to put their thoughts into words. Wait for them to do so. Encourage questions and comments. Ask for examples or illustrations of the fact or concept being discussed. This pause allows your students to reflect on the new material and allows you to test their understanding.

VARIATION

Lesson variation is an essential presentation skill for teachers who want to develop a healthy, vital classroom climate. In analyzing classroom videotapes, Kounin (1977) noticed that satiation results in boredom and inattentiveness. If presentations are monotonous, students will find a way to introduce their own variation by daydreaming, sleeping, fiddling with objects, doodling, or poking their neighbors.

Planning for variation is important whenever you plan a lesson of 30 minutes or longer. Divide your lesson into several segments. Use lecture for only part of the time. For example, include segments of discussion, independent practice, small-group interaction, and application activities. If you cannot break a single lesson into segments, plan to use a variety of strategies during the course of a day. Use quiet, independent work for one subject, group interaction for another, lecture for a third, and hands-on activities for a fourth. In this way, your students will always be expectant and eager for each new lesson of the day. They will feel fresh and highly motivated to learn because of the variations in the way you choose to present material. If teachers attempt to address different learning styles in each lesson, they can't help but provide variation in the classroom. All lessons should be checked for activities that address the different learning modalities. This is discussed in more detail later in this chapter.

INTERACTION

Students thrive on interaction with the teacher and with their classmates. Rather than employing a traditional teacher-to-student, student-to-teacher communication pattern, open up your classroom to a variety of interactive experiences. Pushing the desks into a large circle encourages open-ended discussion from all students. Arranging the desks in small groups encourages highly interactive problem solving. Moving the desks aside leaves a lot of space in the middle of the room for activities. Pairing the desks provides opportunities for peer teaching or partnerships of other kinds. Your presentations can include all these types of activities, and you will find that it is motivating not only to your students but to you as well. You will feel a sense of expectant excitement as you say, "All right, students, let's rearrange the desks."

The need for interaction derives from the powerful motivational need for belonging described by Maslow (1954) and Glasser (1986). When these needs are frustrated or denied, disruptive behavior is likely to occur as a means of satisfying them. When teachers consciously plan interactive learning experiences, they allow students to satisfy their important drive for belonging and thereby prevent unnecessary discipline problems.

ACTIVE, AUTHENTIC LEARNING EXPERIENCES

Teachers who value authentic learning present material in ways that engage their students in active rather than passive learning by including many verbal, visual, or hands-on activities. Consider a lecture on a topic such as the closed circuit in electricity. Ho hum. Add a visual aid—a poster or an overhead projection. Students sit up in their seats to see better. Now add a demonstration. Turn off the lights. Hold up a battery, some copper wire, and a light bulb. Your students watch expectantly with a new sense of interest.

Turn on the lights again. All these techniques are adequate to teach the students a concept, but none is as valuable as a hands-on experience for in-depth learning and understanding. Picture this scene instead. After lunch the students come into their classroom to find a battery, a flashlight bulb, and a piece of copper wire on each desk. After getting their attention, the teacher simply says, "Working independently, try to get your bulb to light up." Lights go on all over the room—in children's eyes and in their minds as they struggle with this problem. The motivation to succeed is intense and intrinsic, not tied to any exterior reward. Each individual has a sense of power and a need to know.

The key to authentic learning is in allowing your students to encounter and master situations that resemble real life. Simulated experiences are often just as valuable as real life for elementary school students and are much safer and more manageable for the beginning teacher. While your students may never invent a marketable product, you can simulate this type of exploration by inventing products that are needed in your classroom. You can simulate the debate and communication skills necessary to solve international crises by creating a mini United Nations in your room, in which each student studies one country in depth and engages in substantive conversations about the varied needs and strengths of each country.

CLOSURE

In the active learning experience example, the teacher can aid the students in comprehending what they've learned by having them share what they did that worked and didn't work. Concepts can be developed by articulating and generalizing what they learned about electricity. Such a teacher-led discussion is an essential part of active, hands-on learning. It provides a sense of closure.

Every lesson or presentation can benefit from some thoughtful consideration to its ending. It is important to allow time for closure. You may use this time to ask questions that check for understanding so that you will know what to plan for the lesson that follows. You may allow the students to close the lesson with their own conclusions and new insights. A few moments spent summarizing what was learned is valuable in any form. If insight is to occur, it will probably occur in this period. At the close of one lesson, you can also indicate what will follow in the next lesson so that your students know what to expect and how to prepare for it.

Systematic Classroom Instruction
DIRECT INSTRUCTION OF NEW KNOWLEDGE AND SKILLS

The curriculum contains a high proportion of basic knowledge and skills that learners must master thoroughly to succeed in the upper grades. Basic language concepts such as letter recognition, phonics, decoding words, writing letters and words, and the conventions of sentence and paragraph construction must be mastered. Basic mathematical concepts such as number recognition, quantity, order, measurement, and the operations used in computation must be learned.

Many models of direct instruction are appropriate for teaching this type of material. They are known as the five-step or seven-step lesson because they have been described in a chronological sequence of steps that results in getting students' attention; reviewing what has been learned up to the current lesson; systematically teaching, modeling, and practicing the new material; then demonstrating individual and independent mastery of what was taught.

The direct instruction model includes the following steps:

1. Create an anticipatory set to interest your students in the lesson by asking a thought-provoking question, providing an interesting visual aid, or using a puzzling and intriguing opening statement about the topic.
2. Connect this lesson with what has come before by providing a short review of previous, prerequisite learning or otherwise describing relationships between the current lesson and other subjects being studied by the class.
3. A short statement of the purpose of learning this new information is likely to convince your students that this lesson has a meaning to their lives beyond just achieving well in school. Tell them what they are going to learn and why it is important.
4. Present new, unfamiliar, and complex material in small steps, modeling each step by doing an example yourself. Give clear and detailed instructions and explanations as you model each process.
5. Provide a high level of active practice for all students. After you model a step, allow every student to practice the example on his or her own or with a learning partner.
6. Monitor students as they practice each new step. Walk around and look at their work as they do their sample problems. Ask a large number of questions to check for student understanding. Try to obtain responses from many students so that you know the concept is being clearly understood by the class. Provide systematic feedback and corrections as you see the needs arise.
7. At the end of each practice session, provide an opportunity for independent student work that synthesizes the many steps students have practiced during the lesson. This may be assigned as seatwork or homework. It is important to check this work and return it to students quickly with assistance for those who have not demonstrated independent mastery of the new material.

When these seven strategies are reviewed quickly, many readers may respond with reactions such as "But isn't that what all teachers do? What is new about these methods?" It is true that many teachers have used these strategies throughout the history of education. Unfortunately, many other teachers have not. We have all observed classroom teachers who take a much less active role than these systematic procedures call for. Teachers who subscribe to the R-A view of teaching and learning often follow only two steps: assigning work and correcting it.

On close examination, these steps are comparable to the C-M view of teaching and learning because they describe methods that would be used by a teacher who expects all students to achieve in school if the teacher takes an active role in helping them process the new information being taught. They are also highly compatible with the concept of authentic learning because students are encouraged to think about what they are learning, construct the new knowledge in a meaningful context, and respond to substantive discussion in a supportive environment for learning. Although direct instruction is frequently associated in peoples' minds with whole-class instruction, you can readily see that these systematic steps can be used during small-group instruction as well.

In selecting appropriate teaching methods and strategies, reflective teachers are likely to look for and discover relationships among various theories of learning and methods of teaching. One such relationship exists between this direct instruction model of systematic teaching and the process of thinking and learning known as *information processing*.

The first step—*begin a lesson with a short review of previous, prerequisite learning*—is a signal to the learner to call up an existing schema that will be expanded and altered in the new lesson. Beginning a lesson with a short statement of goals provides the student with an advance organizer that allows more efficient processing. In practice, these first two steps are often presented together and can be interchangeable with no ill effects.

Current information processing theories suggest that there are limits to the amount of new information that a learner can process effectively at one time (Gagne, 1985). When too much information is presented at one time, the working memory becomes overloaded, causing the learner to become confused, to omit data, or to process new data incorrectly. This overload can be eliminated when teachers *present new material in small steps, with student practice after each step.* This allows learners to concentrate their somewhat limited attention on processing manageably sized pieces of information or skills.

Teachers who *model new skills and give clear and detailed instructions and explanations* are likely to provide students with the support they need while they are processing new information in their working memories.

Providing students with a *high level of active practice* after each step, and again at the conclusion of a series of steps, is important because the practice enhances the likelihood that the new information will be transferred from working memory to long-term memory, where it can be stored for future use. Each time a new skill is practiced, its position in long-term memory is strengthened.

As teachers *guide students during initial practice and ask a large number of questions, check for student understanding, and obtain responses from all students,* they are also encouraging their students to process the information accurately. Learning occurs when schemata stored in long-term memory are expanded, enriched, and reorganized. Effective teacher questions and checks for understanding cause students to think about new ideas from a variety of perspectives and to update their existing schemata accordingly.

Providing systematic feedback and corrections and monitoring students during seatwork also increases the likelihood that students will process the important points and practice the new skills in the most efficient manner.

TEACHER MODELING AND DEMONSTRATION

When teachers present new information to students, they must carefully consider the method they will use to introduce it. For students, it is rarely sufficient for teachers simply to talk about a new idea or skill. A much more powerful method of instruction is to model or demonstrate it first and then give students an opportunity to practice the new learning themselves.

A simple example of this technique occurs at the primary grades when teachers say, "First, I will say the word; then you will say it with me." In the middle grades, the teacher may first demonstrate the procedures used in measuring with a metric ruler and then ask students to repeat them. In the upper grades, teachers may write an outline of a paragraph and then ask students to outline the next one.

Teacher demonstration and modeling is an effective instructional technique for almost every area of the curriculum. It is useful in teaching music: "Clap the same rhythm that I do." It is vital in teaching mathematics: "Watch as I do the first problem on the chalkboard." It can be easily applied to the teaching of creative writing: "I'll read you the poem that I wrote about this topic, and then you will write your own."

When teachers circulate throughout the classroom to monitor students as they practice or create their own work, it is efficient to use modeling and demonstration on a one-to-one basis to assist students in getting started or in correcting mistakes.

SCAFFOLDING

Scaffolding is a variation on the technique of teaching that involves modeling and demonstrating a new skill. It requires a highly interactive relationship between the teacher and the student while the new learning occurs. Anderson (1989a) cites Jerome Bruner's work with mothers and children as the first reference to scaffolding. As a mother reads aloud to a toddler, she may simplify the book to meet the attention span and interests of her child, calling the child's attention to material that is appropriate and eliminating material that is beyond the child's present capacity. She is also likely to allow the child to interact with her as they read and discuss the words and pictures on each page. This flexible and simplified interaction between child and parent allows the child to connect new ideas to existing schemata at his or her own level.

Teachers can apply scaffolding in the classroom by reducing complex tasks to manageable steps; helping students concentrate on one task at a time; being explicit about what is expected and interpreting the task for the student; and coaching the student using familiar, supportive words and actions. When a teacher coaches the student through a difficult task, he or she must provide sufficient scaffolding through the use of hints and cues so that the student can succeed. As students become more skillful, the scaffolding can be reduced and finally eliminated entirely.

Scaffolding is an especially valuable technique for the primary teacher because most young students require supportive interaction and accommodation to their existing vocabularies to learn new skills. But scaffolding is also appropriate for upper-level students when the tasks are complex or the students have difficulty with the language.

Some teachers do not use scaffolding techniques at any level:

> Instead of seeing themselves as supporters of students' constructions of knowl-
> edge, many teachers see themselves as presenters of content (especially facts and
> skills) and as orchestrators of activities that bring students in contact with that
> content. One result is the predominance of the recitation mode of instruction, in
> which the teacher asks a question, students offer answers that the teacher con-
> firms or disconfirms and the cycle is repeated. Teachers spend little time in the
> classroom encouraging students to explain how and what they are thinking, ele-
> ments that are necessary for scaffolded dialogues. (Anderson, 1989a, p. 107)

For some beginning teachers, scaffolding may not come naturally because they may
not have experienced scaffolded learning in their own school experiences. This technique
can be learned only by reflecting on the needs of students, gathering the latest information on such techniques from reading and talking to experienced teachers who have used
the techniques successfully, and gradually adding such strategies to personal repertoires.

STRUCTURING TASKS FOR SUCCESS

Researchers have found that the degree of success that students have on school tasks
correlates highly with achievement in the subject area. This supports the widely known
maxim that "success breeds success." Both formal research and informal discussions
with students reveal that when students experience success on a given task, they are
motivated to continue working at it or to tackle another one. The number and type of
successful learning experiences that students have affect their self-knowledge, leading
them to have expectations regarding probable success or failure in future tasks (Anderson, 1989b, p. 93).

To structure tasks for success, a teacher must create a good fit among his or her
expectations, student ability, and the difficulty of the task. Rimm (1986), who has specialized in assisting underachieving students reach their potential, describes it this way:

> Children must learn early that there is a relationship between their effort and
> the outcome. If their schoolwork is too hard, their efforts do not lead to success-
> ful outcomes but only to failures. If their work is too easy, they learn that it takes
> very little to succeed. Either is inappropriate and provides a pattern which fos-
> ters underachievement. (p. 92)

When teachers select and present academic tasks to their students, they need to reflect
continually on how well the task fits the students' present needs and capacities.

Glasser (1969) has been committed to improving schools throughout his career. As a
psychiatrist, he strongly believes that a person cannot be successful in life "until he can
in some way first experience success in one important part of his life" (p. 5). Glasser
recognizes that children have only two places in which to experience success: home
and school. If they are lucky enough to experience success in both settings, they are
likely to be successful in their adult lives. If they achieve success at home, they succeed
despite a lackluster school experience. But many students come from homes and neighborhoods where failure is pervasive. For these students especially, it is critical that they
experience success in school. Glasser's book, *Schools Without Failure*, offers many real-

istic and practical methods for teachers to develop a classroom environment that breeds success.

MATCHING TEACHING AND LEARNING STYLES

To motivate students fully to learn new material, it is also important to consider each student's particular *learning style*. Dunn, Beaudry, and Klavas (1989) define a learning style as "a biologically and developmentally imposed set of personal characteristics that make the same teaching method effective for some and ineffective for others" (p. 50). In other words, each person has a particular pattern of needs for optimum learning.

Some students learn best in quiet rooms; others prefer a certain level of noise in the room. Students have individual preferences for light and dark, temperature, and seating. Learning styles in enormous variety have been described, including preferences for the structure of tasks and the best time of day for learning. Although you cannot accommodate all the needs of all your students, you will want to become aware of some of the many variations in learning styles so that when a student with an unusual sensitivity or a severe impediment to learning appears in your classroom (and this will happen), you will be able to reflect on the student's particular needs and provide a learning environment or restructure your teaching style to better match the student's learning style.

A set of learning styles based on sensory preferences is especially useful to reflective teachers. Eight studies in the 1980s examined preferences for *visual, auditory,* and *kinesthetic* learning. Most learners were found to prefer receiving information either visually (by viewing or reading), auditorially (by hearing), or kinesthetically (by touching, working with, or otherwise manipulating materials). Teachers have a strong tendency to teach using the modality they prefer as a learning modality. Specifically, visual learners who rely on reading and viewing material to learn tend to rely on reading and other visual aids as teachers. Similarly, if you learn best by hearing, you may assume that others do also; as a result, you may teach primarily using lecture and discussion. Kinesthetic learners who enjoy hands-on activities as students tend to provide many of these active learning materials in their own classrooms.

> When youngsters were taught with instructional resources that both matched and mismatched their preferred modalities, they achieved statistically higher test scores in modality matched, rather than modality mismatched, treatments. (Dunn et al., 1989, p. 52)

Currently, two major approaches exist for solving this educational dilemma. One solution requires schoolwide cooperation. At each grade level, teachers may be identified as having visual, auditory, or kinesthetic preferences. Students are then tested and placed in the classroom with the teacher whose style matches their own. But this approach offers few opportunities for learners to improve their weaker learning modalities.

Another approach is for each teacher to plan conscientiously to teach using all three modalities. For example, when presenting a lesson, the teacher will provide visual aids in the form of pictures and reading material; auditory aids in the form of lecture, a discussion, or tape-recorded material; and kinesthetic aids in the form of models or other manipulative materials. Studies show that providing all three types of learning experiences to all students is likely to result in higher achievement than simply by matching one style. "When students were taught with multisensory resources, but *initially through their most preferred modality*, their scores increased even more" (Dunn et al., 1989, p. 52).

MULTIPLE INTELLIGENCES

The concept of learning styles is related to Gardner's (1983) emerging theory that humans have more than one type of intelligence. He describes seven different intelligences: linguistic, logical-mathematical, spatial, musical, bodily-kinesthetic, interpersonal, and intrapersonal. According to Gardner, each individual has a different profile of strengths and talents among these seven domains. Teachers who wish to acknowledge and support the varied intelligences of their students try to provide learning experiences that allow students to access their special strengths in learning a subject or skill.

For example, when teachers present new material to a class, they are likely to describe it in words and ask for verbal feedback for linguistically talented students. They attempt to provide problem-solving activities related to the subject for logical-mathematically oriented students. They give spatially talented students visual cues and allow them to react to the new material with drawings or diagrams. They may encourage musically talented students to commit the new material to memory via a song or allow them to create a musical response to what they have learned. They set aside time and space for bodily-kinesthetically gifted students to learn with their bodies by modeling, acting out, or pantomiming the material they are learning. For students with a special facility for interpersonal communication, teachers plan stimulating classroom discussions; and for students who are especially good at intrapersonal examination, they provide opportunities for written or oral responses related to how the new material connects with students' own sense of self.

Reflective, caring teachers are likely to value the C-M view of teaching and learning, which holds that students must be active learners rather than passive recipients of knowledge. With this philosophy, reflective teachers attempt to plan varied and interesting lessons, which their students view as authentic, meaningful learning experiences.

In this chapter, we have discussed some general presentation skills that can engage the learner's interest in the lesson that is being taught. We have also focused on the strategies that teachers use to instruct a large group of students in the basic skills of a subject. Because the techniques of direct instruction are used frequently in classrooms, it is important for the beginning teacher to become proficient in planning and teaching lessons of this type.

Although some teachers may rely on direct instruction of the entire class as their major or only teaching strategy, reflective teachers are likely to want to be able to choose from a variety of strategies. The next three chapters offer the beginning teacher a glimpse of a range of teaching methods. From these, you may begin to build a repertoire of teaching strategies to expand your own teaching skills and increase your students' motivation for learning.

⟳ Reflective Actions for Your Professional Portfolio
A Repertoire of Your Teaching Strategies

Perceptiveness: A Successful Teaching Experience

To perceive your own teaching performance, it is important to see yourself in action. Teach a lesson that is videotaped. As you observe the videotape of your own teaching, observe your presentation skills and rate your enthusiasm, clarity, smooth transitions, timing, variation, interaction, active learning, and closure. If possible, teach the lesson again, making improvements according to your perceptions.

Construction of Knowledge: Teaching Strategy Log

Begin to keep a log of all the teaching strategies you observe teachers using in the classrooms you visit. Look for strategies that develop authentic learning. Which strategies encourage students to use higher-order thinking, take part in substantive conversations, or develop depth of knowledge? Which methods allow teachers to connect subject matter to the students' world and provide a good support system for student achievement?

Values and Principles: Your Conception of How Students Learn

How do your values and principles relate to your own conception of how students learn? Is your philosophy more similar to the receptive-accrual belief system or the cognitive-mediational view? Write a statement of your philosophy on how students learn. This statement may become very useful to you when you complete applications for employment later on.

Creativity: Adapting Teaching Strategies

Select one teaching strategy that you have observed a teacher using that does not fit your philosophy of how students learn. Describe the strategy and its effects on students. Then describe what you would do to adapt that strategy to fit your philosophy and values. Tell how these changes would affect students' experiences.

Persistence and Problem Solving: Refining Strategies

Choose one of the presentation skills described in this chapter that you want to improve in your own teaching. For example, you may choose enthusiasm if you feel that your presentation style is low key. For the next four occasions that you have to work with students, focus on the skill and attempt to improve it. Ask the classroom teacher for feedback and work to refine and master this skill to your own satisfaction.

Communication Skills: Learning from Colleagues

Engage a classroom teacher in a dialogue about teaching strategies. Ask questions about why the teacher uses certain strategies and how they fit the teacher's philosophy. Listen carefully and then communicate your own opinions about the value of various strategies. Record in a journal your experiences of sharing this information and how you handled any differences of opinion that may have occurred.

References

Anderson J., & Pearson, P. (1984). A schema theoretic view of basic processes in reading. In P. Pearson (Ed.), *Handbook of reading research* (pp. 255–291). New York: Longman.

Anderson, L. (1989a). Classroom instruction. In M. Reynolds (Ed.), *Knowledge base for the beginning teacher* (pp. 101–115). Upper Saddle River, NJ: Merrill/Prentice Hall.

Anderson, L. (1989b). Learners and learning. In M. Reynolds (Ed.), *Knowledge base for the beginning teacher* (pp. 85–89). Upper Saddle River, NJ: Merrill/Prentice Hall.

Ausubel, D. P. (1960). The use of advance organizers in the learning and retention of meaningful verbal material. *Journal of Educational Psychology, 51,* 267–272.

Bransford, J. (1983). Schema activation—schema acquisition. In R. Anderson, J. Osborn, & R. Tierney (Eds.), *Learning to read in American schools* (pp. 23–37). Hillsdale, NJ: Erlbaum.

Brophy, J., & Good, T. (1986). Teacher behavior and student achievement. In M. Wittrock (Ed.), *Handbook of research on teaching* (3rd ed., pp. 328–375). Upper Saddle River, NJ: Merrill/Prentice Hall.

Dunn, R., Beaudry, J., & Klavas, A. (1989). Survey of research on learning styles. *Educational Leadership, 46*(6), 50–57.

Gagne, E. (1985). *The cognitive psychology of school learning.* Boston: Little, Brown.

Gardner, H. (1983). *Frames of mind.* New York: Basic Books.

Glasser, W. (1969). *Schools without failure.* New York: Harper & Row.

Glasser, W. (1986). *Control theory in the classroom.* New York: Harper & Row.

Good, T., & Brophy, J. (1987). *Looking in classrooms* (4th ed.). New York: Harper & Row.

Hunter, M. (1982). *Mastery teaching.* El Segundo, CA: TIP.

Jones, F. (1987). *Positive classroom discipline.* New York: McGraw-Hill.

Kounin, J. (1977). *Discipline and group management in classrooms.* New York: Kreiger.

Maslow, A. (1954). *Motivation and personality.* New York: Harper & Row.

Newman, F., & Wehlage, G. (1993). Five standards of authentic instruction. *Educational Leadership, 50*(7), 8–12.

Rimm, S. (1986). *Underachievement syndrome: Causes and cures.* Watertown, WI: Apple.

8

Discussion and Questioning Strategies That Make Learning More Authentic

When students become actively and enthusiastically interested in thinking about and discussing an idea, they are experiencing *cognitive engagement,* a powerful new concept for teachers to aim for when they select teaching strategies for their classrooms.

Cognitive engagement results in the opposite of the sterile, passive classroom environment in which students attend listlessly to the lessons and carry out their seat-work and homework with little real effort or interest. When students are fully engaged in reading, listening, discussion, or creation, the classroom climate is likely to be as lively and stimulating as a thundershower. When teachers structure classroom discussions to engage their students fully in substantive, meaningful, and highly interactive exchanges of information and ideas, authentic learning is likely to occur, even without the use of hands-on manipulatives.

Can you recall a classroom learning experience so powerful that you have almost total recall of it many years later? When you recall the event, do you feel as if you are reliving it because the memory is still so vividly etched in your mind? Do you think of this event as life changing? Perhaps it altered the way you think about an issue or caused you to change your career goal or provoked you into making a life-style change. Bloom (1981) calls these relatively rare classroom events *peak experiences.*

For many students, peak learning experiences occur during especially stimulating classroom discussions in which all members of the classroom community are expressing ideas, opinions, and points of view. Students experience these discussions as authentic, substantive, and valuable. Teachers also have a sense of exhilaration and pride when they are able to create the environment and structure needed for such powerful exchanges. In this chapter, we will examine some of the strategies you can use to stimulate and guide substantive and satisfying classroom discussions.

Asking Questions That Stimulate Higher-Level Thinking

Imagine you are observing a classroom discussion after the students have read a biography of Dr. Martin Luther King, Jr. The teacher asks the following questions:

When and where was Dr. King born?

Who were the other members of his family?

How did King's father and mother earn a living?

What career did Dr. King choose?

What does the term *ghetto* mean?

What does *prejudice* mean?

What did Dr. King accomplish that earned him the Nobel Peace Prize?

As you watch and listen to this discussion, you might reflect on the way you would lead it and the questions you would like to ask the students. Perhaps you believe that there are other, very different types of questions that the teacher could use to stimulate higher-level thinking and engage the students in a discussion that connects what they've read to their own lives.

Many reflective teachers use Bloom's taxonomy (Bloom, Engelhart, Furst, Hill, & Krathwohl, 1956) to think of discussion questions that promote the use of higher-level thinking processes. Discussion questions can be readily planned at every level of the taxonomy, just as other learning experiences are planned. The term *higher-level* refers to the top four levels of the hierarchy:

Higher-Level Thinking Processes
>   Evaluation
>   Synthesis
>   Analysis
>   Application

Lower-Level Thinking Processes
>   Comprehension
>   Knowledge

In the previous example, the teacher has asked only lower-level (knowledge and comprehension) questions. But you can plan your discussions to highlight the thinking processes of application, analysis, synthesis, and evaluation. Although this system can be used at any grade level and with any topic, the following examples are taken from the discussion of Dr. King's biography.

KNOWLEDGE LEVEL

At this level, the learners are asked to recall specific bits of information, such as terminology, facts, and details:

>   When and where was King born?
>   Who were the other members of his family?
>   What were the jobs King's father did to earn a living?
>   What jobs did his mother do?
>   What career did Dr. King choose?

COMPREHENSION LEVEL

At this level, the learners are asked to summarize and describe the main ideas of the subject matter in their own words:

>   What does the term *ghetto* mean?
>   What does *prejudice* mean?

How did the church affect King's life?

What did Dr. King accomplish that earned him the Nobel Peace Prize?

While the teacher in the previous example stopped here, a reflective teacher is likely to use those questions only as a beginning to establish the basic facts and ideas so that the class can then begin to engage in a spirited discussion of how Dr. King's life and accomplishments have affected their own lives.

APPLICATION LEVEL

At this level, the learners are asked to apply what they have learned to their own lives or to other situations:

Are there ghettos in this community? What are they and who is affected by them?

Give an example of prejudice that has affected you.

If Dr. King were alive today, what do you think he would be most concerned about? What do you think he would do about it?

ANALYSIS LEVEL

At this level, the learners are asked to describe patterns, cause-and-effect relationships, comparisons, and contrasts:

How did Rosa Parks's decision to sit in the front of the bus change King's life? How did her decision change history?

In what ways was Dr. King a minister, a politician, and a teacher?

If Dr. King had never been born, how would your life be different today?

SYNTHESIS LEVEL

At this level, the learners are asked to contribute a new and original idea on the topic:

Complete this phrase: I have a dream that one day. . . .

If there were suddenly a strong new prejudice against people that look just like you, what would you do about it?

How can we, as a class, put some of Dr. King's dreams into action?

EVALUATION LEVEL

At this level, the learners are asked to express their own opinions or make judgments about some aspect of the topic:

What do you believe was Dr. King's greatest contribution?

Which promotes greater social change: nonviolence or violence? Give a rationale or example to defend your answer.

What social problem do you most want to change in your life?

Some teachers find that Bloom's taxonomy is a useful and comprehensive guide for planning classroom discussion questions as well as other classroom activities. Others find that the taxonomy is more complex than they desire and that it is difficult to discriminate among some of the levels, such as comprehension and analysis or application and synthesis. Other systems of classifying thinking processes are available. Doyle (1986) proposes that teachers plan classroom tasks in four categories that are readily applicable to classroom discussions: (1) memory tasks, (2) procedural or routine tasks, (3) comprehension tasks, and (4) opinion tasks.

Classroom questions and discussion starters can be created to fit these four task levels, as follows:

1. *Memory questions:*   Learners are asked to reproduce information they have read or heard before.
   When and where was Dr. King born?

   Who were the other members of his family?

2. *Procedural or routine questions:*   Learners are asked to supply simple answers with only one correct response.
   What jobs did King's father and mother do to earn a living?

   What career did Dr. King choose?

3. *Comprehension questions:*   Learners are asked to consider known data and apply them to a new and unfamiliar context.
   What does the term *ghetto* mean?

   What does *prejudice* mean?

   How did the church affect King's life?

   What did Dr. King accomplish that earned him the Nobel Peace Prize?

   How did Rosa Parks's decision to sit in the front of the bus change King's life? How did her decision change history?

   In what ways was Dr. King a minister, a politician, a teacher?

4. *Opinion questions:*   Learners are asked to express their own point of view on an issue, with no correct answer expected.
   Are there ghettos in this community? What are they and who is affected by them?

   Give an example of prejudice that has affected you.

   If Dr. King were alive today, what do you think he would be most concerned about? What do you think he would do about it?

   Complete this phrase: I have a dream that one day. . . .

If there were suddenly a strong new prejudice against people who look just like you, what would you do about it?

What do you believe was Dr. King's greatest contribution?

What can we, as a class, do to carry out some of Dr. King's dream?

Which promotes more social change: nonviolence or violence? Give a rationale or example to defend your answer.

What social problem do you most want to change in your life?

You will notice that the questions in Doyle's four categories are the same as the ones listed in the taxonomy's six levels. Questions at the comprehension and analysis levels are both contained in Doyle's comprehension category, and questions at the application, synthesis, and evaluation levels are contained in the opinion category. Both of these systems offer teachers a comprehensive framework for planning a range of thought-provoking questions. You may choose to write out the questions you ask ahead of time, or you may just remind yourself as you participate in a discussion that you need to include questions from the higher-level thinking categories.

Strategies for Authentic Discussions

In some classrooms, what pass for discussions are really dull and repetitive question-and-answer periods. Some teachers may simply read aloud a list of questions from the teachers' manual of the textbook and call on students to recite the answers. As you probably recall from your own school experiences, when this type of "discussion" occurs, many students disengage entirely. They read ahead, doodle, or do homework surreptitiously. They seldom listen to their classmates' responses; and when it is their turn to recite, they frequently cannot find their place in the list of questions.

Reflective teachers value the process of considering alternatives and debating opinions and ideas. That is how reflective teachers approach the world themselves, and they are likely to want to stimulate the same types of behavior among their students.

Authentic learning experiences depend heavily on the promotion of high-quality and actively engaged thinking. Teachers who are committed to creating authentic learning for their students do so by planning discussions that stimulate *higher-level thinking processes, problem-solving skills, critical thinking,* and *creative thinking* and acknowledge the *multiple intelligences* of their students.

These terms and concepts can be confusing and overwhelming for the beginning teacher, who may think it is necessary to establish separate programs for each of them. That is not the case, however. It is possible to discover common attributes among them and plan classroom discussions and other experiences that promote high-level thinking, problem-solving skills, and critical and creative thinking in all seven of the multiple intelligences at the same time. One question may pose a problem; another may call for a creative response; a third may be analytical; and a fourth may ask students to evaluate a situation and make a critical judgment. The best (which is to say, the most highly engaging) classroom discussions do all of these in a spontaneous, nonregimented way.

The following sections describe various thinking processes along with alternatives for planning classroom discussions to promote these processes. As you read these sections, reflect on the similarities and differences; look for patterns and sequences; and consider how you would use, modify, and adapt these systems in your classroom.

Although these processes can be applied to both academic and nonacademic areas of the curriculum, we will illustrate how classroom discussions are created and managed, using the topic of racial discrimination as a common theme. In this example, the operational goal is to promote understanding of how racial discrimination affects the lives of human beings and to generate a sense of respect for individuals who are different from oneself.

PROBLEM-SOLVING DISCUSSIONS

Much has been written about the need for developing students' problem-solving and decision-making abilities. This can be done by presenting students with a complex problem and providing adequate scaffolding support for them to learn how to solve problems. Although some solutions require paper and pencil or a hands-on experimental approach, classroom discussion can solve other problems.

To create productive problem-solving discussions, the teacher must understand the processes involved in problem-solving and then structure the questions to guide students through that process. A problem is said to exist when "one has a goal and has not yet identified a means for reaching that goal. The problem may be wanting to answer a question, to prove a theorem, to be accepted or to get a job" (Gagne, 1985, p. 138).

According to cognitive psychologists, the framework for solving a problem consists of identifying a goal, a starting place, and all possible solution paths from the starting place to the goal. Some individuals are efficient and productive problem solvers; others are not. An excellent classroom goal for the beginning teacher is to help students become more efficient and more productive problem solvers.

Nonproductive problem solvers are likely to have difficulty identifying or defining the problem. They may simply feel that a puzzling situation exists, but they may not be aware of the real nature of the problem. Students who are poor problem solvers need experience in facing puzzling situations and defining problems. They also need experience in identifying and selecting worthwhile goals.

When a problem has been defined and a goal established, it is still possible to be either efficient or inefficient in reaching the goal. Efficiency in problem solving can be increased when students learn how to identify the alternative strategies to reach a chosen goal and recognize which ones are likely to provide the best and quickest routes to success. This can be done by helping students visualize the probable effects of each alternative and applying criteria to help them choose the most valuable means of solving the problem they have defined.

As in the teaching of higher-level thinking processes, several useful systems are available to teachers who want to teach students to become better problem solvers. Osborne (1963) proposed the technique known as *brainstorming*, which includes four basic steps:

1. Defining the problem
2. Generating, without criticism or evaluation, as many solutions as possible

3. Deciding on criteria for judging the solutions generated
4. Using these criteria to select the best possible solution

Brainstorming is an excellent way to generate classroom discussion about a puzzling issue. Rather than formulating a series of questions, the teacher supplies a dilemma or a puzzle, teaches the students the steps involved in brainstorming, and then leads them through the process itself.

In discussing the life of Martin Luther King, Jr., and helping students to understand the effects of racial discrimination, the teacher might use a portion of the classroom discussion to brainstorm answers to one of the most perplexing questions. For example, the teacher might choose to use brainstorming to expand discussion of the following question:

> If Dr. King were alive today, what do you think he would be most concerned about? What do you think he would do about it?

The techniques of brainstorming call for the teacher to pose the question or problem in such a way that it engages students' interest and motivates them to take it seriously. Because students may not be proficient at discussion of this sort, it is frequently necessary for the teacher to give additional cues and suggestions as a scaffold. In this instance, the teacher might need to pose the original question and then follow it up with prompts such as these:

> What do you think he'd be concerned about in our community?
>
> What has been in the news lately that might alarm him?
>
> Who are the people in the world who are presently in need?
>
> What about threats to our environment?

Open-ended questions such as these will generate many more responses than if they were not used. After recording all of the student responses on the chalkboard, the teacher leads the students through a process of selecting the most important items for further consideration. This may be done by a vote or general consensus. When the list has been narrowed to several important issues, the teacher must then lead the students through the process of establishing criteria for judging the items.

Because the question is related to Martin Luther King, Jr.'s, values, one possible criterion is to judge whether King showed concern for the issue in his lifetime. Another criterion might be the number of people who are threatened or hurt by the problem. After judging the items by these criteria, the class makes a judgment about which items would most concern King. Then the process of brainstorming begins again, but this time the problem the class is considering is what King would be likely to do to help solve the problem. Generating responses to the first question—"If Dr. King were alive today, what would he be most concerned about?"—will help students understand the many aspects of racial discrimination that exist today. By selecting one of these as the main concern and generating responses to the question "What do you think he would do about it?" the students will reflect on their own responsibilities to other human beings and on ways to increase tolerance and build a sense of community in their neighborhoods.

To moderate a brainstorming discussion, the teacher faithfully records every response generated by the students, no matter how trivial or impossible it sounds. The teacher then leads students through the process of eliminating the least important items and finally works through a process of establishing criteria to use in evaluating the best possible solutions.

Brainstorming alone does not solve problems. It merely trains students to think productively about problems and consider many alternative solutions. In some classrooms, teachers may wish to extend the hypothetical discussion of possible solutions to an actual attempt to solve a problem or at least contribute to a solution.

GROUP INVESTIGATIONS

Occasionally, a crisis or an unusual event will excite students' interest and concern. When the topic is appropriate, and especially if it relates to the curriculum for that grade level, teachers allow students to participate in an investigation of the puzzling event to learn as much as they can about the subject and, in the process, learn research and communication skills. Often teachers create puzzling situations or present unusual stimuli as a means of causing students to become curious and learn how to inquire and investigate to gather information that leads to accurate assessments and judgments.

Perhaps there is a change in local government or a national election that students want to know more about. Perhaps a change occurs in the way their own school is managed, or a community event that affects their lives unfolds around them. The first hint of student interest may occur in a classroom discussion. To the extent that reflective teachers are sensitive to their students' concerns, they may wish to allow students time to talk about the event.

The first discussion of the event may simply be time to air students' early opinions and express their feelings about the event. If the teacher decides that the event is a worthwhile issue, the class may be encouraged to read about it, ask questions, or interview other members of the community and bring back their findings for more expanded discussions. These, in turn, may lead students to form small investigative groups that attempt to discover as much as they can about the event and even suggest solutions to the problems or issues under discussion.

The teacher's role in this type of investigative discussion is to encourage students to find out more about the subject and to allow them opportunities to express their opinions and share their findings. The discussion may continue for a few days or a few weeks, depending upon the seriousness of the event and its impact on the students' lives. Under the guidance of a caring, reflective teacher, this type of discussion is authentic learning at its very best.

When teachers want to stimulate curiosity and discussion, they may present a social dilemma or demonstrate a strange event. For example, the teacher may drop a number of different fruits and vegetables into a large, clear bowl of water, asking students to predict and observe which will sink and which will float. Students are encouraged to ask the teacher questions and to formulate hypotheses about floating and sinking objects. As the discussion progresses, the large group discussion may be adjourned to allow small groups to make investigations of their own, reaching their own conclusions. After small group investigations are completed, class members reconvene to share their hypotheses, demonstrate their investigations, and present their conclusions.

DISCUSSIONS THAT PROMOTE CRITICAL THINKING

The term *critical thinking* is not a separate and distinct concept that is different from higher-level thinking processes and problem solving. It overlaps both of them. It is presented here in a separate section because, during the past few years, it has become a field of study with its own research base and suggested classroom processes.

The field of study known as critical thinking grew out of the philosophical study of logic, which was designed to train people to think about a single hypothesis deductively to arrive at a rationale conclusion. But in the late 1960s, deBono (1967) observed that, although logical thinkers were prepared to deal with a single issue in depth, they were not prepared to deal with unexpected evidence or ideas.

Using the analogy of digging for treasure, deBono (1967) suggested that, in thinking about a hypothesis, a logical thinker might dig a deeper and bigger hole; but if the hole is not in the right place, then no amount of digging will improve the solution. In contrast, deBono (1967) believed that a critical thinker would be more flexible than a logical thinker; after considering a problem or issue, the critical thinker would be able to select from a toolbox of thinking skills that allows the individual to clarify where to dig, select from alternative digging methods, use a variety of procedures to analyze the contents of the hole, and judge the worth of what is excavated.

Critical thinking, then, is partially defined as a complex set of thinking skills and processes that are believed to lead to fair and useful judgments. Lipman (1988) points out the strong association between the words *criteria* and *critical thinking*. Through the use of problem-solving discussions, students learn the technique of brainstorming and applying criteria to select the best solution.

But critical thinking is a much more multifaceted concept than problem solving. Critical thinking involves more than simply training students to use a set of strategies or procedures. It also involves establishing some affective goals for students to support them in becoming more independent and open-minded. Paul (1988), director of the Center of Critical Thinking at Sonoma State University in Rohnert Park, California, proposes that some of the affective attributes of critical thinking include independence, avoidance of egocentricity and stereotyping, and suspension of judgment until appropriate evidence has been gathered.

Paul recommends that school curricula be designed to teach students cognitive strategies such as observation, focusing on a question, distinguishing facts from opinions, distinguishing relevant from irrelevant information, judging credibility of sources, recognizing contradictions, making inferences, and drawing conclusions. Because almost every specialist in critical thinking proposes a slightly different set of thinking processes and skills that compose critical thinking, reflective teachers need to judge for themselves which of the strategies to stress in their own classrooms.

Raths, Wasserman, Jonas, and Rothstein (1986) describe a set of thinking operations that they believe compose critical thinking and then provide a wealth of practical classroom applications at both the elementary and secondary levels. The operations they emphasize are comparing, summarizing, observing, classifying, interpreting, criticizing, looking for assumptions, imagining, collecting and organizing data, applying facts and principles in new situations, and decision making.

To train students systematically to become better thinkers, Raths et al. (1986) suggest that teachers select one thinking operation at a time and tell the class that they will be focusing on improving this thinking skill. The teacher then proposes a discussion topic, listens attentively to students' responses, and records them if appropriate. In the following sections, some of their specific suggestions are paraphrased.

DISCUSSIONS THAT IMPROVE OBSERVATION SKILLS

Whenever possible in your curriculum, bring in photos or objects related to the subject you are studying. Invite students to read their stories, essays, or poems aloud for other students to listen and respond to. You may even be able to stage an event to elicit student observation skills. For example, as you study the concept of community, ask some students to role-play a disagreement. Then ask them to describe what they observed, using as many details as they can. Call on as many students as possible and encourage each of them to make their own response to the situation. If they seem to be making impetuous or repetitive observations, guide their thinking with questions that ask them to explain or support their observations.

Show your students that they can observe with all five senses, not just sight. As you study nutrition, for example, allow students to taste a variety of foods and describe their taste observations. During a study of sound waves, provide a variety of different sounds and ask students to identify the objects they have heard. The more students use their five senses and discuss what they observe, the more likely they are to develop accurate, detailed schemata for the subject matter they are studying.

DISCUSSIONS THAT ENHANCE COMPARING SKILLS

In classroom discussions, compare two or more objects, stories, characters, or events by asking students first to articulate ways that the two subjects are the same. Take as many responses as possible. Then ask students to tell how the two are different. This type of discussion can occur in any subject area. You may ask them to compare fractions with percentages in math, George Washington and Abraham Lincoln in history, Somalia and the United States in geography, electric- and gasoline-powered engines in science, or the wording and effects of two different classroom rules in a classroom meeting.

DISCUSSIONS THAT GUIDE CLASSIFICATION SKILLS

Introduce a collection of words or, for young children, a set of manipulative materials appropriate to their grade level. For example, you may use a collection of buttons, small toys, macaroni shapes, or shells. When possible, conduct this type of discussion using cooperative groups. Ask each group to examine the collection, look for distinguishing attributes, and create a system for classifying the objects into groups. During follow-up discussions, a spokesperson for each group can describe the attributes they observed and present a rationale for the classification system they used.

Older children can classify the words on their spelling lists, books or stories they have read, foods, games, clothing, famous people, or television programs. The best results occur when the teacher has no preestablished criteria or notion of right or wrong classification systems. As children discuss the characteristics of the shells or television programs they are classifying, they may discover some of the same attributes that adults have already described, or they may discover a completely original rationale on which to base their categories. The object of the discussion is not to get the most "right" answers but to participate in the open-ended process of sharing their observations and making critical judgments they can defend with evidence.

DISCUSSIONS THAT IDENTIFY ASSUMPTIONS

Use advertisements for products your students want to buy as a means of stimulating a discussion to identify assumptions people make. Show a newspaper ad for a product and ask students to describe what they believe the product will be like based on the advertisement alone. Then discuss the actual product and compare the students' prior assumptions with the real item.

Talk about assumptions human beings make about each other. Ask students to examine the meaning of clothing fads in their lives. Whenever a subject arises that illustrates the effects of making decisions based on assumptions, take the time to discuss these events with your class. For example, ask students to discuss what assumptions are being made when they hear someone say, "He's wrong," or "She's the smartest girl in the class."

SOCRATIC DIALOGUES

One form of discussion that reveals individual assumptions to the speaker and the listeners at the same time is the technique known as *Socratic dialogue,* in which the teacher probes to stimulate more in-depth thinking among students. Teachers who use this method believe that individuals have many legitimate differences in opinion and values. They want to encourage their students to listen to each other to learn different points of view.

To conduct a Socratic dialogue, the teacher presents an interesting issue to the class and asks an individual to state an opinion on the case. With each participant, the teacher probes by asking the student to identify the assumptions and values that led to this opinion. Further questions may be posed to the same student to encourage clarification of the consequences of the student's opinion or the relative importance it has in the student's priorities.

This type of exchange between the teacher and one student may take several minutes and from 3 to 10 questions. While the teacher conducts the discussion with one student, the others are expected to listen carefully, comparing what they believe to what is being said by their classmate. Another student with a different opinion is likely to be the next subject of the Socratic dialogue. When the teacher believes that the most important issues have been raised by the dialogues, then a general class discussion can be used to express how opinions may have been changed by listening or participating in the Socratic dialogues.

DISCUSSIONS THAT ENHANCE CREATIVE THINKING

Can individuals learn to be creative? Perhaps the more important question is, Do individuals learn to be uncreative? A century ago, William James (1890) stated his belief that education trains students to become "old fogies" in the early grades by training them to adopt habits of convergent, conformist thinking.

Divergent thinking is the opposite of convergent thinking in that it deviates from common understanding and accepted patterns. Guilford (1967) contributed a definition of divergent thinking that is still well accepted and has become the basis for E. Paul Torrance's (1966–1984) well-known tests for creativity. Guilford describes (and Torrance's test measures) four attributes of divergent thinking: *fluency, flexibility, originality,* and *elaboration.* In other words, a divergent thinker is one who generates many ideas (fluency), is able to break with conformist or set ideas (flexibility), suggests ideas that are new in the present context (originality), and contributes details that extend or support the idea beyond a single thought (elaboration).

Classroom discussions can be designed to help students develop these four attributes of creativity. In a technique similar to brainstorming, the teacher can ask students to generate many responses to a single question as a means of helping them to become more fluent in their thinking. For example, given our topic of King's "I have a dream" speech, the teacher may begin the process with the unfinished sentence, "I have a dream that someday. . . . "

Students may be asked to write their own responses for several minutes before the actual discussion begins. This allows each student to work for fluency individually. Then the ideas on paper are shared, and other new ideas are created as a result of the discussion. To promote flexibility, the teacher may ask students to imagine making their dreams come true and suggest ways that they could do this, using flexible and original strategies rather than rigid and ordinary methods. Finally, to extend the students' elaborative thought, the teacher may select one dream and ask the entire class to focus on it and create a more detailed vision and a more in-depth plan to accomplish it.

Einstein and Infeld (1938) add a further dimension to our understanding of creative thinking:

> The formulation of a problem is often more essential than its solution, which may be merely a matter of mathematical or experimental skill. To raise new questions, new possibilities, to regard old problems from a new angle, requires creative imagination and marks real advance in science. (p. 92)

Problem solving, then, is related to creative thinking. It is readily apparent that the methods described for improving problem solving involve critical thinking and that both involve the use of higher-level thinking processes. Whatever we call it, the goal of aiding students in developing better thinking skills is an integral part of any classroom discussion.

Just as we respect Einstein's ability to pose new problems, so should we respect and develop our own and our students' capacity to ask questions and suggest new ways of solving age-old problems. Certainly, the teaching profession needs people with the capability of regarding old educational problems from a new angle. Often it is the newest and youngest members of a faculty who see things from a helpful new perspective and suggest new ways of dealing with difficult school issues.

Another dimension of creativity involves the production of something useful, interesting, or otherwise valued by at least a small segment of society. In synthesis, a creative thinker is one who poses new problems, raises new questions, and then suggests solutions that are characterized by fluency, flexibility, originality, and elaboration. The solutions result in a product unique for that individual in those circumstances.

DISCUSSIONS THAT ENCOURAGE IMAGINATION AND INVENTIVENESS

In the process of discussing almost any type of subject, teachers always have opportunities to ask students to consider, "What if . . . ?"

> Imagine living on an island with no electricity. What would your life be like? How would it be different than it is now?
>
> What could we do to make our school a better place?
>
> What would you do if you were the main character in the story? How would your actions change the ending of the book?

For many reflective teachers, these questions are as important as those that test student recall of information or understanding of the main idea. While it is seldom necessary to plan a discussion with the sole intent of stimulating children's imagination, it is a worthy goal to include these types of questions in any classroom discussion.

Another technique is to assign a group of students a certain task that requires them to discuss strategies and invent a method to carry it out. For example, give students a single dollar bill and ask them to discover how high a stack of one million dollar bills would be. Give them a few pieces of cloth and some string and ask them to make an effective parachute. Have each group work together to design one map of the school property. These real-life and simulated tasks provide incentives for authentic discussions on substantive and meaningful topics.

PREWRITING DISCUSSIONS

Another method teachers may use is to focus on images, analogies, and metaphors in creative discussions. These are very effective discussions before students begin writing, encouraging students to use these word pictures in their writing as well. Gordon and Poze (1975) suggest that analogies allow us to make the strange familiar and the familiar strange. In discussions, teachers can present an unfamiliar idea or object and assist students in describing it using sensory images or comparing it with another, more familiar concept. For example, when presented with a rusty old lawnmower engine, students may be led to describe it according to size, shape, imaginary sounds, or uses. They can compare it to other, more familiar objects. The teacher may ask students what the machine reminds them of. This may generate responses such as "The machine is like my old shoes." Then the teacher probes by asking the child to tell why the machine and the old shoes are alike: "Because they are both old and muddy." Another child may see the machine in a whole different context: "The machine is like a kangaroo because it has a lot of secret compartments." Discussions like this can begin to have a life of their own and can lead to fresh new ways to express one's ideas.

Do schools enhance or undermine the conditions and processes that encourage creativity? Do textbooks, curriculum guides, rules, regulations, and expectations support the development of creative thinking and the process needed to create a unique product? Caring and reflective teachers do. They work very hard to create stimulating classroom discussions that assist students in learning to become creative thinkers rather than nine-year-old fogies.

DISCUSSIONS THAT ADDRESS MULTIPLE INTELLIGENCES

Thomas Armstrong was asked by a Wisconsin school district to create a format for teaching children to tell time, using all seven of the multiple intelligences described by Gardner (1983) in *Frames of Mind.* To create this set of learning experiences, he linked his instructional objective to "words, numbers or logic, pictures, music, the body, social interaction, and/or personal experience" (Armstrong, 1994, p. 26).

Armstrong told a story about a land of No Time and how confusing it was for people who lived there. The king and queen sent a group of explorers in quest of time, which was rumored to exist beyond their horizons. The explorers met a family named the O'Clocks, who had 12 children: one, two, three . . . twelve.

After telling the story, Armstrong engaged the students in verbal experiences of retelling and restating what they had learned. He asked questions that engaged students in logical and mathematical problem solving to figure out the relationships among the O'Clocks. He used visual aids such as clock faces for spatially talented learners and allowed bodily-kinesthetic learners to act out the times while musically oriented youngsters sang special rhyming songs for each hour.

> My name's One O'clock
> I tell time
> Listen while I sing
> My timely little chime
> BONG! (Armstrong, 1994, p. 26)

Everyone danced to the tune of Bill Haley's "Rock Around the Clock," and students wrote stories illustrated with clock faces showing different times. In a subsequent discussion, they read aloud and shared their pictures and stories.

As Armstrong plans classroom discussions, he asks himself the following questions to guide himself through the planning process (Armstrong, 1994, p. 29):

Linguistic: How can I use the spoken or written word?

Logical-mathematical: How can I bring in numbers, calculations, logic, classifications, or critical thinking?

Spatial: How can I use visual aids, visualization, color, art, metaphor, or visual organizers?

Musical: How can I bring in music or environmental sounds, or set key points in a rhythm or melody?

Bodily-kinesthetic: How can I involve the whole body, or hands-on experiences?

Interpersonal: How can I engage students in peer or cross-age sharing, cooperative learning, or large group simulation?

Intrapersonal: How can I evoke personal feelings or memories or give students choices?

THE ROLE OF THE TEACHER IN LEADING DISCUSSIONS

Discussions that promote the use of critical thinking can be exciting classroom events for both students and teachers, but beginning teachers may find it difficult to elicit responses from students who are not used to taking part in such activities. Raths et al. (1986) asks:

> What if you ask a wonderful question and the pupils don't respond?
> There is nothing quite so demoralizing for a teacher as a lack of response from students.
> "Now boys and girls, how do you think the sound got onto this tape?"
> No response. Interminable silence. Finally the teacher leaps in to break the tension and gives the answer. Everybody, including the teacher, visibly relaxes. Whew! Let's not try that again. (p. 183)

This example of a nondiscussion is more common than is desirable. Students in your classroom may not have had opportunities to think creatively and express their own ideas. If not, they may be reluctant to do so at first. They may believe that you expect one right answer, just as most of their teachers have in the past. Because they do not know the one right answer, they may prefer to remain quiet rather than embarrass themselves by giving a wrong answer. Your response to their silence will tell them a great deal. If you jump in with your own response, they will learn that their own responses were not really wanted after all.

Scaffolding is a necessary component of teaching critical thinking and discussion strategies to students. Be explicit about what you do expect from them in a discussion. Tell them that there are no wrong answers and that all opinions are valued. If they still hesitate, provide cues and prompts without providing answers. Simplify or rephrase the question so that they are able to answer it. If the question "How do you think the sound got on this tape?" gets no response, rephrase it. "What sounds do you hear on this tape? Can you imagine how those sounds were captured on a piece of plastic like this? Do you think machinery was used? What kinds of machines are able to copy sounds?" These supporting questions provide scaffolds for thinking and talking about unknown and unfamiliar ideas.

In the following reflection, Mary O'Donnell, a high school history teacher who has been teaching for two years, describes how she works to develop a classroom climate that encourages active discussion and provides a support system for reluctant participants.

Case 8.1 ⊃ Reflective Action
Developing a Classroom Climate to Encourage Discussion

Mary O'Donnell, History Teacher
Crystal Lake South High School, Crystal Lake, Illinois

Perceptiveness

In my classroom, I want to make history come alive so that my students will feel like they not only understand history, but that they feel that they are part of history. To capture my students' interest and give them a sense of ownership, I use a variety of teaching strategies, including having students go out into the community to write and create their own local history. However, it isn't always possible to do such projects. So, even when we are stuck in the classroom, I want to make our discussions about historical events and issues dynamic and exciting.

Constructing Knowledge

The questions I continually ask myself are "How do I make history relevant to my students' lives? How do I encourage lively discussions that involve as many students as possible? What can I do to help insecure students recognize that their view of history is valid and important to our class so that they will feel comfortable speaking up?"

Whenever I get an opportunity to observe other teachers, I focus on their discussion strategies. Craig Pfannkuche, my cooperating teacher during student teaching, was an especially valuable resource for me. His classes always had the liveliest (and loudest) discussions of any I've ever observed. At the end of a class periods, his students would often stay to continue the discussion they had started in class. I wanted to develop that same kind of climate in my classroom.

What I discovered from my observations was that the most successful discussions were led by teachers who had created a classroom climate that made their students feel secure. Students in these classrooms seemed to believe that their opinions were valuable not just to the teacher but to their classmates as well. There was a sense of mutual respect that made the majority of students feel comfortable contributing to the discussions. I knew then that in order to encourage lively and active discussion in my classroom, I had to create a safe and supportive emotional climate for my students.

Clarifying Values and Principles

One major reason that I became a history teacher is to encourage students to take an active civic role as adults in their community. Students who recognize that they have the ability to analyze historical and current events and make critical decisions and judgments about these events will be empowered to become voters, community leaders, and political leaders. Another strong belief that I hold is that each individual should respect the values and opinions of every other individual in our society. Based on these beliefs, I have tried to establish an understanding with my students that respect is the basic social rule of my classroom.

Creativity

To reach my goal of having lively, diverse, and mutually respectful discussions, I considered using cooperative learning. Although I do find cooperative learning useful for small group discussions, I still find it necessary to allow the class as a whole to the various opinions they hold on each important issue.

Early in my teaching career, I considered using wide-open, unrestrained discussions in the hope that the students would take the class into all the possible realms, but I quickly found that these discussions could become chaotic and uncomfortable to manage.

Persistence and Problem Solving

To make my discussions exciting but manageable, I realized that I would have to establish some way to make sure that only one person spoke at a time. I set up a modified form of parliamentary procedure, which requires that the class recognize that the person speaking has the right to the floor until he or she is finished talking. In my classroom discussions, I take the role of parliamentarian. Sometimes I call on students to recognize their right to speak, but as the year progresses and the students show an understanding of parliamentary procedures themselves, I have been able to allow students to speak up when they want to comment without raising their hands. When a person begins to speak in my classroom, the rest of the class has learned to recognize that the speaker "has the floor" until he or she is finished, at which time someone else can feel free to speak.

To make these discussions work, I have learned that I must be well prepared with a good list of questions that will elicit the types of student responses that I want. I design my questions to confront students with tough issues and encourage them to use critical thinking in response.

For example, in discussing Christopher Columbus, I may begin with such simple questions as "What were the names of the three ships?" Then I ask, "Why are you all able to recite these names so easily? Why is Columbus so important? Wasn't he just a bad navigator who happened to land on an island in the Bahamas? Does he really deserve the credit he receives?"

Communication Skills

The first week of school, I plan discussions on interesting topics to train my students to use parliamentary rules and to encourage all of them to contribute to discussions. I tell them that we all want to hear what they have to say. I explain that when someone is speaking, they have the right to speak without interruption until they are finished. For the first few weeks of school, I have to remind students to remain quiet while a classmate is speaking. I try to call on quiet students and encourage them to say what they are thinking. I may stop the discussion for a minute and ask students to reflect on what has been said so far. Then I will ask a quiet student, "Which of the opinions that you've heard do you believe has the most historical merit?" That allows the listener to become an active participant.

The most dramatic results of our discussions are evident in my students' essays and other writing assignments. In their written work, students remember and sometimes even paraphrase what they've learned from other students. I find myself using their views as well. My students enjoy our discussions so much that they frequently initiate discussions themselves. I get excited when I notice that my students are beginning to ask one another what they think. As the year progresses, the most outgoing students will call on their quieter classmates to ask them their opinions. When this happens, I believe that my principles of mutual respect for diverse opinions and equal access to knowledge are being successfully passed on to my students.

Another consideration in leading discussions is to *value* silence rather than fear it. Silence can indicate that students are truly engaged in reflection. By allowing a few moments of silence, a teacher may find that the resulting discussions are much more creative and productive. Students need time to process the question. They need time to bring forward the necessary schema to their working memories and to consider the question in light of what they already know about the topic. Some students need more time than others to see connections between new ideas and already stored information and to generate a response of their own.

Some teachers consciously use *wait time*, requiring a short period of silence after each significant question is asked. Students are taught to listen quietly, then think quietly for several seconds and not raise their hands to respond until the wait time has passed. Rowe (1974) found that when teachers used a wait time of 3–5 seconds, more students were able to generate a response to the question. Without a planned wait time, the same group of fast-thinking students are likely to dominate all discussions. With the wait time, even slower-thinking students will have an opportunity to consider what it is they do believe before hearing the opinions of others.

Lyman (1989) recommends that teachers employ a system called *listen, think, pair, share* to improve both the quantity and the quality of discussion responses. This technique employs a structured wait time at two different points in the discussion. When a question is asked, wait time goes into effect while students jot down ideas and think about their responses. Students are then expected to discuss their ideas in pairs for a minute. Then a general discussion takes place. After each student makes a contribution, other members of the class are expected to employ a second wait time of 3–5 seconds to process what their classmate has said before they raise their hands to respond.

The quantity and quality of students' responses may be improved by introducing the questions early in the class period, followed by reading, a lecture, or another type of presentation and actual discussion of the questions themselves. This strategy follows the principle of using the question as an advance organizer. Giving students the question before presentation of new material alerts them to what to listen or read for and allows sufficient time for them to process the information they receive in terms of the question. When teachers use this technique, they rarely experience a silent response.

Another strategy that promotes highly interactive discussions involves the physical setup in the classroom. To facilitate critical and creative thinking, students must be able to hear and see one another during the discussion. Arranging the chairs in a circle, rectangle, U-shape, or semicircle will ensure that each student feels like a contributing member of a group.

Meyers (1986) notes that a hospitable classroom environment is the most important factor in engaging students' attention and interest and promoting their creative responses during discussion:

> Much of the success in teaching critical thinking rests with the tone that teachers set in their classrooms. Students must be led gently into the active roles of discussing, dialoguing, and problem-solving. They will watch very carefully to see how respectfully teachers field comments and will quickly pick up nonverbal cues that show how open teachers really are to student questions and contributions. (p. 67)

Reflective teachers are critical and creative thinkers themselves. They welcome opportunities to model their own thinking strategies for their students and plan experiences that encourage the development of their students' higher-level thinking processes. They are likely to make even the simplest discussion an exercise in problem solving, reasoning, logic, and creative and independent thinking. They examine the subjects taught in the curriculum in search of ways to allow their students to learn to think and communicate their ideas. They plan discussions involving the creation and testing of hypotheses in science. They promote thinking that avoids stereotypes and egocentricity in social studies. They teach their students to suspend judgment when they lack sufficient evidence in discussions of math problems. They promote flexible, original thinking in discussions of literature. Discussions in every part of the curriculum can be crafted in ways that teach individuals to think reflectively, critically, and creatively.

⊃ Reflective Actions for Your Professional Portfolio
Videotape and Reflection of Your Class Discussion

Perceptiveness: Assess Your Previous Experiences
Write about your own experiences as a participant in discussions. Do you enjoy contributing ideas? What type of support do you need from a teacher or a discussion leader to encourage you to take a more active role?

Write about your own experiences in leading discussions. Are you comfortable in the role of leader? Do you tend to ask good questions spontaneously? Do you need to prepare carefully and write questions ahead of time?

Construction of Knowledge: Gather Information
What type of discussion leader do you want to be? What do you need to do to improve your ability to be that kind of facilitator? Follow up some of the leads in the references in this chapter to read more about strategies that you can incorporate into your repertoire.

Values and Principles: Clarify Your Expectations
Despite what people say about their values, what one values is often evidenced by the amount of time given to it. Observe a classroom and record the amount of time spent on teacher talk and on authentic student discussions. What amount of time do you want to set aside each day for students to express their ideas in discussion?

Creativity: Plan and Lead a Discussion
Select a topic appropriate for the grade level of a class you are visiting. Ask the teacher to allow you to plan and lead a discussion on that topic. Write the student outcomes you hope to achieve. Do you wish to emphasize students' critical thinking, creativity, or concept formation? Have someone videotape the discussion.

Persistence and Problem Solving: Reflect and Revise
In response to the videotape of the classroom discussion you planned and led, write a reflective critique, comparing the result to the outcomes you had hoped for.

As you watch the video, transcribe the questions you asked and categorize them according to Bloom's taxonomy. Keep a tally of the students you called on during the discussion. Were you equitable in calling on students of both genders? How did you encourage students who were reluctant to participate? If you were given an opportunity to repeat this discussion, what would you change?

Communication Skills: Gather and Use Feedback

Confer with the classroom teacher about the classroom discussion you led. Ask for feedback on your questioning techniques and responses to students' ideas. Incorporate this feedback into your revised plan.

References

Armstrong, T. (1994). Multiple intelligences: Seven ways to approach curriculum. *Educational Leadership, 52*(3), 26–28.

Bloom, B. (1981). *All our children learning.* New York: McGraw-Hill.

Bloom, B., Engelhart, M., Furst, E., Hill, W., & Krathwohl, D. (1956). *Taxonomy of educational objectives: Cognitive domain.* New York: Longman.

deBono, E. (1967). *New think.* New York: Basic Books.

Doyle, W. (1986). Classroom organization and management. In M. Wittrock (Ed.), *Handbook of research on teaching* (3rd ed.) (pp. 392–420). Upper Saddle River, NJ: Merrill/Prentice Hall.

Einstein, A., & Infeld, L. (1938). *The evolution of physics.* New York: Simon & Schuster.

Gagne, E. (1985). *The cognitive psychology of school learning.* Boston: Little, Brown.

Gardner, H. (1983). *Frames of mind.* New York: Basic Books.

Gordon, W., & Poze, T. (1975). *Strange and familiar.* Cambridge: Porpoise.

Guilford, J. (1967). *The nature of human intelligence.* New York: McGraw-Hill.

James, W. (1890). *Principles of psychology.* New York: Holt.

Lipman, M. (1988). Critical thinking—what can it be? *Educational Leadership, 46*(1), 38—43.

Lyman, F. (1989). Rechoreographing the middle-level minuet. *Early Adolescence Magazine, 4*(1), 22–24.

Meyers, C. (1986). *Teaching students to think critically.* San Francisco: Jossey-Bass.

Osborne, P. (1963). *Applied imagination.* New York: Scribner's.

Paul, R. (1988). *31 Principles of critical thinking.* Rohnert Park, CA: Center for Critical Thinking and Moral Critique.

Raths, L., Wasserman, S., Jonas, A., & Rothstein, A. (1986). *Teaching for thinking.* New York: Teachers College Press.

Rowe, M. (1974). Wait time and reward as instructional variables, their influence on language, logic and fate control. Part 1: Wait time. *Journal of Research on Science Teaching, 11,* 81–94.

Torrance, E. (1966–1984). *Torrance tests of creative thinking.* Bensenville, IL: Scholastic Testing Service.

chapter
9

Cooperative Learning Strategies

Many reflective teachers are reconsidering the use of traditional practices that emphasize competition over cooperation in the classroom. Teachers are reevaluating the conventional wisdom that individuals should work quietly, in isolation, hiding their findings from one another so that no cheating can occur. Instead, many teachers are experimenting with a variety of strategies that promote student interaction and encourage them to share their skills, knowledge, and understandings.

But experimentation may not lead to success unless it is based on an understanding of the principles and methods that successfully promote cooperative learning in the classroom. Sometimes teachers hear about a new strategy and quickly decide that they like the idea and will use it immediately. Without taking adequate time to gather the necessary information and evaluate it carefully in light of their own students' needs, they may simply try it out the very next day. This premature adoption of a new teaching method can have disastrous results.

Imagine, for example, that a teacher hears some general ideas about cooperative groups at a conference or reads the first few paragraphs of an article on the strategy. Thinking that it seems to be an intriguing idea, the teacher may hurry back to the classroom, divide the class into several small groups, and tell them to study the Civil War together for a test that will be held next Friday. After a few moments of discussing what they have (or have not) read about the Civil War, the groups are likely to dissolve into chaos or, at best, evolve into groups who sit near one another and talk as each person studies the text in isolation.

Johnson and Johnson (1984) provide this description of what cooperative learning is *not:*

> Cooperation is *not* having students sit side-by-side at the same table to talk with one another as they do their individual assignments.
>
> Cooperation is *not* having students do a task with instructions that whoever finishes first is to help the slower students.
>
> Cooperation is *not* assigning a report to a group of students wherein one student does all the work and the others put their names on the product, as well. (p. 8)

Teachers who wish to become knowledgeable and proficient in the use of cooperative learning in their classrooms must take the time to seek out information from books, journals, conferences, and visits to classrooms where the techniques are being used. This chapter provides a cursory overview of the multifaceted strategy and lists some references for your own follow-up study of the subject.

Models of Cooperative Learning

GROUP INVESTIGATION

The strategy or model known as group investigation is a good place to begin the search. Dewey (1910, 1916) believed that students can only learn to live in a democratic society if their education provides them with actual experiences of democratic decision making and problem solving. He envisioned classrooms in which students participate fully in the democratic process by investigating real problems.

Thelen (1960) adapted Dewey's educational philosophy into the *group investigation* model for the study and improvement of social issues and concerns. In this model, a class of students encounters a puzzling situation that they are encouraged to discuss freely. It is expected that individual views will differ and that values and assumptions will clash. The teacher's role is to facilitate the discussion without offering too much direction and lead the group to make a plan for studying and investigating the issue further. The larger group is divided into smaller study groups with various assignments to gather data and information to present to the larger group. An extended time is given to the small-group investigations. Finally, the small groups report their findings and suggest their ideas or solutions to the entire group. This may lead to a resolution of the problem. If it does not, the investigation continues.

An excellent example of group investigation at the middle school level occurred in Jean Malvaso-Zingaro's sixth-grade classroom (Case 9.1). The students encountered a real problem in their neighborhood. At school the students voiced strong concerns, and their teacher encouraged the discussion and guided their investigation into the matter. She allowed students to take school time to study the matter and, in effect, built the investigation into her social studies curriculum. Guest speakers were invited, field trips were taken, and the class took an active role in proposing a solution to the city council and defending it with data they had collected.

Case 9.1 ⊃ Reflective Action
Community Action Unit: A Group Investigation

Jean Malvaso-Zingaro, Sixth-Grade Teacher
School No. 6, Rochester, New York

Perceptiveness

The curriculum must be meaningful to students. They are concerned with immediate, real problems that touch their lives. When the curriculum also includes these issues, students want to learn.

As a recent example, a historic church was going to be torn down in the inner-city neighborhood of our school. This was going to happen because it was deteriorating due to lack of maintenance.

Clarification of Values and Principles

The children in my class were alarmed. They didn't want another vacant lot where drug dealers would sell their drugs, the homeless would congregate, and garbage would be dumped. As a class we discussed this situation many times. We all agreed that our school would be safer next to a church than it would be next to a vacant lot.

Proactive Construction of Knowledge

So the students wrote letters voicing their concerns to the city council. The letters were also published in the local newspaper. They invited speakers to come to our class to speak on both sides of the issue. Four representatives of various groups came to our school to share with us their reasons for either demolishing or preserving the church. The class also went on a walking field trip to the church to examine the architecture of the period in which it was built and to assess the extent of the damage. They compared the cost analysis of preserving the church with the estimates of the cost of tearing it down.

Creativity, Persistence, and Communication

We began working with the Rochester Historical Society to have the church declared a landmark. The children brainstormed different ways the church could be used. Finally, the children were asked to speak in front of the city council. The children prepared well for the event, writing and practicing their speeches. Two hundred people were at the council meeting that night. The students spoke with pride about their neighborhood and what they foresaw for the church.

At least in part because of the efforts of my sixth-grade class, the city council elected to preserve the church and declare it a historic landmark.

Sharan (1984) adapted the group investigation procedures to include opportunities for students to participate in all aspects of planning the investigation. In his model, the teacher proposes a general topic for study and asks students to organize themselves into small, academically and ethnically heterogeneous groups to be responsible for subtopics. The students are allowed more choice in what they study and who they study with, but they are led by the teacher to make responsible choices and ensure that the groups are heterogeneous. Sharing this responsibility promotes awareness and tolerance of individual differences among students.

In Sharan's (1984) model, students also participate in deciding on the methods they will use in the investigation and the types of products the groups will produce. In studying the human body, the class may decide to produce booklets, charts, and diagrams or entirely different products. Teacher and students negotiate together to decide on methods and products the groups will use. During final presentations, the teacher asks students to assist in evaluating the contributions each group made to the class as a whole.

Group investigation is a relatively unstructured form of cooperative learning. The role of the teacher is fairly nondirective, and the goals of the learning situations are almost always social or affective rather than academic. Cognitive learning may take place, but it is a by-product of the investigative process into the social issue. Recently, educational researchers have been adapting the notion of cooperative learning to include more highly structured models that can be used to teach students academic material as well.

JIGSAW MODEL

Aronson, Blaney, Sikes, and Snapp (1978) propose a model known as *jigsaw* that was developed to foster understanding among students from various racial and ethnic groups. In this model, cooperative groups are made up of students from a variety of ethnic groups. Each student is given a different portion of the total task to do to foster mutual interdependence. Often, each student is also given a different portion of the materials or information needed to complete the entire task.

For example, if the class is studying the human body, the teacher may form heterogeneous primary groups of five students to work together. The teacher then assigns each primary group responsibility for doing research on a different system in the human body. For example, one group studies the nervous system, another the circulatory system, another the respiratory system, another the digestive system, and another the skeletal system. After the primary groups have had sufficient time to learn about the systems they have studied, the teacher reassigns students to groups consisting of one student from each of the primary groups. In the groups, the student who had previously studied the nervous system is considered the expert on that system. For example, the student who had previously been part of the circulatory system research group is now the expert on that system.

In the groups, a typical assignment may be to work together to create a life-sized mural of a human body, showing all the systems and major organs of the body. As they work on this mural, students take responsibility for drawing and labeling the parts of the body associated with the systems they had studied in their primary groups. Each student who has studied one system teaches the others in the group what he or she has learned. Because the final exam will cover all of the systems of the body, students depend on other members of their group for learning about the systems they did not study. This interdependence motivates students to listen carefully to one another and to offer assistance and encouragement to one another as needed (Stallings & Stipek, 1986, p. 749).

LEARNING TEAMS

Slavin (1995) emphasizes the team concept in several variations of cooperative learning that are designed to accompany the regular academic curriculum of the school. In a model called *student teams achievement division (STAD)*, the teacher presents information to the entire class in the form of lectures, discussion, or readings. As a follow-up, students are formed into four- or five-member heterogeneous teams to learn the new material or practice the new skills.

Learning teams were designed to provide a way to encourage both individual accountability and group efforts at the same time. A baseline score is computed for each team by combining the data from individual pretests. Students then work together and assist each other in learning new material. At the conclusion of the study period, individual posttests are given to determine how well each member of the group has learned the material. Students are not allowed to help one another on the tests, only during the practice sessions. The individual test scores are then combined to produce a team score. But the winning team is not necessarily the team with the highest combined score. The results that count are the *improvement scores,* computed by determining the difference between each individual's original baseline pretest score and the final posttest results and adding these individual improvement scores together to create a final group improvement score.

For example, students may be pretested on 20-word spelling lists. High-scoring students are grouped with lower-scoring students to study and practice together, with the goal of having all students in the group earn improvement points for their team. One group's scores and points might look like this example:

Name	Pretest Score	Posttest Score	Difference = Improvement Points
John	13	15	+2
Mary	17	14	−3
Jorge	12	19	+7
Carla	10	18	+10

The teacher may use the total score of 16 or calculate an average improvement score for this group, which is 16 divided by 4, for an average group improvement score of 4. This group's score can then be compared with other groups in the class, and a competition among the study groups may be used to stimulate interest and motivation in working together to improve everyone's scores. If all groups do well and achieve impressive group improvement scores, then all groups can earn awards or extra privileges. Teachers can design award certificates or plan a menu of extra privileges to encourage students to work hard individually and in cooperation with each other.

In a variation on this approach, Slavin's (1995) *teams-games-tournaments (TGT)* model, tournaments replace tests and groups work to prepare students for the event. In the tournament, individuals from each team compete against others of similar ability, and the results are combined to produce a total team score. This method appeals to teachers who prefer this lively, oral assessment of learning to the written testing used in STAD.

Team-accelerated instruction (TAI) is a third model created by Slavin (1995). This approach combines cooperative learning with individualized instruction. It was designed especially to teach mathematics to students in grades three through six. TAI students are given placement tests in math, and each student enters a sequential mathematics curriculum made up of many units at the appropriate starting level. Students work individually at their own rates on the math assignments in the sequence. Tutoring teams are heterogeneous, with students at all levels on a single team. Teammates check one another's work using answer sheets and help one another understand their errors and learn new concepts. On completing a unit, the student takes a unit test. Each week the teacher totals the number of units completed by all team members and gives certificates and other rewards to teams for homework and completed units and extra points for perfect papers.

Because students are responsible for monitoring and assisting one another, the teacher is free to spend class time presenting lessons to small groups of students drawn from the various teams. For example, the teacher may call together all students in the fraction unit, present a lesson, check on their understanding, and then send them back to their teams to work on their assignments.

Cooperative integrated reading and composition (CIRC) is designed to enrich conventional methods for teaching reading and writing in the elementary grades. Pairs of students are assigned to encourage and support one another in their reading and writing efforts. In Ginny Bailey's first-grade classroom, these pairs of students are known as *reading buddies.* Although the teacher works with a reading group, pairs of students read aloud to one another, summarize stories to one another, and write and edit stories and poems.

PEACEMAKING GROUPS

Some cooperative groups are formed for the social purpose of teaching students how to resolve conflicts, handle anger, and avoid violence in their lives. Many schools are taking an active role in training their students to incorporate conflict-management skills into their daily lives. Johnson and Johnson (1991) have created a series of learning experiences that teachers can use for this purpose. Students are taught to recognize that conflict is inevitable and that they can choose between entering into destructive or constructive conflicts. They learn how to recognize a constructive conflict through cooperative group experiences and simulations.

For example, a group of students may be told that they have just won an all-expense-paid field trip to the destination of their choice. Now comes the hard part. Where will the group choose to go? Pairs of students are formed to list their choices and create a rationale for them. Through negotiation, the group must resolve the dilemma and make a plan by consensus.

In other group sessions, students learn to identify how they personally react to conflicts and learn how to be assertive rather than aggressive or withdraw from arguments. For example, one session may be devoted to assisting students in dealing with insulting remarks and put-downs. In another they may deal with a simulated situation in which one student refuses to do her part in a cooperative group assignment. Cooperative group activities such as these are designed to encourage students to seek peaceful solutions in their school environment. Teachers who use these methods are also likely to believe they may be useful to their students as adults and may lead to future generations' seeking more peaceful solutions in business, politics, or other issues in their families and communities.

The Purpose of Cooperative Learning

Although many variations of cooperative learning have been proposed, Stallings and Stipek (1986) found that most models have a common set of purposes, which, in turn, are founded on certain assumptions and beliefs.

Cooperative learning is designed to encourage students to help and support their peers in a group rather than compete against them. This purpose assumes that the perceived value of academic achievement increases when students are all working toward the same goal. Cooperative groups emphasize the notion of pride in one's "team" in much the same way that sports teams do.

Another major purpose of cooperative learning is to boost the achievement of students of all ability levels. The assumption is that when high-achieving students work with low-achieving students, they both benefit. Compared to tracking systems that separate the high achievers from the low achievers, cooperative groups are composed of students at all levels so that the low-achieving students can benefit from the modeling and interaction with their more capable peers. It is also believed that high-achieving students can learn to be more tolerant and understanding of individual differences through this type of experience than if they are separated from low achievers.

Still another point is that cooperative teams are believed to be more motivating for the majority of students because they have a greater opportunity to experience the joy of winning and success. In a competitive environment, the same few high-achieving students are likely to win over and over again. But a classroom divided into cooperative teams, each with its own high- and low-achieving students, more evenly distributes the opportunity to succeed. To this end, the reward systems do not honor individuals but depend on a group effort. As in a sports team, individual performances are encouraged because they benefit the whole team.

SELECTING AND ADAPTING MODELS

After researching the various models of cooperative learning that are being written about and discussed, reflective teachers must consider which model fits the goals they have established for each learning experience. Some models are most appropriate when the goal is to develop cooperation and communication skills; other models are more appropriate when the major goal is to motivate students to learn cognitive material accurately and efficiently. In many cases, reflective teachers adapt and change the models they read about to fit the unique needs of their own classes.

In *Circles of Learning*, Johnson and Johnson (1984) describe in detail how to implement cooperative learning in a classroom, but they do not prescribe a certain set of guidelines or steps for teachers to follow. They believe that, for most teachers, prepackaged programs will not work. Creative teachers may feel too constricted by rigid rules and procedures. Instead, they propose a set of principles that reflective teachers can use as the basis for creating their own models of cooperative learning.

According to Johnson and Johnson (1984), productive and mutually beneficial cooperative groups contain four basic elements: positive interdependence, face-to-face interaction, individual accountability, and the development of interpersonal skills.

The tasks and goals assigned to the cooperative group must use the skills of all members and require that all members take an active role in completing the job. When this *positive interdependence* occurs, there is a sense that each member of the group is making a valuable contribution toward the common goal. To achieve this, the teacher needs to assign a singular role to each member, to divide the tasks among members, or to provide each member with some materials and information the group needs. Through any or a combination of these means, the teacher engineers the group's perception of "all for one and one for all."

Individual members could conceivably complete their tasks separately and turn them in together. But to encourage the maximum benefit from the cooperative effort, the teacher must allow class time for students to work *face to face* with one another. When this occurs, the groups have an opportunity to increase their communication skills as well as work to achieve other academic goals.

When a well-defined group goal and an incentive are established, cooperative groups tend to resolve differences and follow through to the completion of their tasks. But in addition to the group goal, a system of *individual accountability* needs to be established. Individuals must each be responsible for demonstrating their own mastery of the subject matter by completing and turning in assignments or by performing well on written or oral quizzes and tests. Without a system of individual accountability, what begins as a group effort can turn into the efforts of a few carrying the rest of the group. High-achieving students may become impatient with slower classmates and want to take over the entire task. Low-achieving students may be fearful of making errors or holding the others back, so they pass off their work to be completed by others.

Whenever students are assigned to work in cooperative groups, they need guidance from the teacher to recognize, practice, and enhance their *interpersonal skills*. They will need to employ effective listening and speaking skills to work productively together. Students need to learn how to manage conflicts and be assertive. Teachers can help by training students in these skills and designing tasks that encourage their development. When students are initially introduced to working cooperatively, the tasks may be simple so that the groups can succeed. Early experiences will require simple communication and problem-solving skills. But as groups become more experienced and mature, it is possible to increase the complexity of the tasks so that the members continually enhance and develop their communication and problem-solving skills.

How Cooperative Learning Is Used in Classrooms

Cooperative groups can be used in almost every part of the curriculum. Various models may be more appropriate for different subjects and grade levels. The uses and adaptations of the cooperative group strategy are limitless, depending only on the classroom teacher's imagination and style.

Some teachers may divide students into long-term cooperative groups: pairs or small groups of students who sit near one another and assist one another in all subject areas. Other teachers may prefer to create cooperative groups for a single purpose only, changing the membership of groups for each new project.

The following examples describe a typical classroom task as it would be taught using conventional methods. Then it is revised to show how the subject could be taught using cooperative group strategies. The examples are not in any way limited to one grade level. Any of these examples may be adapted to another grade level with modifications for the particular group you are teaching.

KINDERGARTEN APPLICATIONS

A major component of the kindergarten curriculum is learning to recognize letters and the sounds they represent. In a conventional classroom, the day may begin with a large group meeting to discuss the day, the weather, and the season. Students may then be encouraged to share important news with one another in a "show and tell" format. The teacher may then teach the group the shape and sound of the letter B and, as a follow-up exercise, ask students to go to their desks and do phonics worksheets emphasizing this letter.

Because kindergarten classes emphasize socialization as part of their curriculum, it is natural to introduce children to cooperative groups at this early age. The lesson on the letter B can easily be adapted to a cooperative venture. When the large group meets in a circle for opening exercises and sharing time, the teacher may initiate a search for things in the room that have the B sound. The teacher can then assign students to cooperative groups, taking care to include both readers and nonreaders in each group. The teacher gives each group a stack of old magazines and asks them to work together to find and cut out pictures of objects that begin with B and paste them onto a large piece of paper. The student with the most advanced skills can then write the name of each object as a label for each picture. Roles that can be assigned to each student in the group include finder, cutter, paster, and labeler. On successive days, these tasks can be reassigned to give all students an opportunity to perform each task they are capable of doing.

As a group goal, the task is to find as many objects as possible in a given time. Incorrect items do not count toward the final tally. The group reward may be a minute of free play for each item or a similar number of grapes or crackers for snack time. As a measure of individual accountability, the teacher may meet with each student individually and have each student "read" aloud the names of the objects on the poster.

First-Grade Applications

At the first-grade level, students may be studying a science lesson on nutrition that could be handled in a similar fashion. The conventional method might be to read and discuss the four food groups, followed by an activity in which individual students search for examples of foods that fit each group. To make the task more interesting, the teacher may choose to assign students to cooperative groups and tell them that each group is going to be responsible for starting a new restaurant. Their first task will be to name the restaurant. Then they must work together to plan three menus: one each for breakfast, lunch, and dinner.

Given large sheets of construction paper, the groups will create menus that include all four food groups for each meal. The division of labor can be handled by having three students per group, one responsible for each meal. When the menus are completed, the groups can interact by having students role-play the act of visiting one another's restaurants as customers and choosing a well-balanced meal. Individual accountability can be built in by giving a quiz at a later date. Groups can earn certificates of merit if their group menus are accurate and well prepared and if the individuals in their group meet minimum criteria on the follow-up quizzes.

In an activity-centered math program or a whole language reading and writing program, pairs of learning partners are vital to success. By pairing a high achiever with a low achiever, the teacher can ensure that students are actively learning each new concept and will get the scaffolding necessary to understand difficult new concepts. For example, in teaching addition without learning partners, the teacher usually models the operation on the chalkboard and asks students to duplicate the process at their desks. As learning partners, students work on their problems and then check one another's work. If there is a difference between the two answers, they redo their work until they both have the correct answer.

Tim Curbo, who teaches first-grade at Hawthorne School in San Francisco, describes in Case 9.2 how he uses cooperative groups to encourage students to develop their language, problem-solving, and cooperation skills simultaneously.

Case 9.2 ⊃ Reflective Action
Cooperative Groups: A First-Grade Activity

Tim Curbo, First-Grade Teacher
Hawthorne School, San Francisco

Perceptiveness

First graders need time to work in groups. They need opportunities for socializing and learning how to communicate and solve problems together, especially the population at Hawthorne School, where we may have students from as many as 35 different countries, with different languages, customs, and learning patterns. So every Friday I plan special cooperative group activities.

Creativity

I divide the class into groups of four. Because I have many bilingual students in my class, I make sure each group has a combination of English-speaking and Spanish-speaking children.

In each group there are four different jobs or roles for children to take. I post the roles on the bulletin board. For example:

> Maria: materials
>
> Jed: reporter
>
> Carlos: facilitator
>
> Ana: writer

The materials person gets all the necessary materials for the task. The facilitator makes sure everyone is participating and solves any problems that arise. The writer keeps a written record of the activity. Because this is first grade, the writer may just draw illustrations; and as I circulate through the room, I record the observations of the other members of the groups. The reporter gives a report of what the group accomplished. Children get a different role each time we do cooperative group activities.

Communication Skills

Before the first task we talk about the various responsibilities. I usually choose a simple task initially, such as a puzzle. All of the students work together to solve the puzzle. Then the writer may draw the finished puzzle, and the reporter describes the process the group used to solve the puzzle.

One of the first tasks of the group is to select a name. This is then posted on the board. The writer's report is posted next to the group's name. Other products can also be posted in this space.

Persistence and Problem Solving

From the beginning I turn questions and problems that arise back to the group. I encourage the facilitator to take leadership but to involve the others in trying to solve the problems. I tell them, "Four heads are better than one." I keep myself free to circulate, clarifying, extending the activity, and making encouraging remarks.

Clarification of Values and Principles

It's always noisy, and things are bumpy at first. Children aren't sure of their roles. There are personality clashes. We process or talk about all of these issues. Most issues are worked out with time. My students enjoy the spirit of cooperation that develops and the social interaction. Through repeated use of this strategy, it becomes evident that cooperation and problem-solving skills are prominent shared values in our classroom.

SECOND-GRADE APPLICATIONS

The second-grade curriculum emphasizes the concept of community. Reflective teachers recognize that, to truly understand the concept of community, students need to live it. Using a jigsaw approach, small groups can each study one element of a community and report their findings to the class. Using a group investigation approach, students may discover a controversy in their own community that they wish to study and then take a stand on.

As an example of a cooperative learning unit on communities, the teacher may choose to begin with the local community or neighborhood if the school is located in a large city. Beginning with a walking or bus tour of the commercial area, the entire group discusses the various elements that are needed for a successful community. If possible, some teachers extend the tour to pass by the houses of each person in the class. Given a map of the area, cooperative groups can be formed with an initial assignment of depicting on the map the important sites they observed on the tour. Each person in the group can be given the job of locating and recording an equal number of sites on the map.

Later, the same cooperative groups can select one aspect of the community to study, such as the hospital, fire station, police station, city hall, library, churches, or the school itself. With the teacher's help, each group can invite speakers to come to the class to discuss their jobs and responsibilities to the community. Each group can also prepare a short skit (including all the members of the group) that informs the rest of the class about the roles and responsibilities of the community helpers they studied.

After a thorough study of the local community, this unit can be expanded to include a study of very different communities around the world or how one community has changed with time. Again, cooperative groups can each take responsibility for researching one type of community and creating a model of it for others to see. Roles and tasks may have to be assigned to ensure that everyone in the group is included in the project. These roles could include reader, writer, builder, and painter.

THIRD-GRADE APPLICATIONS

At the third-grade level, students are expected to demonstrate mastery of the basic skills taught during the primary grades. Standardized achievement or criterion-referenced tests may be given to document students' gains as a class and as individuals. For example, many third graders are expected to demonstrate that they can meet the school's criteria for computing the basic addition, subtraction, and multiplication facts. In a traditional classroom, teachers may prepare students for this assessment by providing them with daily worksheets for practicing and memorizing the math facts. In an effort to motivate students to improve their skills, conventional teachers may post charts for all to read that display the names of students who have reached the criteria and those who have not.

Although this type of competitive environment may please and motivate the high achievers, it is not likely to encourage the remainder of the class. To modify the process of learning math facts from a competitive to a cooperative experience, teachers could adapt the student team achievement division model to fit the needs of their classrooms.

Using a STAD approach, the teacher would begin by giving a pretest of 100 math facts to the entire class. By sorting the pretests into high, medium, and low scores, the teacher can divide the class into heterogeneous groups with equivalent ability in math facts. Each group would contain one of the top scorers, one of the lowest scorers, and two in the middle range.

How the teacher sets up the conditions and expectations for this cooperative learning experience is very important. The achievement goal and the behavioral expectations must be clearly explained at the outset. For example, the teacher may state that the groups are expected to practice math facts for a given time each day. Worksheets, flash cards, and other materials will be provided, and the teams are free to choose the means they use to practice. The goal, in this instance, is to raise all scores from pretest levels as much as possible. A posttest will be given on a certain day, and each individual will have an improvement score, which is the difference between the correct responses on the posttest and the correct responses on the pretest. The group improvement score will be computed by adding up the individual improvement scores. This method of scoring encourages the group to give extra energy to raise the scores of the lowest scorers because they have the most to gain. Top scorers, in fact, may not gain many points at all because their pretests may already be near the total. Added incentives for this group may be devised, such as a certain number of points for a perfect paper.

The incentives that will be awarded for success depend a great deal on the class itself. The teacher may choose to offer one reward for the group whose scores improve the most or reward each group, depending on their gains. For example, a single reward for the most improved group may be tangible, such as a certificate of success or temporary possession of a traveling math trophy. Less tangible incentives are also important to third graders, such as the opportunity to be first in line for a week, go to the library together during a math class, or eat lunch with the teacher. To spread the incentives to all groups, the points that each group earns may be translated into an award such as 1 minute of free time per point or the opportunity to "buy" special opportunities and materials.

Once students become accustomed to helping their classmates in one subject area, they are likely to take considerable interest in assisting and supporting their members in doing well in other subjects as well. Similar groups could operate to improve spelling, vocabulary, the mechanics of writing, or other basic skills. The membership of each group would be different because students are likely to score differently on pretests for various subjects.

FOURTH-GRADE APPLICATIONS

While math computation lends itself to a STAD approach, math problem solving can be enhanced by the extra incentive of working toward participation in a tournament in the TGT model of cooperative learning. Traditional methods of teaching math problem solving involve individual students' doing pages of story problems on paper and having the papers corrected and graded. When students have difficulty with story problems, the teacher must work personally with them to help them understand the processes and operations needed to solve the problems.

Using a team approach, pretests or other measures of past performance in math problem solving are used to form heterogeneous groups consisting of high, middle, and low achievers. Textbooks, worksheets, and other practice problems can be given to groups of students to prepare them for tournaments to be held once or twice a week. During a tournament, the groups are divided again so that each student is assigned to a table or a station to compete individually against students of similar achievement levels from other teams. Problems can be presented orally or in written form during the tournaments. The difficulty of problems can be varied to match the achievement levels of students at each station.

Slavin (1995) recommends cumulative scoring of tournaments. The top scorer from each table receives six points, the middle scorer four points, and the low scorer two points. Team scores are then calculated by simply adding the results for the teammates. These scores are added to the team's tallies from previous sessions. Team standings are then publicized in newsletters that go home to parents.

FIFTH-GRADE APPLICATIONS

In many classrooms, the conventional approach to teaching science once centered on textbook reading, discussion, an occasional demonstration by the teacher, and written tests of understanding. But more recently, science curricula have been revised to include many more hands-on experiments and investigations. The current philosophy is that students need to learn how to *do* science rather than simply learn about it.

Hands-on science is an area that has a natural fit with cooperative group strategies. By participating in cooperative science investigations, students learn how scientists themselves interact to share observations, hypotheses, and methods. Although many teachers value these current science goals, they may be reluctant to try them because they are unsure of how to manage the high level of activity in the classroom when science experiments are happening. Cooperative groups can provide the support and structure needed to manage successful science investigation in the classroom.

When a topic or unit approach is taken for teaching science, each unit offers opportunities for cooperative learning. For example, jigsaw groups may study the topic of astronomy, with each studying one planet, creating models and charts of information about that planet, and reporting the group's findings to others.

Investigations into the properties of simple machines, magnets, electricity, and other topics in physics can be designed by establishing a challenge or a complex goal for groups to meet by a given date. Groups may be given a set of identical materials and told to create a product that has certain characteristics and can perform a specific function. For example, given a supply of toothpicks and glue, groups are challenged to construct a bridge that can hold a pound of weight without breaking. Given a raw egg and an assortment of materials, groups work together to create ways to protect their eggs when they are dropped from a high window onto the pavement below.

Science groups can be mixed and matched frequently during the year, offering students an opportunity to work cooperatively with most other members of their class. This strategy is likely to reinforce the principles of social science as well. As Johnson and Johnson (1984) recommend, one interpersonal skill can be learned and practiced during each academic group experience. For example, during the astronomy unit, the emphasis could be on learning how to come together as a group quickly, quietly, and efficiently when getting started on the day's project. During the bridge-building unit, the groups could practice encouraging everyone to participate, taking time to ask for opinions and suggestions from every member of the group before making an important decision. After completing each unit, the groups should participate in evaluating how they worked together and how well they demonstrated the interpersonal skill emphasized during that unit.

SIXTH-GRADE APPLICATIONS

The sixth-grade reading curriculum is designed to introduce students to a variety of literary forms. Using conventional methods of teaching reading, three homogeneous reading groups based on ability may still be used at the sixth-grade level. Each group reads stories, essays, poems, and plays collected in a basal reader geared for that group's reading ability. The teacher leads discussions of reading materials and assigns seatwork to be done while he or she works with other groups.

Many upper elementary teachers, however, prefer to use literary materials in their own format rather than as collections in basal readers or anthologies. They believe that students' motivation to read will improve if they are encouraged to choose and read whole books, novels, poetry collections, and plays. A variety of paperback books in sets of six to eight books apiece are needed to carry out this type of reading program.

At Our Lady of Mercy School in Chicago, sixth-grade teacher Roxanne Farwick-Owens has developed a system that allows choice, maximizes cooperative efforts, and holds individuals accountable. She has woven elements of the CIRC, jigsaw, TGT, and Sharan's group investigation models into her own unique system of cooperative learning.

To maximize student motivation and enjoyment of reading, Roxanne believes students must be allowed to choose their reading materials. Each month she provides three or four reading selections, in the form of paperback books, to the class. Students are allowed to choose the book they want to read, and groups are formed according to interest rather than ability level. Roxanne may advise students about their selections and try to steer them toward appropriate selections, but in the end she believes that they have the right to choose for themselves what they will read, especially because she has provided only books that have inherent value for sixth graders.

During initial group meetings, students decide for themselves how much to read at a time. They assign themselves due dates for each chapter. Periodically, each group meets with Roxanne to discuss what they are reading, but most discussions are held without her leadership. Usually, she holds the groups responsible for generating their own discussion on the book. To prepare for this discussion, all members are expected to prepare questions as they read. For example, each person in the group may be expected to contribute three "why" questions and two detail questions per session. Roxanne reviews the questions each day as a means of holding each individual accountable for reading the material and contributing to the group.

Another task is to plan a presentation about the books (using art, music, drama, and other media) to share with the rest of the class at the end of the month. This allows groups to introduce the books they have read to the other members of the class, who are then likely to choose them at a later date. One group made wooden puppets and a puppet stage to portray an event from Mark Twain's *The Adventures of Tom Sawyer*. After reading Judy Blume's *Superfudge*, a group created a radio commercial for the book complete with sound effects and background music. Familiar television interview shows are sometimes used as a format, as are music videos.

About once per quarter, two teams are formed to compete in a game show–type tournament. Questions about the books are separated into categories such as characters, plot, setting, authors, and miscellaneous. Each person is responsible for writing five questions and answers on index cards to prepare for the tournament. One student acts as emcee, while another keeps track of the points. The team with the most points wins the tournament.

Roxanne finds that this cooperative group structure increases her students' social skills, especially their ability to work with others and to find effective ways to handle disagreements. But the primary reason for the program is to help her students see that reading can be enjoyable and that, instead of being a solitary pursuit, reading can have a social aspect. Roxanne believes many of her students may become lifelong readers from this one-year experience.

In other subjects, study groups can participate in selecting incentives they want to achieve. Weekly incentives can be used to encourage members to learn enough to do well on the quizzes or tournaments. A whole class incentive can be planned, with the goal that every member of the class passes the test on the first or second try.

MIDDLE SCHOOL APPLICATIONS

When middle school students are invited to participate in planning their own learning, they are likely to show interest, energy, and responsibility in handling the task.

Theodosia Jackson teaches in an urban middle school. Her college education was interrupted early when she gave birth to her son in her freshman year. She was a full-time mom and worked full time as well for about eight years. A divorce caused her to rethink her life goals. She wanted to be an example for her own children of what a person can accomplish if he or she is willing to persevere, so she went back to college and worked part time as a teacher's aide. As an aide, she worked with low-achieving students who seemed to be missing a great many basic skills. She decided to become a teacher and completed the teacher education program at San Diego State University at the age of 31.

Her first assignment was in an urban school with a large population of minority students. Being African American herself, and coming from the same type of working-class background, Theo believes that it is her responsibility to inspire the next generation to succeed. She concentrates her efforts on prompting students to think about college as a goal. She especially wants her students to know that no matter what background they may come from, they can set their goals to attend college and achieve those goals.

To make these goals real for her students, she established six cooperative groups in her classes. Each group of students selects a college or university for its group name. Students must pay tuition and rent once a month and buy their books and materials as they need them. At first the students didn't understand the reasons for Theo's unusual methods. But she explained to them that when you get to college, nothing is free. She told them that she wanted them to see a realistic picture of what college life entails. Gradually, her students began to budget their money carefully so that they had enough money to pay their tuition each month. Within their colleges, students are able to cooperate and support each other to earn their tuition money and share scarce supplies. By the middle of the year, her students began to show a great interest in going to college. When I visited her classroom, I heard many of her students tell about their determination to go to college themselves one day.

Laurie Mednick, of Kellogg School in Chula Vista, California, uses permanent cooperative groups in her middle school classroom. At the beginning of the year, she assigns students to a "tribe" consisting of four or five members who are expected to work on all their assignments together, supporting and teaching one another as needed. Tribes create their own names and rules for working together and assign duties to each member. Laurie uses the term *tribe* to connote a group of individuals who may not be related genetically but are all interdependent on each other. As a result, Laurie's students take their work very seriously and show pride in their group's accomplishments. They have learned to solve problems without relying on adult intervention.

HIGH SCHOOL APPLICATIONS

Students in cooperative groups in high school classes are generally given a great deal of responsibility for their own learning. They are asked to do their own research, solve their own problems, and support one another as they plan and carry out learning investigations.

In her global studies course that is required for freshmen at Crystal Lake South High School, Mary O'Donnell planned a jigsaw cooperative learning experience on traditional Chinese culture and civilization. After reading assigned material about class distinctions in China, students were divided into seven small groups. Each group represented one social class and was assigned the responsibility of finding out what that social class in China experienced. One group became the peasants, and others became the merchants, government officials, scholars, gentry, scientists, and soldiers. In their small groups, the students reread the assigned material and then discussed what it meant to be a member of their assigned social class and what the life-style was like in traditional Chinese society.

Using the jigsaw approach, one student from each social class group was then reassigned to form secondary cooperative groups. Each secondary group consisted of one member from each original social class assignment. In these secondary groups, each student became the expert on one social class and assumed responsibility for teaching what he or she had learned to the others. Students did this by role-playing the social class they had studied in their first group and introducing themselves to one another. Together, the secondary groups created skits to demonstrate the various roles and responsibilities of each social class.

In her U.S. history course, Mary used a different form of cooperative learning to encourage students to explore the concept of imperialism. She divided students into groups of three students and asked them to decide whether or not they supported the concept of U.S. imperialism. She assigned one student the role of reader. This student had the responsibility of reading and reporting on the information from the textbook. Another was a note checker, who reviewed notes taken from previous class lectures and discussions. The third member was the recorder, who prepared the new notes and plans for this group assignment.

After studying and discussing the concept of imperialism in their groups, the students decided whether the United States should act as an imperialistic power. To back up their opinions, they selected and described three historical events that supported their points of view. Each group presented its arguments and then defended its views against classmates' questions.

Science teachers typically use cooperative groups to encourage investigation and experimentation and to allow students to create their own hypotheses and test them together. Math teachers at the high school level engage their students in learning experiences that require problem solving and communication of their findings to others.

Classroom Conditions That Encourage Cooperation

Cooperative groups are a welcome change of pace for many students. They enjoy the opportunity to interact with their peers for part of the school day. But teachers may be hesitant to try the strategy for fear that the students will play or talk about outside interests rather than work at the task assigned. Cooperative groups can degenerate to chaotic groups if they do not meet certain conditions.

When the group has a poor understanding of the goals of the task, the results may be unproductive and frustrating. To prevent this, the teacher must clearly state the goals and expectations of each group task and provide a copy of them in writing so the group can refer to them from time to time.

In addition to being clear, the goal or task must have some inherent value, and the group must perceive it as worth their time and effort. When students care about the outcome, they are more likely to take one another seriously and ask one another for help in achieving the goal (Slavin, 1995).

To encourage high-quality effort and achievement, groups must view incentives as meaningful and valuable. The incentives may be extrinsic, in the form of a certificate, points, grades, a pizza party, or an extra-long recess. In some cases, there may be intrinsic incentives as well, such as enhanced group pride or the good feeling that comes from having contributed to the well-being of other people. Each teacher and school community has different needs and values that must be taken into account as incentives are planned and communicated to the students.

Johnson and Johnson (1984) suggest a number of ways to implement successful cooperative groups. The size of the group may vary from task to task. Generally, groups consist of two to six students, with smaller groups in the primary grades and larger groups in the upper grades. Pairs are excellent for monitoring and checking tasks. Groups of three to six are used for study teams and investigations. The shorter the time, the smaller the groups should be. Small groups can be more efficient because they take less time to get organized, they operate more quickly, and each member has more "air time."

Assigning students to cooperative groups can be the most difficult part of the process for teachers. The philosophy of heterogeneous grouping is excellent in theory but is difficult to achieve in a real-life classroom. A classroom is likely to have one or two superstars whose ability cannot be matched in some subject areas. Similarly, one or two students may have very unusual learning difficulties or behavior problems. For most types of learning situations, the teacher must simply make the best judgment about the combinations that are approximately equivalent in ability.

It is advisable to put non-task-oriented students into groups with highly task-oriented teammates so that peer pressure will work to keep them on task. This theory, however, does not always work out in the classroom. Angry or highly restless students may refuse to participate or otherwise prevent their team from succeeding. When this happens, the group itself should be encouraged to deal with the problem as a means of learning how to cope with and resolve such occurrences in real life.

In arranging the room during cooperative group activities, each group should have a comfortable space, and members should be able to face one another and have eye contact with every other member of the group. Separating the groups from one another is also necessary so they can each work undisturbed by the conversations and activities taking place in other groups.

Materials intended for cooperative groups may differ from those used in conventional teaching and learning situations. It is suggested that only one set of materials explaining the task and the expectations be distributed. This causes students in the group to work together from the very beginning. In some cases, each member of the group may receive different information from other members. This promotes interdependence because each member has something important to share with the others.

Interdependence can also be encouraged by the assignment of "complementary and interconnected roles" to group members. These roles will vary with the type of learning and task but might include discussion leader, recorder of ideas, runner for information, researcher, encourager, and observer.

Tasks that result in the creation of products rather than participation in a test or tournament are more likely to succeed if the group is limited to the production of one product. If more than one product is allowed, students may simply work independently on their own products. Members of the group should also be asked to sign a statement saying that they participated in the development of the group's product.

To ensure individual accountability, students must know that they will all be held responsible for learning and presenting what they learned. During the final presentations, the teacher may ask any member of the group to answer a question, describe an aspect of the group's final product, or present a rationale for a group decision.

The Effects of Cooperative Learning

To compare the academic achievement of students using the cooperative learning methods with other more conventional approaches, Slavin (1987) compared pre- and posttest scores for students in math, writing, reading, social studies, science, and language arts. "Of 38 studies of at least four weeks' duration comparing cooperative methods of this type to traditional control methods, 33 found significantly greater achievement for the cooperatively taught classes" (Slavin, 1987, p. 10). In addition, positive effects were found on higher-order objectives as well as on basic skills. But perhaps the most striking effects of cooperative learning are affective rather than cognitive.

In a school setting, students learn in classes made up of their agemates, for the most part. With conventional teaching methods, relationships among peers in a class are likely to become somewhat competitive because most students are aware of how well they are doing in relation to their classmates. Grading systems reinforce the competitive nature of school, as do standardized tests and entrance exams.

It is recognized that individual competition can enhance the motivation for high-achieving students who perceive that they have a possibility of winning or being the best. However, the public nature of competitive rewards and incentives leads to embarrassment and anxiety for students who fail to succeed. When the anxiety and embarrassment are intense, students who recognize that they are not likely to win no matter how hard they work eventually drop out of the competition in one way or another.

Even when the anxiety over competition is less intense and under control by students with average or high-average achievement, they may become preoccupied with grades to the extent that they avoid complex or challenging tasks that will risk their academic standing and grades (Doyle, 1983).

Despite these negative effects of competition, it is difficult to imagine a classroom without some type of competitive spirit or reward system, and despite its obvious flaws, competition does create an energetic response from many students. Slavin's (1995) models of cooperative group structures are designed to maintain the positive value of competition by adapting it in the form of team competition so that each student is equally capable of winning.

Team competition, then, has motivational advantages for low- and middle-achieving students that individual competition does not. Still, any competitive situation has winners and losers, and Johnson and Johnson (1984) caution that losing team members may blame one another and hold as scapegoats individual members of their team whom they believe to be responsible for the team's loss.

Reflective teachers who undertake some form of cooperative learning will need to be aware of all possible effects and observe for both positive and negative interactions among teammates. When using competitive teams, teachers should take steps to ensure that every team has an equal chance to win and that attention is focused more on the learning task than on who wins and loses. When anger or conflict arises within groups, teachers must be ready to mediate and assist students as they gain the interpersonal and communication skills necessary to learn from their team losses.

Johnson and Johnson (1984) report that when cooperative groups are well planned and managed, they "promote considerably more liking among students" than do competitive and individualistic structures. "This is true regardless of differences in ability level, sex, handicapping conditions, ethnic membership, social class differences, or task orientation. Students who collaborate on their studies develop considerable commitment and caring for one another no matter what their initial impressions of and attitudes toward one another were" (p. 18).

Slavin (1995) and Sharan (1984) also report that cooperative groups may actually improve race relations within a classroom. When students participate in multiracial teams, studies show that they choose one another for friends more often than do students in control groups. Researchers attribute this effect to the fact that working together in a group as a part of a team causes students to promote more differentiated, dynamic, and realistic views (and therefore less stereotyped and static views) of other students (including handicapped peers and students from different ethnic groups) than do competitive and individualistic learning experiences (Johnson & Johnson, 1984).

Slavin (1995) also reports that cooperative groups have a positive influence on the successful mainstreaming of handicapped students into the regular classroom. Research on the use of cooperative groups to facilitate mainstreaming and meet the needs of remedial readers has found positive effects on both the achievement and the social acceptance of these learners. This is believed to occur because students generalize the concept of helping one another learn from the team efforts in cooperative groups to become a fundamental principle of classroom organization.

Cooperative learning experiences have also been shown to promote higher levels of self-esteem. Johnson and Johnson (1984) attributed this effect to a connection between cooperative relationships with peers and basic, unconditional self-acceptance. In contrast, they found that competitiveness promotes conditional self-acceptance and that highly individualistic attitudes tended to be related to self-rejection.

Cooperative learning experiences also have been shown to affect student relationships with adults in the school. "Students participating in cooperative learning experiences, compared with students participating in competitive and individualistic learning experiences, like the teacher better and perceive the teacher as being more supportive and accepting academically and personally" (Johnson & Johnson, 1984, pp. 21–22).

Slavin (1987) also believes the effects of cooperative groups can lead to the concept of a cooperative school, in which it becomes the norm for students to help one another and for teachers to coach and support one another as well. Administrators, parents, teachers, and students could work together to develop a community sense that "every student's learning is everyone's responsibility, that every student's success is everyone's success" (p. 12).

⊃ Reflective Actions for Your Professional Portfolio
Your Plan for Using Cooperative Groups

Perceptiveness: Assessing Your Own Experience

Do you believe in using competition or cooperation to motivate your students to learn? From your own experience, do you find cooperative groups enjoyable and stimulating or frustrating and discouraging? What type of role do you usually take in a cooperative group? Do you get impatient with others in your group and wish you could work on the assignment by yourself? How could the structure of the groups you participated in have been improved? Based on your own experience as a learner, are you likely to use cooperative groups in your classroom? Why or why not?

Construction of Knowledge: Cooperative Groups in Action

Visit a number of classrooms that are using cooperative groups. This is one strategy that cannot be learned by reading alone. Observe the methods other teachers use to form the groups and to assign tasks and responsibilities. Keep a log of the best ideas you see.

Values and Principles: Competition versus Cooperation

In the classrooms you are visiting, is competition or cooperation more highly valued? Give examples of classroom events or incentive structures to support your observation. What would you emphasize in your class? What strategies will you employ to encourage more cooperation? How can you create more positive interdependence? Describe an example of a recent classroom event that you observed and tell what you would do to enhance a cooperative attitude among the students. Describe how you will create a climate for cooperation in your classroom.

Creativity: Your Plan for Cooperative Groups

Write a brief plan for using cooperative groups in the grade level you hope to teach. Organize your plan according to subject matter or thematic units. Describe three to five types of cooperative groups you will use to accomplish different purposes.

Persistence and Problem Solving: Cooperative Group Field Test

In a classroom you are visiting, ask for an opportunity to field test a cooperative group. Implement it and have someone videotape the students working on the task while you assist them.

Communication Skills: Reflecting on Your Field Test

Describe the field test for your portfolio. How did you form the groups? What was the task? How did you communicate the task to the students? How did you assign roles and responsibilities? How did you interact with groups as they worked on the task? Critique the results with honesty and reflectiveness, describing what you have learned in the process.

References

Aronson, E., Blaney, S., Sikes, J., & Snapp, M. (1978). *The jigsaw classroom.* Beverly Hills: Sage.

Dewey, J. (1910). *How we think.* Boston: Heath.

Dewey, J. (1916). *Democracy and education.* Upper Saddle River, NJ: Merrill/Prentice Hall.

Doyle, W. (1983). Academic work. *Review of Educational Research, 53,* 159–199.

Johnson, D., & Johnson, R. (1984). *Circles of learning.* Alexandria, VA: Association of Supervision and Curriculum Development.

Johnson, D., & Johnson, R. (1991). *Teaching students to be peacemakers.* Edina, MN: Interaction.

Sharan, S. (1984). *Cooperative learning in the classroom: Research in desegregated schools.* Hillsdale, NJ: Erlbaum.

Slavin, R. (1987). Cooperative learning and the cooperative school. *Educational Leadership, 45*(3), 7–13.

Slavin, R. (1995). *Cooperative learning* (2nd ed.). Boston: Allyn & Bacon.

Stallings, J., & Stipek, D. (1986). Research on early childhood and elementary school teaching programs. In M. Wittrock (Ed.), *Handbook of research on teaching* (3rd ed., pp. 727–753). Upper Saddle River, NJ: Merrill/Prentice Hall.

Thelen, H. (1960). *Education and the human quest.* New York: Harper & Row.

Using Technology and Other Teaching Strategies to Increase Authentic Learning

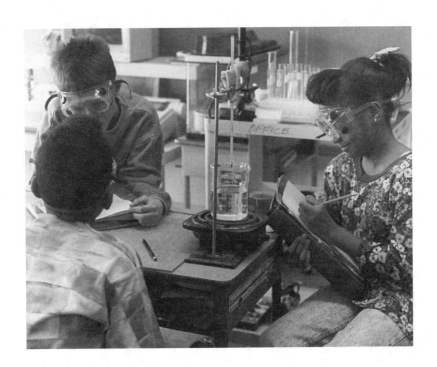

School experiences can be enjoyable for both teachers and students. One way of heightening the enjoyment is by using a variety of teaching strategies and activities. When learning experiences are varied, students are more likely to become actively engaged in the learning process. Their intrinsic motivation to learn is also likely to improve if the skill or knowledge they are learning is presented in a novel and unusual format. To promote the enjoyment of teaching and learning, many reflective teachers are continually searching for new methods and strategies to motivate and engage their students in the learning process. Developing a repertoire of teaching strategies is also necessary because students' needs and learning styles are diverse. For this reason, teachers must be ready to modify lesson plans and present information in more than one way.

Teachers are also searching for effective ways to use computers and other technological advances to enhance their curricula. In the past decade, classroom uses for computers have expanded and become a great deal more varied. Many schools have invested in technology so they can offer students more diverse learning opportunities and prepare them to use the technology that is becoming commonplace in the world of work. In the next decade, the investment must be made in providing teachers with the information and skills they need to be able to use the full potential of the technology available to them.

The purpose of this chapter is to introduce you to a repertoire of teaching strategies, highlighting methods that employ computers and related systems as teaching and learning tools. As you consider each strategy, you will quickly recognize that the descriptions in this chapter are not sufficiently detailed for you to become proficient in using the new strategy. This book can provide only an overview of the descriptions, illustrations, and examples you will need to employ these methods successfully. For strategies that you wish to implement in your classroom, you will need to use the reflective action of initiating an active search for more detailed descriptions of these strategies in books and journal articles or in observations of experienced teachers.

As you read about or select a strategy to try out in a laboratory or classroom, you will find that some of them work for you and others do not. You will need to reflect about what works for you and your students and why. As you think about what works for you, it is quite acceptable for you to combine, adapt, modify, and add your own strategies to the ones you read about or observe. Through this process of practice and reflection, you will discover, create, and refine your own unique teaching style.

Technology Can Increase Authentic Learning

Although some teachers, because of their fear of the unknown, may still be reluctant to use computers in their classrooms, many others believe that having a computer in the classroom is like having another teacher. When computers were first introduced in classrooms in the 1970s, few software programs were available. The first educational goals established at that time involved teaching students about how computers function and how to write their own computer programs. This goal contributed greatly to the fear that many classroom teachers still have. Not being computer programmers, they rarely felt comfortable teaching these skills to students.

Until recently, computer-assisted instruction was the primary emphasis for classroom uses of technology. This philosophy assumed that computers could provide one-to-one tutoring in the basic skills. As a result, many software programs were developed that provided drill and practice in mathematics and other routine tasks. Teachers tended to use these programs sparingly.

Currently, classrooms use computer technology very differently. Using stimulating, challenging, user-friendly software programs, teachers are creating many projects that have all the characteristics of authentic learning. That is, they create computer-based tasks that are meaningful and productive and that encourage creative expression. When students become engaged in a computer activity that challenges their motor skills, brain power, and creativity to figure out solutions and strategies, they see the activities as worthwhile.

Still, mastering the use of a computer program can be a challenge in its own right, and knowing which programs to use for which learning experiences is another complex matter. Hundreds of computer programs are now available that can be used to accomplish many useful tasks. Here are a few recommendations from teachers who use technology in their classrooms.

WORD PROCESSING PROGRAMS

Word processing programs are among the most versatile software available for classrooms. Early experiences, especially in the primary grades, may be devoted to very simple writing assignments with a dual purpose: composing and learning keyboarding. Many programs are available to teach students how to type and use the special function keys on the keyboard. As students learn to identify letters and numbers, they can often begin to type them before they can hold a pencil and write them on paper.

Learning to operate a keyboard also provides new opportunities for older students with special needs related to small motor functioning. Students with visual and motor difficulties that prevent them from writing neatly or cause them to erase and redo their work can now create neat papers. The delete key may save students from embarrassment and frustration, just as it does for you and me. For this reason, I recommend allowing students to learn keyboarding skills at the same time they are learning to write with a pen or a pencil and then allowing them to choose which form they prefer to use for assignments.

When students master keyboarding skills, they are free to compose many types of verbal products, including letters, stories, poems, essays, reports, and plays. Studies have shown that students write longer pieces on a word processor than they do by hand. The other major benefit is that the word processor greatly simplifies the editing and revision processes. Students can learn to use spelling checkers, grammar checkers, and thesaurus programs. Their motivation to write is increased in part because of the attraction of working on a computer but also because the final printed products are neat and relatively error-free. Rather than experiencing writing as drudgery, students are likely to feel pride and success related to the writing process when they are allowed to compose and edit using a word processing program.

Students with limited English proficiency can also benefit from writing and composing with a word processor. If a teaching pairs a proficient English speaker with a less proficient student, the two can work together at the computer to compose and illustrate stories and poems. In the process, they are communicating orally as well as on in writing, giving the less proficient English speaker an opportunity to use the new language in a meaningful context.

Using word processing programs or more specialized desktop publishing programs, students can create newspapers, magazines, posters, invitations to events, and other materials that have the appeal of a professionally published product. Many teachers are employing these media to help students create gifts for families, such as published books of poetry or calendars illustrated by the class.

COMPUTER-ASSISTED RESEARCH PROJECTS

CD-ROM disks are fast replacing the traditional encyclopedia in most school media centers. Students are able to type in a key word to call up an article on almost any subject. For many topics, they also see a picture or even a short video of the subject they are researching.

At the Open School, an inner-city elementary school in Los Angeles, research begins early. In a combined first and second grade, Jan Ng uses a HyperCard program called *Dino Hunt* (Smithsonian) to take her students to an archaeological dig where their task is to identify a dinosaur bone. The program gives clues that students use to begin their research using books and maps.

Cliff Gilkey, a multi-age fourth/fifth/sixth-grade teacher at Frank Paul Elementary School in Salinas, California, was searching for a method to engage the interest of his students, many of whom were from families of migrant workers with limited English proficiency. The social studies material he had available neither matched his students' interests nor gave them positive role models. To meet these needs, Cliff created the Local Heroes Project, a social studies investigation and oral history of local Hispanic, African American, and Vietnamese leaders (such as political figures, businesspeople, researchers, and teachers).

The students decided that they would produce videotapes and publish booklets about the local heroes that students in other classes could use as well. Students were asked to identify local heroes that they would like to know more about. The heroes they selected included a Mexican American school board member, a Latina news anchorwoman, an African American police chief, the Cuban American city manager, and a Miwok Indian leader.

For this project, students worked in teams of three to four. They developed a set of interview questions by reading and analyzing biographies to see what other biographers included. After preparing the interview questions, they set up appointments to meet the individual local heroes they wanted to interview. One student asked questions as another operated the video camera. They transcribed the words of their heroes onto word processors so that they could create booklets about each hero.

This year Cliff plans to do the project again with even more technology at his command. He has a new Hyper Studio program that will allow the students to create multimedia presentations and a VCR companion they plan to use to create special effects and credits for their video production.

NETWORKING TO SHARE INFORMATION

Dawn Morden, a sixth-grade teacher in Altoona, Pennsylvania, wanted to provide more relevant, authentic learning experiences to motivate her students to want to learn social studies. She noticed that her students seemed uninterested in the social studies text because they saw little relationship between the text and their own lives. Dawn and a colleague, Connie Letscher, teamed up to create an interdisciplinary, technology-based project that they call "Crossroads to the World."

They begin with literature that stimulates students' interest in traveling, then introduce computer programs that simulate travel, such as *Oregon Trail* (MECC), *Cross-Country Canada* (Didatech), and *Where in the World Is Carmen Sandiego?* (Broderbund). They have also subscribed to an on-line educational telecommunications network, *WorldClassroom*, that allows students in Altoona to communicate with people all over the world. When students make contacts in other parts of the world, they share firsthand information about their communities. Turning next to word processing programs, students write letters to their new friends.

Each student selects a travel destination and writes business letters or sends e-mail messages to chambers of commerce, tourist bureaus, and embassies to gather information about that destination. To prepare their budget for the trip, they use a spreadsheet. They consult newspapers and other media to learn about current events or natural disasters in their chosen destinations. Before their journeys, they plan a bon voyage party, complete with party invitations to friends and family, using *Print Shop* (Broderbund).

During the actual "travel," students gather information using CD-ROM, laser disks, and other more traditional resources. They document their trips by keeping a daily log on audiotape or a word processor.

High school students are learning to do research on line in many different types of classroom activities. By logging on to the Internet, students may be able to discover up-to-the-minute information on the topics that interest them. When you give students assignments to research a topic on the Internet, you are wise to search for the information first, just as you would preread an assigned book or preview a film. Then be as specific as possible about the expectations you have for the project so that your students stay focused on the assignment you have given.

MATHEMATICS AND PROBLEM-SOLVING PROGRAMS

Computer programs are now available for classroom use that can diagnose students' skill levels in math, reading, vocabulary, and other basic skills and prescribe lessons at the appropriate level. In "teaching" the lessons, computers make excellent tutors because they are endlessly patient in waiting for a student response and give the appropriate feedback without emotional side effects. An excellent example is IBM's *Write to Read* program, which teaches primary students how to plan, write, and edit stories and poems. Josten Integrated Learning Systems offers an integrated package of reading and mathematics programs for the elementary school. Students are pretested on the computer in reading and math. They then begin to work at their own individual levels of mastery and progress through a series of learning activities that emphasizes comprehension and problem solving.

Like manipulatives in mathematics, many computer games provide students with realistic or simulated experiences that allow them to experiment, observe relationships, test hypotheses, and use data to reach conclusions supported by evidence. Programs such as *Gertrude's Secrets* (Learning Company) offer students the opportunity to manipulate objects.

Some gamelike programs are useful in expanding students' experiences beyond the classroom walls into simulated journeys, laboratories, foreign countries, earlier periods of history, and the future. Many of these programs increase students' decision-making and problem-solving abilities by offering them opportunities to make choices and get immediate feedback on the consequences of their decisions. An example is the program known as *Oregon Trail*, which allows students to simulate the experience of a wagon train journey with full decision-making power over how many supplies to bring, when to stop and restock, and how to deal with emergencies along the way. Poor choices in any of these areas leads to death on the trail. It takes most students many attempts to reach Oregon alive.

Another MECC program known as *Lemonade* plunges students into the economic decision making necessary to market a product to make a profit. Students must decide how many lemons to buy, how many glasses to make each day, how much advertising is needed, and what price to charge based on the weather report. Good choices lead to profits, and poor choices lead to losses.

Teachers can access both the *Oregon Trail* and *Lemonade* programs through the Minnesota Educational Computer Consortium (MECC), which is available in many school districts and libraries throughout the country. MECC offers its programs to teachers for classroom use for a minimal expense. By taking their own computer disks to a MECC software library, teachers are able to copy the programs they would like to use in their own classrooms.

Where in the World Is Carmen Sandiego? (Broderbund) is a multidisciplinary adventure program that allows students to explore the world in search of clues to solve a mystery. In the process, they learn about various countries and use logic and deduction to hypothesize about the solution to the mystery. After the initial success of this program, Broderbund used the same approach to encourage students to learn history in *Where in History Is Carmen Sandiego?* Programs such as these can be incorporated into unit plans or as a part of a learning contract. Students work with a partner to solve the mysteries and record the results in a notebook.

Many excellent software programs provide students with a blank slate for creating, inventing, and composing original works. *KidPix* (Broderbund) is a paint program that uses tools very similar to the ones used by professional artists and architects. Students can draw, paint, or use stamps to create designs and pictures. Patterns can be replicated and inverted, illustrating the mathematical relationships of patterns for students to see and manipulate. By becoming proficient with this child-centered program, students will be able to easily master the adult versions in later life.

Another interesting synthesis of learning materials and experiences is the program called *Lego/Logo* (Lego Dacta). Students create objects with Lego building blocks and then wire their moving parts to a computer terminal. Using the computer language known as LOGO, students can type in commands that control the movement of their logo machines and inventions from a computer terminal. This provides students with an authentic experience similar to the processes inventors now use in the computer age.

High school science and mathematics teachers are learning to employ image processing projects as a way to motivate students to learn about the environment, astronomy, physics, and biology. Instead of learning these subjects by reading textbooks, students are able to manipulate images of weather phenomena, CAT scans of the human brain, or constellation maps. A program called Image Processing for Teaching, in Tucson, Arizona, trains teachers in the art of using computer scanners, CD-ROMs, and software developed by the National Institute of Health that is in the public domain, which allows teachers to access hundreds of thousands of images from federal research projects. For more information, contact the Center for Image Processing in Education at (800) 322-9884.

RECORD KEEPING AND GRADING

In addition to student uses, teachers can use computers to create classroom materials, keep records, and compute grades. Many teachers use word processing programs to create and store curriculum plans, student worksheets, quizzes, and tests. They may also use them to write reports, proposals, and newsletters. Specialized record-keeping programs are available that allow teachers to record students' achievement. Many of these will compute average grades for report cards.

The major limitations on the use of computers in the classroom are money, availability of high-quality programs, and management concerns. Because of the expense of equipment, many schools have only a few computers that many classrooms must share. In some cases, computers are placed on traveling carts and moved from room to room according to a schedule. In this case, teachers must coordinate their plans to fit the computer schedule. In other instances, the computers are all housed in a single classroom designated as a computer lab, and teachers must arrange to bring their students to the lab when they wish to incorporate computers into their plans.

Even if each classroom has its own computer, locating high-quality computer software can be difficult. Most software is expensive, and much of it is of minimal value. Many programs that purport to teach math or language skills are little better than workbooks. Teachers must review software carefully before purchasing it. The criteria for selecting programs vary from class to class; but at a minimum, computer programs should be selected only if they are user-friendly and easy to load and start with simple directions. They should also be interesting and should actively engage the learner in a meaningful learning experience.

When teachers have access to computers in the classroom, they must learn to manage computer use efficiently. In some cases, the computer is available for a variety of student uses; in others, teachers may dedicate the use of the computer for a specific purpose for a period of time. Students may work singly or in pairs at a computer terminal. With 30 students, this means that each student gets to use the computer for only a short time each day.

Despite the management problems, computers are valuable tools with many uses in remediation, tutoring, and creative efforts. Additionally, when students are able to use computers frequently for a variety of purposes, they learn to accept and understand the

place of computers in society and are more likely to be ready to accept further technological advances of the 21st century.

CALCULATORS

Calculators are increasingly viewed as a valuable tool for investigating mathematical
and scientific relationships that are complex and difficult to compute with pencil and
paper. Teachers must consider which tasks are appropriate for calculators and which
are not. Many teachers separate learning arithmetic skills from other problem-solving
activities. When students are being asked to master the process of calculating multiplication or division or comparing fractions and decimals, then calculators are not used.
But for tasks designed to encourage students to explore patterns and functions, search
for a variety of ways to solve problems, or create and test hypotheses, calculators facilitate and encourage the students to accept and master complex investigations.

The California Mathematics Frameworks (1992) recommends viewing calculators as
the electronic pencils of today's world. Teachers are encouraged to provide every student with a calculator and to teach them to use the device to check paper and pencil
calculations as well as to use them in experiments and other mathematical explorations.

AUDIO-VIDEO TECHNOLOGY

Teachers have long used films, filmstrips, and audiotapes to supplement their classroom
instruction. Many of these resources can be ordered through the media center located
in the school. They can be used for whole class instruction, or they can be set up at a
learning center so that individuals or groups of students may listen to tapes or watch a
filmstrip on their own.

With the advent of video cameras, many new teaching strategies have emerged.
Video disks used along with computers have produced the capability of employing
interactive video for classroom use. An interactive format means that visual images
stored on the video disk can be programmed to play on a television monitor. The order
of the images can be completely controlled by the teacher or the students by typing
commands on the computer. If teachers wish to teach students about recent historical
events, they can obtain a video disk of recorded speeches and newscasts from specific
times. For example, as the teacher discusses Martin Luther King, Jr., the television
monitor can display him speaking in public. When the subject is earth science, a video
disk can be programmed to display various land forms at the teacher's command.

Video cameras provide the teacher with many exciting new strategies. Students'
products and performances can be recorded by the teacher or an assistant for future
evaluation purposes or to document that the event took place. Students can rehearse
their presentations on videotape and watch the recording to see what they need to
improve. I used the video camera to record the speeches my students gave in a unit
called "Panorama of the Presidents." In the early stages, students used the video camera to practice their speeches so they could see themselves and hear their own voices.
These preliminary looks at their own performance caused the students to study and
practice harder. We also videotaped the assembly in which they gave their final presen-

tations. Afterward, we had a permanent record of their accomplishments and were able to share the videotape with family members who had not been present at the event.

MANAGING TECHNOLOGY IN THE CLASSROOM

School computers are usually located in the classroom, the media center, or, in some cases, a computer laboratory with its own staff. Computer labs typically have from 15 to 30 computers that students use alone or in pairs under the direction or guidance of the computer lab teacher. The learning experiences planned for a class of students in a computer lab may include instruction about the use of computers or software programs so that the students will be able to put these skills to use in other settings.

In some cases, computer labs are used for students' homework or independent projects from other classes. Often, the classroom teacher and the computer specialist confer about what the students need to accomplish when they come into the laboratory. Occasionally, the computer specialist will initiate and manage a series of experiences for each grade level.

Having computer activities in a centralized laboratory has certain advantages. The teacher in the lab is likely to be more familiar with various programs and can efficiently select and instruct students in their use. Computer programs can be stored in the lab and distributed easily when students need them. On the negative side, when the entire school must be scheduled for time in the lab, each class may get only an hour or two per week to spend working with the computers.

This problem is not as serious if students have access to computers in their classrooms and in the media center as well as in the laboratory. Media center computers are managed by media center personnel. They may designate one or more computers to be used for CD-ROM research stations. Students use these computers whenever they want to search for information on the CD-ROM encyclopedia, atlas, or other data base. Other computers in the media center may be available for a variety of uses, including word processing, tutoring programs, and literature-based software packages. When the media center has a collection of software programs available, students may be allowed to check them out and use them on a computer in the room, getting assistance from media center personnel when needed.

In the classroom, teachers may have from one to six computers for use by the students and the teacher. Teachers may designate one or more computers for a specific use. In the primary grades, rotating schedules are often created that allow each child to use a computer to accomplish a specified task for the week. For example, while studying addition, students may rotate through four to six stations that allow them to practice addition. One of the stations may be a computer with a program like *Number Muncher* (MECC), an addition learning activity.

In the upper grades, schedules are often created so that students can sign up to use a computer. Cliff Gilkey, for example, has four computers in his classroom. He has collected a variety of software programs over the years. For some projects, he uses a rotation system that allows one cooperative group to use the computers at a time. He tries to keep the computers busy as much as possible during the day, so he rotates students to the computers for one task or another. During free time, students can choose to use the computer to play educational games.

Cliff keeps experimenting to find the most workable management plan for his computers. Even though he has used computers successfully for many years, he still feels like he is exploring their potential along with his students. "Computers change every year and we are all learning together. That's how the kids learn, by exploring, and so do I. Computers are a wonderful tool to open doors and that's what I want for my students. I know that because they have learned to use computers in the classroom, they won't be afraid of computer technology in the workplace."

Teaching Strategies That Fit Bloom's Taxonomy

In this section, brief descriptions of some of the most frequently used teaching strategies are presented to give you an overview of the rich and varied methods that are available. They are organized within the framework of the *Taxonomy of Educational Objectives* (Bloom, Engelhart, Furst, Hill, & Krathwohl, 1956) so that you can understand the relationship between planning an objective at a certain level of the taxonomy and selecting a teaching strategy or method to achieve that objective in the classroom. As you will see, some strategies, such as class discussion or cooperative groups, can be used to accomplish objectives at several levels of the taxonomy, depending on what the class is asked to discuss or what task the group is asked to do.

TEACHING STRATEGIES THAT DEVELOP A KNOWLEDGE BASE

The most common teaching strategies used to help students learn a knowledge base of facts, information, and skills are reading for information and the method known as *direct instruction*, described in Chapter 7. Many teachers also employ *drill and practice* strategies, having students repeat what they have learned in an oral recitation or in written exercises to reinforce their understanding of the new facts or skills and commit them to memory.

Drill, practice, lecture, reading, and recitation: are these the only strategies that teachers must master to teach the basic facts and skills that students need to know in each content area? These were the traditional teaching strategies that schools used until educational psychologists such as Ausubel (1960) showed that meaningful learning consists of linking new bits of knowledge to already known facts and ideas gained from previous learning experiences. Reflective teachers have learned from cognitive psychology that a key to successful learning of a knowledge base is providing rich and *varied* learning experiences, not just relying on drill and practice.

The curriculum emphasizes the learning of basic facts, skills, processes, and concepts in all subject areas. As students experience the complexities of the world they inhabit, they gather many unrelated verbal and numerical symbols, facts, data, concepts, and ideas. When these bits of knowledge are successfully integrated in the brain, they can be stored and recalled on demand. Cognitive psychologists use *schema theory* to explain this process of sensing, storing, and recalling information. Each separate schema is a storehouse of images, sensations, symbols, and words that are somehow related in an individual's mind (Anderson, 1977; Bransford, 1983).

For students to develop a knowledge base for a particular subject, they need first to create a simple, rudimentary, or basic schema on that topic through direct or vicarious experience. For example, consider how students learn about animals. Many students have an experience with a dog or a cat before coming to school. They store the sensations (furry, barking, wet nose and tongue, four legs, petting, tail) in a schema often labeled *doggy* or *kitty*. Images of stuffed teddy bears or goats in story books may be included in the student's schema labeled *doggy* for a time, until the child is able to differentiate among these four-legged creatures.

Children need additional experiences in school that will help them to develop richly detailed and accurate schemata on a variety of topics. This statement implies several teaching responsibilities. First, the teacher must choose teaching strategies and plan learning activities that provide students with appropriate experiences so that they gain new bits of knowledge and create new schemata. Second, the teacher must assist students in ordering and classifying the knowledge they have stored so that it is readily accessible.

Teachers can use many teaching strategies to provide students with new experiences, sensations, and ideas. Very young children can gain knowledge through vicarious experiences such as listening to the teacher read aloud, while older students can read for themselves. Hands-on activities are also important for schema development in the elementary grades. When children play with balls, rocket ships, measuring cups, dolls, and other objects, they develop increasingly complex schemata for these things. Field trips are especially likely to cause students of all ages to create new schemata. Taking students out of their familiar environments to go to a zoo, a museum, a play, or a concert is likely to result in the formation of new schemata.

Teachers assist students in classifying and ordering their existing schemata by planning verbal discussions and explications of what students are seeing and experiencing. Children may develop a schema for *alphabet* by viewing *Sesame Street* or singing the ABC song. But teachers must assist their students in making these symbols meaningful by explaining the relationship between a visual symbol and its meaning or use.

Manual tasks such as copying the letters of the alphabet help children differentiate among these symbols. Oral exercises make them aware of the sound that each letter represents. Matching pictures of familiar objects with the same sound as the letter helps children connect the symbol-sound-use relationship. With each new experience, their schema for alphabet becomes increasingly complex but also much better organized and accurate.

Drill, practice, memorization, and recitation may help students strengthen existing schemata, but they cannot replace authentic learning experience for schema creation or development. Reflective teachers are likely to plan active, creative, hands-on lessons to teach knowledge-level objectives.

TEACHING STRATEGIES THAT PROMOTE COMPREHENSION

Is comprehension the same as decoding? "Decoding means cracking a code, and this is exactly the function of decoding processes—they crack the code of print to make print meaningful" (Gagne, 1985, p. 167). Decoding strategies include (1) instructing students to match unknown printed words to their previously learned sight word vocabularies and (2) teaching students to use phonics to sound out unfamiliar words. Although these strategies are useful in the literal comprehension of words, reflective teachers know that students need to learn to comprehend ideas and concepts, not just single words.

To teach comprehension at ideas level, teachers often use a strategy known as an *advance organizer.* Ausubel (1960) demonstrated that teachers can increase student comprehension by introducing unfamiliar material with a statement showing how the new material is related to knowledge the student has already learned. This introduction allows the student to recall related schema before reading or hearing the new material. When the unknown ideas are encountered, the student has an existing schema in mind that makes the new idea more meaningful.

For example, when asking students to read a passage about the boundaries between nations, the teacher may describe how fences in a neighborhood are used to protect private property and maintain relationships among neighbors. This description uses language and concepts that students understand. It allows the student to call up an existing schema, *fences,* and be ready to construct a new schema called *boundaries.* After the passage is read, the teacher may ask students to tell how boundaries and fences are alike. The strategy of following up the reading with a discussion that includes the advance organizer and the new material strengthens the students' understanding of the new concept.

Teachers may use questions, clues, and suggestions to alert students to look, listen, or search for some new, previously unknown element. Madeline Hunter (1976) encourages teachers to use a variety of introductory experiences to motivate students to want to find out more about a subject. This strategy, the use of an *anticipatory set,* creates a positive anticipation for the student. For example, a teacher might preface the reading of a passage on water evaporation by wiping a wet sponge on the blackboard and drying it with a hair dryer. Students would then be asked to read the passage to discover what happened to the water.

Discussion is an important strategy that teachers use for increasing student comprehension of a new subject. As students state their ideas aloud, they are reinforcing their own understanding of the topic. When teachers respond to students' ideas by showing agreement or by giving useful feedback and clarification, they are further enhancing students' understanding. Class members who listen to their classmates' ideas and teacher's responses also may gain new perspectives and greater understanding of the subject.

One of the most frequent methods that teachers use to evaluate student comprehension is to ask students to say or write the meaning of something in their own words. In the example of water evaporation, a teacher may conduct a demonstration or allow students to experiment with water properties at various temperatures and then ask them to summarize in writing how water evaporates. When students are able to do this, the teacher knows that the concept has been successfully understood. If the students are unable to state or write a summary of the concept, the teacher knows that the material must be retaught.

To reteach, it is necessary to present a subject differently from the way it was taught the first time. When descriptions and explanations of unfamiliar material do not work, many teachers find that the use of *analogies* helps students understand a difficult new concept by building a bridge between unknown or abstract concepts and known, concrete experience. The use of the phrase *building a bridge* in the preceding sentence is itself an analogy for the abstraction known as *analogy.*

By describing how a fence is similar to an international boundary, the teacher makes an abstract concept more concrete. In a class discussion or lecture, the teacher may extend this analogy to describe how family loyalty resembles patriotism, how economies of nations are similar to the economies of families, and how the decisions about land use may vary from nation to nation as well as from family to family.

Another teaching strategy that promotes comprehension is to provide graphic examples and illustrations to assist students in interpreting new information. Just as a picture is worth a thousand words, a graph or a chart can summarize a great deal of data in a form that students can comprehend. Bar graphs show temperature comparisons much better than lists of figures do. Pie charts vividly demonstrate the amount of time or money spent on various pursuits better than paragraphs can. Reflective teachers frequently employ visual or graphic aids in their teaching. They also ask their students to create illustrations, graphs, diagrams, and charts to demonstrate that they have interpreted data or new concepts successfully.

TEACHING STRATEGIES THAT ALLOW STUDENTS TO APPLY WHAT THEY LEARN

A widely accepted principle of learning is that "if a student really comprehends something, then he can apply it" (Bloom et al., 1956, p. 120). The fact that most of what we learn is intended for application to problem situations in real life indicates the importance of application objectives in the general curriculum.

Reflective teachers are eager to offer students opportunities to apply what they've learned in most of the subjects in the curriculum. *Discussion*, as a teaching strategy, can be an occasion for application as well as for comprehension. For example, a teacher-led discussion on current events may focus on the way in which a news item affects the lives of students in the class. Literary discussions are valuable for the exchange of views on how characters deal with situations and how class members might act under those circumstances.

Many teachers employ *inquiry training, dilemmas, simulations,* and *role playing* to bring the world into the classroom. These strategies are described in greater detail in this book, but all have in common the presentation of a puzzling situation and the opportunity to discuss alternatives and generate solutions to problems. Their function is to assist students in clarifying what they know and believe about situations that they may well encounter throughout their lives. These strategies allow students to rehearse difficult decisions in the safe environment of their classroom so that later in life they will be able to make real decisions with more confidence.

Discovery learning is another strategy that classroom teachers can successfully use to cause their students to apply not only what they have already learned but also what they are currently learning, and thereby learning by doing. Instead of telling students a rule, principle, or concept, the teacher sets up conditions in the classroom so that students may discover it on their own. Math teachers frequently use this technique when they ask students to solve several equations and then state the rule or algorithm discovered in the process. Science processes frequently require students to discover a principle through experimentation. In both of these cases, students are applying known ideas to unknown situations and generating both solutions and insight in the process. This strategy is described in greater detail later in this chapter.

Another application strategy that reflective teachers employ is *model making,* as when students are asked to build or replicate a model of a Native American village, a simple machine, a heart that pumps simulated blood, or a volcano. Teachers also use *cooperative groups* as a strategy for having students apply communication and problem-solving skills to solve problems or do meaningful work together.

TEACHING STRATEGIES THAT REQUIRE ANALYSIS

As students apply what they have learned, they often think inductively about the specific cases they are working on and make generalizations about the ideas they are applying. Analysis calls on students to do the opposite: begin with a generalization and break it down into its constituent parts, separating elements and looking for relationships and organizational principles.

Teaching strategies that stimulate analytical thinking include *discussions* that focus on identifying the elements of an argument: assumptions, hypotheses, facts, opinions, inferences, and conclusions. For example, after reading an article on a controversial topic such as the relationship between drugs and gang membership, the teacher may ask students to separate the facts from the opinions in the article and to identify the author's assumptions and hypotheses.

Expanding on the analysis of separate elements, the teacher may then guide students in recognizing how the elements relate to one another. Discussion may focus on whether the data presented in the article are consistent with the author's original assumptions and how that affects the conclusions.

Analysis of relationships also can focus on comparisons, similarities, differences, and cause and effect. A strategy other than discussion that is appropriate to this level of Bloom's taxonomy is *independent research* to compare and contrast or show cause and effect. After the research is complete, teachers usually ask that students prepare written or oral reports on their findings. They may require students to prepare charts that classify the elements they've studied or graphs showing relationships. As an example, the teacher may assign students (individually or in cooperative groups) to investigate one of the systems of the human body. Students researching the skeletal system will have to describe, illustrate, and analyze the bones (elements) and how they fit together (relationships). They may also prepare charts that show the cause-and-effect relationship of good and bad nutrition on bone development.

Analytical thinking has much in common with what is now known as *critical thinking.* The discussion strategies to promote critical thinking described in Chapter 8 also help students think and communicate with one another in an analytical way.

TEACHING STRATEGIES THAT ENCOURAGE SYNTHESIS

Synthesis is another word for creativity; it occurs when students express what they have learned in an original way. According to Bloom et al. (1956), synthesis involves "recombination of parts of previous experience with new material, reconstructed into a new and more or less well-integrated whole" (p. 162). Synthesis requires that an individual or a group create a unique communication or product. The teacher establishes criteria to make sure the students' products fit the subject and demonstrate that learning has taken place.

In the classroom, synthesis is usually expressed through *art, music, creative writing, storytelling,* and *drama* activities related to the subject being taught. Criteria may specify that these products include a number of facts in the stories or plays, show realistic details in the drawings, or suggest new ways of solving the problems or issues in the subject being taught.

After students study the first Thanksgiving, many teachers allow them to dramatize the event with simple costumes and a real or simulated feast. In a unit on the prairie, a teacher may allow students to create a mural of the prairie along one side of the classroom. Students are allowed to draw and paint their pictures of prairie grasses, animals, and insects on the mural. After reading a story, students may be asked to write a new ending for it or to extend a book by writing a new chapter.

The primary reason for including synthesis activities and products in the curriculum is because they emphasize and encourage personal expression rather than passive participation, independence of thought and action rather than dependence (Bloom et al., 1956).

TEACHING STRATEGIES THAT GENERATE EVALUATION

The highest level of Bloom's taxonomy is evaluation because it represents an end process in the range of cognitive behaviors in which students are asked to make judgments about some aspect of what they have studied. A key element of evaluation is that the students are expected to use criteria in making their judgments, although these criteria can be determined by the students or given to them by the teacher. It is believed that students can make the most informed judgments after experiencing all of the other levels of the taxonomy (Bloom et al., 1956).

For example, a unit on economics may begin with preliminary discussions that encourage the students to give their opinions about how to spend their allowances, but by the end of the unit it is expected that their opinions will become better informed and that they will be able to make judgments about money using criteria such as supply and demand.

Teaching strategies that generate useful, valid evaluations are those that involve students in *discussion, writing, problem solving, debate,* and any other activities in which students express their own views and opinions on a subject. In the classroom, one of the most frequently used strategies is a class discussion after reading a story or a chapter in a book. Students are asked to say whether they agree or disagree with the character or the issue and to state why.

Group problem-solving endeavors on controversial issues may cause students to clarify and articulate their attitudes and opinions about how to solve a problem. Simulations may be used to illustrate the complex nature of real-life problems. For example, students may be given roles to play in a simulation of where to locate a new city dump. They must use criteria to persuade the group to locate the dump somewhere other than their own backyards.

It is not easy for teachers to assess their students' evaluation activities. Because free expression of opinions and judgments is expected, perhaps the only fair way to assess student products is to determine the extent to which the students use evidence and criteria to support their judgments.

Classroom Examples of Teaching Strategies

You may read or hear about a variety of interesting teaching strategies that you would like to add to your own repertoire. To assist you as you reflect on which strategies are appropriate for you, this section provides a brief overview of some innovative methods. Not all of them will appeal to you, but many of them can be employed to provide variety and spice to your classroom curriculum. As you read these brief descriptions, keep in mind that you must look for more detailed sources of information to truly understand the model and how it can be used.

DISCOVERY LEARNING

In the 1960s and 1970s a phenomenon known as the *open classroom* bloomed, mushroomed, and then faded into obscurity. The underlying philosophy of the open classroom was that students would become more active and responsible for their own learning in an environment that allowed them to make choices and encouraged them to take initiative. To this end, the rows of desks in many classrooms were rearranged to provide more space for activity and learning centers. The curriculum of the open classroom was revised to allow students to choose from among many alternatives and schedule their own time to learn what they wanted to learn when they wanted to learn it (Silberman, 1973).

One of the teaching strategies emphasized in the open classroom was known as *discovery learning*. The principle of discovery learning is that students learn best by doing rather than by hearing or reading about a concept. Teachers may still find this strategy an excellent addition to their repertoire. It can be used occasionally to provide real, rather than vicarious, experience in a classroom.

In employing discovery learning, the teacher's role is to gather and provide equipment and materials related to a concept that the teacher wants the students to learn. Sufficient materials should be available so that every student or pair of students has immediate access to them. Materials that are unfamiliar, interesting, and stimulating are especially important to a successful discovery learning experience. After providing the materials, the teacher may ask a question or offer a challenge that causes students to discover the properties of the materials. Then, as the students begin to work or "mess about" with the materials, the teacher's role is to monitor and observe as the students discover the properties and relationships inherent in the materials, asking occasional questions or making suggestions that will guide the students in seeing the relationships and understanding the concepts. The period of manipulation and discovery is then followed by a discussion in which students verbalize what they have observed and learned from the experience (Hawkins, 1965).

A simple example at the primary level is the use of discovery learning to teach the concept of colors and their relationships to one another. Rather than telling students that blue and yellow make green or demonstrating that they do while students watch, the strategy of discovery learning is to provide every student with a brush and two small puddles of blue and yellow paint on white paper and allow them to discover it for themselves. In this case, the opening question may simply be "What happens when you mix blue and yellow together?" When this relationship becomes apparent and students verbalize it, the teacher can then provide additional puddles of red and white paint and challenge students to "create as many different colors as you can." Experiences can be easily designed to allow students to discover how and why some things float, what makes a light bulb light, how electricity travels in circuits, and the difference between solutions and mixtures.

Math relationships also can be discovered. Beans, buttons, coins, dice, straws, and toothpicks can be sorted according to size, shape, color, and other attributes. Objects can be weighed and measured and compared with one another. The concept of multiplication can be discovered when students make sets of objects in rows and columns. Many resources in the form of math curriculum projects involving discovery learning are presently being developed for schools because discovery is a part of the problem-solving process, a current hot topic in education.

INQUIRY TRAINING

Closely linked to the discovery method is a strategy known as inquiry training. Teachers who believe that their students must learn how to ask questions and carry out other types of investigations to become active learners often plan lessons that stimulate their students' curiosity and then train them in asking productive questions and using critical thinking, observation skills, and variations of the scientific method to gather information, make informed estimates or predictions, and then design investigations to test their hypotheses.

For example, a classroom teacher wanted to train her students to think like scientists do, using the skills of observation, inquiry, prediction, hypotheses testing, and experiment designing to find out what they need to know. She grouped her students into pairs and distributed a clear plastic glass and five raisins to each dyad. She asked them to predict what would happen to the raisins if they were dropped into a glass of water. Most students correctly guessed that the raisins would sink to the bottom of the glass. The teacher then discussed with her students the need to keep an open mind and not jump to easy conclusions based on prior knowledge. She poured a carbonated lemon-lime beverage into the students' glasses and asked them to predict whether the raisins would sink or float. Each pair of students wrote down a prediction. The teacher generated a chart on the board showing the class predictions.

After recording the predictions, the teacher allowed the students to drop the raisins into their glasses. At first it appeared that the students who predicted that the raisins would sink were correct because the raisins fell to the bottom of the glasses. But as the students watched, several raisins began to rise to the top. In the next few minutes, the students observed a puzzling phenomenon. Raisins moved up and down in the glasses, each at its own pace.

At this stage in the lesson, the teacher encouraged the students to ask questions of her and of each other as they all tried to make sense out of what they were observing. The teacher answered their questions with yes and no answers, giving her students the responsibility of articulating the questions and gathering the information they needed to make meaning out of the situation. Soon they began to generate new investigations that they would have to undertake to discover why some raisins moved up and down more quickly and why some settled to the bottom.

To stimulate your own curiosity and encourage you to use the reflective actions of gathering information, being creative, and being persistent in solving problems, I will not disclose the reasons for the raisins' movement. Try the experiment yourself and try to think like a scientist. If you have opportunities to learn like this yourself, you will be better able to provide your students with the encouragement and support they need without rushing to provide them with answers. You will allow them to take the time they need to inquire and experiment so that they can succeed and fully experience the "aha" moment, just as scientists do when their inquiries lead them to new understandings.

ROLE PLAYING

When problems or issues involving human relationships are part of the curriculum, teachers may choose to use role playing to help students explore and understand the whole range of human feelings that surround any issue. This strategy is frequently used to resolve personal problems or dilemmas, but it can also be employed to gain understanding about the feelings and values of groups outside of the classroom.

For example, to help students understand the depth of emotions experienced by immigrants coming to a new and unfamiliar country, the teacher may ask students to role-play the interactions among family members who are separated or the dilemmas of the Vietnamese boat people or others who want to emigrate to the United States but are stopped by immigration quotas.

Successful and meaningful role playing has two major phases: the role playing itself and the subsequent discussion and evaluation period. In the first phase, the teacher's responsibility is to give students an overview of both phases of role playing so that they know what to expect. The teacher then introduces and describes a problem or dilemma, identifies the roles to be taken, assigns the roles, and begins the action by setting the stage and describing the immediate problem that the actors must confront. Roles must be assigned carefully. Usually teachers select students who are involved in the problem to play the role. In an academic dilemma, the roles may be assigned to students who most need to expand their experience with and understanding of the issue. Students who are not assigned roles are expected to be careful observers.

To set up the role-playing situation, the teacher can arrange some chairs to suggest the setting of the event to be played out. During the role play itself, the actors are expected to get inside the problem and "live" it spontaneously, responding realistically to one another. The role play may not flow smoothly; actors may experience uncertainty and be at a loss for words just as they would in real life. The first time a role is played, the problem may not be solved at all. The action may simply establish the problem, which in later enactments can be probed and resolved.

To increase the effect of role playing, Leyser (1982) suggests that, after playing a scene out once, the actors may exchange roles and play out the same scene so that they grow to understand the other characters' points of view. Actors may be allowed to select consultants to discuss and improve the roles they are playing.

In the second phase, the observers discuss the actions and words of the initial role players. The teacher helps the observers review what they have seen and heard, discuss the main events, and predict the consequences of actions taken by the role players. Following the initial discussion, the teacher will probably decide to have new class members replay the role to show an alternative way of handling the problem. The situation can be replayed a number of times if necessary. When a role-played situation generates a useful solution or suggests an effective way of handling a problem, the situation can be adapted, and subsequent role plays can focus on communication skills that will enhance or improve the situation even further.

Role playing has many applications in both the cognitive and affective goals of the curriculum. Through role playing, students can experience history by researching the life of a public figure and taking the role in a historical interaction. Each student in the class, for example, can study the life of a U.S. president and be the president for a day. Frequently, teachers ask students to play the role of characters in books that they have read as a means of reporting their own reading and stimulating others in the class to read the book. Students can enact the feelings of slaves and slave traders, the roles of scientists as they are doing science, or the interaction between an author and an editor as they try to perfect a piece of writing.

Students can learn new behaviors and social skills that may help them win greater peer acceptance and enhance their own self-esteem. Interpersonal conflicts that arise in the classroom can be role-played as a means of helping students discover more productive and responsible ways of behaving. For example, when two students argue about taking turns with a toy in the kindergarten class, the teacher can ask the students to role-play the situation in an effort to learn new ways of speaking to one another, asserting their own desires, and creating a plan for sharing the scarce resource. In a classroom, the teacher may notice that one student is isolated and treated like a scapegoat by others in the class. The dilemma can be role-played with the role of the isolated student assigned to some of the students who have been most critical and aggressive toward the student. Through this active, vicarious experience, students may learn to be more tolerant and accepting of one another.

SIMULATION

Student drivers drive simulated vehicles before they learn to drive a real car on the highway. Airplane simulators provide a realistic but safe way for student pilots to practice flying, in which mistakes lead to realistic consequences without threatening lives. Simulations usually involve some type of role playing but also include other gamelike features, such as a set of rules, time limits, tokens, or other objects that are gained or lost through the action of the simulation, and a way of recording the results of the players' decisions and actions. Simulations almost always focus on dilemmas in which the players must make choices, take actions, and then experience feedback in the form of consequences of their actions. The purpose of simulations is primarily to allow young people to experience tough, real-life problems and learn from the consequences in the safe, controlled environment of the classroom.

One of the longest-running international simulation projects in the world is the Model United Nations project, which was begun in 1926 and is still going strong. Each year more than 60,000 students from middle schools, high schools, and colleges participate in role-play simulations of U.N. meetings. Students are assigned the roles of ambassadors of U.N. member nations and learn how to debate and negotiate the many diverse global problems on the U.N.'s agenda for that year. Model United Nations can be conducted in a classroom or as an extracurricular club. The United Nations Association publishes resource materials for students and teachers interested in the project. Contact them at UNA-USA, 485 Fifth Avenue, New York, NY 10017; (212) 697-3232 or fax (212) 682-9185.

Many valuable academic and social simulations can be used to enrich the classroom experience and cause students to understand the relationship among choices, actions, and consequences. The teacher can purchase or create simulation games. A company named Interact publishes catalogs of simulations in all areas of the curriculum that can be purchased for a relatively small price. These kits include teacher's manuals describing the rules, time limits, and procedures to follow and a set of student materials that may include fact sheets, game pieces, and record-keeping devices. Titles of some of the simulations they publish include *Zoo, Dinosaur, King Lexicon, Shopping Spree,* and *Classroom City.*

The role of the teacher during a simulation is to explain the conditions, concepts to be covered, and expectations at the outset of the event. A practice session may be held to familiarize participants with the rules and procedures that govern the simulation. After assigning roles or creating groups that will interact, the teacher moderates, keeps time, clarifies misconceptions, and provides feedback and consequences in response to the participants' actions. At the conclusion of the simulation, the teacher leads a discussion of what occurred and what was learned by asking students to summarize events and problems and to share their perceptions and insights with one another. At the end of the discussion, the teacher may compare the simulation to its real-life counterpart and ask students to think critically about what they would do in real life as a result of having taken part in the simulation.

An example of a simulation in economics involves the creation of small companies or stores in which students decide on a product, create the product, set up the store, price and sell the product, and keep records on the transactions. The purpose, of course, is to learn about the principles of supply and demand as well as the practical skills of exchanging money and making change. Along with the primary goals of the simulation, there are secondary learning experiences. Students are also likely to increase their capacity for critical thinking and to learn about their own actions and decisions regarding competition, cooperation, commitment to a goal, and communication.

Students may simulate the writing of the U.S. Constitution by writing a classroom constitution. After studying various countries of the world, sixth-grade students may take part in a mock United Nations simulation in which students are delegates and face daily world problems presented to them by the teacher.

In language arts, students may establish a class newspaper to learn how news is gathered and printed in the real world. They may even establish a number of competitive newspapers to add another dimension of reality to the simulation. Students may simulate the writing, editing, and publishing processes as they write, print, and distribute their own original books.

An excellent example of a classroom simulation that provoked students to think critically and change their views on an important human issue is described in *A Class Divided* (1984) by William Peters. Jane Elliott, a third-grade teacher in Riceland, Iowa, taught her students to think critically about racial prejudice by randomly dividing the class into two groups: those with brown eyes and those with blue eyes. She actively discriminated against the students with blue eyes for a full school day. Mimicking behaviors of people who exhibit racial prejudice, she called the blue-eyed students names, did not let them play on the swings, and criticized their work and behavior. She successfully influenced the brown-eyed students to follow her lead and convinced them to avoid social contact with their inferior blue-eyed classmates.

The next day, Jane reversed the process and discriminated against the brown-eyed students in much the same way. Blue-eyed students were now considered superior to brown-eyed students in her eyes and their own. At the conclusion of the second day, Jane led a discussion of the effects of the entire learning experience. Twenty years later, at their high school reunion, her students reported that their understanding of prejudice and their attitudes toward people of different races were radically restructured as a result of this classroom experience.

Before the experience they had not been critical thinkers about racial prejudice. They easily accepted the prevailing notion that some people are superior to others. Afterward, they had grown in empathy, had recognized points of view different from their own, and had become more self-directed or independent in their thinking than they were before the experience.

Simulations may be used to introduce a unit or as the culminating activity of a unit. They may take a few minutes or the entire year. They may be continued from week to week but played for only a specified amount of time during each session. Some may take a full day or longer. Simulations are powerful learning experiences that may change the way that students view themselves and the world, as it did for the participants in the blue eyes/brown eyes experience.

MASTERY LEARNING

Teaching strategies known as *mastery learning* derive from the philosophy that all students can learn if the task fits their aptitude and they have sufficient time to master the new skill or concept. The theoretical model for mastery learning was inspired by Carroll's (1963) observation that students with low aptitude for a particular subject could still learn that subject but that it would take them more time to do so. He proposed that students have different *learning rates* rather than different ability levels.

Bloom (1974) created a practical system for instruction using mastery learning based on Carroll's (1963) theoretical model. Carroll observed that most schools are established on the assumption that learners vary in their ability to achieve. Bloom disagrees. Studies conducted under his guidance have shown that 95 percent of the students in our schools can achieve the educational objectives established for them; but because they learn at different rates, some students appear to be better or worse than others.

Bloom (1984) points to cases in which students are tutored to prove his point. In a controlled experiment, he demonstrated that "the average tutored student outperformed 98% of the students in the control class" (p. 5). He attributes this finding to the fact that a tutor is able to determine what each student knows in a given subject and is then able to plan an educational program that begins instruction at the student's level and proceeds at the student's own pace.

The basic structure of the mastery learning model, including adaptations known as *individually prescribed instruction (IPI)* and *continuous progress,* lend themselves best to the learning of basic skills in sequentially structured subjects. Very specific behavioral objectives are written for each unit of study. Pretests are used to assess students' prior knowledge, which then determines their placement or starting level. Working individually, as students master each objective in the sequence of learning, they are able to proceed to the next one. Periodically, unit tests covering several objectives are given to check on the mastery and retention of a whole range of knowledge and skills.

The teacher's role in this process is quite different from teaching skills with a whole class approach. The teacher rarely instructs the entire class at one time. Instead, as students work independently, the teacher monitors their progress by walking around the classroom and responding to requests for assistance. In a cooperative version of mastery learning, Slavin (1987) proposes the TAI model (see Chapter 9), which pairs students as monitors and assistants for one another during a mastery learning experience. This frees the teacher to work with small groups of students rather than devoting all of the time to responding to individual needs.

The value of mastery learning is that it allows students to actively learn new material and skills on a continuous basis. Motivation to achieve also presumably increases because students are working at their own pace and have the prerequisite skills necessary for success. Also, because testing is done individually and students have opportunities to repeat what they did not learn, they should suffer less embarrassment when they make mistakes. The primary goal of mastery learning programs is to help students become independent, self-directed learners.

CONTRACTS FOR INDEPENDENT LEARNING

While mastery learning is appropriate for use only in sequential subjects that require a great deal of independent practice, many teachers are searching for methods of promoting independence and self-directed learning in other subjects as well. An alternative to direct, whole-class instruction is the use of independent or group academic learning contracts. A learning contract such as the one in Figure 10.1 is usually created by the teacher at the beginning of a unit of study. The contract specifies one list of required activities, such as reading a chapter in the textbook, finding a library resource and writing a summary of the topic, completing a fact sheet, and other necessary prerequisites for developing a knowledge base on the subject.

A second list of activities is offered as choices or alternatives for students to pursue. This list includes opportunities to do additional independent research or create plays, stories, songs, and artwork on the topic. When learning contracts are offered to develop

Westward Expansion of the United States
Required Learning Activities

Date   Approval

_____ _____   Read Chapter 6 in the social studies textbook.

_____ _____   Write answers to the questions at the end of the unit.

_____ _____   Locate and read a book on the American West or Indians.

_____ _____   Write a 2–4 page summary of the book

_____ _____   Play the computer game *Oregon Trail* until you successfully reach the state of Oregon alive.

Alternative Learning Activities

_____ _____   Imagine that you are a member of a wagon train heading west. Write a series of letters back "home" describing your journey.

_____ _____   Write a play about a meeting between Indians and settlers. Find a cast for your play and present it to the class assembly.

_____ _____   Draw or paint a large picture of a scene that you imagine took place during the westward expansion.

_____ _____   Create a song or ballad about life in the west. Be prepared to play and sing it for the assembly.

_____ _____   Create a diorama or a model of a Plains Indian village.

_____ _____   Research the lives of the Plains Indians today. Be prepared to give a speech about the conditions in which they live now and how this is related to the westward expansion.

_____ _____   Create an alternative plan for a learning experience on this topic.

- -

I, _____, agree to complete the following required learning activities
by the date_____. In addition, I select two to five alternative activities to pursue on my
own. I will present my creative work to my classmates at our assembly on _____.

_____   I have reviewed this contract and understand the work
            student signature   my child has agreed to do. I agree to support this effort.

_____   _____
            teacher signature   parent signature

Figure 10.1   Independent learning contract.

independence, individuals usually select the activities they want to accomplish. A variation on this strategy would be to combine the concepts of cooperative groups and learning contracts and allow each group to sign a joint contract specifying the tasks and products they will complete.

Science investigations, social studies research projects, and creative language-arts activities can be described in learning contracts. The primary advantage of this strategy is that it allows individuals at various ability levels to work on an appropriate amount and type of work during the unit of study. High-achieving students can select the maximum number of tasks and products, and lower-achieving students can select fewer tasks. Theoretically, both types of students can actively learn and experience success during the same amount of time.

GROUP ROTATIONS USING LEARNING CENTERS

Learning centers or stations are areas of the classroom where students can go to do independent or group work on a given subject or topic. Learning centers vary enormously in appearance, use, and length of time for which they are set up. Teachers who use learning centers use them for a variety of purposes and with a variety of expectations.

Some centers may be informal and unstructured in their use. For example, a classroom may have a permanent science center containing a variety of science equipment and materials. Students are free to go to the center to do science experiments in their free time. The same classroom may have a permanent reading center furnished with a rug, comfortable chairs, and shelves or racks of books where students can go to read quietly.

Other centers are set up for a limited amount of time and have highly structured expectations. For example, to accompany the unit on settling the western United States described in the learning contract, the teacher may have set up an area of the classroom as a research center. It would contain a computer with the MECC computer program called *Oregon Trail* turned on and ready for students to use. It would also contain posters and maps of the western United States and a variety of reading materials on the topic. When the unit is finished, the center will be redesigned; new learning materials will replace the ones in the finished unit, and the center will become the focus of a new unit of study.

In primary classrooms, learning centers are often an important adjunct to reading and language arts. Many teachers set up four or five learning centers or stations with different activities each week. Students in small groups travel from one station to another according to a prespecified schedule. For example, Ginny Bailey uses a weekly theme as the basis for her first-grade language-arts program. Each week she sets up activities related to that theme in her five stations: art, math, writing, listening, and reading. To accompany her butterfly theme, students will find books on butterflies to read at the reading station, paper and directions for a writing project at the writing center, paint and brushes to create a picture at the art station, a prerecorded tape to listen to at the listening station, and a math game involving butterflies and caterpillars at the math station.

Ginny uses five centers—one for each day—and that means each group can visit each center once a week. A poster on the wall shows the schedule of groups and centers:

Learning Station Schedule					
Group	**Monday**	**Tuesday**	**Wednesday**	**Thursday**	**Friday**
Blue	Art	Math	Writing	Reading	Listening
Green	Math	Writing	Reading	Listening	Art
Red	Writing	Reading	Listening	Art	Math
Yellow	Reading	Listening	Art	Math	Writing
Orange	Listening	Art	Math	Writing	Reading

In Ginny's classroom, students can go to their stations only after completing their daily work assignments. In her system, the stations extend the students' learning experiences on the weekly theme but are also used as an incentive system for students to complete their required work.

Teachers who work with students who have limited English proficiency are finding that rotations from one learning center to another give the students many rich opportunities to use the English language with their peers as well as with adults. In a kindergarten classroom at Hamilton School in mid-city San Diego, Susan King recently completed her Cultural, Language, and Academic Development (CLAD) teaching credential. In her classroom, she wants to create a learning environment that enables her Limited English Proficient (LEP) students to take risks with English so that they develop oral fluency in their new language. In Case 10.1, you can read about how she changed her entire system of teaching within a few months when she became aware that her LEP students were becoming less proficient and quieter under the conventional teacher-centered system she had been using.

Case 10.1 ⊃ Reflective Action
Establishing Learning Centers

Susan King, CLAD Kindergarten Teacher
Hamilton School, San Diego

Perceptiveness

At the beginning of my first year as a kindergarten teacher, I organized my classroom for whole-group instruction in reading and language arts. I used conventional methods in which my students all worked at the same task at the same time, with a great deal of direct instruction from me. Then I began to take course work to get my Cultural, Language, and Academic Development (CLAD) teaching credential. The new knowledge I gained in these courses caused me to become aware of the needs of the Limited English Proficient (LEP) students in my class. What I first perceived was that the room was too quiet. Students sat quietly, waiting passively for me to tell them what to do. There were very few opportunities for oral language development using this teacher-centered approach to teaching. So I decided to take some risks myself and reorganize my entire classroom system to stimulate talking, problem solving, and cooperative learning.

Constructing a Knowledge Base

Through my CLAD training, I became aware of how important it was to include parent volunteers or peer tutors who are familiar with the primary or first language (L-1) of LEP students in my program. In my classroom, these L-1 languages include Spanish and Laotian. I recruited Spanish- and Laotian-speaking parents and upper-grade students to assist me in my classroom. I also decided to use the resources of my own students who are bilingual. After five months of conventional instruction, I decided to abandon my whole-group approach to teaching language arts except for the opening activities. In my CLAD course work, I learned about sheltered teaching instructions that emphasize using guided reading in small groups to develop language.

In order to be able to give my full attention to the students in the guided reading group, I had to find a way to organize the learning environment so that the other 25 students were busy and would not need to interrupt me. This felt like a real challenge to me because even though I had recruited parent volunteers, they did not come consistently. So I went to my colleagues who teach upper grades and asked them to send me some helpers who would like to help in the kindergarten. The response was overwhelmingly positive. Just as my students needed peer tutors, the older students need this type of responsibility to enhance their own self-image.

I talked with the peer tutors and parent volunteers and asked them to assist without taking over. I want my kindergarten students to communicate and become better problem solvers.

Our district has designated mentor teachers who are willing to share the teaching strategies they employ with beginning teachers. I arranged to visit a mentor teacher who uses a rotation schedule for her kindergarten/first-grade classroom and I learned more in that one day than I could imagine. I was able to see the physical arrangement of her classroom and watch her students travel from one learning center to another. I took pictures of the charts and schedules she used to direct traffic in her room. I also took pictures of the students working at the various centers she had established. From this visit, I was able to envision the changes that would need to be made in my classroom.

Creativity

During winter break, I began to design the materials I would need to get started. When we returned to school in January, I plunged into the whole new system. I set up four different learning stations in my classroom: journal writing, a reading basket, a structured activity center, and the guided reading group. Peer tutors supervised the structured activity center to help students with science, math, and social studies. In all the centers I encouraged my students to talk with each other, share ideas, help each other, and solve whatever problems were at hand. I instructed them to ask everyone in their group for help and then ask the peer tutor or group captain before coming to ask me for help. With this management system, I was free to work with the guided reading group without interruptions.

I grouped the students according to their oral language proficiency and made up a chart to display how the groups would rotate through the various centers. They went from guided reading to journal writing, then to structured center activities, and then to the reading basket.

Clarification of Values and Principles

It took about two weeks for the students to be accustomed to the movement from one area to the next. It took even longer for them to become independent learners. At first they would stand still, waiting for me to come give them direct teaching or instruction about every little step. When I saw this response, of stillness and waiting to be spoon-fed, I thought to myself, What a disservice we are doing to students when we train them to be passive learners. I realized that the whole-group teaching I had done for the first five months had caused this response. I had trained them to wait for my every word and not to think for themselves.

Persistence and Problem Solving

Every day for the first month, I spent time in my opening activities talking to students about problem solving, independent working, cooperative learning. "When you go to your journal writing center, open your books and begin. Don't wait for me or anyone else to come help you. When you finish writing, share what you've written with the rest of the group." What I was promoting was that they would be in charge of their own learning. I began to see more interaction among students first at the reading basket. I saw them pairing off to read books, using sentence strips to quiz each other. Then I saw it begin at the journal center. There were a few students who resisted taking responsibility for their own learning, and I had to set up consequences.

I had taken these steps in order to encourage more risk taking and oral language development, and I soon began to see that I had done the right thing. In the guided reading groups, I began to hear my LEP students speak up. They raised their hands and seemed eager to participate in the small group where before, in a group of 30, they had been very quiet and timid. They showed excitement about talking to me and their classmates. I saw their eyes gleaming; I heard their laughter as they showed eagerness to read and talk about what they read. What amazed me most is that I discovered that they knew more English than I thought they knew. I thought that they were still at a stage where they were only able to point in response to my questions. Instead, I found that they were able to speak whole sentences when they felt safe and encouraged to speak by their small group of classmates.

In my classroom, I encourage my students to use both their native language (L-1) and their new language (L-2) as they need it. By the end of the year, they were so confident about speaking and problem solving with their classmates that they all wanted to be peer tutors themselves. As the students grew in independence, I was able to give my time to the students who needed me most.

Communication Skills

I learned a great deal from several mentor teachers whom I visited before and during the transformation of my classroom organization. Someday, I may want to become a mentor teacher for other beginning teachers and invite them to observe my classroom. But I'm not ready for that yet. I'm still going to give my energy to making this system work for me and my students. However, when other adults visit my classroom now to observe me or a student, they are intrigued with the independence and interdependence of my students. A resource teacher who visited recently to watch the behavior of a troubled child observed my guided reading group and then looked around to see the other students working so independently—solving problems and taking charge of their own learning. As he left, he told me, "I can't believe this is a kindergarten class. The students are so responsible—so in charge of their own learning."

YOUR OWN REPERTOIRE OF TEACHING STRATEGIES

With a repertoire of teaching strategies from which to choose, you can expect to create a stimulating classroom that appeals to students from a range of backgrounds and with a variety of learning style preferences. You can be flexible and creative. When one teaching strategy does not work, you can select another and reteach the lesson. You can look forward to a year of varied experiences for yourself and your students.

The strategies described in this book are only the tip of the iceberg. Each one has dozens of variations, and many additional strategies can be successfully employed to build a classroom environment that meets the needs of all of your students and creates new horizons and new interests that they did not have when they entered your classroom.

To continue to expand your repertoire, plan to conduct an active search for new ideas, methods, and learning activities. Consult your professors for sources of interesting learning materials. Talk to classroom teachers you admire and ask them for copies of their favorite ideas and activities. Read educational journals and magazines and clip out the best ideas. Begin now to build a file of interesting classroom materials that you can adapt and use throughout your career.

➲ Reflective Actions for Your Professional Portfolio
Your Repertoire of Teaching Strategies

Perceptiveness: Observe Strategies in Action
Make a classroom observation for the purpose of identifying the types of instructional strategies used by the person teaching the lesson. Note the effects each strategy has on the students' interest and comprehension.

Construction of Knowledge: Expand Your Repertoire
Consider some of the strategies you have observed, heard, or read about. Select one or more and do the research necessary to have a basic understanding of how you could employ these strategies in a classroom situation.

Clarification of Values: Learning Strategies You Prefer
Which teaching strategies are you most likely to employ in your classroom? Why? How do they fit your emerging style of teaching? Have you selected an adequate variety of strategies to motivate students with different learning styles and needs? Which strategies would you avoid using? Why?

Creativity: Plan a Lesson Using Your Favorite New Strategies
Arrange with the classroom teacher to let you plan and teach a lesson to a group of students. Incorporate some of the strategies you most prefer. Select your teaching strategies to fit the lesson and the needs of your students.

Persistence and Problem Solving: Review and Revise
Videotape your lesson and review it to observe how well the strategies fit the subject and your students' needs. Replan the lesson, making adjustments as necessary. If possible, reteach it to the same or a different group of students to see how effective the changes are.

Communication Skills: Self-Evaluation
Write a reflective evaluation of your lesson, describing the effects of each teaching strategy you used. Were some more effective with one set of students than with another?

References

Anderson, R. (1977). The notion of schemata and the educational enterprise. In R. Anderson, R. Spiro, & W. Montague (Eds.), *Schooling and the acquisition of knowledge* (pp. 415–431). Hillsdale, NJ: Erlbaum.

Ausubel, D. P. (1960). The use of advance organizers in the learning and retention of meaningful verbal material. *Journal of Educational Psychology, 51,* 267–272.

Bloom, B., Engelhart, M., Furst, E., Hill, W., & Krathwohl, D. (1956). *Taxonomy of educational objectives: Cognitive domain.* New York: Longman.

Bloom, B. (1974). An introduction to mastery learning theory. In J. H. Block (Ed.), *Schools, society and mastery learning* (pp. 12–21). New York: Holt, Rinehart, & Winston.

Bloom, B. (1984). The search for methods of group instruction as effective as one-to-one tutoring. *Educational Leadership, 41*(8), 4–17.

Bransford, J. (1983). Schema activation–schema acquisition. In R. Anderson, J. Osborn, & R. Tierney (Eds.), *Learning to read in American schools* (pp. 23–37). Hillsdale, NJ: Erlbaum.

California State Department of Education. (1992). *Mathematics frameworks.* Sacramento: Bureau of Publication Sales, P.O. Box 271, Sacramento, CA 95802-0271.

Carroll, J. (1963). A model of school learning. *Teachers College Record, 64,* 723–733.

Gagne, E. (1985). *The cognitive psychology of school learning.* Boston: Little, Brown.

Hawkins, D. (1965). Messing about in science. *Science and Children, 2*(5), 5–9.

Leyser, Y. (1982). Role playing in the classroom: A threat or a promise. *Contemporary Education, 53,* 70–74.

Peters, W. (1984). *A class divided: Then and now.* New Haven, CT: Yale University Press.

Silberman, C. (Ed.). (1973). *The open classroom reader.* New York: Vintage.

Slavin, R. (1987). Cooperative learning and the cooperative school. *Educational Leadership, 45*(3), 7–13.

Authentic Assessment

W hat is good work? As a teacher, you may find evaluating students' accomplishments among the most difficult judgments you have to make. You have worked hard to create authentic learning experiences. Now, how can you create an assessment system that allows students to demonstrate what they have learned? How can you create an assessment system that allows students a range of possibilities to demonstrate their own particular strengths and talents? How can you create an assessment system that is fair and that your students can understand?

To be able to make fair and reasonable judgments about your students' work, you must think out the assessment process before teaching the lesson and communicate this process to your students. Assessment issues are present at every stage of the planning and teaching processes. That is why they are described frequently in earlier chapters of this book. Chapter 3, which outlines the processes that teachers use to diagnose the needs of their students before teaching, describes many assessment devices. Cumulative files of information about students' past performance, standardized test scores describing levels of present achievement, and placement exams are all methods of assessing student accomplishments and are part of the reflective teacher's continual process of evaluation.

Chapter 4 describes long-term goals and outcome statements. These serve as the basis for later evaluation of what students gained from their school experience. Assessment of student accomplishment is primarily concerned with measuring how much students gained and comparing the actual gain with the original goal or outcome statement.

Chapters 5 and 6 describe the creation of learning objectives that specify what teachers *expect* their students to gain during short-term learning events such as a single lesson or a short sequence of lessons. To evaluate student accomplishment in these areas, the teacher must measure what students actually gained during the lesson and compare that gain with the criteria established for each objective.

Chapters 7 through 10 describe methods that teachers select for instructing students or facilitating their learning. These methods have an impact on the amount and type of accomplishment that students are able to achieve. Therefore, reflective teachers are continually assessing student progress and achievement during every learning experience to verify that the teaching strategy they have selected is working or to alter it if they find that students are not accomplishing the objective for that lesson.

These final chapters on assessment and reporting on student achievement only fall at the end because of the linear nature of books. Genuine understanding of what students have accomplished in a given school year requires that reflective teachers employ a systematic process of evaluation that includes observations, testing, collecting samples of students' typical work, and collecting portfolios of their best work. This process begins before the first day of school and continues until the last dismissal bell rings.

Assessment Terminology

The terms used in discussing student assessment can be confusing. This brief set of definitions is provided to make it easier to comprehend what each term means in this text.

To begin, there are subtle differences among measurement, assessment, and evaluation. In this textbook, *measurement* is a broad term referring to the process of obtaining a number of correct responses or a raw score for a student on any type of assessment device. A *criterion* is a preestablished number or score that a teacher believes will demonstrate mastery of the planned objective (*criteria* is the plural form of *criterion*). The teacher makes an *assessment* by comparing the student's raw score with the criterion score and determining whether the student successfully accomplished the objective. *Evaluation,* in this text, is the reflective process of gathering objective and subjective data on a student and making a decision about how best to help that student succeed.

The current trend is to create *authentic assessment systems.* These are evaluation plans that incorporate learning of both content and thinking processes in a realistic setting. An authentic assessment is most often a task that students perform that allows them to demonstrate what they have learned as well as the thinking processes they employ in completing the task. To assess student performance equitably and efficiently, many teachers establish *performance tasks* that describe what they expect their students to be able to do at the end of the period of learning. They also create *benchmarks,* which are steps that mark student progress from initial introduction of a new skill to demonstrating mastery of the skill in an authentic performance task.

Some authentic assessment systems contain very specific, detailed descriptions of student performance that are often called *performance standards.* Teachers evaluate each student's work by comparing it to a set of preestablished learning levels. These systems are also known as *rubric grading* systems. For example, a four-level rubric system may describe observable characteristics that can help gauge student performance. Level 4 describes the highest expectation, while level 1 describes a minimal performance level.

In this text, the term *student achievement* is used to describe the degree to which a student has demonstrated mastery of a subject or objective (usually paper-and-pencil) tests. *Student accomplishment* is meant to be a more inclusive term that indicates the degree to which a student has completed or demonstrated knowledge or skill on a variety of assessment devices, including tests, products, projects, oral presentations, performances, and creative works.

As described in Chapter 3, *criterion-referenced tests* are those created by teachers themselves in which the test items match the specific objectives they plan to teach. Scores on criterion-referenced tests can be used to assess how well students did in relation to the criterion for success on the planned objectives. In contrast, *norm-referenced tests* are written by professional test writers and are published widely. The items may or may not match the school's curriculum. Scores on norm-referenced tests tell teachers how much a student achieved compared to other students of the same age or grade throughout the country.

Many types of tests are used in an educational program. Teachers use *diagnostic tests* before teaching to assess students' prior learning, especially gaps in their prior learning that must be addressed. *Placement tests* are a form of diagnostic test that teachers use to help them make decisions about the level of difficulty of material that will best match the student's present knowledge level.

A significant distinction exists between formative tests and summative tests. Although they may look exactly alike, they are used differently. *Formative tests* measure the student's progress during a set of lessons or learning experiences so that the teacher can provide appropriate feedback and help the student correct errors in understanding or skill. They are *not* graded and are *not* used to make final judgments or evaluations of student achievement.

Summative tests are used at the end of a set of learning experiences to measure the progress a student has made over time. They *are* usually graded and *are* used to make final judgments or evaluations about student achievement.

Pretests are given before teaching a new unit or set of skills or knowledge. *Posttests* are given directly after teaching the new set of skills. Comparing posttest and pretest scores can be an important way for teachers to learn how much their students gained from a specific lesson, sequence of lessons, or unit of study. Pre- and posttests are often used in research to demonstrate gains that students make under a certain set of conditions. Reflective teachers are likely to use pre- and posttests just as researchers do—as a means of gathering data about the value of various teaching strategies or sets of learning materials.

Nontest measures of student achievement and accomplishment also exist. These include informal observation, student products, presentations, and portfolios. Teachers use informal observation of their students' efforts and accomplishments continually. It may be planned or unplanned. Teachers may observe a single student or a group of students as they work together. Although it is difficult to measure any specific achievement during an informal observation, the technique does provide subjective data that teachers need to understand the objective data gathered using other assessment devices.

In this text, a *student product* or *performance task* is meant to include any form of written work, such as essays, stories, reports, poems, and plays, that are handed in to be assessed and evaluated by the teacher. A variety of student products are not written but are completed works of art, music, models, machines, or other student-created items. A student product can be assessed by comparing it against a criterion or a set of criteria that fits that product type.

A *portfolio* denotes a collection of student products designed to show a progression of accomplishment from early undertakings to more recent and advanced efforts. By gathering portfolios of students' work, teachers may assess the accomplishments made over time in a given type of endeavor. There may be portfolios of drawings, showing increasing attention to detail and craftsmanship, or portfolios of student writing, showing growth in letter formation or use of grammatical conventions.

Objective measures imply that, no matter who scores the assessment device, all scorers will get the same score. This occurs only on tests with items that have clearcut right and wrong answers. *Subjective measures* are those that different scorers will score differently, depending on their own interpretations and values. These include essays, artwork, and any other creative products or performances.

Reliability is related to objectivity. Reliable tests consistently measure the same thing time after time. *Validity* means that a test is appropriate for the subject and contains items that will provide useful information about student achievement in that content area. Construction of both test and nontest assessment devices should take reliability and validity into account. When assessment devices are reliable and valid for their purpose, the information they provide can be used with confidence to make decisions about children's school experiences.

Public Interest in Student Achievement

Who cares about students' accomplishments in public schools? Who wants to know the difference between achievement of students in the suburbs and students in the inner cities? Why is so much energy, time, and money spent on assessment procedures in public education today? The answer is that we all care, and we all want to know at every level of society: national, state, local community, family, and individual.

At the national level, we care because we have seen signs that students educated in the United States are falling behind students from other industrialized nations. The National Assessment of Educational Progress (NAEP) measures the academic achievement of students in the basic skills in elementary, junior high, and high schools. These statistics are not reported to students or their parents. They are collected for the purpose of comparing achievement of U.S. students from year to year. Reports are made to the public and to policymakers about the achievement levels of various age groups, the changes over time, and differences in achievement in terms of gender and racial and ethnic groups. The NAEP uses the results of these tests to spot trends and forecast future needs of U.S. schools.

State governments are also vitally interested in assessing the achievement of students within their boundaries. As Chapter 4 described, each state government has established a state department of education responsible for providing guidance and standards to local school districts in curriculum development. The state departments are also responsible for holding school districts accountable for achieving the curriculum standards. Many state governments use *minimum competency tests* to measure whether districts are accomplishing the state guidelines.

Classroom teachers administer minimum competency tests on a specified date. Average scores are computed for various subjects and grade levels for each school district. In some states, these average scores are ranked and reported to the public in what is known as a *school district report card.* Districts with scores above the state mean are believed to be doing a better job of educating their students than are school districts with scores below the mean. The purpose of this practice is to strengthen the feelings of accountability among school district administrators.

In some school districts, administrators choose to rank and report the results of the test by schools. In this way, they hold the principal and faculty of each school accountable for the school's educational program.

Many questions remain unanswered about the value of minimum competency tests and the practice of using the results to label schools and districts *poor, good, better,* and *best.* Some educators question whether the tests measure important student accomplishments or simply discrete, unconnected bits of knowledge. Others question whether the practice of reporting results is a valid measure of educational programming because the socioeconomic status of each school is also believed to affect test scores.

Standardized norm-referenced tests of achievement in the basic skills are a fact of life in most school districts today, and teachers must learn how to interpret and use productively the information these tests provide. But just as tests are gaining prominence in measuring and comparing achievement among school districts and states, they are also drawing severe criticism from many educators. Critics charge that testing takes too much time away from the curriculum. Schools may spend one to two weeks of a 30-week school year on district, state, and national achievement testing.

Another criticism is that norm-referenced tests may measure only limited aspects of what students have learned during the school year. Because they are written and distributed nationally by test publishers, the items on the tests are generic rather than specifically written to match what was taught in a particular school. Many items on a test may be unfamiliar to students because the material was not part of their school's curriculum.

A further criticism of standardized tests is that they cause unfair and unrealistic labeling and categorization of students. There is great concern, for example, that generic achievement tests have a built-in bias against minority students. Critics point to items, pictures, and language in early editions of such tests that were geared to the vocabulary and culture of the white middle class. Although test manufacturers now employ writers who represent various racial and ethnic minorities to develop fairer tests, the concern remains that students from minority groups may have less opportunity to learn the content of the tests, which causes them to earn unrealistically low scores.

Test results must be interpreted with caution and compared with other measures of student achievement. It is a serious breach of ethics when school districts misuse the data from standardized tests to classify students as learning disabled or gifted. Neither diagnosis can be made from the limited information of a generic test of basic skills. In fact, no serious educational decision should be made using only the data from standardized, norm-referenced tests of basic skills. Overemphasizing and generalizing from test scores is likely to damage students' self-concepts and may even create self-fulfilling prophecies.

The emphasis given to standardized test scores varies from state to state and district to district. Some states and districts give standardized achievement tests enormous weight in labeling students as gifted or low achieving, in determining children's placement in special programs, and in determining who wins awards for merit. Reflective teachers who work in schools using these practices are likely to experience discomfort. It is important, then, to challenge such practices and encourage the use of a more balanced assessment and evaluation system.

How Teachers Select and Use Assessment Methods

It is the responsibility of educators in state departments of education to create a balanced method of assessing whether students are meeting the state's standards. District administrators are responsible for creating a fair and useful collection of data about the achievement of students in the schools they serve. The principal of a single school provides guidance to classroom teachers in determining methods for evaluating the progress of the students in that school. But even with all of the direction and guidance from administrators and supervisors, individual classroom teachers retain a great deal of leeway in the area of student assessment.

Individual classroom teachers have varied philosophies of life and related curriculum orientations. Just as teachers' philosophies and curriculum orientations influence their methods of teaching, these values also greatly influence the types of assessment procedures they select and the weight they give to various measures of student accomplishment.

Teachers who believe that some students are smarter than others and can learn more difficult material more easily than their classmates are likely to employ summative tests early and often, recording the results in their grade books as evidence of how each student's achievement matches the ability or IQ tests recorded in the student's cumulative file. In my view, these teachers are very susceptible to the practice of making and ensuring self-fulfilling prophecies about their students.

Teachers who think children's accomplishments are linked to the richness of their experiences and self-esteem are likely to employ many formative evaluation procedures in their effort to identify students' learning gaps and assist them in overcoming their cognitive processing errors. Using the information they gain from a variety of formative evaluation strategies, these teachers provide the scaffolding necessary for students to achieve mastery and succeed in their classroom. Reflective teachers are likely to hold this view of teaching and learning and use evaluation not as a reward or caste system but as an integral part of the learning process.

Educators committed to providing authentic learning for their students are also searching for meaningful and useful assessment systems that provide the kinds of information that allow students to move ahead and develop their skills and knowledge base.

One piece of the authentic learning puzzle is to be sure to link your grading and reporting criteria with the criteria used in the learning process. When students know what the criteria for success are and see how they are linked to the learning experiences in the classroom, the learning environment seems fair to them (Guskey, 1994). Varying evaluation procedures are also seen as beneficial. No one evaluation strategy works well for all subjects, grade levels, or student learning styles. For that reason, students should have a variety of ways to earn their grades.

Imagine you are a teacher planning a unit on astronomy for your classroom. You have gathered some very interesting learning materials, including filmstrips on the solar system, National Aeronautics and Space Administration (NASA) material on space shuttles and telescopes, and many exciting books with vivid illustrations. You've planned a field trip to an observatory and invited an astronomer to visit the classroom. You have worked out a time line for several weeks' worth of individual and group investigations and projects.

But now it is time for you to think about evaluation for yourself and to clarify your values regarding complex evaluation issues. How will you know what students have learned at the end of this unit? What do you expect them to learn? What techniques will you use to find out whether they have learned what you expect? What about the possibility that they may learn something different from what you expect or even that some students who become very actively engaged in the study may learn more than you expect? How will you know what they have learned? How will you assign students science grades at the end of this unit? How will you communicate to parents what each student has gained from it?

The following sections describe a variety of assessment devices. Each one has a number of uses and applications. Each one provides answers to different questions that teachers have about evaluation. To illustrate how they compare with and complement one another, each will be applied to the astronomy unit described previously.

Reflective teachers will consider each alternative and decide whether and how to use such measures in their own classrooms. Recognizing that this introductory text can only provide minimal information about each assessment method, the reflective teacher will want to search actively for more information about certain methods in order to understand fully their value and use before incorporating them into a program that affects children's lives.

INFORMAL OBSERVATIONS

Teachers use informal observation intuitively from the first moment that the students enter the classroom at the beginning of the term. They watch groups to see how students relate to one another; they watch individuals to spot patterns of behavior that are either unusually disruptive or extremely productive. To manage a classroom effectively, "withit" teachers are alert to the overt and covert actions of their students at all times.

Informal observations also have academic implications. Teachers who observe their students while teaching a lesson are able to evaluate their understanding. Spotting a blank look, a nervous pencil tapping, or a grimace of discomfort on a student's face, the teacher can stop the lesson, check for understanding, and reteach the material to meet the needs of the students who didn't understand.

As students read aloud, primary teachers observe and listen for patterns of errors in decoding words. They may also listen to the expression in the student's voice to determine whether the student is comprehending the material or simply saying words aloud. They listen for signs that indicate whether the student is interested in or bored with the material. An additional tool in informal observation is asking the student pertinent questions to check for understanding and determine the student's thought processes. This one-to-one interaction provides data and information not measured in any paper-and-pencil test.

By observing the student read, asking a few questions, and comparing the results with other students of the same grade or age, the teacher is able to assess many things, including (1) the extent to which the student is able to use phonics and context clues to decode reading material, (2) the student's approximate reading level in terms of sight vocabulary, and (3) the student's comprehension level. In addition, the reflective teacher uses the informal observation to gather information about the student's affective qualities, including confidence level, interest in the subject or in reading itself, amount of effort the student is willing to give to the task, and expectations the student has about success or failure in the subject.

By observing as students write or by reading what they have written, teachers can gather similar data about children's writing abilities, interests, and expectations. As students work out unfamiliar math problems, teachers are careful to observe who works quickly and who is struggling. Then they can gather the struggling students together for an extra tutoring session.

In the astronomy unit, the teacher may observe as students take part in discussions to determine the extent to which various students understand the concepts. When students are visiting the observatory, the teacher will watch them to learn about their interests in various aspects of the topic. When an astronomer visits the classroom, the teacher will listen to the students' questions to assess the depth of understanding they have achieved.

Informal observations are one of the most powerful assessment devices the teacher can use to gather new information about children's learning patterns and needs. Teachers may gather data about a student from academic and psychological tests, but in the end it is the informal observation that most teachers rely on to understand the test data and make a final evaluation about appropriate placement or a grade value for a student's work.

PERFORMANCE TASKS TO DEMONSTRATE MASTERY OF OUTCOMES

In contrast to informal evaluations, which provide useful subjective information, well-designed student outcomes are a relatively formal method used to provide useful objective data about what students have learned. Many reflective teachers know that it is valuable to gather both objective and subjective data. They want to design a method for gathering hard data about what students have achieved during classroom learning experiences and compare those data with the subjective information they have gathered during their informal observations.

To plan an assessment system based on students' showing mastery of certain specified outcomes, the teacher must begin before teaching the lesson. By preplanning a unit with specific outcomes or a lesson with very concrete behavioral objectives, the teacher specifies the skills that students should be able to demonstrate at the conclusion of the lesson and the criterion for success. Teachers then plan learning experiences that are linked with the outcomes. After each objective has been taught and students have had an opportunity to practice the new skill, a quiz, worksheet, or other assessment product asks students to demonstrate that they have mastered the new skill and can perform it with few errors.

When each lesson is introduced, the teacher describes the prespecified criterion for success to the students. The criterion for success may be specified as a percentage or as a minimum number of correct responses. For example, the following behavioral objective specifies 80 percent (or 16 of the 20 possible items) as the acceptable demonstration of mastery of this objective:

> *Spelling objective:* When the teacher reads the list of 20 spelling words aloud, students will write 80 percent of the words, using correct spelling and legible handwriting.

A criterion-referenced test such as the weekly spelling test common in many classrooms demonstrates whether the students have mastered the new skill. To record student achievement, teachers may write the percentage of correct responses that each student attained in a grade book.

For more complex student outcomes, teachers design performance tasks that ask students to demonstrate what they have learned. Marzano, Pickering, and McTighe (1993) describe a system that allows teachers to design performance tasks for affective, cognitive, and process outcomes. Tasks can be designed by teachers at all grade levels to measure students' attitudes toward learning, complex thinking, information processing, communication skills, collaboration abilities, and behavior habits.

For example, high school students may be exposed to learning experiences about the effects of illegal drugs. At the conclusion of the learning experiences, they may be asked to collaborate to complete the following performance task:

Drug education performance task: Imagine that you have been hired by the city to design a program to discourage drug use among teenagers in this community. Use a variety of resources to learn about the issue and plan a campaign that will work to decrease illegal drug use. Present your ideas to the class and plan to present them to another appropriate audience as well.

This type of performance task calls upon students to demonstrate knowledge of the effects of drug use on society, their understanding of individual rights versus societal expectations, and their complex thinking ability to create viable alternatives for overcoming the problem. In addition, by communicating their program to others, they are demonstrating communication skills and their ability to collaborate to complete a task.

When students are ready to present their campaigns to their classmates, the teacher may provide them with rubric guidelines for their communication of ideas, such as the following (Marzano et al., 1993, p. 85):

Rubric for Communication Skills in Oral Presentations
  4   Clearly and effectively communicates the main idea or theme and provides support that contains rich, vivid, and powerful detail.

  3   Clearly communicates the main idea or theme and provides suitable support and detail.

  2   Communicates important information but not a clear theme or overall structure.

  1   Communicates information as isolated pieces in a random fashion.

CRITERION-REFERENCED QUIZZES AND TESTS

Quizzes are frequently used with behavioral objectives to determine whether students are successfully gaining each new skill or bit of knowledge in a unit of study. Quizzes are generally short, consisting of only a few questions or items, and are thought of as formative assessments, providing teachers with a way to know whether the students are learning the material day by day.

Tests, however, may consist of many items and are generally thought of as summative assessments. Tests are often given at the end of a unit and contain a variety of items that measure students' achievement of content and skills that have been taught during a period.

In both cases, the term *criterion-referenced* refers directly to the criterion established for each behavioral objective. Each item on a criterion-referenced test should match a preestablished criterion. Criterion referencing provides objective data about material that all students in the class have had an equal opportunity to learn.

Objective tests may take a variety of forms. The most common are matching, true-false, multiple choice, and short answer or completion forms.

Matching items are those that provide both the question and the response. Students have only to recognize the correct response for each item and draw a line to connect the two. Items appear in a column on one side of the paper and the responses in a different order on the other side. In terms of Bloom's taxonomy, matching items are an excellent way of measuring knowledge-level objectives that require students to recognize correct responses. An example of a matching quiz related to the astronomy unit might look like this:

Jupiter	Planet with rings and many moons
Earth	Planet closest to the sun
Mercury	Planet that is ⅗ water
Saturn	Largest planet

To construct fair matching items, each right-column response must be clearly identified with only one item on the left. In our astronomy test, for example, descriptions of the planets need to contain unambiguous elements so that only one matches each planet. If several responses are vaguely correct, the reliability and therefore the objectivity of the test decline.

True-false items are also knowledge-level items, consisting of a statement that students must recognize as either true or false. These items are difficult to write because they must be factual and objective if they are to provide useful data. If items contain unsupported opinions or generalizations, the students must guess what the teacher has intended.

For our astronomy unit, we might construct a quiz with statements such as these:

True	False	The sun orbits the Earth.
True	False	Venus is smaller than Jupiter.
True	False	Mars is closer to the sun than Neptune is.

These items are reliable in that the correct responses are not likely to change in our lifetime. They are also valid because every item is an element directly related to our objective of teaching students about the physical characteristics of the solar system.

As examples of less reliable and less valid items, consider these:

True	False	Venus is a more interesting planet than Uranus is.
True	False	The sun will never stop shining on the Earth.

Multiple-choice items also measure knowledge-level objectives because they call for the student to recognize a fact or an idea. A multiple-choice item contains a question, a problem, or an unfinished statement followed by several responses. The directions tell the student to mark the one correct answer. While college admission tests may contain several near-right responses and students are expected to use reasoning to determine which one is best, classroom tests should probably be constructed with only one correct response. As in other objective measures, reliability and validity of each item must be considered.

To fit the astronomy unit, here are two valid and reliable items:

1. Which planet is known as the red planet?
   a. Venus
   b. Orion

    c. Mars

    d. Jupiter

2. It would take longest to travel from Earth to . . .

    a. Neptune.

    b. Mercury.

    c. Venus.

    d. Saturn.

Short answer or *completion* items supply a question or an unfinished statement, and students are expected to supply a word, phrase, number, or symbol. These items are used primarily to test students' knowledge of specific facts and terminology. For our astronomy unit, here are two examples:

1. The planet Saturn has _____ rings around it.
2. Which planet has the most moons?

The advantage of the four types of objective items that compose most criterion-referenced tests is that they objectively measure students' knowledge of the basic content of a subject. They can be written to match directly the criteria of the teacher's objectives for the lessons. They are also relatively easy to correct, and the scores are easily recorded and can be averaged together to provide the basis for report card grades.

The disadvantage of such items is that they only measure students' understanding of basic knowledge-level content and skills. They do not provide information about what students comprehend, how they would apply the knowledge they've gained, what they would create, or how they analyze and evaluate the ideas they've learned.

MASTERY LEARNING

Some teachers prefer to use a teaching strategy known as *mastery learning* to motivate students to learn a sequence of skills. In mastery learning, individual students work through a series of learning experiences at their own pace and demonstrate mastery as they complete each objective. The teacher uses the information gained on the tests to provide helpful feedback for reteaching rather than as a record of achievement. Summative evaluations occur only at the end of a unit of study, when students are expected to demonstrate mastery of a whole sequence or unit of learning. Grades of unit tests are recorded and become the basis for determining students' grades.

In the astronomy unit, the teacher may have written a number of outcome statements, such as these:

After viewing the filmstrip on the solar system, the students will be able to match pictures of each planet with its name, with no more than one error.

Students will be able to draw and label an illustration of the solar system with the sun and the nine planets in their respective orbits, with 100 percent accuracy.

Together these two outcomes will inform the teacher whether students have learned the names, distinctive visual elements, and locations of the planets in the solar system. To measure whether students have mastered this content, the teacher simply carries out the tasks described in the objectives after students have had sufficient opportunity to learn the material. The teacher prepares a matching quiz with a column of nine names and another column of nine pictures of the planets. For those who do not achieve the criterion of eight correct answers, the teacher can provide a reteaching experience or require students to do additional reading on their own. They can be retested until they achieve the criterion.

On another occasion, the teacher distributes blank paper and asks students to draw and label the solar system. From these two objectives and others like them, the teacher can begin to answer the question "How will I know what they have learned?" Also, the data gathered from this assessment system are more readily translated into letter grades than are the data from informal observations.

ESSAYS EVALUATED WITH RUBRIC GUIDELINES

Essays have the exact opposite advantages and disadvantages of criterion-referenced tests. They are subjective rather than objective. Unless they are given very specific criteria upon which to base their ratings, two or more teachers rarely evaluate an essay the same way. Essays are also very time-consuming to read and mark.

However, essays provide teachers with an excellent means of knowing what students comprehend, how they would apply their new learning, and how they analyze and evaluate the ideas and concepts. Essays also provide students with opportunities to be creative by asking them to synthesize a number of previously unrelated notions into an original expression of their own. Essays can answer the question "How much more have they learned than what I taught in this unit?"

To improve the way in which teachers rate essays, many school systems employ a rubric guide that specifies what an essay must contain and how it must appear on the page to earn a specific mark or grade. Teachers who use a rubric to guide their assessment of essays usually limit the topic of the essay within specific parameters and may even specify what must be included in the response. For example, in the astronomy unit, the teacher may want to assess whether students can describe the concept of outer space in their own words. This will provide information about how much students truly comprehend about the subject rather than what they simply remember. For example, a teacher may present students with these guidelines for writing their essays on the solar system:

> Write a two-paragraph essay in your own words comparing the Earth's atmosphere with space. Tell why humans cannot live in outer space without life support. Use examples and provide evidence to support your ideas.

These guidelines are fairly explicit in terms of both length and content. For these reasons, this form of essay is relatively objective. To make it even more likely that two or more teachers would look for similar elements when correcting the papers, school systems may provide teachers with *rubric evaluation* samples of student work, along with specific descriptions for measuring success on a particular essay topic.

Grade	Characteristics of Essay
A	Paragraphs are well organized and contain at least six sentences. Facts are accurate, and evidence is clearly given to support the student's viewpoints.
B	Paragraphs contain at least four sentences. Most facts are accurate. Examples are given to support ideas.
C	Paragraphs contain at least three sentences. Some facts are accurate, although one or more errors are present. One example is given.
D	Paper contains only one paragraph. Some facts are accurate, although no evidence or examples are given to support them.
F	Unconnected sentences contain few accurate facts. Many errors are stated. No examples given.

This format for essay evaluation is especially useful for assessing students' levels of comprehension on a topic. It also provides an opportunity for students to demonstrate their ability to analyze the topic but limits the use of synthesis and evaluation. If students are provided with the rubric system before they begin writing, they are more likely to know what the teacher expects of them and thus be able to deliver it.

For other purposes, the *extended response essay* gives students more freedom to express ideas and opinions and to use synthesis-level thinking skills to transform knowledge into a creative new idea. In the astronomy unit the teacher may hope that students will gain a sense of responsibility for the Earth after studying its place in the universe. This affective goal for the unit may also be expressed as a series of problem-solving or expressive objectives. Here is an example:

> At the end of the unit, students will write an essay entitled "The Big Blue Marble," in which they express their own hopes and fears for the future of the Earth. The essays will be edited, rewritten, and illustrated and then displayed for parents to view on parents' night.

This extended-response essay calls on students to integrate all that they have learned in this unit and combine it with previous learning from geography and social studies units. Their individual experiences and outside readings are likely to affect their responses as well. Objectivity in marking this essay is very low. It is quite likely that one teacher will view the responses very differently from another teacher. Nevertheless, within a single classroom, a teacher can say or state a set of criteria or expectations that can lead students to write a successful essay. In this instance, as the objective stated, students will have an opportunity to receive critical feedback and make corrections on their essays before the final products are displayed.

Despite the lack of objectivity of extended-response essays, there is good reason to include them in an educational program. They provide invaluable information about the creativity, values, philosophy, and maturity of students. Moreover, they encourage students to become more creative and give them practice in making difficult judgments. One of the most effective ways to give students the information they need to succeed is to provide them with the rubric descriptions before the time they write their essays. When students can see the criteria upon which their work will be evaluated, they are able to meet the expectations with much greater degrees of success than when they try to guess what the teacher expects or wants from them.

ORAL REPORTS AND EXAMINATIONS

Like essays, *oral reports* can be restricted or unrestricted depending on the type of assessment the teacher wants to generate. To increase objectivity and communicate expectations to students, teachers can create rubric systems describing the length and format of the oral report as well as what must be included. Examples of *restricted* oral reports include book reports in which students are expected to describe the main characters, the setting, the plot, and their favorite part of the story. In a restricted oral examination, teachers may ask questions that students must answer within specified parameters. In the astronomy unit, an oral examination may be scheduled for a certain day. Students are told to prepare for it by reading material supplied by NASA on the U.S. space program. In the examination, teachers ask questions taken from the reading material, and students are expected to respond in their own words. Here is an example:

> Tell how the astronauts prepared for weightlessness.
>
> Describe the food astronauts eat in space.

As they listen to the students' responses, teachers will find it possible to make a judgment about whether the answers are right or wrong. It is also possible to assess whether the students have a poor, average, or unusually good understanding of the ideas they speak about. The teacher's evaluation of the students' responses can be recorded in some form to be shared with the student later.

Unrestricted oral reports allow students more opportunities to speak about matters of great interest and importance to them. They encourage students to use their imagination to generate synthesis-level responses or to be persuasive about a matter of opinion or judgment. Here is an example:

> Describe the space journey you'd like to take.
>
> Tell what you think should be NASA's next big undertaking.

Debate is a form of oral examination because it provides students with an opportunity to prepare to speak about a subject by learning a great deal of content and evidence for opinions before the event. During the debate, teachers can assess the students' energy and effort in gathering information as well as their understanding of the topic.

In evaluating oral presentations, teachers may write comments as they listen, or they may videotape the presentations so that they can evaluate them more comprehensively later. Students may be involved in self-evaluation of their own efforts as well. They can view the videotapes and discuss with the teacher what they did well and what they need to improve.

DESIGNING AUTHENTIC ASSESSMENT PERFORMANCE TASKS

It is possible to construct assessment tasks that measure student performance in terms of using higher-level thinking skills of analysis and evaluation as well as critical thinking skills of observation and inference and problem-solving strategies such as the creation and testing of hypotheses. These tests can be constructed as paper-and-pencil exams, presenting a situation or a dilemma and asking students to respond to it in various ways. Such a test may consist of a passage to be read that describes a problem or dilemma. Maps, charts, graphs, or other forms of data might also be available on the test. The test items then consist of questions that allow the student to observe, infer, formulate a hypothesis, design methods of testing the hypothesis, and speculate about the possible outcome.

For example, in the astronomy unit, students may be presented with reprints from journals and magazines describing various theories about the evolution of the universe. From these articles, students are asked to respond to the following questions, citing evidence from the articles to support their answers:

1. Approximately how old is the universe?
2. Describe the contents of the universe, including the matter that resides between the planets and stars.
3. In your opinion, will the universe continue to expand indefinitely, or will it reach a maximum size and begin to collapse?

This test may appear to be very difficult, but its scoring does not depend on whether the students have knowledge about the actual contents of the universe. Instead, the scoring should reflect how accurately they have observed the data presented to them and whether their inferences can be supported by their observations.

For intermediate students, a simpler test may focus on the orbit of the Earth around the sun and its relationship to the seasons of the year. A diagram of Earth's orbit would be displayed along with a chart about the dates of the four seasons in the northern hemisphere and questions such as these:

1. What do you *see* about the path that the Earth takes around the sun?
2. What do you *see* on the chart about when seasons begin?
3. What connection do you think there is between the beginning of summer and the Earth's position in its orbit?
4. What other connections do you see?
5. What do you think the tilt of the Earth has to do with seasons?

Even primary students can be tested for their inquiry skills, although the tests will probably have to be oral rather than written. The teacher may ask students to observe a demonstration of the rotation of the Earth on its axis, using a flashlight on a beach ball in a dark room. After the demonstration, students can be asked to describe their observations, make inferences, and then respond to unfinished questions beginning with "What if . . . ?"

Another common method of assessing students' authentic learning is to encourage them to do independent research on one aspect of a unit theme and to create a product that shows what they have learned. This method allows students to demonstrate their knowledge, comprehension, and all four of the higher-level thinking skills on a topic. This assessment technique is appropriate for every area of the curriculum. Students can do independent research or make an independent investigation in math, science, social studies, literature, music, or art. This method lends itself especially well to interdisciplinary units.

The strategy is for the teacher to introduce a unit or theme and provide some teacher-centered instruction on it at the outset. Readings may be assigned, and quizzes and worksheets may be used to assess the extent to which the student is developing a knowledge base about the topic. Essays or oral presentations may be assigned to assess whether students comprehend the main ideas and concepts of the topic. Finally, each student selects one aspect of the main topic on the basis of individual preference or interest and begins to research that subtopic independently. Each student decides on a final product that will demonstrate what has been learned and achieved during the independent study.

The kinds of products that students might create as a result of this type of investigation are limitless. Many teachers prefer to plan their evaluations of student accomplishment to correspond with Bloom's taxonomy. Specific student products are appropriate for learning objectives at all six levels. A sample of them can be found in Figure 11.1.

Teachers may evaluate these student products using a rubric checklist or rating scale. Very specific rubric systems may be prespecified so that students know exactly what their product must demonstrate to earn a high mark or positive evaluation from the teacher. Reflective teachers who wish to encourage critical thinking and reflectiveness among their students are also very likely to involve the students in self-evaluation of their own products. When students evaluate their work critically, they are learning how to become more independent and responsible for revising and improving their work without an outside evaluator.

RUBRICS, CHECKLISTS, AND RATING SCALES

When teachers wish to assess students' products or presentations, they can tell the students their reactions in a conference or write comments on a piece of paper and give these comments to the students. These methods suffice for informing the students, in a general way, whether they have met the teacher's expectations in the product; and they may be adequate for evaluating an unrestricted product or presentation.

When the teacher has prespecified the criteria for a product or presentation and several important elements must be included, the teacher may choose to create a *rubric* or *checklist* to use for notation when listening, for example, to the speech. This is fre-

Characteristics of Each Level	Products Associated with Each Level
Knowledge Level Can recognize and recall specific terms, facts, and symbols.	**Knowledge Level** Worksheet, Label a given diagram, Memorize poem or song, List, Quiz, Recognition of math symbols, Spelling bee, Response to flashcard.
Comprehension Level Can understand the main idea of material heard, viewed, or read. Is able to interpret or summarize the ideas in own words.	**Comprehension Level** Written paragraph or summary of main idea, Oral retelling of story, Use of math symbols and numbers in simple calculations, Report.
Application Level Is able to apply an abstract idea in a concrete situation, to solve a problem, or relate it to prior experiences.	**Application Level** Diagram, Map, Model, Illustration, Analogy, Mental problem solving, Action plan, Teaches others, Diorama, Costume, Diary, Journal.
Analysis Level Can break down a concept or idea into its constituent parts. Is able to identify relationships among elements, cause and effect, similarities and differences.	**Analysis Level** Graph, Survey, Chart, Diagram, Report showing cause and effect, differences and similarities, comparisons and contrasts.
Synthesis Level Is able to put together elements in new and original ways. Creates patterns or structures that were not there before.	**Synthesis Level** Artwork, Story, Play, Skit, Poetry, Invention, Song, Composition, Game, Collection, Hypothesis, Essay, Speech, Videotape, Film, Computer program.
Evaluation Level Makes informed judgments about the value of ideas or materials. Uses standards and criteria to support opinions and views.	**Evaluation Level** Debate, Discussion, Recommendation, Letter to editor, Court trial, Panel, Chart showing hierarchies, rank order, or priorities.

Figure 11.1   Student products related to Bloom's taxonomy.

Source: Created by Judy Eby from TAXONOMY OF EDUCATIONAL OBJECTIVES: Handbook I: Cognitive Domain, by Benjamin S. Bloom et al. Copyright 1956, 1984 by Longman Publishing Group.

quently done when the objective is for students to use effective speaking skills in a presentation. In preparing the students for the speech, the teacher will likely specify several important elements that the students should incorporate, such as maintaining eye contact with the audience, using appropriate volume to be heard by everyone in the room, and speaking rather than reading during the presentation. By preparing a simple checklist with these items on it, the teacher can quickly and accurately record whether each student used these skills in their presentations. To make the whole system even more valuable, when the teacher shares the rubrics with the students ahead of time, students are able to make much better judgments about what to study, what to include, or how to present the information they have learned.

Rubrics and checklists can record mastery of many basic skills in the primary grades. Each item on the checklist can correspond directly to a behavioral objective. Together the items on a checklist provide an overview of a sequence of objectives. Kindergarten teachers frequently employ checklists to record the letter recognition of each pupil, letter by letter. Primary teachers use checklists to record mastery of basic math operations. Intermediate and middle school teachers may use checklists to record whether students have demonstrated fundamental research skills. In our astronomy unit, for example, the teacher may combine a goal of developing research and study skills with the goal of content mastery. To record the accomplishment of these skills the teacher may use a checklist such as the one in Figure 11.2.

Checklists provide useful and efficient means of recording information about the accomplishments of individual students. They are also valuable during a student-teacher conference. Both teacher and student can quickly see what has been achieved and what still lies ahead. Checklists are also valuable when teachers confer with parents about the student's progress along a set of learning objectives.

Name _____ **Grade** _____

This is a record of research and study skills demonstrated by this student. The teacher's initials and date indicate when the skill was successfully demonstrated.

Date	Initials	Skill Area
_____	_____	A. Located a book on astronomy in the card catalog
_____	_____	B. Located a book on astronomy on the library shelves
_____	_____	C. Used the table of contents to find a topic
_____	_____	D. Used the index to find a subtopic
_____	_____	E. Orally interpreted a graph or chart
_____	_____	F. Took notes on a chapter in a book on astronomy
_____	_____	G. Summarized the chapter from notes
_____	_____	H. Wrote the bibliography for the book

Figure 11.2   Astronomy unit checklist of research and study skills.

Rating scales are used in circumstances similar to those of checklists. They provide additional information, however, in the form of a rating of how well the student achieved each element or skill on the list. Rating scales are useful in providing students with feedback that rates their performance on an objective. In the astronomy unit, for example, students' products may be turned in and evaluated by the teacher, who is using a rating scale of important elements. In many classrooms, teachers involve the student in their own evaluation of the product and the efforts expended in creating them. In Figure 11.3, a rating scale is structured so that both the student and the teacher rate the finished product.

A rubric system is similar to a checklist but also employs very detailed descriptions of the specific levels of mastery that the teacher hopes students will attain. Student products are then compared to the levels of mastery described in the rubric system. In Figure 11.4, a rubric system is shown that allows the teacher to compare student products related to the astronomy research project against a set of specific criteria. As I have suggested earlier, if students are given this rubric system before beginning the unit, they are empowered to make better choices about how to use their time, what to study, and how to present the material they have learned.

LEARNING CONTRACTS

A learning contract is a device that can be thought of both as a teaching strategy and a means of assessment. The learning contract described in Chapter 10 listed several required activities and a number of options for the unit on settling the western United States. Teachers using this strategy meet with individual students to agree on a suitable number and type of optional activities. The activities on the contract then provide the

---

Name _____ **Grade** _____

To the student: Please evaluate your own product, using the following scale:

O = OUTSTANDING; one of my best efforts
S = SATISFACTORY; I accomplished what I set out to do
N = NEEDS IMPROVEMENT; I need to revise and improve this element

Student's Rating	Skill Area	Teacher's Rating
_____	Did adequate research and information gathering	_____
_____	Elements of the model are accurate in shape	_____
_____	Elements of the model are accurate in scale (except for orbits of planets)	_____
_____	Labeling is accurate and legible	_____
_____	Legend is accurate and legible	_____
_____	Model is visually interesting and pleasing	_____

Figure 11.3   Astronomy unit rating scale of the solar system model.

To the student: Read these criteria before you begin your research so that you will know how to earn the level you want to attain.

Turn in a 5–10 page booklet on the solar system. The booklet may contain a combination of words, pictures, graphs, and any other types of illustrations that show an understanding of the physical elements of the planets, moons, and sun that make up our solar system. The booklets will be evaluated according to the following criteria:

Level 4: The student clearly and completely identifies the important planets and moons of the solar system and shows how they are related to the sun and each other in size and space. There is a combination of verbal descriptions and visual illustrations that make the distinguishing features of each planet very evident. The writing is well organized, and references are given for sources of information. At least four references are provided.

Level 3: The student clearly identifies the planets and some of the most important moons of the solar system. Relationships of size and space are given, though they may be distorted in some cases. Verbal information is fairly well organized, and illustrations are useful in distinguishing among the planets. At least two references are given as sources of information.

Level 2: The student correctly names the nine planets and shows that they travel around the sun. Relationships among planets are not accurate. The booklet uses more pictures than words. Only one source of information is provided.

Level 1: The student incorrectly labels planets and shows little understanding of their relationship to the sun and to each other. Verbal information is given as captions for illustrations only. No source of information is given.

Figure 11.4   Rubric grading evaluation system for astronomy research project.

structure for daily learning experiences. When the unit is complete, the contract is used as the basis for assessing what each student has accomplished. Just as in adult life, students are held accountable for meeting the terms of their contracts. If they succeed, they can expect a positive evaluation. If they have not met the terms of their contract, they can expect to have to explain why and describe what they will do to honor their contract.

Learning contracts can take several forms and can even be structured so that the student makes a contract to receive a certain grade for a specified amount of work. A point system can be employed to allow students to select from among options and earn the grade they desire. Using our example of the astronomy unit, Figure 11.5 shows a learning contract with a built-in point system for earning a grade.

Learning contracts also serve as the basis for recording accomplishments. In the sample learning contract for the astronomy unit, the parent is also required to sign the contract, agreeing to support the student's efforts. This strategy is a very efficient way

Astronomy Unit Learning Contract

I, _____ , a student in the fifth grade at Otis School, do hereby contract to complete the following tasks during my investigation of the solar system.

Furthermore, I agree to complete these tasks by _____ .

I understand that I am agreeing to earn _____ points, which will earn a grade of _____ if my work is evaluated to be acceptable.
I understand that the point values listed below are the maximum number that can be earned for each task and that fewer points may be awarded.

Points Needed to Earn Specific Grades

> 90 = A	> 80 = B	> 70 = C	> 60 = D	< 60 = F

_____	10 pts	Read Chapter 7 in the science text. Do exercises, pp. 145–146.
_____	10 pts	Matching quiz
_____	10 pts	True-false quiz
_____	10 pts	Multiple-choice quiz
_____	10 pts	Short-answer quiz
_____	15 pts	Drawing of the solar system, labeled correctly
_____	20 pts	Model of the solar system, labeled and scaled to size
_____	10 pts	Essay on Earth's atmosphere and outer space
_____	10 pts	Essay on "The Big Blue Marble"
_____	05 pts	Per answer on NASA oral exam
_____	10 pts	Oral report on "A Space Journey I'd Like to Take"
_____	10 pts	Finished checklist on research skills

Signed this day _____ 19_____ at _____School.

_____   _____
      student signature   teacher signature

_____   _____
      parent signature   witness signature

Figure 11.5 Sample learning contract.

to communicate with parents about the goals and expectations of the class. Later, during parent-teacher conferences, the parent can see the work that was accomplished. If a student did not complete the contract, the parent can see what was left undone.

PORTFOLIOS OF STUDENT PRODUCTS

Portfolios are collections of work samples designed to illustrate a person's accomplishments in a talent area. Photographers collect portfolios of their best photos; artists collect their artwork; composers collect their compositions. Assessment portfolios are used to document what a student has achieved in school. To use this technique, teachers collect samples of each student's work and put them into a file folder with that student's name on it. Some teachers collect many types of work in a single portfolio; others have writing portfolios that contain only writing samples, math portfolios filled with worksheets and tests, and other portfolios for other subject areas.

Teachers may collect only samples of a student's very best work in a portfolio to demonstrate the maximum performance of that student. However, an argument can be made for collecting samples of ordinary or typical work as well. These samples demonstrate how well the individual is performing on a day-to-day basis.

Portfolios may be kept for a long or short time. Many teachers collect writing samples in the first week of school, then periodically throughout the school year. In some cases the teacher may assign a writing topic during the first week and then assign the very same topic during the last week of school. When the two samples on the same topic are compared, the growth and development of students' writing abilities are plain for everyone to see.

A short-term portfolio may be collected for the duration of a learning unit. For example, in the astronomy unit, all of the student's work, including quizzes, essays, pictures, and photos of the model solar system, can be collected in a portfolio to document that student's accomplishment during the unit. If a contract was used during the unit, the contract will be included in the portfolio along with the work samples.

Portfolios may be used at all grade levels and for any subject or course a student takes. When portfolios are meant to be used to document student accomplishment, they must be organized so that they reveal the development of a skill or the growing understanding of a set of ideas. To demonstrate growth and change, Wolf (1989) suggests collecting "biographies of works, a range of works and reflections" (p. 37).

The biography of a work consists of several drafts of a work, showing the student's initial conception of the project, the first attempts, and the final product. By collecting these items, the teacher can document the growth and development of the student. Wolf (1989) further recommends that, after completing this collection, the teacher may ask the student to reexamine all the stages of the work and reflect on the process and the products from beginning to end. The student's reflection may be done in writing or captured on audiotape (and later transcribed onto paper) and should then be included in the portfolio itself. This self-evaluation is valuable in helping the student develop metacognitive abilities that then can be applied to future projects.

Wolf (1989) also suggests that teachers deliberately collect a range of works, meaning a diverse collection, consisting of journals, essays, poems, drawings, charts, graphs, letters, tests, and samples of daily work. When using the portfolios as a basis for a parent-teacher conference, the teacher can take advantage of this range to discuss and document many different aspects of the student's school accomplishments.

Primary teachers must take responsibility for collecting and filing all items in students' portfolios. At the upper grades, however, students may be asked to keep their own. The teacher may suggest items to be included, and the student may decide on others. At the end of a people and nature unit, for example, each student may have a portfolio containing the tests, lab reports, essays, creative writing, and charts created for the unit.

At the end of a unit or term, the teacher can collect the portfolios, examine them, ask for reflections on certain items or sets of items, and arrange the materials in chronological order in preparation for parent-teacher conferences. Teachers often ask students to create covers for their portfolios, which are then on display during parent open-house visits or conferences.

Portfolios of student work are an excellent way to communicate with parents about a student's accomplishments. When the parent and teacher look at the writing sample together, they can both understand what the student's strengths and weaknesses are at a glance. When a parent sees the signed contract and the completed work, both parent and teacher see the same evidence to support the resulting grades.

The transition from traditional grade reports to portfolio assessment is not easy. Interpretation of student work is subjective and value-based. Challenges such as questions about validity and gender and racial equity in portfolios are likely to emerge. But those who support the move to portfolio assessment believe that it offers real hope for creating assessment systems that promote high-quality work, critical thinking, and success motivation rather than simply labeling past achievements.

In Case 11.1 Pam Knight provides an example of the reflective processes used by a classroom teacher who is setting up a portfolio assessment plan for her classroom.

Case 11.1 ⊃ Reflective Action
Designing an Authentic Assessment

Pam Knight, Middle School Math Teacher
Twin Peaks Middle School, Poway, California

Perceptiveness

For a long time I have been concerned about the assessment techniques in my math classes. I often see student classwork that shows clear understanding and mastery. Sometimes I hear a student explain a process to another student but then not do as well on the math test as the person he or she was helping. I have also observed a student who does no homework, shows little work on math problems, and is often absent from class score high on tests that require only replication of algorithms from the textbook.

Constructing a Knowledge Base

Are students such as the second example superior at math just because they do well on tests? If I were in a position to hire a student, which one would I prefer to employ? Which one exhibits traits that will make him or her successful in the future? If I grade only on tests, the second student always comes out ahead, but I think that the other type of student possesses many valuable skills that will contribute to future success. How do I structure an assessment system that will show the many facets of a successful mathematics student?

When I went back to school to work on an advanced degree, I began to read about newer methods of assessment that I had not known about before. I discovered the term *authentic assessment*. The key element of authentic assessment is to gather representative examples of each student's work for a portfolio that will demonstrate the student's real capabilities.

Since little had been done about portfolio assessments in mathematics, I gained most of my information by researching the portfolio work being done in the field of language arts. I joined a portfolio network at the San Diego County Office of Education that met monthly to support each other and share ideas.

Clarifying Values and Principles

In my quest, I discovered that the few efforts in mathematics portfolios involved folders collecting homework and tests or portfolios which were collections of weekly problem-solving activities. I wanted something that assessed what I covered in my mathematics class: long-term situational problem solving, scale drawing, experiments as well as math problems from the text.

Clarification of Values and Principles

For many years, I have believed that a student's work ethic often determines his or her success in life. I want to encourage my students to develop a positive work ethic. To do this, I believe that it is important for students to complete their homework, show their work in computation, attend class regularly, work successfully in group activities, and communicate their knowledge both in written and oral forms. I believe that each of these skills is important for their future. Based on this belief, I decided to create an assessment plan that would assess these skills. I felt that it would be most valuable if the assessment were filled out first by the student as a form of self-assessment and then by the teacher.

Creativity

From my research, I found that journals are a popular method of self-evaluation in language arts. Could they be applied to mathematics?

I also knew that I had to create more situational problems that could be used in an assessment plan. My goal was to have the students create a mathematics portfolio that had all the projects, journals, notes, investigations of the year that would show the next year's teacher more about the student's skills, attitudes, and knowledge of mathematics than test scores ever could.

In the first year, my portfolio assessment plan included a situational long-term problem for each quarter that included some type of project. Most of the projects involve the collection of data, some work analyzing the data using mathematical processes, and a written conclusion. At the end of the year, students wrote reflective statements about the value of the work they had done. They also included their best and worst tests in their portfolio.

Persistence and Problem Solving

I was proud and amazed at the diversity, creativity, and excellence the portfolios displayed. As I expected, the portfolios often had little relationship to the students' average test scores. Is this a problem? Should these two types of assessment concur? I had students that are experts on the computer produce portfolios that were visual treats. These portfolios had so much glitz that it was difficult for me to assess the actual content. To solve the credibility problem of my first portfolios, I began the entire reflective process again. The second year, I added both a skills assessment that included test score averages and an attitude assessment to be filled out by the student and verified by me, their teacher.

Communication Skills

I wrote an article about my portfolio assessment plan for *Educational Leadership*. It was published in May 1992 (Knight, 1992). I have also presented my plan at several conferences and institutes. From each of these efforts, I have received valuable feedback from other teachers wrestling with similar endeavors. Where do I go from here? The next step is to get a group of teachers willing to do some classroom research. We need to try to establish a model of portfolio assessment that fits the field of mathematics.

VIDEOTAPE RECORDS

When the purpose of evaluation is to record the accomplishment of a student and allow later analysis and more comprehensive evaluation, a videotape is an excellent way to capture and store a variety of learning events. Speeches can be videotaped easily. So can dramas, skits, presentations, and displays of students products.

Videos are also excellent ways to communicate to parents the accomplishments of a student or the entire class. They allow all interested parties to view the final products or performances of a unit of study. Teachers can store on tape a whole year's worth of accomplishments.

Video recordings also provide teachers with data they need to evaluate their own plans. By reviewing a video of a classroom learning event, reflective teachers are able to gain new understandings about what students need from their learning environment to be successful.

COOPERATIVE GROUP PROJECTS AND PRODUCTS

Many of the assessment methods described in this chapter can be adapted for cooperative groups. Evaluation of cooperative group efforts should include an assessment of both a task that requires a group effort to complete and an assessment of individual efforts to ensure that each member of the group takes responsibility for doing personal reading and preparation.

As an illustration of how to adapt ordinary lessons and units into cooperative lessons and units, consider the astronomy unit. To adapt this unit for use by cooperative groups, each group can function as a study team with directions to assist one another in reading and preparing for the quizzes. Group scores can be computed and recorded for each quiz at the same time that individual scores are recorded.

Rather than 30 individual models of the solar system, there will be five or six for each group in the class. The oral examination can be undertaken as a team effort, as proposed by Slavin's (1987) TGT model of cooperative learning. Essays and written reports can be combined as a group report.

The contract system works very well with cooperative groups. When used in this way, there is one contract per group instead of per individual. Each group negotiates what it will accomplish together. Evaluations can include peer assessments, with members of the group providing critical feedback for one another.

Assessment of student accomplishment is a complex and multifaceted undertaking. There is no one best way to assess what students have learned or accomplished in school. Some methods work better than others at various grade levels. Some work better than others with different individuals. This chapter has provided you with a number of assessment methods so that you can develop a repertoire of assessment devices to use as the basis for making judgments about the accomplishments of your students.

⟳ Reflective Actions for Your Professional Portfolio
A Plan for Authentic Assessment

Perceptiveness: Reflect on Your Own Experiences

What type of assessment systems have you experienced in your own schooling? How did these systems affect your success as a student? How did they affect your attitudes about learning?

Construction of Knowledge: Authentic Assessment

What does authentic assessment mean to you? What do you need to know to organize such a system in your own class? Find current articles and read more about this topic.

Clarification of Values: Your Philosophy of Assessment

What assessment devices are you most likely to use in your classroom? Why do you prefer them? What methods are you least likely to choose? Why?

Creativity: Thematic Unit Assessment Plan

For a thematic unit plan, create an assessment system that is an authentic assessment of the work that students are expected to do. Consider providing more than one method for students to demonstrate what they have learned.

Persistence, Problem Solving, and Communication Skills: Collegial Feedback

Exchange assessment plans with your classmates and give each other feedback on the systems you have created for assessing student accomplishment. Ask each other how you can make your assessment more authentic. From the feedback you receive, make revisions to your assessment plan.

References

Guskey, T. (1994). Making the grade: What benefits students? *Educational Leadership, 52*(2), 14–19.

Knight, P. (1992). How I use portfolios in mathematics. *Educational Leadership, 49*(8), 71–72.

Marzano, R., Pickering, D., & McTighe, J. (1993). *Assessing student outcomes.* Alexandria, VA: Association for Supervision and Curriculum Development.

Slavin, R. (1987). Cooperative learning and the cooperative school. *Educational Leadership, 45*(3), 7–13.

Wolf, D. (1989). Portfolio assessment: Sampling student work. *Educational Leadership, 46*(7), 35–39.

12

Recording and Reporting Student Accomplishments

Report cards. These two words are likely to elicit memories filled with anxiety and a variety of other conflicting emotions for most people.

In your many years of schooling, you have probably received more than 50 report cards. You probably viewed many with relief and happiness and proudly displayed them to your parents; others may have caused torment and disbelief. On occasion, you may have questioned the teacher's fairness or integrity; you may have questioned whether the teacher really got to know you or understood the effort you put into your work. Perhaps you have even approached a teacher and challenged the grade you received, showing evidence of why the assigned grade was unjustified.

Eight or nine weeks into your first school year, you will face the task of deciding on and recording report card grades for your students. Many first-year teachers consider the responsibility one of their most difficult challenges. Experienced teachers often report that the task doesn't seem to get easier as the years pass. In fact, many reflective teachers find that the more they know about grades and children, the more difficult it is to sum up the work and efforts of a student in a single letter grade.

In Tracy Kidder's (1989) description of a year in a fifth-grade classroom, entitled *Among Schoolchildren,* the teacher, Chris Zajac, takes a group of social studies tests home to grade:

> A stack of social studies tests lay before her on the table, slippery sheets of ditto paper, the questions in purple ink—fill in the blank questions that asked for definitions of terms such as "Tory." The test closed, as always, with an essay question; the students had to describe briefly a Famous Patriot. She stared at the stack of tests for a moment. "Do I want to?" she murmured to herself, and took the first test, Arabella's, off the pile. Chris's pen made a one-part scratching sound, inscribing red C's down most of the page, and she began to smile.
> "84 = B," Chris wrote across the top of Arabella's test. (pp. 72–73)

Although Arabella's paper proves to be a pleasure to grade, Chris later encounters the test turned in by Jimmy:

> Chris stared at Jimmy's test. He had not tried to answer more than half the questions, and had not written an essay. Jimmy was the sleepiest boy Chris had encountered in years, also one of the stubbornest when it came to evading work that required thought. . . .
> Chris would explain an assignment. Jimmy would say, "I don't understand." Chris would explain again. Jimmy would say, "I don't understand." Of course, he was waiting for her to do it for him. . . .
> Chris stared at the window. Maybe tomorrow, she thought, she'd make Jimmy take this test again. She went back to the pile. (p. 76)

Still later in the evening:

> Chris sat down again at the table. Pedro's test lay on top of the pile. She read,
> Tory. Like a grup of sogrs.
> Chris placed her hand like a visor on her forehead. She stared at the blackened window across the room and slowly shook her head. "Poor kid."

. . . He didn't often talk. He never misbehaved. He almost always tried to do his homework. It was as another teacher had said, "Poor Pedro. He works so hard to get an F." His situation had seemed intolerable to Chris the very first day when, after assigning some simple classwork, she stopped to look over Pedro's shoulder, and he looked up at her and asked, "Did I do good, Mrs. Zajac?" (pp. 79–80).

"36 = F," Chris wrote on Pedro's social studies test. If she was not honest, she would never have the tangible evidence of progress or decline. (p. 85)

In carefully correcting and grading these tests, Chris Zajac is performing an important part of her job. She is holding students accountable for learning what they have been taught in her classroom. She is also providing them with feedback so that they can understand what they have accomplished and what they still need to work on. She is also contributing data to a growing record kept on each student so that assistance and special educational opportunities can be provided if necessary. But the task of grading is an arduous and time-consuming one, and the teacher may feel as emotional about giving grades to students as the students feel about receiving them.

Varied Perspectives about the Purpose of Evaluation

As I described in Chapter 11, many people want to know about student achievement in the elementary schools. Although the state and federal governments and school district administrators are interested in data about the average achievement levels of all students in a given grade, it is the student's parents and teachers who are most interested in the achievement of an individual student.

Teachers want to know what the student has gained from each learning event as a means of planning further experiences and as a measure of their own teaching methods. Parents want three very different types of information from an evaluation (Oakes & Lipton, 1990):

1. What has my child learned?
2. How well is my child doing in school?
3. What about my child's future?

The question of what each student has learned focuses on an individual. It does not ask for comparisons among students and assigns no value to the student's achievement. To evaluate what a student has learned, teachers select from a variety of assessment methods such as those described in Chapter 11. Informal observations, checklists of accomplishments, and data from tests and other assessment devices allow a teacher to describe what a student knows about each subject in the curriculum and what skills the student has mastered. Compiling an accurate record of what each student has learned is an important part of the teacher's responsibility to the student and the parents. The record of what each student has achieved at each grade level is also valuable because it certifies whether the student has accomplished the expectations for that grade.

Reports of what a student has learned can take the form of oral descriptions during a conference, accompanied by a portfolio of work samples, or they can be written reports called *anecdotal records* that describe what the student has learned during a specific period. An anecdotal record might read as follows:

> In kindergarten, this student mastered letter recognition of all 26 capital letters of the alphabet. He has almost mastered the recognition of small letters, but at present he still confuses *b*, *d*, and *p*. He can give an example of a word that starts with each letter of the alphabet.

Another example might read:

> *Third grade, second quarter report:* Although she is still quite shy with other students, she has participated actively in her writing group. She writes full and complete sentences with interesting and detailed descriptions. She recently wrote a paragraph on dinosaurs and read it aloud to her group. They responded with much interest and enthusiasm to her vivid descriptions of various types of dinosaurs. She accepted suggestions from the group and incorporated their ideas into her revision of the work.

Such reports are valuable because they allow the parents to understand the objectives of the school and whether their child is achieving the intended learning outcomes. When parents understand the school's objectives, they are better able to join with school personnel in supporting their child's learning and affective development. Also, having accurate information about their child's achievements, failures, strengths, and weaknesses enables the parents to give their child the support and encouragement he or she needs to succeed in school.

School evaluation would be a relatively simple endeavor if it only concerned the question of how much each student has learned during a given time. Unfortunately, few parents are satisfied with that descriptive evaluation alone. Parents often ask teachers, "How is my child doing in school?" This question could mean "in relation to the curriculum" or "compared to his or her achievement at the beginning of the year." In response, teachers must be able to respond to the question "How much of what I taught did this student learn?" (Oakes & Lipton, 1990, p. 136).

To answer this question accurately, the teacher must be able to compare the achievement of a student with a standard or criterion for success. This is the reason for the current strong interest in assessment by behavioral objectives. Each objective is written with a built-in criterion. Students who meet the criterion can be recorded to have passed or mastered the material. Students who did not meet the criterion are recorded to have failed or to be deficient in this learning task. Students who exceed the criterion can be reported to have excelled.

For example, consider the objective that students will apply recently learned math skills to calculate the answers to 100 problems; the criterion for success is 90 of 100 correct. If Joan gets 91 correct, she is reported to have met the criterion and passed. If Sam gets 74 correct, he is reported to have failed; and if Greg gets 98 correct, he is reported to have done excellent work.

A second way to interpret the question "How is my child doing?" reflects a strong parental interest in knowing how the student is doing *compared to others* of the same age or grade. This is the question that causes evaluations to become competitive. In recording or reporting this information to parents, the teacher must not only tell how the student did in relation to the objective criterion but also how the student's performance compared to others in the class.

Using the same example as above, imagine that out of the class of 30 students, 5 got scores of 95 or above, 15 got scores of 90 to 95, and 10 got scores below 90. Then the report on each student may contain the information that allows the parents to see how well the student is doing compared to the rest of the class. Joan met the criterion, but so did half the class, so her performance is reported to be near the mean or average. Sam got only 74 correct, but six other students made even more errors than he did. This means that Sam is in the bottom half of the class but above those who are in the bottom fifth. Greg, with his score of 98, was also the top scorer in the class, which may please his parents even more than knowing that he exceeded the criterion.

Standardized achievement test data can also be interpreted to inform parents where their child stands in relation to students in the same grade throughout the United States. In most elementary schools, the classroom teacher must be able to interpret the data from classroom events and from achievement tests for the parents to indicate how well the student is doing compared to others at the same grade level.

The third question parents ask in many school evaluations is "What about my child's future?" This really means "What does the present performance tell us about this child's future?" In other words, "Is my child college material?" or "Is it likely that my child will be able to earn a good living?" These questions call for more than simple descriptions or comparisons. The teacher is expected to be a forecaster, predicting a student's future achievements based on present school performance. This is not as difficult as it may sound, at least as far as the prediction of future success in school is concerned. Studies show that present performance in school is a fairly accurate predictor of future performance in school (Bloom, 1982).

Teachers are not usually required to speculate about future performance in their records or reports of student achievement. But many do so informally. They predict success or failure to other teachers in the school: for example, "Oh, you have Greg this year? I had him last year. He's a straight A student." They may also offer conjectures to the parents such as "If we don't get this kid's behavior straightened out now, I'm afraid he'll end up behind bars."

Teachers' predictions are often made as recommendations for special gifted or enrichment programs, college-bound or vocational curricula, and ability tracks when the student leaves the elementary school for junior and senior high school. These predictions may contribute to a self-fulfilling prophecy. It is certainly true that the students who are recommended for enriched educational opportunities are more likely to succeed in school than their classmates are. But some reflective teachers wonder which comes first: the enriched opportunity or the success? They'd like to see how well average students would do if they were offered the types of enriched learning experiences available to students selected for elementary gifted programs.

Philosophies Underlying Various Evaluation Systems

Reflective teachers struggle with many conflicting ideas, thoughts, and concerns when they confront existing evaluation systems. Systems using letter grades are likely to be based on the assumption that students vary in ability and acquire learning by passively receiving knowledge from the teacher. From this assumption, it is logical to conclude that students should be evaluated by determining what they have learned and how this compares to other students of the same age. Categorizing and rank ordering of students is the next step and is done by assigning letter grades to label their respective categories of ability. Teachers with this perspective can be overheard saying, "John is an A student, and Sally is a C student."

Reflective, caring teachers are often very uncomfortable with such statements. They recognize the complex mix of environmental, nutritional, genetic, and experiential factors that contribute to each student's success or lack of success in school. Moreover, according to their view of teaching and learning, it is the teachers' responsibility to diagnose their students' needs and then plan a series of learning experiences and the scaffolding each student needs to experience success. The competitive nature of letter grades contrasts sharply with this philosophy.

How Curriculum Orientations Influence Evaluation

In addition to having a general overarching philosophy of teaching and learning, each teacher may prefer one or more of the five curriculum orientations described by Eisner (1985). Just as a teacher's curriculum orientation influences the learning activities that take place in that classroom, it also influences the types of assessment methods used to evaluate what students have learned and how well they have learned it. A teacher with only one strongly held curriculum orientation is likely to use similar methods of assessment day after day in every subject of the curriculum. For example, a teacher with a strong academic rationalism orientation will use tests and restricted essays as the preferred method of evaluating student performance.

Students who do well on the teacher's preferred type of assessment are likely to be perceived as being successful by that teacher. They will get As in the class. Students who do less well on that type of assessment will get lower grades. The teacher will predict the students' future success based on this strongly held curriculum orientation. Teachers who do not know or understand the variations in curriculum orientations may assume that their own perspective is the only way, or the best way, to view schooling.

Many teachers have more than one curriculum orientation. They may combine several or have one orientation for one school subject and a different orientation for the arts or another academic area. These teachers are likely to select a variety of assessment devices because their vision of the curriculum is multifaceted. Students in their classrooms may do well on one type of assessment and poorly on another. This varied performance will be recorded and reported.

The purpose of describing how a teacher's curriculum orientation affects the types of assessment methods chosen and the evaluation is to allow you to begin to clarify your own curriculum orientation(s) and to help you see how your orientation(s) can influence your choice of assessment methods and your vision of how well a student is achieving in your classroom. It can also help you to interpret other teachers' judgments and recommendations about your students.

HOW VARIOUS ORIENTATIONS AFFECT TEACHERS' OBSERVATIONS

Teachers with all curriculum orientations use informal observations as a means of evaluating what students know and what they need to know. Teachers oriented to the use of curriculum technology plan their curriculum with behavioral objectives or performance tasks linked to very specific learning standards and benchmarks for success. As they observe and listen to their students, they are assessing whether the student is reaching the criterion established for the lesson.

Academic rationalists are interested in assessing what has been termed *cultural literacy* (Hirsch, 1987). They assume that there is a body of traditional knowledge that all students should learn in school. As they listen to students discuss the content and ideas expressed in a classic text or literary work, they assess whether students have a mature understanding of the ideas or whether they require greater explication and perhaps a rereading of the text to gain the desirable degree of understanding.

Teachers with a social perspective plan a curriculum that emphasizes social awareness and responsibility. As they observe their students working, they are likely to be assessing the degree to which the students interact cooperatively or the extent to which a student is taking an active role in solving a social dilemma.

Teachers with a cognitive processes orientation emphasize the learning of processes over the mastery of content. As students work on problems, the teacher is likely to interrupt their independent practice to ask them to describe how they are attempting to solve the problem. As students describe their thinking processes, the teacher assesses whether they are using an appropriate process. The teacher also makes a judgment about whether their thinking is efficient and likely to lead to a correct solution or whether the teacher should provide the student with scaffolding that will lead to a more strategic problem-solving process.

Teachers with a personal relevance orientation emphasize the affective domain over the cognitive domain. They are interested in helping students develop positive self-esteem and intrinsic interest in learning. Their observations monitor student interest and engagement in the learning events.

HOW CURRICULUM ORIENTATIONS RELATE TO TEST CONSTRUCTION

Teachers with all five curriculum orientations are likely to use occasional short-answer quizzes and tests. However, academic rationalists and curriculum technologists are likely to use more of them than teachers with the other three orientations.

The type of tests used by curriculum technologists has been fairly well described in the section on mastery of learning objectives in Chapter 11. These teachers create both formative and summative quizzes and tests that are designed, item by item, to be related to their preplanned behavioral objectives.

Academic rationalists frequently use summative tests to assess whether students have gained knowledge about the identity of the world's great thinkers and the contributions each has made to our culture. For example, a teacher with an academic rationalist orientation would create tests that ask students to match the author with an idea or a title.

Teachers with a cognitive processing orientation are likely to use tests in which students solve problems. They are also likely to ask students to show their work rather than simply provide an answer. This is because these teachers are primarily concerned with assessing how students think, and they can evaluate that more accurately if they can see the steps the student has used in thinking through a problem.

Teachers with a social perspective design tests to assess whether their students are able to understand and solve difficult social problems. Tests and quizzes would likely consist of some short-answer items designed to test the student's knowledge base on each subject, but most items would probably ask students to apply this knowledge to social concerns.

Teachers with a personal relevance orientation may include a few short-answer knowledge-based questions, but most items will ask students to apply the new information to their own lives or give their opinions on the ideas they've read about. It is also likely that these teachers would write the test to allow students to choose to answer some items and omit others that have less interest for them. Directions for tests given by this type of teacher usually include "Choose three of the five questions."

How Curriculum Orientations Affect the Selection of Assessment Devices

Aside from informal observations and tests, teachers with a curriculum technology orientation are likely to use checklists and rating scales describing the mastery of skills. They are less likely to use essays because these are less objective than a curriculum technologist prefers. They may use learning contracts, but these would resemble checklists of skills and would simply be used as a reminder to students of where they are in the sequence of objectives that must be mastered. They are very unlikely to use tests of inquiry, creative products, or performances to evaluate student progress. Portfolios of student products would contain primarily worksheets and formative and summative tests.

Academic rationalists emphasize the assessment of students' knowledge and comprehension of a large body of content in classic literature and subject areas. They are quite likely to use essays as a means of assessing the students' comprehension of historically valued information, principles, and works of art and literature that make up the bulk of their curriculum. Oral presentations and debates are also likely to be employed for the same reason. They are less likely to use checklists and rating scales because these typically emphasize skills rather than content. The portfolios kept by academic rationalists would contain mainly tests and essays.

In contrast, teachers with a cognitive processes orientation are more interested in process than content. When they evaluate essays, they are more likely to look for evidence of the students' application of ideas, research skills, and hypothesis testing than the content itself. Oral presentations would also be evaluated more on process than on content. These teachers are likely to use tests of inquiry more frequently than objective tests because they believe in teaching students how to use inquiry and critical thinking skills to gain knowledge. Individual creative products and performances are likely to be assigned and evaluated with an emphasis on how well the students are progressing in processing information through the use of research, investigations, experiments, and reporting of findings. Portfolios are likely to contain "before" and "after" work samples and a variety of students' products to demonstrate how each student's skill in cognitive processing is growing and developing with time.

Teachers with a social perspective are likely to emphasize cooperative group projects and products over individual ones. Group learning contracts may be employed to assess cooperative efforts. In assessing individual work, these teachers are likely to use many expressive essays and oral presentations on social topics and problems to evaluate the extent to which each individual is growing in awareness of social needs and taking responsibility for creating solutions. Tests of inquiry into social concerns are also likely to be given. Portfolios are likely to contain these essays, letters to the editor, political cartoons, and other work that shows evidence of social awareness and concern.

Teachers with a personal relevance orientation are most likely to use learning contracts with many options for self-selection as a measure of student accomplishment. These teachers believe it is important to match the interests and individual needs of students with the topic being learned. They also believe self-selection encourages intrinsic interest and motivation in completing school assignments. Essays are likely to be quite open-ended and expressive in nature. The teacher encourages students to create individual products and performances and probably prizes them as evidence of student accomplishment and achievement. Portfolios of creative efforts and videotapes of performances are likely to be used to display students' accomplishments to others.

Although Dewey (1933) exhibited a combined orientation toward cognitive processing, social perspectives, and personal relevance, his influence did not fundamentally change the orientation of school personnel in the early 20th century. Since the 1960s, these three orientations have grown in strength, number, and influence. When you enter the teaching profession, you will see and hear evidence of all five orientations whenever teachers meet to discuss curriculum concerns. You will also see and hear the philosophies of all five orientations being debated when teachers get together to discuss how to assess student learning. It will serve you well to clarify which of these orientations you hold so that you can assert your own views on the appropriate methods to assess your students' accomplishments.

Methods of Reporting Student Accomplishment

Due to the time-consuming nature of the task of correcting students' work and the complexities of the evaluation processes described previously, it is easy to see why school personnel have resorted to a form of shorthand to record and report student progress. Most teachers have too many students and too little time to hold discussions with each student's parents or to write extensive narratives of each student's learning on a regular basis. Schools use standardized shorthand methods known as *grades* and *test scores* to communicate with parents, future teachers, college admissions personnel, and future employers (Oakes & Lipton, 1990).

The practice of awarding letter grades as measures of individual achievement has been part of the U.S. educational scene for many decades. In the 1960s and 1970s, personnel in some school districts attempted to replace conventional report cards with detailed anecdotal records describing what each student had accomplished in each subject area during the course or term. But these attempts to change the prevailing evaluation system met with opposition from parents, who insisted on a return to the letter grade system with which they had grown up. Parents were not satisfied with a description of their own child's achievements. They wanted to know how their child compared with other students. They expressed concern that these records would not be accepted at the most prestigious colleges.

In response to these debates, school boards and administrators in most school districts arrived at a compromise. While they reestablished the letter grade report cards for the intermediate and upper elementary grades, they retained the use of anecdotal report cards for the primary grades. This is the prevailing practice today. That means that if you are planning to teach at the primary grades (kindergarten through the second or third grades), you will be expected to write anecdotal report cards describing and documenting what each student in your classroom has learned. If you are planning to teach at the upper elementary, middle school, or high school levels, you may be expected to compute letter grades every quarter for the students' report cards.

COMBINING EVALUATION DATA

There is no formula that beginning teachers can learn from experienced teachers to guide them in selecting appropriate assessment devices and combining the data into a rationale for a grade. That is because no two teachers have the same philosophies or combination of curriculum orientations. Consider what would happen, for example, if Mary, an experienced teacher with a strong academic rationalist curriculum orientation, tells Pam, a beginning teacher with a mix of curriculum orientations, how to compute grades for report cards. Their conversation might sound like this:

> *Pam:* Mary, can you tell me how to figure my report card grades?
>
> *Mary:* Sure. Here are the tests I use. They are fill-in-the-blank and short-essay items. I use a straight percentage to figure my grades. Ninety percent and above is an A, eighty is a B, and so on. Then, for report cards, I just average the results of the tests.
>
> *Pam:* But how do you count in projects like the models my students made of the Indian villages during colonial times?
>
> *Mary:* I don't count those at all, except maybe for extra credit. If a student is on the borderline, I might give him the higher grade if he did a nice project.
>
> *Pam:* Well, then what do you do about students who try very hard but don't do well on the tests?

Mary: I just give them what they earn. That's what grades are supposed to do—communicate whether students learned what we taught them.

Pam: But what if they cooperated very well with their groups and helped to put on a great dramatic skit about the Pilgrims and the Indians but still did not retain the facts and dates on these tests? How can I give those students a flunking grade?

Mary: That's easy. You don't need to do so many of those *extra* projects. They just confuse you and the students. Spend more time on reading, recitation, and worksheets, and they'll do better on the tests. Grades are supposed to reflect knowledge of content, not fluff like group projects, models, and plays.

Pam is likely to come away from this exchange discouraged and more confused than ever. Mary makes it sound so easy. She seems to have an efficient system for deciding on grades, but it just does not fit Pam's curriculum or her philosophy that every student can accomplish something valuable in school, although not all students can be expected to learn in the same way or accomplish the same goals. In an attempt to gather more useful information, Pam may consult a second experienced teacher named Tom, who is known for his creative projects and highly interactive relationships with his students. "I like the way he teaches," Pam thinks. "Perhaps his system of grading will work for me, too."

Pam: Can you tell me how you figure your report card grades?

Tom: Oh, I wish you hadn't asked me that. Its not something I feel very sure about.

Pam: But you've been teaching for several years. How have you figured your grades up to now?

Tom: Well, I mostly go with student effort. If a student is willing to work and takes an active part in our class projects, I give her an A.

Pam: What kinds of tests do you give? How do you record what students have learned?

Tom: That's why I wish you hadn't asked. I use my gradebook for attendance only. If I had to show evidence of why a student got a certain grade, I'd be in trouble.

Pam: Well, don't you have to show that kind of data to the parents during the conferences?

Tom: So far, I've avoided it. They're usually so happy with the high grades their kids are getting that they don't ask me for too many details.

If you are like Pam, you are probably not satisfied with either of these explanations. You probably feel a need for answers to such questions as these (Linn & Gronlund, 1995, p. 343):

1. What should be included in a letter grade?
2. How should achievement data be combined in assigning letter grades?
3. What frame of reference should be used in grading?
4. How should distribution of grades be determined?

Linn and Gronlund (1995) respond to each of these questions as follows:

What should be included in a letter grade?   Traditionally, there are five letter grades (A, B, C, D, F), although some schools reduce this number to three (E = Excellent, S = Satisfactory, U = Unsatisfactory). According to Linn and Gronlund (1995), letter grades are efficient systems for communicating student achievement to parents and students when they are used for evaluation of academic achievement only. When extraneous factors such as behavior and effort are combined with achievement data, letter grades lose their meaning. For example, if effort and achievement are combined in the teacher's mind, a grade of C may mean excellent achievement combined with little or no effort, or it could mean excellent effort combined with very low achievement, or it could mean a moderate amount of effort and achievement. Therefore, the first recommendation is to use separate systems for communicating student behavior and effort and to compute the letter grades on achievement data alone.

In addition, "if letter grades are to serve as valid indicators of achievement, they must be based on valid measures of achievement" (Linn & Gronlund, 1995, p. 344). This means that the assessment devices the teacher selects or creates need to fit the objectives of the learning experience.

How should achievement data be combined?   The emphasis given to tests, essays, ratings, and other measures of achievement should be guided by the type of objectives that were planned and covered in the course or term. The more important the objective in the curriculum, the greater weight it should receive in the final grade.

Teachers with various curriculum orientations are likely to establish different objectives for their classrooms or give varying weights to the same type of item. The variation among teachers cannot be eliminated, but each teacher must be able to define the learning objectives he or she has established for the subject area and to base the letter grade on a reasonable combination of all of these objectives.

Combining data is difficult because various assessment measures are often not different from each other. Some tests may contain 100 items, and others contain only 25. If two measures are not equivalent, the grades on each one should be given different weights.

For example, if a student receives an A on the 100-item test and a C on the 25-item test, what grade does he or she deserve when the two items are combined? The average of an A and a C is typically a B, but that is only if the tests are equivalent. In this case, the 100-item test is worth four times as much as the 25-item test. That can be taken into account in at least two ways. One way is to multiply the value of the 100-item test by four when combining it with the 25-item test. That means that it is worth four As. Four As and one C will compute to a final grade of A.

What frame of reference should be used in grading?   Linn and Gronlund (1995) suggest that three typical frames of reference are used in grading decisions:

1. Performance in relation to other groups (relative grading)

2. Performance in relation to prespecified standards (absolute grading)
3. Performance in relation to learning ability or amount of improvement

Relative grading involves determining grades by comparing one student's achievement with the achievement of the other members of the class. An individual's grade is influenced by both the student's and the group's performance. A student is likely to receive a better grade in a low-achieving group than in a high-achieving group.

Absolute grading is the method of establishing a standard for mastery and awarding grades according to the extent of mastery each student achieves. The most common system of this type used in elementary schools is the percentage system.

The system of grading performance *in relation to learning ability* or amount of improvement is used fairly widely in elementary schools, but, as employed, it is seldom a reliable assessment. Reliable measures of growth or improvement are difficult to achieve with or without tests. Teachers may use the system to motivate low-achieving students, but Linn and Gronlund (1995) believe that the available measures are so undependable that achievement should be reported using one of the other two frames of reference and that improvement should be reported as a secondary or supplemental grade.

How should the distribution of grades be determined?   Relative grading is also known as *grading on the curve.* This is because it was developed to coincide with the normal curve of distribution, but this is not a reasonable possibility in a group the size of a single class. Instead, Linn and Gronlund suggest that a reasonable distribution may be in the following ranges (1995, p. 349):

A = 10% to 20% of the pupils
B = 20% to 30% of the pupils
C = 30% to 50% of the pupils
D = 10% to 20% of the pupils
F = 0% to 10% of the pupils

These ranges are not scientifically determined, but they represent a general target for this type of grading. Final decisions regarding the actual distribution should take into account the school's philosophy, the population served, and the purpose of the grades. One element that distinguishes this distribution from the normal curve is that it does not require some students to fail because they are at the bottom of the distribution.

Using an absolute grading system, Linn and Gronlund (1995) recommend the following distribution ranges (p. 350):

A = 95% to 100% correct
B = 85% to 94% correct
C = 75% to 84% correct
D = 65% to 74% correct
F = below 65% correct

Many teachers may prefer to alter these ranges to create more opportunities for earning the highest grade. With absolute grading systems such as this, grade distribution does not depend on the achievement of others. If all pupils demonstrate a high level of mastery, they can all receive high grades. Whether students pass or fail a course should depend not on their ranking within the class but on their absolute level of learning. If all low-ranking students have mastered the material sufficiently, they should all pass.

AN AUTHENTIC GRADING SYSTEM THAT ENCOURAGES SUCCESS

A major reason for failure in elementary schools is that too often the students do not know what they are expected to do to succeed. In some classrooms, the teacher's expectations may be vague and unclear. The students know only that they are supposed to work hard and do well on all of the classwork and tests that come their way. But some students may not be good at guessing what the teacher's real priorities are. This may be because the teacher has not sorted out these priorities either.

No two grading systems are alike. Teachers have different expectations due to their philosophies and views of how students learn. They have widely different priorities because of their curriculum orientations. They also have many other personality traits, interests, and values that influence their expectations for their students.

How can students be expected to adapt to so many different teachers with such a variety of expectations? It appears that most students can and do adapt if they are clearly and precisely informed about the expectations in each class. On entering a class for the first time, students want to know what the rules and expectations are in *this* class. Just as a clear statement of behavior rules and procedures is important, so is a clear statement of how to get a good grade on each project, paper, or test.

To be able to describe clearly to your students what you expect, it is essential to first clarify your expectations for yourself. A synthesis of research on effective evaluation suggests that you are most likely to clarify your own expectations and communicate them effectively to your students if you use the following steps for each subject area that you are grading:

1. Plan a set of educational objectives or outcomes.
2. Decide which of the outcomes are most important. Plan how you will weight them when you combine their data.
3. Plan learning experiences for each objective.
4. Create a performance task that can be used to measure the students' accomplishments for each objective.
5. Create a clear criterion for success for each performance task that will be used to measure students' achievement.
6. At the beginning of each learning event, inform students about
   a. the goal or purpose of the learning activity.
   b. the performance task they will be required to complete at the end of the unit and the criteria or standards they should be trying to achieve.
   c. what you will be looking for when you correct their work and precisely how you will score their work.
   d. what they may do if their first attempt is not acceptable.
7. When you correct and mark students' work, provide adequate feedback on what was done correctly and what needs to be improved. Give sug-

gestions for improvement. Encourage students to confer with you about how to improve their work.

8. Well before report card grades are due, inform students about
   a. what work will count toward the report card grade.
   b. what work will be given the greatest weight for the report card.
   c. what students may do to improve work for a higher grade.
9. When report cards are distributed, have a conference with each student and explain the reason for each grade. Describe the good work that resulted in good grades and describe the unacceptable work that resulted in poor grades. Help students to see how to make improvements in the unacceptable work during the next term.

Although some of these nine steps are commonly used in elementary classrooms, many are not. Most teachers do plan learning objectives, but many do not consider which ones are most important. Often, teachers treat all objectives as if they are equal, at least on paper. They may have priorities, but do not communicate them well to their students. Few teachers have clarified the weight they plan to give to each type of work and each objective. This situation was illustrated by Pam's dilemma. She had carefully planned a stimulating set of learning activities but had given no thought to how she would combine and weigh the outcomes until the last moment.

Another rarity in most classrooms is the practice of telling students how each piece of work will be scored and graded. Some teachers, exemplified by Tom, don't appear to know what they are really looking for in student work, apart from enthusiasm and participation. Others may have a much clearer understanding of this issue, but they do not believe that students need to know their conclusions.

Reflective teachers are likely to disagree. Rather than keeping the evaluation process a mystery, these teachers believe strongly that students *need to know* exactly how to succeed and what is expected of them. If they know these things, they can learn to take an active role in monitoring and evaluating their own work. One of the cognitive processes that reflective teachers want students to learn is *metacognition,* the capacity to monitor and regulate their own work. They plan learning activities that promote independence and personal responsibility. Informing students of exactly what is expected, how each piece of work will be scored and graded, and how various assignments and assessments will be weighed in determining the final grade gives students the information they need to regulate their own work. With this knowledge, they can make well-informed decisions about how much time and energy to spend on each assignment or task. They can learn to recognize when they should revise and improve a piece of work before turning it in or when to revise their work further after the first attempt.

Teachers who plan their evaluation systems to assist students in developing metacognition need to recognize that the capacity for self-regulation entails the use of a very complex set of cognitive processes, such as recognition of whether they comprehend an idea and whether the learning strategy they are using is appropriate. The development of metacognition takes time. It also takes many learning experiences in which students practice it. In the elementary grades, students need a great deal of scaffolding to help them gain these skills. Clear statements of what is expected and how to succeed, examples of what a good piece of work contains and what a poor piece of work looks like, precise and detailed feedback, and suggestions for improvement are all scaffolds that students need at this age.

USING PERFORMANCE TASKS TO CREATE AN AUTHENTIC EVALUATION SYSTEM

Imagine that teachers in a particular school collaborate to plan a nine-week interdisciplinary unit on people and their environment. The cognitive goal of the unit is to inform students about the present dangers to the natural environment. The affective goal is to create in each student a sense of responsibility toward the environment. The psychomotor goal stresses how to live in the environment, using it wisely.

The primary learning activities of this unit will include four weeks devoted to developing a knowledge base and understanding the basic concepts related to environmental concerns. Readings are assigned, discussions planned, guest lecturers invited, and films ordered. During the fifth week, the entire group is scheduled to spend a week at an outdoor education site learning how to use natural products and how to test for environmental hazards and to create artwork and write poems, stories, essays, and dramas about the relationship of people to their environment. During the final four weeks, students will work in cooperative groups to investigate one environmental problem and present their findings and solutions to their peers in a science exhibit at the conclusion of the unit.

The primary objectives of this unit, with the criteria for success underlined in each, are described in the following performance tasks. The number of asterisks next to each performance task indicates the importance of that objective and the weight that will be given to its product in the final determination of grades.

Knowledge-Level Performance Task

>   *1. On a matching test, students will be able to *identify 7 out of 10 sites* of environmental pollution and connect them with the type of hazard that exists at that site.

Grade equivalents:

>   A = 10 correct
>
>   B = 9 correct
>
>   C = 8 correct
>
>   D = 7 correct
>
>   F = fewer than 7 correct

Comprehension-Level Performance Task

>   *2. On a short answer test, students will be able to write the definitions of *10 terms* related to the environment *with no more than 2 errors.*

Grade equivalents:

>   A = 10 correct

> B = 9 correct
>
> C = 8 correct
>
> D = 7 correct
>
> F = fewer than 7 correct

Application-Level Performance Tasks

**3. Students will conduct *two tests* for water and air pollution during the outdoor education experience. They will write laboratory reports worth *10 points each* that include their observations, hypotheses, tests, and the results of their tests.

Grade equivalents:

> A = 20 points
>
> B = 18 points
>
> C = 16 points
>
> D = 14 points
>
> F = fewer than 14 points

*4. Students will demonstrate that they can find food and create a safe shelter in the natural environment. They will *identify at least 10 edible foods for 0.5 points each and draw a picture worth five points* of the shelter they would create of natural materials.

Grade equivalents:

> A = 10 points
>
> B = 9 points
>
> C = 8 points
>
> D = 7 points
>
> F = fewer than 7 points

Analysis-Level Objective

*5. Students will create a chart showing cause and effect or a comparison between environmentally safe and hazardous practices for their cooperative group display at the science fair. The chart will contain *at least 10 comparison or cause-and-effect elements*.

Grade equivalents:

> A = 10 or more points
>
> B = 9 points
>
> C = 8 points
>
> D = fewer than 7 points
>
> F = not done or not handed in

Synthesis-Level Performance Task

*6. Students will create a song, poem, story, essay, play, or skit to read aloud or perform at an assembly during the outdoor education week. Each work will contain a description of how people interact with nature and stress the importance of good ecology. *Criteria: Each work will receive 0, 1, or 2 points for each of the following three elements: fits topic, clarity, interest, length, and originality.*

Grade equivalents:

A = 9–10 points

B = 7–8 points

C = 5–6 points

D = 3–4 points

F = not done or not handed in

Evaluation-Level Performance Task

***7. Students will write a three-page essay giving their opinions of the most serious concern related to the environment. The essay will contain *at least five elements* as supporting evidence for this evaluation and will suggest *at least three ways* people can solve the problem and alleviate the hazard. *Criteria: 1 point for each element stated above. In addition, each essay will receive 0, 1, or 2 points for the writing elements of clarity and originality, for a possible total of 12 points.*

Grade equivalents:

A = 10 points

B = 8 points

C = 6 points

D = 4 points

F = not done or not handed in

Note that these seven performance tasks have a total of 10 asterisks. That means that each asterisk symbolizes a value worth 10 percent of the final grade. Most objectives are each worth 10 percent, the set of experiments is worth 20 percent, and the final essay is worth 30 percent of the final grade. The teachers planned their unit in this way so they could easily weigh the value of each assessment in determining the students' final grades for the unit. They plan to distribute a list of all of the requirements—with their criteria for grades and the weight of each grade—to the students on the first day of the unit so they will know at the outset what is expected of them and how they can succeed.

When they correct each of the seven assignments, the teachers plan to provide adequate feedback in their written comments or in a conference with the students so they know what they did that was successful and what did not meet the criteria. Then the students will have one week to make revisions and improvements on all performance tasks except the two objective tests if they wish to raise their grades.

At the end of the unit, the grades may be recorded in the teachers' gradebooks as shown in Figure 12.1.

COMPUTATION OF GRADES

Computation of the final grades for the unit is shown in Figure 12.2. It involves a straightforward computation of an average grade by awarding numerical equivalents to each letter grade, multiplying each grade times its weighted value, adding the seven items, and dividing the total score by 10. Note that although there are seven items, the average score is computed by a factor of 10 to take into account the greater weight placed on two of the items.

An alternative method for computing grades is to award points for each performance task, add up the points, and compare the total to a predetermined scale. In this unit, each of the seven assessments could be assigned a certain point value. Refer back to the objectives with their point values. Notice that objectives 1, 2, 4, 5, and 6 are each worth 10 points. Objective 3, which is considered to be twice as important as the others, has a point count that is double in value. Only objective 7 must be weighed to reflect its relative value. The logical method for calculating a student's total points for the unit, then, is to record the raw score or points in the gradebook, multiplying objective 7 by three before recording it. This produces a total of 100 points for all the assessments in the unit. Using 10 percent increments, the grades can be assigned as follows:

A = > 90 points
B = > 80 points
C = > 70 points
D = > 60 points
F = <\> 60 points

The rationale for using this system instead of the first one is that it diminishes the focus on grades during the unit itself. Rather than receiving a C on a paper, the student receives a certain number of points. With appropriate critical feedback, students may

	Graded Objectives						
Name of Student	***1**	***2**	****3**	***4**	***5**	***6**	*****7**
Jane	A	B	B	A	C	A	B
Bill	B	C	A	B	C	C	B
Gary	D	C	A	C	B	F	C

Figure 12.1 Teacher's grade book.

			Value of Grade ($\times$) Weight (*)					
Name	*1	*2	**3	*4	*5	*6	***7	Final Grade
Jane	A	B	B	A	C	A	A	
	4×1	3×1	3×2	4×1	2×1	4×1	4×3	
								35/10 =
	4 +	3 +	6 +	4 +	2 +	4 +	12	3.5 = A
Bill	B	C	A	B	C	C	B	
	3×1	2×1	4×2	3×1	2×1	2×1	3×3	
								29/10 =
	3 +	2 +	8 +	3 +	2 +	2 +	9	2.9 = B
Gary	D	C	A	C	B	F	C	
	1×1	2×1	4×2	2×1	3×1	0×1	2×3	
								22/10 =
	1 +	2 +	8 +	2 +	3 +	0 +	6	2.2 = C

Values of grades for computation purposes

A = 4.0   B = 3.0   C = 2.0   D = 1.0   F = 0.0

Final grade point averages equivalent to final letter grade

A = 3.5–4.0   B = 2.5–3.4   C = 1.5–2.4   D = 0.5–1.4   F = 0.0–0.4

Figure 12.2   Teacher's computations of grades.

be able to revise their first attempts to earn more points. When students are allowed and encouraged to revise and return their work, they are able to monitor their own progress. By keeping track of how many points they have earned to date, they can decide for themselves whether they need to revise and return their work for additional points. Deadlines for revisions, such as one week from receiving the corrected paper, can be used to hold students accountable for timely efforts on their own behalf. This system encourages students to use metacognitive skills in evaluating and taking control of their own school achievements.

Whatever method you choose for determining grades, after they are computed, they are recorded in the student's cumulative folder and on the report cards that are sent home to parents. Report cards for upper elementary, middle school, and high schools are likely to use letter grades to sum up the student's achievement in each academic subject. Some report cards may also provide checklists of subskills beneath the letter grade as a means of explaining to parents how the letter grade was determined. Because few report cards have categories for interdisciplinary units such as the one on people and the environment, it is likely that the teachers in this example would record the "people and nature" grade under science or social studies and explain in an accompanying note what the grade represents.

Within this unit, many learning experiences are planned, but only these seven performance tasks will be assessed as a means of determining a final grade. The teachers who created this unit are very proud of the way these assessments evaluate learning at all six levels of Bloom's taxonomy. They are also pleased that the assessments allow students with different learning styles to demonstrate what they have learned.

They have agreed that they will inform students of exactly what is expected at each stage of the learning process. During the first four weeks, when the students are reading and doing assignments to establish a knowledge base, the teachers will inform them of the nature of the two objective tests and provide them with samples of the items on the test.

When the classes go to the outdoor education site, the teachers will inform the students which activities are to be graded and how much each grade is worth. They will provide examples of well-written lab reports and will demonstrate the difference between a creative writing product that fits the topic and has clarity and originality and one that misses the topic and lacks clarity and originality (for example, one that borrows heavily from an existing nursery rhyme or song).

Back in the classroom, as students begin their individual investigations, the teachers will show examples of well-researched charts and give examples of evaluation essays that contain all of the important elements. At all stages of the evaluation process, the teachers will encourage their students to revise and return their first attempts so that they can experience the good feelings of being in control of their own success in school.

WRITING ANECDOTAL RECORDS

In most school districts, teachers are responsible for writing three or four report cards per year. These contain descriptions of each student's current level of accomplishment in each of the major areas of the curriculum, plus a summary of the student's work habits and social adjustment to school and peers. At the primary grades, report cards usually consist of either anecdotal records or checklists of skills rather than letter grades. Some school districts may use both. The advantage of this double format is that it allows teachers to describe and report their direct observations of a student's actual behaviors and accomplishments with sufficient detail so that parents understand the student's strengths and deficiencies. This is especially useful for skill areas such as listening, speaking, writing, study habits, social skills, and interests.

When a concern about a student arises, the teacher's daily observations of the student's work habits or social interactions can be important sources of data to help parents or other school personnel understand the student's particular needs and strengths. These observations may be augmented by the use of written anecdotal records of what the teacher observes. For example, if a student comes to school late, appears tired, and has difficulty sitting still in her desk, the teacher may want to document these observations by keeping a short anecdotal record for a week, recording how late the student is every morning, and describing episodes of falling asleep or inattentiveness. When this written record is shown to the parents, it is more likely to enlist their cooperation with the teacher in seeking answers to the problem than if the teacher simply reports orally that the student is "always late and too tired to work."

To be used to their best advantage, anecdotal records should be limited to observations of specific skills, social problems, or behavioral concerns. If a teacher sets out to record every behavior and event in a student's school day, the process will become too tiring and difficult to be feasible. Instead, when a student is exhibiting a particular behavior or deficiency in a skill area, the teacher can focus on daily descriptions of that one area and be successful in producing a useful document.

The major limitation or disadvantage of the anecdotal record is the difficulty of being objective when reporting student behavior. Many teachers have a tendency to project their own value judgments into the description of a student's behavior or accomplishment. This is due, in part, to the tendency to observe what fits one's preconceived notions. "For example, they will tend to notice more desirable qualities in those pupils they like best and more undesirable qualities in those they like least" (Linn & Gronlund, 1995, p. 270). The recommended way to avoid this tendency is to keep descriptions of observed incidents separate from your interpretation. First, state exactly what happened in nonjudgmental words. Then, if you wish to add your interpretation of the event, do so in a separate paragraph and label it as such.

In general, a single observation is seldom as meaningful as a series of events in understanding a student's behavior. Therefore, anecdotal records should contain brief descriptions of related incidents over time to provide a reliable picture of a student's behavior.

ORGANIZING PORTFOLIOS TO DOCUMENT ACCOMPLISHMENTS

Portfolios are used extensively in schools that prize authentic learning and assessment. They provide an excellent source of data when accompanied by an anecdotal record. As mentioned in Chapter 11, they may contain work samples in one subject area alone or reflect the student's work across the entire curriculum. Teachers who tend to think of the curriculum as a number of separate subjects are likely to use separate portfolios of work, and teachers who think of the curriculum as multidimensional are likely to include all relevant work samples in one portfolio. Some teachers may create portfolio categories such as *verbal work, technical work,* and *artistic work.*

At the middle school and high school levels, portfolios may be maintained for each subject that the student is taking. The Performance Assessment Collaborative for Education (PACE), directed by Dennie Wolf at the Harvard Graduate School of Education, has been investigating portfolio assessment as a tool for reforming schools. In collaboration with a number of school districts across the country, PACE has created a vision of what a school that uses performance tasks and portfolios would look like (Wolf, LeMahieu, & Eresh, 1992).

Students in the PACE school are expected to become responsible partners in documenting their own learning. In every class, a student puts together a folder that contains classwork, journals, and projects. At the end of the first nine-week marking period, an *initial portfolio* is created by students in every class. These portfolios replace or supplement quarterly tests that may be given in the course, but they do more than that. Students gain reflective awareness of how much progress they have made as they gather and evaluate the material for their portfolios. Teachers use the portfolios as the basis for computing grades and communicating with parents about what the students have accomplished. Grades and written reports are sent to parents accompanied by some items from the portfolios. Parents are asked to respond in writing or by telephone.

Nine weeks later, it is time for students and teachers to collect the material for their *semester portfolios.* At the visionary PACE school, a *portfolio week* is held instead of a finals week. During this week, students attend at least one *conference* with an adult advisor to discuss past accomplishments and future goals the student has for the second half of the year. At this conference the student and advisor also write a *letter to parents.* This letter is sent home with the student's report card.

At the end of the school year, a *year-end portfolio* is created as students draw on all of their best work of the year to provide current evidence of their progress on the essential learning tasks. In addition, the PACE school envisions holding *portfolio exhibitions* where students can display their finest accomplishments and committees composed of teachers, other students, and family members can ask questions about their work.

When it is evident to the teacher and other readers that a student's portfolio contains incomplete or unsuccessful work, the consequences may include assignment to summer school courses or placement in special programs or courses for the following year.

To establish reasonably consistent standards throughout the school district, the PACE school recommends that teachers *cross-read* portfolios from other teachers' classes. For example, the science teacher at one school reads four portfolios from another school. The four portfolios selected for this cross reading could include one from a superstar, one created by a low achiever, one average portfolio, and one puzzling one. Teachers who cross-read must become fair and honest critics of one another, asking whether the curriculum is challenging enough, whether teachers are providing enough commentary and feedback to students, and whether substantial learning appears to be occurring.

To validate the accuracy of portfolio assessment, the PACE school employs a process of auditing by external readers. A community-wide audit committee made up of businesspeople, educators from neighboring districts, and subject-matter experts may examine a sample of portfolios from each school. They will look at the quality of work, skills of teacher responses, appropriateness of grades awarded, and whether all students had access to the type of learning they needed. The committee will then report its findings to the community and make recommendations to the school board to suggest planning, budgeting, and other changes and improvements.

As you enter the field of education, the debate about portfolio assessment procedures will undoubtedly continue. Challenges and questions about portfolio validity will be raised, and conflicts about benefits and deficiencies will occur within schools and school districts. Reflective teachers will rise to this challenge by becoming well informed about both standardized and portfolio assessment procedures so that they can make fair and principled judgments about which to use and how to adapt and create new models of assessment that combine the best of both methods.

INVOLVING STUDENTS IN EVALUATION PROCEDURES

For reflective teachers, the natural extension of the teaching process is the interactive evaluation process that encourages students to become active evaluators of their own efforts and products. The current writing programs organized around periodic student-teacher conferences and the grouping of students who edit one another's work are excellent examples of this type of evaluation. In classrooms that feature such writing programs, the teacher's role in evaluation is to confer with the students about their current writing projects and to ask questions that engage them in analyzing what they have written.

Teachers may use open-ended questions designed to gather information on what the student has intended to do in a piece of writing. When the teacher has a sufficient understanding of the student's goal, the teacher and student may begin to zero in on ways to improve the quality of the writing so that it more nearly matches the student's purpose. This may mean correcting the mechanics of the writing so that it can be understood by others, or it may mean guiding the student to rethink the way in which a passage is written and to consider new ways of stating the ideas.

The editing groups used in such writing programs encourage students to learn how to listen to and respect the work that their peers are creating. Typically, students in a group each read aloud from a current piece of writing and then answer questions about the content from the other students in the group. Through this type of interactive evaluation, students may be learning how to work cooperatively, accept critical feedback, and write better at the same time.

This interactive evaluation system can be used in other parts of the curriculum as well. "What did you learn?" should form the core of the classroom evaluation. The more often this question is asked, the easier it is for students to identify and receive the help they need. It is a question children can learn to ask themselves (Oakes & Lipton, 1990, p. 132).

Providing students with self-evaluation checklists or rating scales assists them in learning more specific types of questions about their own progress and achievement. Checklists and rating scales that ask the student to evaluate specific outcomes may be developed for any learning activity, especially a unit of study that takes place over several weeks. Teacher evaluations may be entered on the same form to allow students and their parents to compare the student's self-evaluation with the teacher's assessment of the student's accomplishments. For example, in Figure 12.3, students are allowed to assess themselves after completing a research unit on leadership.

Interactive evaluation procedures are designed to breed success and enhance students' metacognitive capacities. They are as much a part of the *learning process* as they are a part of the assessment process. In fact, the long-term goals of most caring, reflective teachers are likely to emphasize the development of independence, self-responsibility, self-discipline, and self-evaluation as important affective goals of education. These goals are achieved through the development of metacognitive processes as children learn to understand how to succeed in any learning environment.

```
┌─────────────────────────────────────────────────────────────────────┐
│                         Leadership Unit                               │
│                    Student/Teacher Evaluation                         │
├─────────────────────────────────────────────────────────────────────┤
```

Name of student_____ **Grade**_____ **Date**_____

Leader selected for research _____

The student completes the left side of this evaluation and then the teacher will complete the right side. Afterward, student and teacher discuss the accomplishments made by the student, decide on areas that need to be improved, and plan goals for future learning experiences.

O = Outstanding   S = Satisfactory   N = Needs Improvement

Student Evaluation: **Teacher Evaluation:**

____   I completed the readings and assignments for this unit on time.   ____

____   I showed responsibility by bringing appropriate materials to class.   ____

____   I showed growth in my planning, decision-making, and organizational skills.   ____

____   I have gained skills in doing research and taking notes to gather information.   ____

____   I used a variety of relevant and challenging resources to learn about my subject.   ____

____   I improved my ability to speak in public.   ____

____   I gained confidence in my ability to speak in public.   ____

____   I gained independence in working on my own to achieve a goal.   ____

____   I am able to evaluate my own accomplishments and identify what   ____
         I need to improve with accuracy and honesty.

The most important thing I learned in this unit was:

Regarding my work in this unit, I am most proud of:

Figure 12.3   Sample student/teacher evaluation.

⊃ Reflective Actions for Your Professional Portfolio
Your Design for an Interactive Portfolio Assessment System

Perceptiveness: Observe a Portfolio Assessment System

Visit a classroom in which the teacher uses an interactive portfolio assessment system. What system does this teacher use for recording grades? Are there elements of this system that seem useful to you? Does the teacher use an absolute or a relative frame of reference? Which would you use? Do the students appear to understand the teacher's grading policies and expectations? What would you do to improve their understanding?

Construction of Knowledge: Portfolios

Read more about portfolio assessment, especially current material by Dennie Palmer Wolf. Visit classrooms to observe the systems other teachers use to collect student work in portfolios.
Clarification of Values: What Do Grades Mean to You?
Did you get good grades in elementary school? Do you believe that the grades you received were an accurate reflection of your effort and achievement? How will you determine grades in your classroom? If you choose not to use letter grades, what will you use instead to report student progress?

Creativity: An Interactive Assessment System

For the unit plan you are working on, plan an interactive student-teacher evaluation system that encourages students to use metacognitive processes to assess their own performance. Create a contract, checklist, or rating scale that students and teachers can use to look at the students' positive achievements as well as providing realistic and useful information about what students need to improve.

Persistence and Problem Solving: Refine Your Plan

Your plan is probably a product of your own curriculum orientation and learning style. Examine it again and look for ways to include more variety so that students with different learning styles will have an opportunity to succeed in your unit.

Communication Skills: Use Feedback to Improve Your Plan

Share your assessment plan with other prospective teachers. Get feedback from them on how clear and understandable your system is likely to be with students. Then try using the system with one student. Ask the student to tell you what is needed to make the plan clear, useful, and fair.

References

Bloom, B. (1982). *Human characteristics and school learning.* New York: McGraw-Hill.

Dewey, J. (1933). *How we think* (rev. ed.). Lexington, MA: Heath.

Eisner, E. (1985). *Educational imagination* (2nd ed.). Upper Saddle River, NJ: Merrill/Prentice Hall.

Hirsch, E. (1987). *Cultural literacy: What every American needs to know.* Boston: Houghton Mifflin.

Kidder, T. (1989). *Among schoolchildren.* Boston: Houghton Mifflin.

Linn, R., & Gronlund, N. (1995). *Measurement and assessment in teaching* (7th ed.). Upper Saddle River, NJ: Merrill/Prentice Hall.

Oakes, J., & Lipton, M. (1990). *Making the best of schools.* New Haven, CT: Yale University Press.

Wolf, D., LeMahieu, P., & Eresh, J. (1992). Good measure: Assessment as a tool for educational reform. *Educational Leadership, 49*(8), 8–13.

13

Reflective Teachers and the School Community

The teacher's role in the school community becomes more complex each day. Most school districts are undergoing some form of restructuring or systemic change that calls upon teachers to take more responsibility for planning and evaluating school programs beyond their own classrooms. School restructuring is often compared to piloting an airplane and conducting a major overhaul while in flight.

While attempting to maintain a stable environment for students and faculty, many schools are overhauling their curriculum, schedules, student evaluation systems, and administrative relationships. Schlechtly defines restructuring or systemic change as "changing the system of rules, roles, and relationships that govern the way time, people, space, knowledge, and technology are used and deployed" (Brandt, 1993, p. 8).

All of these changes make a difference in teachers' day-to-day activities as well as having long-term effects on their career paths. When restructuring is successful, teachers begin to see themselves as leaders and as inventors. "The job of the teacher, often working with other teachers, is to invent work that kids will do, and to lead them to do it" Schlechtly believes. "And if teachers are leaders, then the principal is a leader of leaders" (Brandt, 1993, p. 8).

The motivation for many of these changes appears to be a shift in what people see as the basic purpose of schools. One of the first tasks of systematic change is for the faculty of the school to gather information from members of the community about what they want and need from each other and what they believe to be the purpose of the school in their community. Synthesizing the information from many disparate members of the school community into a vision, articulating it in a mission statement, and operationalizing it with a plan of action take courage, patience, and many, many meetings.

Principals, teachers, and other staff must respond by working harder and longer hours to accomplish the many complex tasks needed for a successful restructuring. They must also be able to reduce a natural tendency to become defensive upon hearing criticism. Instead, teachers must be able to examine what it is the community wants them to accomplish and communicate to the community what they view as important. This process is likely to generate conflict. It is probably unavoidable and may perhaps be necessary to induce change. But reflective teachers are not afraid of conflict. Instead, they are willing to invest time and energy into building their own conflict-resolution skills and using them to gain important information from all members of the school community.

Two-Way Communication with Parents

At the beginning of Chapter 4, Lori Shoults described the many thoughts, feelings, and decisions she had to make on her first day of teaching. In the week before that first day, Lori spent a lot of time in her classroom setting up bulletin boards and learning centers. As she worked that week, many of her new students and their parents who had come to the school for registration stopped by her classroom to see the "new teacher." Some stood outside her door looking in quietly until she approached them and introduced herself. Others came into the room and looked around, exclaiming over the brightly decorated walls. The children were all interested in trying to discern whether the new teacher was "nice" and whether they thought they would be happy in her class.

Their visits, before the first day of school had even arrived, alerted Lori to the fact that she had more than the needs of 28 students to consider. She also had to be aware of and concerned with their parents' needs.

Some parents of primary children may be especially reluctant to see the beginning of school because, for them, it marks an end of an important phase in their lives. For five years, they've had complete jurisdiction over the lives of their children. Now they recognize that the teacher may have almost as much influence over their children as they have. I have observed the parent of a first grader, for example, standing outside the school after dropping off the child, saying tearfully, "But we've had lunch together every day of his life."

For the majority of parents, many of whom work outside the home and whose children have gone to day-care centers and preschools, this leave taking may not be so abrupt, but it is still a significant event in their own lives as well as those of their children. Many parents feel a strong interest in, and responsibility for, determining whether this particular classroom is a healthy and welcoming environment for their children. For this reason, parents of primary schoolchildren are likely to come to school, on one pretext or another, in the first days of school, just to see for themselves that their children are in good hands.

Beginning teachers may feel somewhat overwhelmed by these visits. All of their available energy has gone into planning the curriculum, moving furniture, decorating the classroom, and meeting and becoming acquainted with other teachers in the school. When a parent suddenly shows up, unannounced, it can be unsettling, especially if the parent wants to ask questions when the students are present. When this occurs, it is necessary for the teacher to suggest, politely but assertively, another time for this impromptu conference: "I'm sorry, Mrs. Jones, but all of my attention is needed in the class right now. Would you prefer to talk about this after school or tomorrow morning at 8:15?"

On many occasions throughout the school year, the teacher is expected to communicate with parents either singly or in large groups. In addition, many classroom teachers invite parents to become involved in the life of the classroom. Some students come from single-parent families, blended families in which divorced parents have remarried and have children with previous and current spouses, foster parents, and guardians. Teachers meet students who do not have the same last names as their parents. Teachers must recognize that the home lives they may have experienced may be different from those of their students. When *parents* are mentioned in this chapter, the term is meant to refer to the people who are being contacted or are meeting with the teacher on behalf of a particular child.

FALL OPEN HOUSE

When parents come to visit the classroom early in the year, one method of deflecting their concerns is to suggest that they will be able to have many of their questions answered within a few weeks at the annual fall open house (sometimes called "back to school" night). This event is planned especially for that purpose in many school districts.

The fall open house is usually held on an evening in late September. To prepare for the event, teachers are asked to be ready to describe their goals for the year and give an overall picture of the school's curriculum at that grade level. The event usually begins in the school auditorium or other large meeting room, where the principal welcomes everyone to the school and describes the important events that the entire school has planned for the coming year. The teachers, counselors, other administrators, and some-times the president of the parent-teacher organization are introduced. Special attention is given to introducing any new teachers on the faculty. At the conclusion of this general meeting, the teachers are released to go to their classrooms and make themselves ready for the open house. After a few minutes, the visitors are dismissed from the general meeting to find their children's classrooms.

When the parents assemble in the classroom, the teacher makes a short presentation to the entire group, describing what is planned for the year. A time for questions and answers of interest to the entire group is also likely to occur. Because most school districts intend the fall open house to be a time for general discussions of goals and curriculum, there is no planned opportunity for individual parents to ask teachers for specific information about their child's achievement or behavior. If parents approach the teacher and begin to discuss personal concerns, it is expected that the teacher will suggest an alternate time and place for an individual conference.

PARENT-TEACHER CONFERENCES

Conferences between individual parents and teachers vary greatly in purpose. Some are primarily used for diagnosing a problem or concern, and others are set up to report to the parents about a child's progress in school. Diagnostic conferences were described in Chapter 3 but are discussed briefly in this context as well because they are such a valuable means of evaluation.

If either the teacher or the parent has a serious concern about a child, one or the other may arrange a conference in the first weeks of school. When teachers, for example, observe unusually aggressive, passive, depressed, or antisocial behavior in a child, they are wise to call home immediately and set up a conference right away to gain information about the nature of the child's problems. This is especially true when a child's behavior disrupts other students in the class.

Setting up a conference sends an important signal to a student who is exhibiting unusual or unacceptable behavior. It tells the student that the teacher has withitness and is going to take action to correct the problem rather than let it go. It allows the teacher to seek information about the underlying reasons for the observed behavior. In a conference of this type, it is recommended that the student attend with the parents to gain a better understanding of the adults' views of the behavior.

When the conference takes place, the teacher should describe the behavior and, if possible, supplement the oral description with written anecdotal reports of examples of the behavior. The teacher should express concern about the behavior and then ask both the student and the parents to explain why it is occurring.

"Students usually cannot explain fully why they act as they do, and teachers should not expect them to be able to do this. If the students had such insight, they probably would not be behaving symptomatically in the first place. Instead, the hope is that clues or helpful information will emerge from the discussion" (Good & Brophy, 1987, p. 293).

When the parents discuss their own views of the child's problem, the teacher may gain significant insight by learning about the home environment. For example, the parents may agree that they have observed the same behavior at home and that it seems to be related to a crisis the family is dealing with, such as a death, divorce, drugs, a lost job, or a move. When the teacher, the child, and the parents confront this matter together, they can begin to put together a workable plan to help support the student during this difficult period and, at the same time, help the child gain awareness about the effects of the behavior on others.

Conferences don't always result in such harmonious cooperation. Parents may not present much useful information. On occasion, they may become very defensive or resentful of the suggestion that their child's behavior is unacceptable. In their family, this behavior may be okay. For example, a fifth-grade teacher was alarmed to see a boy walk into her class on the first day of school wearing a T-shirt that read, "Born to Raise Hell!" True to the message on the shirt, the child fought with other children at least once a day. When the parents were called in for a conference and the teacher described this behavior to them, the father replied, "So what? I tell my kids not to let anyone get the best of them." From the words and the father's tone of voice, the teacher learned that fighting was an acceptable behavior in that family. No happy resolution was discovered in this conference, but it did give the teacher some additional insight into the source and the depth of the boy's difficulties in social interactions with his peers.

At times, a teacher may need to involve others in the conference. Counselors may need to be present to suggest alternative ways of dealing with problems. If the teacher, parents, and counselor cannot effectively address a problem with the student, additional professional help may need to be offered to the parents. At times, parents admit that they cannot even handle their child at home.

Conferences designed for reporting on student progress rather than for diagnostic purposes usually take place in the late fall to coincide with the end of the first marking period and the first report card. In many districts, the parents are asked to come to the school for a conference with the teacher shortly after report cards are sent home. This gives the parents an opportunity to look at the report card and think about the questions and concerns they may want to raise at the conference. Some school districts require parents to come to the school to pick up the child's report card and have a conference with the teacher. In this case, the teacher explains the grades and observations to the parent as the parent views the report card for the first time. This second strategy is used primarily to make sure that parents do attend the conference.

Report card conferences are generally 15 to 30 minutes in length. They may be offered during the day and at night so that parents who work during the day may choose a night conference. Usually one or two school days are used for the fall conferences. In some school districts, the entire process is repeated in the spring. In the elementary school, a schedule of 30 conferences over a period of one or two days is a very tiring experience for most teachers, who may find that conference days are more exhausting than regular teaching days. This is due primarily to the tension caused by the teachers' recognition that they are responsible for the smooth flow of conversation and information. When this feeling of responsibility is multiplied by a factor of 30 or more in a few short days, it is easy to see how draining it can be.

To minimize the tension, it is extremely important that teachers plan each conference very carefully. Before the event, reflective teachers often write a page of notes about each student, highlighting the accomplishments and the matters of concern that the teacher wants to discuss with the parents. It is important for the teacher to be able to identify the child correctly in the conference. Teachers have mentioned embarrassing moments when parents have a puzzled look on their faces, only to discover that the teacher was talking about another student and not their child.

In addition to planning what you want to say about each child, it is a good idea to make a general plan for how you will conduct your conferences. The primary purpose of report card conferences is for you to inform the parents about the child's progress in your class. But the conference is also designed to elicit information from the parents that may help you to help the child. The parents may also have concerns that they wish to discuss. To accomplish all of these things in 20 minutes is very difficult. To do so, you must act as the timekeeper and allot a reasonable amount of time to each purpose. The parent will not be concerned about going over time, but you will because you will be aware that the next set of parents is waiting outside the door for their appointment with you.

Linn and Gronlund (1995) suggest considering the following elements when you plan your conferences:

1. Make plans for each conference. For each child, make a list of the points you want to cover and the questions you want to ask.
2. Begin the conference in a positive manner. Making a positive statement about the child, such as "Betty really enjoys helping others" or "Derek is an expert on dinosaurs," is likely to create a cooperative and friendly atmosphere.
3. Present the student's strong points before describing areas needing improvement. Present samples of work and focus on what the child can do and what he or she still has to learn.
4. Encourage parents to participate and share information. You must be willing to listen as well as talk. They may have questions and concerns about the school and about their child's behavior that need to be brought out into the open before constructive, cooperative action can take place.
5. Plan a course of action cooperatively. Guide the discussion toward a series of steps that can be taken by the teacher and the parents to assist the child. At the end of the conference, review these steps with the parents.
6. End the conference with a positive comment. Thank the parents for coming and say something positive about the student, such as "Erik has a good sense of humor, and I enjoy having him in my class."

The regularly scheduled report card conferences may be the only time you will meet with the parents of most of your students. For others, those whose behavior or learning problems are quite serious, you will need to continue to contact the parents by telephone or in follow-up conferences to monitor whether the cooperative plan of action is being implemented and what effects it is having.

Effective two-way communication with parents is essential for assisting students with severe problems. In working with children whose behavior interferes with their learning in school, an excellent resource for both teachers and parents is Rimm's (1995) *Why Bright Kids Get Poor Grades.* This book describes many of the most feared behavior problems that teachers must face: hyperactivity, passiveness, perfectionism, rebellion, bullying, and manipulative behaviors. Rimm believes these behaviors cause children to achieve much less than they are capable of in school. In her studies of underachievement, Rimm has discovered that children learned most of these behaviors in response to some elements of their home environment. Changing the behavior takes a concerted effort by the parents to isolate the causes and create new procedures to help children learn healthier, more productive behavior patterns that can lead to success.

Often it is the teacher who spots the self-defeating behavior. Parents have been living with the child for so long that they may not see that the child's behavior is unusual, and they may not be able to recognize how it affects the child's school achievement. Some examples of home situations that may lead to underachievement include the following:

The overwelcome child: Although it has long been recognized that an unwelcome or rejected child is likely to have problems in life, it is also likely that excessive attention can cause achievement and emotional problems. When parents overprotect and overindulge, the child may develop a pattern of not taking initiative and of waiting for others to do his or her bidding.

Early health problems: When children are born with allergies, birth defects, or other disabilities and parents respond by investing themselves almost totally in the child's well-being, a set of behaviors similar to those of the overwelcome child can develop.

Particular sibling combinations: Birth order and sibling rivalry affect all children, but some combinations may be particularly damaging to a child's achievement. A student who is the sibling of a child with severe health problems or is considered to be extremely gifted may feel left out or inadequate in comparison to the sibling. This can lead to the development of attention-getting behavior patterns, such as clowning or mischief making, that may prevent the child from achieving fully.

Specific marital problems: A single parent may develop a very close relationship with the child as a result of seeing the child as the only purpose for living. The parent may treat the child more like a spouse or a partner than a child, thus giving the child too much power. The child may learn to expect power and may not be willing to give it up to conform to the requirements of school (Rimm, 1995).

These are only four of many possible situations that can cause children to develop behaviors that may prevent them from achieving well in school. When a teacher spots a child who is exhibiting overly dependent or overly aggressive behaviors, it is important to confer with the child's parents, to report the problem, and to learn how the behavior first developed and how the parents are responding to it. The first step toward a positive behavior change is for the teacher to describe and give examples of the behavior and its effects on the child's achievement. The parents may deny that the behavior exists or that it is serious; but if the teacher can establish a cooperative two-way dialogue with the parents, it may lead to new insights for all of them.

If parents do acknowledge the behavior, the next step is for you to describe the changes you are going to make at school to support the development of new, more positive behavior patterns and to suggest modifications that the parents may make at home. Together with the parents, set some reasonable goals for the child in terms of both behaviors and grades. Discuss methods of helping the child reach these goals, and agree on a plan that fits the child and the situation.

Rimm cautions that children will not change their behavior just because the adults in their lives want them to do so. The child must want to break the underachieving patterns and substitute them for behaviors that lead to success. Both the teacher and the parents must also confer with the child, describing the behaviors and their effects in words the child can understand and accept. When the teacher, parent, and child all have the same goal and are working together on a plan of action tailored to fit the needs of the child, it is quite possible that the child will succeed.

Independent contracts are also useful support systems for helping children change behavior. A contract can specify work the child is to do, with deadlines and expectations for success. It can also be used to specify behavioral expectations. When the teacher negotiates the contract with the child ahead of time, the child has an intrinsic incentive to complete it: after all, the child helped to create it and decide what would be required. A sense of ownership is likely to increase the likelihood of the contract's being fulfilled (see Figure 13.1).

The teacher may employ additional extrinsic incentives if these seem useful in a given circumstance. It is most often recommended that students receive a reward that supports academics. For example, a student could earn points toward additional time at a learning activity or game. The major point is that the reward is something a student really would like to receive. Some things a teacher thinks would be rewarding are not rewarding to students. The types of rewards would vary by grade level.

This type of plan may be created as a result of a successful parent-teacher conference, a visit by the teacher to the student's home, or by telephone, followed by written documents specifying what the teacher expects, what the parents agree to take responsibility for, and what the student agrees to do to earn the agreed-upon incentive.

For example, if the teacher observes that a student is not turning in homework, the teacher may call the students' parents and ask for a conference at school or suggest that the teacher come to visit the home to discuss the matter. Alerting the parents to this concern is likely to result in a discussion of probable causes. The parents may or may not accept the teacher's perceptions of the problem and its negative consequences for their child's achievement. After a frank discussion of conditions at home that may support or interfere with the student's doing homework, the parents may come to recognize that the major cause might be the fact that the child and the family watch a great deal of television, beginning right after school and continuing up to bedtime. If the parents express a willingness to do their part to help change the child's behavior, then together they can draft an agreement or contract, specifying when the student will do homework and when he or she can watch television. It is a good idea for the teacher to follow up on this

Daily Evaluation Form

Student   Teacher
name _____   name _____   Date _____

Assignments completed: ___ All   ___ Most   ___ Less than half

Classroom effort: ___ Excellent   ___ Satisfactory
                          ___ Fair   ___ Unsatisfactory

Behavior   ___ Excellent   ___ Satisfactory
                          ___ Fair   ___ Unsatisfactory

Comments and missing assignments:

_____

_____

_____

_____

Thank you very much for your help.

Figure 13.1   Daily evaluation form.

Source: From WHY BRIGHT KIDS GET POOR GRADES by Dr. Sylvia Rimm. Copyright © 1995 by Dr. Sylvia Rimm. Reprinted by permission of Crown Publishers, Inc.

type of agreement by sending the parents daily or weekly reports specifying whether the homework is actually being turned in. These daily reports are likely to help everyone remember the commitment they have made. Later, when the student appears to have learned the new pattern of behavior and is more consistent about turning in homework, the reports can be sent home less frequently (see Figures 13.2 and 13.3).

I have one final caution about conducting parent-teacher conferences: occasionally, participants in the conference may reveal a family problem that is unusual and extremely serious. The students or parents may describe extreme poverty, desertion, or physical or sexual abuse to a teacher as a desperate attempt to get help. The classroom teacher is well advised not to try to deal with such problems alone. If this happens to you, ask the parent to allow you to discuss this matter with the school's social services personnel and immediately contact the principal, school psychologist, social worker, and other members of the crisis team to assist in the matter.

THROUGH THE EYES OF PARENTS

When parents send their children to school, they have many hopes and fears for their children's future. They want to be able to trust the school to create a safe, stable, nur-

Weekly Evaluation Form

Name _____   Grade _____   Date _____

Week of _____

Subject	Behavior	Effort	Grade this week (optional)	Grade to date (optional)	Teacher initials
1.					
2.					
3.					
4.					
5.					
6.					
7.					
8.					
9.					

Comments and missing assignments:

_____

_____

_____

Please use the same rating for effort, behavior, and achievement:
A – Excellent   C – Average   F – Failing
B – Above average   D – Below average

Figure 13.2   Weekly evaluation form.

Source: From WHY BRIGHT KIDS GET POOR GRADES by Dr. Sylvia Rimm. Copyright © 1995 by Dr. Sylvia Rimm. Reprinted by permission of Crown Publishers, Inc.

turing environment for their students. They want their students' developing sense of self to be enhanced and their individual talents to be appreciated. But many parents feel left out of the decision-making process of their children's schools. If teachers describe their goals or programs using unfamiliar educational jargon, parents may be reluctant to attend conferences or meetings at the school.

When parents are involved in establishing the school's vision statement or invited to participate on advisory groups, they may contribute many valuable ideas. In Jefferson County, Colorado, a school created a parent-teacher focus group to provide teachers

---

Sample Study Plan Contract

Richard, his mom, his dad, and Mrs. Norbert agree that Richard will spend at least one hour each day, five days a week, studying and doing his homework independently at his desk in his room. He will do this before he watches TV and there will be no radio, stereo, or TV on in his room during study time. After his work is complete, his dad will review his materials. At the end of the week, if all work is complete in class and homework has been handed in on time, Richard will receive ten points, which may be saved toward a bicycle. Each point is worth one dollar toward the price of the bike. Richard may also receive extra credit points for doing special projects. Richard's mom and dad will not remind him to study, and he will take the initiative independently. If Richard has not completed his homework, he will bring all his books home on Friday and Richard will not be allowed any weekend activities until he completes all missing work.

Richard
Dad
Mom
Mrs. Norbert

Figure 13.3   Sample study plan contract.
Source: From WHY BRIGHT KIDS GET POOR GRADES by Dr. Sylvia Rimm. Copyright © 1995 by Dr. Sylvia Rimm. Reprinted by permission of Crown Publishers, Inc.

with feedback on how to increase student self-esteem. At first, teachers were reluctant to have the parent observers visit their classrooms. But team members worked collaboratively to design a set of guidelines for the observations and agreed to provide teachers with copies of their observation notes after each visit. A parent-teacher retreat was held to build trust and clarify roles and expectations. After observing classrooms and playgrounds, the parent observers worked with faculty to develop a statement of their beliefs about how the schools could enhance students' self-esteem. Their statement of beliefs includes the following (Meadows, 1993, p. 32):

> Provide experiences that allow for individual differences
>
> Provide opportunities to express creativity
>
> View mistakes as learning opportunities
>
> Provide a safe/clean learning environment

While these recommendations were not new to the faculty, they were helpful in clarifying what the community wanted and expected from their school. From the team effort, both teachers and parents had a better understanding of the complexity of education.

In some communities, parents take a very active role in governance. Parents serve as members of school boards or advisory groups that work closely with the school administrators to make the important decisions about school funding and hiring and firing or personnel. On occasion, some parents have very strong views about a single issue and may try to influence school boards or administrators to provide a certain program or modify an existing program to coincide with the parents' values or philosophy. When this occurs, opinions can become very strongly stated, and conflict is likely to arise among parent factions and faculty. For the beginning teacher, it is important to try to learn as much as you can about the values of a school community before submitting an application for employment or accepting a teaching contract. If your own values and philosophy differ greatly from that of the majority of the school governance teams, then you are unlikely to feel at home teaching in that school district.

Teaching and Learning in a Multicultural Community

When the language, culture, and values of the parents match those of the teachers in the child's school, communication is likely to be relatively clear and agreements relatively simple to achieve. When the culture of the child's home differs significantly from the culture of the teacher, the teacher must be especially willing to listen as well as talk during parent-teacher conferences.

Before the *Brown v. Board of Education* Supreme Court decision in 1954, children who were racially different from the "white majority" were often segregated in separate (and inferior) schools. Since that time, federal mandates have required school systems to integrate both the student bodies and the faculties of their schools. But federal laws have not been able to mitigate the subtler forms of racism that still exist in some educational settings.

Although the United States is known as a nation of immigrants, a melting pot of cultures, the traditionally accepted cultural norm has mirrored the philosophy of the white Anglo-Saxon majority. Other cultures have been known as minority cultures. The prevailing belief is that children from minority cultures must be taught the language and habits of the majority. Researchers have found that, "to the extent that the home culture's practices and values are not acknowledged or incorporated by the school, parents may find that they are not able to support children in their academic pursuits even when it is their fervent wish to do so" (Florio-Ruane, 1989, p. 169).

Reflective teachers are aware that their own values and expectations may vary considerably from those of the families in their school community. But rather than assume that the children and their parents should be taught to mimic the language, behavior, and norms of the teacher's own culture, reflective teachers strive to gain a better understanding of the various cultures that make up the school community and to celebrate these differences by incorporating them into the curriculum.

In parent-teacher conferences, the reflective teacher is likely to ask with great interest about the home environment and the parents' cultural values as a means of better understanding the various cultures and conveying respect to the parents. When parents sense this respect from the teacher, they are more likely to return it and to believe that the teacher shares their own concerns for their child. The teacher may need to be especially encouraging to parents of other cultures, urging them to share their own concerns and ask questions. People from many cultures were not raised to ask questions of teachers and may be very reluctant to do so. But if the teacher encourages them to ask questions or make suggestions for the child's benefit, they may feel comfortable enough to do so. This two-way communication and mutual understanding can lead to a more productive arrangement to work together in supporting the child's achievement at home and at school.

The needs of children and their parents who have emigrated to the United States are especially important, as First (1988) found when she interviewed them:

> Immigrant children and adolescents, many of whom have survived wars, political oppression, and economic deprivation, find that their problems are not over when they enter American schools. Confronted with hatred, prejudice, and violence in U.S. schools, many newcomers are left asking what they have done to deserve such treatment. One Vietnamese student spoke for many when he said, "I like school here. But I wish there would be more friendships among immigrants and American students." (p. 210)

A Spanish child revealed the following:

> I came upon a world unknown to me, a language I did not understand, and a school administration which made ugly faces at me every time I spoke Spanish. Many teachers referred to us as animals. Believe me, maintaining a half-decent image of yourself wasn't an easy thing. . . . I had enough strength of character to withstand the many school personnel who tried to destroy my motivation. But many of my classmates didn't make it. (p. 210)

The classroom teacher must demonstrate a willingness to assist culturally different children and their parents as they make the difficult transition from one land to another. One of the best ways to accomplish this is to show sensitivity and respect for the various cultures of all the children in the class. Each year, the teacher may plan a special unit of study on the contribution of the cultures represented by the class members. Parents can be invited to participate in the learning experience by visiting the classroom and sharing with children the crafts and food of their countries. They can teach the children the songs and games of their homelands. First (1988) believes that when teachers involve the parents in their children's education, they send a powerful message that the school cares about them.

However, a teacher should not feel offended if the parent does not want to be involved. This could be viewed as disinterest. But in some cultures parents have been taught that the school is responsible for their youngster's education, and they should not be involved in the process on the school campus.

VISITS TO STUDENTS' HOMES

When teachers care sufficiently about understanding the particular home and cultural environments that surround their students, one way to seek information is to visit the children and their families in their homes. Teachers may do this by sending home a newsletter early in the year, announcing that the teacher would enjoy meeting the parents and seeing the children in their homes and that invitations to do so will be gladly received. This allows the parents to invite the teacher when it is a good time for them.

The visit will probably take place after school or during the evening meal. No agendas need to be established for such a visit; in fact, doing so would be counterproductive. The visit is not a structured parent-teacher conference at all. It is simply an opportunity for the teacher to understand more fully the conditions in which the child lives. Having the teacher share the family's meal, look at their photographs, and hear some of the family stories greatly enhances the feelings of the child and the parents that they are respected members of the school community.

On occasion, it may become necessary for school personnel to make a more structured visit with an agenda. This may occur if a child is having extremely serious problems and is referred for special services and a psychological evaluation. In that case, the school social worker or psychologist may visit the home to determine what factor in the home environment may be causing the child's problems.

Newsletters and Notes

Many elementary teachers communicate with parents by sending home handwritten notes describing a particular behavior or accomplishment of their child. In some classrooms, a note from the teacher signifies only bad news that is sent home when the teacher wants to describe an incident or pattern of misbehavior, a poor test result, or excessive tardiness. More recently, many reflective teachers have considered how to use the note home to encourage good behavior and reward achievement. Many teachers now send home notes describing a special accomplishment, an improvement in classwork, or an act of friendliness or generosity shown by the child.

To ensure that all children benefit from this system, the teacher may send a note of good news home to a certain number of children per week until every child has had one. Others prefer not to use a schedule but send a note whenever they observe a child doing something especially well. Without a schedule, however, it is important that teachers be careful not to favor some children over others.

In some classrooms, teachers prepare and send home classroom newsletters describing the important events planned for that week or month. The newsletter may contain items describing completed projects and new ones just getting underway. In the newsletter, the teacher can request parent volunteers for various projects and write notes of appreciation to parents who have recently helped out in some way.

In primary classrooms, the teacher generally takes full responsibility for creating the newsletter. But in intermediate and upper elementary classrooms, many teachers allow students to help write the items. They may use a computer program designed for creating newspaperlike formats. In this case, the production of the newsletter becomes more than just a method of communicating with parents. It becomes an enriching learning experience as well.

PARENT SUPPORT OF EDUCATIONAL ACTIVITIES

If teachers can communicate the classroom goals for that year of school and can supply parents with regular newsletters or other reports of student progress, this increases the likelihood that the parents will support the school's educational goals at home.

Parents can support their child's education and increase the chances for his or her success in school if they understand what they can do to help and are capable of giving that help at home. Teachers vary considerably in what they ask parents to do to support their children's education. The variation seems to reflect the different expectations teachers have about what parents are capable of and willing to do. Some teachers ask parents to read aloud to their children or allow the child to read aloud to them. To support this request, many teachers are willing to lend school books and other materials to parents to use at home.

Other teachers ask parents to take their children to the library. Many also suggest that parents ask their children what they did that day in school and discuss it with them. When asked for suggested activities and games that can be used at home to support the class's educational goals, most teachers attempt to provide parents with a list of ideas.

Most parents welcome the opportunity to support their children in school-related activities. Teachers who regularly report to parents on classroom events and ask parents to participate by doing parallel activities in the home are likely to develop very productive two-way relationships with parents that can increase the child's self-esteem and achievement and, at the same time, add to the teacher's understanding of the student's home environment.

TELEPHONE CALLS

The telephone provides an important link between school and home. Teachers often call students' homes for the same reasons that they write notes. Some use a telephone call to report a child's misbehavior and poor achievement and to enlist the support and assistance of parents in correcting the problems. Other teachers try to call home to report both positive and negative news. They may make their first call to report a problem or concern and follow up several days later with a second telephone call to report that the student is making progress in solving the problem.

Teachers are often on the receiving end of telephone calls from students' parents as well. Parents may call to clarify something about an assignment or an announcement that they cannot understand from their child's description. If parents hear confusing stories about something that happened during the school day, they may call the teacher to find out what really occurred. Responding to these promptly and in an open and informative manner promotes a positive pattern of communication between home and school.

Occasionally parents call in anger or frustration. They may disagree with the contents of the curriculum, the way a test was graded, or the way a classroom incident was handled. The teacher receiving one of these calls may easily become defensive and angry as well. Dealing effectively with these calls takes mature, well-developed communication skills. It is difficult, but very important, to listen empathetically to what the parent says. Even when the instinctive reaction of most teachers is to break into the parent's statements and present their own side of the situation, it is more productive if the teacher's initial responses encourage the parent to describe the problem in more detail and express personal feelings.

After the parent has had an opportunity to describe fully the reason for the telephone call, the teacher's side of the story can be presented in a quiet, nonthreatening, and nondefensive voice. In a situation such as this, the teacher has the responsibility for attempting to resolve the conflict and creating a mutually acceptable solution.

For example, suppose a fight occurs in the classroom during the day and John is punched in the face by Dean, a much stronger boy. Because John's lip is bleeding, the teacher decides to send him to the nurse. She then tries to talk to Dean to find out what prompted the fight. Dean claims that he was provoked by John's name calling, and many children in the class support that claim. When John returns from the nurse, the teacher tells him that both he and Dean will have to stay in during recess for fighting. John seethes with anger for the rest of the day.

After school, the teacher is called to the telephone to find John's very angry parent on the other end. "Why did you keep my son in for recess when he got hit by that bully? And why didn't you call me immediately when he got hit? Did you know he was bleeding? I'm going to come in right now and talk to your principal about this matter, and you will be sorry you treated my son this way!"

The instinctive reaction for most teachers is to jump in and explain after the first few words are spoken. If the parent continues to question the teacher's judgment, the teacher may soon feel as angry as the parent does. But reflective teachers recognize that there will be days like this in the classroom with 30 students and one adult. They will try to keep their feelings in control and say something to soothe the parent's hurt pride and upset feelings.

"I'm glad you called, Mrs. Jones. I can understand how you feel. Tell me how John's lip is now." This type of comment will help the teacher gather information and gain time to formulate a good response. Not all such problems can be readily resolved. Perhaps the teacher and the parent will continue to have different points of view no matter how much they discuss it. If this is the case, it is necessary to acknowledge it and end the conversation with a comment such as "I recognize how you feel about this situation. I'm sorry John got hurt today, and I'll do my best to see that he is not involved in any more fights this year."

The key point of this section is expressed in the phrase "reflective teachers recognize that there will be days like this." Every school year has days like these. Values clash, and feelings are hurt. The beginning teacher may be shocked the first time this happens and overreact by feeling angry, guilty, or defensive. If possible, when incidents such as these occur in your classroom, remember that every teacher experiences conflict. Conflict is unavoidable in this career, and the first step in learning how to handle it is learning to expect and accept it as part of the job.

SPRING OPEN HOUSE AND OTHER SPECIAL EVENTS

In the fall, the purpose of most conferences and open house events is to allow parents and teachers to get to know each other, communicate their goals for their children (students), and make plans for accomplishing these goals. As the year goes by, the focus of most meetings between parents and teachers is for the teacher to demonstrate to the parents how these goals are being met.

Many classroom teachers invite parents frequently, perhaps as often as once a month, to attend exhibits, plays, assemblies, or other occasions for students to display what they are learning and what they have accomplished. Some of these events may be schoolwide assemblies, such as Thanksgiving plays, concerts, and feasts; winter pageants; midwinter cultural fairs; and spring open houses in which collections of student work are displayed throughout the school.

Individual teachers may also invite their students' parents to school to view the performances or an exhibit of products resulting from a unit of study. These events are usually highly prized by students and parents and are an excellent way for the teacher to interact and communicate continually with the parents.

Consider, though, how some parents might feel if they attend a spring open house and find that their own child's work is not displayed. In some competitive classrooms, teachers tend to display only the papers with "100%" written across the top. For those children who rarely get perfect papers, this can be a discouraging experience; for their parents, it is likely to be equally discouraging. If classroom displays include examples of students' work, it is important to display the best works of every student in approximately equal numbers.

To avoid creating a competitive environment, you may want to display students' work inside their portfolios on their desks so that each parent can view the work done by his or her own child alone. General classroom displays can consist of group projects and murals so that every child and parent can take equal pride in the classroom.

Community Involvement in Classroom Activities

PARENTS AS VOLUNTEERS

Parents volunteer to do many things in schools to benefit their own children and the larger community. Many parents enjoy being members of an all-school organization known as the *parent-teacher association (PTA)* or *parent-teacher organization (PTO)*. These organizations have regularly scheduled meetings and yearly fundraising events to serve the needs of the school. In most cases, parents do the greatest part of the work on the committees, although teachers are usually represented as well.

Many elementary schools encourage parents to volunteer their time during the school day to assist teachers in educational or extracurricular programs. Parents can serve as coaches, assistant coaches, or referees for some sports events such as all-school field day events. They often serve as helpers on class field trips, accompanying the class on the bus ride and throughout the day. Usually, teachers ask each adult to be responsible for a small group of children during the trip, reducing the adult/child ratio from 28:1 down to 4:1 or 5:1.

In the classroom, many primary teachers invite parent volunteers to serve as assistants in the reading and language-arts program. A parent can work with one small group while the teacher works with another or with the rest of the class. In this way, parents can serve many important functions. They can read aloud to a group of children or listen to an individual or a small group of children read aloud to them. Parents can write the words as a child dictates a story or can edit a piece of writing done by a child. Parents can listen to book reports and keep records of the number and type of books each child has read.

With the advent of computers in the classroom, many teachers appreciate having parents who are knowledgeable about computers volunteer to work with groups of children as they learn to operate a computer or to monitor students' progress as they work with tutorial or problem-solving computer programs.

During individualized mathematics or spelling programs or those structured on a mastery learning model, parents can serve as assistants who correct formative tests and provide feedback to students. They can also help to organize the large amounts of paperwork, filing, and record keeping that often accompany individualized instructional programs.

Having parents volunteer to work in your classroom has many benefits, and often you will find knowledgeable and experienced parents who enjoy this type of work. Many parents have interrupted their own careers to raise children and look forward to having a regular volunteer job.

Not all teachers, however, enjoy having parent volunteers in their classrooms. Some teachers are reluctant to have parents view the ups and downs that occur in any school day. Other teachers are not comfortable with parent volunteers because the teacher must be ready with activities and materials whenever the parent arrives. For some teachers, this is a burden that outweighs the benefit of having the extra help. It is true that working with parent volunteers means greater responsibility for the teacher, who must manage the other adults as well as the students in the class.

Whether you wish to use parents as volunteers in your classroom is one of those issues that you will need to reflect on, considering the benefits against the costs. One of the best ways to gather information about the efficacy of this practice in your classroom is to try it out with one subject area and a knowledgeable, experienced parent volunteer to see if it is a system you want to employ.

To increase the likelihood that the practice will work in your room, you and the parent volunteer should discuss in advance what you expect the parent to do and agree on the times the parent will visit. Usually parents do only routine tasks or monitor students as they work on a program planned by you and your colleagues. When these matters are clarified, you will probably find the volunteer effort to be very productive, allowing you to reduce the amount of time you spend on routine tasks.

COMMUNITY RESOURCES

Parents or other community members with special interests, abilities, careers, and accomplishments can also enrich your program by visiting to speak to the class about their specialties. A unit on community helpers can certainly benefit from visits by parents who are nurses, police officers, fire fighters, or others who perform community services. Parents who are manufacturers or waste haulers can provide their input during a unit on ecology. When the class is studying economics, parents who work as merchants can describe the theory of supply and demand to the class.

During the first parent-teacher conference in the fall, you may be able to discover what talents your students' parents possess and create a community resource file to draw on throughout the year. In some schools, these files are kept schoolwide, and parents in the file are happy to come to any classroom in the school to share their knowledge and experience with the children. The file may also contain names of adults in the community who are not parents of children attending the school but who are willing to visit as a service to the community.

Many communities are searching for ways to attract volunteers into the schools to provide important services to students. An organization called Rolling Readers based in San Diego, California, serves as a liaison between volunteers and the public schools. Rolling Readers recruits volunteers who want to read aloud to children in large groups as well as volunteers who want to tutor students in reading skills on a one-to-one basis. The number of volunteers in this program grows steadily because it serves the needs of the adult volunteers who are looking for a way to serve their community and make a difference in the lives of children. For information about how you can duplicate such a program in your community, call Rolling Readers at (800) 390-READ.

CHARACTER EDUCATION PROGRAMS

The interaction between home and school becomes more complex and controversial when the school's objective changes from supporting the child's academic development to supporting the child's moral development. Nevertheless, schools in the 1990s and the 21st century are likely to be at the center of a growing concern about the need for greater emphasis on moral education. This concern grows out of an awareness that schools must take more responsibility for countering the influence of drugs, violence on television and other media, the fragmentation of the family, and the publicity about questionable ethical practices in business and industry (ASCD, 1988).

A panel of educators met in the summer of 1988 to discuss the schools' role in teaching values. The educators agreed that, due to the enormous temptations and distractions facing children today, schools must take an active role in teaching children about the nature of right and wrong. Although the panel recognized that the increasing social, religious, and ethnic diversity of the schools makes it difficult to agree on one set of values, a few common themes appear in almost every culture. The panel recommends that schools develop community-supported programs centering on at least these four themes: *justice, altruism, diligence,* and *respect for human dignity.*

Lickona (1988) recommends that each school recruit local parents to serve on a school-parent support group to (1) arrive at a consensus of the moral values most important to that community and (2) write a moral education curriculum that will be taught at school and in the home at the same time (p. 36).

Mary Ellen Saterlie (1988), a school administrator in Baltimore, illustrates how such a parent-school partnership can be formed and what it can produce. She describes the Baltimore public schools' experience, in which school administrators created a community task force to participate in an open dialogue on community values. They purposely invited people with very different religious and political beliefs to serve on the task force. After extensive reading and debate, the task force was able to agree upon a common core of values appropriate for a democratic and pluralistic society:

> compassion, courtesy, critical inquiry, due process, equality of opportunity, freedom of thought and action, honesty, human worth and dignity, integrity, justice, knowledge, loyalty, objectivity, order, patriotism, rational consent, reasoned argument, respect for others' rights, responsible citizenship, rule of law, self-respect, tolerance and truth. (pp. 46–47)

After identifying these community-acknowledged values, the task force wrote outcome statements for development of these moral values. The board of education then discussed and ratified their report. The PTA developed a brochure on the values education program and distributed it to all parents in the system.

The method used to implement this program allowed each of the 148 schools in the district to appoint its own values committee, which was encouraged to select certain of the task force–identified values to emphasize in its own school projects. This encouraged a creative response from most schools. Some addressed additional values such as computer ethics or academic honesty as well as those identified by the task force. The Baltimore model linked parents, schools, and the community in a unified examination of moral and ethical issues to "strengthen the character of our students, which in turn will contribute to strengthening our free society" (Saterlie, 1988, p. 47).

As a beginning teacher, you may find that your school district is taking similar measures, and you may wish to become an active part of the task force that identifies the moral values of your community and creates school programs to educate students in these values. If you find that your school district has not yet considered such a challenge, perhaps you can be the one who initiates the idea. Reflective individuals who are committed to upholding the moral values of the community can serve as important role models for the students they teach.

Collegial Relationships

TEACHER EMPOWERMENT

The focus of the current research on educational reform and the restructuring of schools centers on the teacher, indicating why the role of the teacher is growing in responsibility and respect. Some use the term *teacher empowerment* to describe the teacher's new role. Teachers are gaining power by showing a growing willingness to take responsibility for all aspects of planning, teaching, and evaluation.

The whole language movement is one example of how curricula are being restructured as a result of classroom teachers' perceptions about what their students need. Frustrated with the status quo of reading programs that rely on vocabulary-controlled stories in basal readers, workbooks full of meaningless seatwork, and few opportunities for students to read or write about their own experiences, many teachers have sought new methods for teaching language arts.

After learning about the whole language approach through conferences, books, and articles or by visiting a classroom in which students selected and read books that mattered to them and wrote about things they cared about, many teachers began to invent ways to use these methods in their own classrooms. Because they needed different materials to teach this way, they began to make their needs known at faculty and board meetings.

Frequently, teachers who believed that the new whole language methods were more responsive to their students' needs and interests conferred with and supported each other in their efforts to make changes in their schools. Other teachers in the school may have different views and wish to retain the "tried and true" basal reader systems. The school administrators have their own views, as do parents and other members of the community. All of these voices have been raised in a professional dialogue about the purpose of the reading and language-arts curriculum. Schools where this conflict has occurred have seen a healthy reexamination of the philosophy, goals, beliefs, and outcomes hoped for and expected of students and teachers alike.

Teacher empowerment means that teachers have more opportunities to make choices and decisions, a necessary ingredient for reflectiveness. For without the right and responsibility to make decisions, reflecting on the way to improve one's teaching and improve the lives of one's students would be fruitless.

TEACHERS MENTORING AND COACHING ONE ANOTHER

Before restructuring, the school principal was responsible for observing and evaluating teachers' classroom performance. In many school systems today, however, teachers are sharing their own perspectives with each other as part of the evaluation process. Experienced classroom teachers, sometimes called *coaches* or *mentor teachers,* observe less experienced teachers as they work with children in their classrooms. Afterward, the two teachers discuss the observed classroom events. This practice allows the mentor teacher to provide critical feedback and to share personal knowledge with colleagues. It also encourages the beginning teachers to reflect on what they do, the effects of their actions, and decisions and ways to improve their teaching.

In Watsonville, California, teachers in two schools created a program called Professional Partnerships to decrease isolation and build collegial support systems. In this program, two teachers selected each other on a voluntary basis to become teaching partners. They observed one another's classrooms each month for a minimum of 30 minutes each visit. The partners meet before each observation to define the focus of the lesson and then discuss the visit afterward. Quarterly, the partners meet with the principal and two additional teachers in the school, who serve as facilitators. Here are how two of the teacher partners described the project:

> My partner is coming to visit so I don't let things slide. My area of interest is improving the quality of student interactions. But I've also improved management, groupings, and materials because everything surrounding the lesson affected what I wanted to have happen.
>
> The postconferences give me a chance to talk about the details of the lesson that I couldn't pay attention to while I was teaching. My partner always gives me new ideas. I feel very supported, and I'm making changes. (Stobbe, 1993, p. 41)

Teachers are also actively involved in selecting the type of staff development they need to accomplish the goals they've established for themselves. When teachers get interested in a new curriculum such as the whole language approach or mathematics programs that emphasize problem solving, they are likely to propose conferences they'd like to attend and arrange to bring in consultants knowledgeable about the new methods.

Another powerful new result of the restructured school environment is the increase in the role of the teacher as a researcher. Teachers are becoming more committed than ever before to investigating areas of concern and doing active research to improve their own instructional practices. When they learn something valuable about their own efforts, they are increasingly taking the role of collaborating with other educators to focus their inquiry on issues larger than those in a single classroom.

To share the results of their investigations, many teachers are writing about their experiences and describing the investigations they've made. They submit their papers to journals and take part as presenters in local and regional conferences.

At the center of all of this change is the teacher and the growing power, responsibility, and respect the teacher has earned. Porter and Brophy (1988) report that since the early 1970s there has been a surge of activity in research on teaching. Much of it has been predicated on a deceptively simple thesis: effective school learning requires good teaching, and good teachers are those who exercise good judgment in constructing the education of their students (p. 74). In other words, as described in Chapter 1 of this text, good teachers are those who use reflective thinking, based on moral principles, in making judgments about classroom events. There is a strong, undeniable link between *reflective* and *effective* teachers.

As discussed in Chapter 2, research shows that the most effective teachers are good classroom managers. This management skill grows directly out of reflective, empathetic, and democratic leadership from the first day of school. As shown in Chapter 3, the role of the teacher includes the responsibility for making accurate diagnoses, which occurs when teachers use formal and informal sources of information as a means of making reflective judgments about appropriate placements of students in the curriculum so that they can achieve success.

Throughout the research on effective teaching and effective schools, the attribute of *teacher clarity* surfaces again and again. "Effective teachers are clear about what they intend to accomplish through their instruction, and they keep these goals in mind both in designing instruction and in communicating its purposes to the students" (Porter & Brophy, 1988, p. 81). Clarity of goal setting requires the reflective planning practices described in Chapter 4.

It is also becoming apparent that it is very effective to combine or integrate subjects into multidisciplinary units of study, as described in Chapters 5 and 6. Rather than being textbook technicians, reflective teachers prefer to create their own learning experiences either individually or with teammates. They frequently focus on interesting themes or topics in which students use and develop their reading, writing, and research skills as they gain new knowledge about a variety of subjects.

Another common element identified throughout the literature on effective teaching is that effective teachers create learning experiences in which students are not simply passive recipients of fact-based knowledge; instead, they teach their students how to use many *cognitive processes*, how to organize information in new ways, and how to solve problems for themselves. It takes a reflective teacher with a cognitive-mediational view of learning to recognize and select the appropriate teaching strategies that will engage students in active learning, as described in Chapters 7, 8, 9, and 10.

Reflective teachers are willing to use a variety of assessment techniques, such as those described in Chapter 11, rather than rely on one objective method. This is an especially effective practice because it allows students with a variety of learning styles to demonstrate their accomplishments and succeed. Effective practitioners are also talented at providing students with useful, timely, and detailed *critical feedback* so that students know what is expected and what they must do to succeed. But we now know that simply being a good evaluator is not enough; the most effective teachers are those described in Chapter 12, who cause their students to take an active role in the evaluation of their own learning by teaching them how to apply *metacognitive strategies* to become independent and self-reliant, able to monitor and regulate their own learning.

In addition to their responsibilities to their students, effective teachers are able to communicate well with the parents and other members of the school community in order to support the moral development of students.

The teacher's role in the educational community is changing. Teaching shows considerable promise of becoming a highly respected profession in the United States during the 21st century. This is largely due to the efforts of reflective teachers who are asking important questions about how they can improve classroom events and children's lives. Alone or in collaboration, reflective teachers are seeking out new alternatives and selecting the ones they believe might improve their teaching. They are taking responsibility for evaluating their classroom practices by gathering data from their own observations and from the current research and knowledge base on teaching and learning. They are disseminating what works for them in faculty meetings, workshops, conferences, and articles in professional journals. The result is a new emphasis on inquiry, reflection, and building a knowledge base about the most successful and effective practices that create a stimulating and healthy learning community.

⮌ Reflective Actions for Your Professional Portfolio
Your Professional Role in the School Community

Perceptiveness: Teacher Empowerment

Ask several teachers to discuss the roles and responsibilities they take beyond their classroom expectations. Do they believe they are empowered to make the important decisions they think are necessary to meet students' needs? What are some examples of teacher empowerment that you have observed? Ask your cooperating teacher to discuss the changes in teacher power that have occurred in the past few years.

Construction of Knowledge: Observe a Faculty Meeting

Arrange to observe a faculty meeting or another decision-making body at a school you are visiting. How are decisions made? Do teachers work as colleagues to propose programs or solve problems? Does the administrator respect the ideas of the faculty? Visualize yourself as a member of this faculty. What responsibilities would you be willing to assume?

Clarification of Values: Decision Making

Are you a person who is comfortable or uncomfortable with decision-making power? If you work in a school district that encourages teachers to take responsibility for many important decisions, will you welcome this as an opportunity or look on it as a burden? Would you prefer to make decisions about your own classroom independently, or would you rather share the power and the responsibility with your teammates?

Creativity: An Action Plan

Choose an educational issue or dilemma that you are observing in schools you visit. Create an action plan to approach this problem that you would propose to your colleagues if you were a full-time faculty member at the school. Include a method to gather information from a variety of people who make up the school community.

Persistence and Problem Solving: Get Feedback

Show your action plan to an experienced teacher. Get feedback on how to improve your plan or make it more realistic. Revise your plan.

Communication Skills: Present Your Plan

Role-play presenting your action plan to a group of colleagues, who take the roles of other faculty members with different points of view. Respond to their questions and concerns. Use your assertiveness and conflict-resolution skills to convince your colleagues of the importance of the issue and the worthiness of your plan.

References

Association of Supervision and Curriculum Development (ASCD). (1988). Moral education in the life of the school. *Educational Leadership, 45*(8), 4–8.

Brandt, R. (1993). On restructuring roles and relationships: A conversation with Phil Schlechtly. *Educational Leadership, 51*(2), 8–12.

First, J. (1988). Immigrant students in U.S. public schools: Challenges with solutions. *Phi Delta Kappan, 70*(3), 205–210.

Florio-Ruane, S. (1989). Social organization of classes and schools. In M. Reynolds (Ed.), *Knowledge base for beginning teachers* (pp. 163–172). Oxford: Pergamon.

Good, T., & Brophy, J. (1987). *Looking in classrooms* (4th ed.). New York: Harper & Row.

Lickona, T. (1988). How parents and schools can work together to raise moral children. *Educational Leadership, 45*(8), 36–38.

Linn, R., & Gronlund, N. (1995). *Measurement and assessment in teaching* (7th ed.). Upper Saddle River, NJ: Merrill/Prentice Hall.

Meadows, B. (1993). Through the eyes of parents. *Educational Leadership, 51*(2), 31–34.

Porter, A., & Brophy, J. (1988). Synthesis of research on good teaching. *Educational Leadership, 45*(4), 74–85.

Rimm, S. (1995). *Why bright kids get poor grades.* New York: Crown.

Saterlie, M. (1988). Developing a community consensus for teaching values. *Educational Leadership, 45*(8), 44–47.

Stobbe, C. (1993). Professional partnerships. *Educational Leadership, 51*(2), 40–41.

Name Index

Anderson, J., 185–186, 203
Anderson, L., 66, 68, 78, 86, 186, 199, 203
Anderson, R., 260, 280
Armstrong, T., 219–220, 226
Aronson, E., 231, 249
Ausubel, D., 188, 203, 260, 262, 280

Bailey, G., 105–108, 124, 130–134, 274–275
Bailey, R., 79–82
Banks, J., 102, 121
Beane, J., 103, 121
Beaudry, J., 73, 86, 200, 203
Bell, M., 89, 121
Blaney, S., 231, 249
Bloom, B., 97, 121, 152, 155–157, 158, 164–167, 182,
    206–209, 226, 260, 271–272, 280, 313, 335
Blume, J., 242, 249
Bonstingl, J., 51, 60
Boone, T., 48
Boston, B., 76, 86
Bragaw, D., 115, 121
Brandt, R., 338, 360
Bransford, J., 260, 280
Bridwell, N., 106
Brophy, J., 57, 60, 69, 86, 103, 121, 190–193, 203, 341,
    358, 361

Canter, L., 43, 60
Canter, M., 43, 60
Carroll, J., 271, 280
Cassel, E., 39, 61
Charles, C., 57–59, 60
Chiaverina, C., 111, 114–115, 161–162, 176–179
Chinn, P., 84, 86
Chomsky, C., 104–105, 121

Cleveland, H., 114
Cox, J., 76, 86
Cskikszentmihalyi, M., 47–48, 60
Curbo, T., 55–56, 237–238
Curci, L., 18

Daniel, N., 76, 86
deBono, E., 214, 226
Dewey, J., 7–8, 24, 228, 249, 317, 335
Doyle, W., 27, 61, 209–210, 226, 246, 249
Dreikurs, R., 39, 61
Dunn, R., 73, 86, 200, 203

Eby, J., 77, 84, 86
Einstein, A., 217–218, 226
Eisner, E., 94–98, 121, 153–155, 182, 314, 335
Elliott, J., 271
Ellison, L., 72
Elrich, M., 75
Emmer, E., 35, 61
Encinas, C., 180–181
Engelhart, M., 97, 121, 260, 280
Eresh, J., 330, 335
Evertson, C., 35, 61

Fadley, J., 73, 86
Farwick–Owens, R., 242
First, J., 349, 361
Florio-Ruane, S., 348, 361
Furst, E., 97, 121, 260, 280

Gagne, E., 197, 203, 211, 226, 261, 280
Gaidimas, L., 92, 100–102, 121
Gardner, H., 72, 86, 201–202, 203, 219, 226
Gilkey, C., 254, 259

Gilligan, C., 11, 24
Glasser, W., 48–51, 61, 194, 199, 203
Good, T., 57, 60, 69, 86, 190–192, 203, 341, 361
Grant, C., 72–73, 86, 102, 121
Graves, D., 105, 121
Gronlund, N., 319–321, 330, 335, 343, 361
Guilford, J., 217, 226
Guskey, T., 287, 308

Hartoonian, M., 115, 121
Hawkins, D., 266, 280
Hicks, J., 111, 114–115, 161–162, 178–180
Hill, W., 97, 121, 260, 280
Hirsch, E., 315, 335
Hosler, V., 73, 86
Hunter, M., 189, 203, 262, 280

Infeld, L., 217, 226

Jackson, T., 243
Jacobsen, L., 57, 61
James, W., 217, 226
Johnson, D., 51, 61, 228, 234, 241, 245, 247, 249
Johnson, R., 51, 61, 228, 234, 241, 245, 247, 249
Jonas, A., 215, 226
Jones, F., 27–29, 36–37, 42–43, 61, 193, 203

Kendall, J., 91, 110, 121
Kidder, T., 69, 86, 310–311, 335
King, M., 206–212,
King, S., 275–278
Klavas, A., 73, 86, 200, 203
Klein, R., 189
Knight, P., 112–113, 171, 173–174, 304–306, 308
Kohlberg, L., 10–11, 24
Kounin, J., 13, 24, 37–39, 61, 189, 191–194, 203
Krakow, S., 106–108, 130–134
Kratwohl, D., 97, 121, 260, 280
Kurusa, D., 109, 121

LeMahieu, P., 330, 335
Letscher, C., 255
Leyser, Y., 268, 280
Lickona, T., 46–47, 61, 355, 361
Linn, R., 319–321, 330, 335, 342, 361
Lipman, M., 214, 226
Lipton, M., 312, 318, 332, 335
Lyman, F., 224, 226

Mallory, V., 43–46
Malvaso-Zingaro, J., 229–230
Marzano, R., 91, 110, 121, 289–290, 308
Maslow, A., 49, 61, 77, 86, 194, 203
McConnell, K., 46
McCormack, J., 47–48, 60
McTighe, J., 289, 308
Meadows, B., 347, 361
Mednick, L., 52–53, 243
Meyers, C., 224, 226
Mullenix, C., 18–21
Murray, D., 105, 121
Muther, C., 93–94, 121

Newman, F., 184, 203
Ng, J., 254
Noddings, N., 11, 24

O'Connor, T., 68, 86
O'Donnell, M., 221–223, 243
Oakes, J., 312, 318, 332, 335
Osborne, P., 211, 226
Osterman, K., 16, 24

Patterson, P., 48
Paul, R., 214, 226
Peters, J., 9, 13, 24
Peters, W., 271, 280
Pickering, D., 289, 308
Porter, A., 358, 361
Poze, T., 218, 226

Raths, L., 49, 61, 215, 220, 226
Reissman, R., 102, 121
Reyes, R., 108–110, 124,
Rimm, S., 42, 61, 75, 86, 199, 203, 343–347, 361
Romo, Y., 65–68
Rosenthal, R., 57, 61
Rothstein, A., 215, 226
Rowe, M., 223, 226
Ryan, K., 10, 24

Saterlie, M., 355–356, 361
Schon, D., 8–9, 12, 24
Schulman, L., 13, 24
Sharan, S., 230, 247, 249
Shotwell, L., 168, 182
Shoults, Lori, 88–89, 338

Sikes, J., 231, 249
Silberman, C., 266, 280
Slavin, R., 231, 240, 245, 246–247, 249, 272, 280, 307, 308
Sleeter, C., 72–73, 86, 103, 121
Smutny, J., 77, 84, 86
Snapp, M., 231, 249
Stallings, J., 233, 249
Stipek, D., 233, 249
Stobbe, C., 357, 361
Strike, K., 10, 24
Sulzby, E., 105, 121

Teale, W., 105, 121

Torrance, E., 217, 226
Tyler, R., 96–98, 121, 128, 149, 171, 182

Viadero, D., 90, 121

Walters, S., 92, 121
Wasserman, S., 215, 226
Wehlage, G., 184, 203
Wick, J., 72, 86
Wolf, D., 303, 308, 330–331,335

Yount, J., 106–108, 130–134

Zajac, C., 69, 310–311

Subject Index

Academic needs of students, assessing, 68–77
Acceleration in curriculum planning, 169
Achievement tests, 71–72
Active learning, 194–195
Advance organizers, 187–188, 262
Affective needs, meeting students', 49–50, 77–84
Americans with Disabilities Act (ADA), 79
Anecdotal records, how to write, 329–330
Aptitude tests, 71–72
Assessment methods, how teachers select, 286–289
Assessment procedures, involving students in, 332–333
Assessment rubrics, checklists and rating scales, 297,
    299–300
Assessment terminology, 282–284
Assessment
    designing authentic performance tasks, 289–290,
      296–297
    informal observations, 288–289
    oral reports and examinations, 295–296
Assessments, planning to fit objectives, 164–167
Attention deficit disorder, (ADD), 73
Attention, getting students', 189–190
Audio-video technology in classroom, 258–259
Authentic assessment system, grading, 322–329
Authentic discussions, 210–219
Authentic learning, 184, 194–195

Behavioral objectives in lesson planning, 153
Bilingual and bicultural students' needs, 65–68
Bilingual lesson plan sample, 177, 180–181
Bloom's Taxonomy in curriculum planning, 152,
    155–158
Bloom's Taxonomy
    student products, 298
    teaching strategies to fit, 260–266

    use in lesson planning, 155–158
Body language, teachers', 36–37

Calculators, use in mathematics programs, 258
California State Department of Education, 91
Character education programs, 355–356
Clarity in presentation of information, 188–195
Classroom environment, physical, 27–31
Classroom meetings, 54–56
Closure, 195
Cognitive processing, 4–6
Cognitive-mediational conception of learning, 185–186
Common core curriculum, 100–102
Communication
    with newsletters and notes, 350
    with parents, two way, 338–348
    with telephone calls, 351–352
Communities, classrooms as, 50–51
Community involvement in classroom events, 353–356
Community resources, 354–355
Comprehension, teaching strategies promote, 261–263
Computer-assisted research projects, 254
Conflict resolution, taught to students, 51–54
Contracts for independent learning, 272–274, 300–303
Cooperation, classroom conditions, 244–246
Cooperative learning
    effects of, 246–248
    gradelevel applications, 235–244
    how used in classroom, 235–244
    models of, 228–233
    selecting and adapting, 234–235
    the purpose of, 233–235
Creative thinking, discussions to enhance, 217–218
Criterion-referenced tests and quizzes, 70, 167, 283,
    290–292

Critical thinking, discussions to promote, 214–215
Cultural diversity in the classroom, 64–68
Cultural, Language, and Academic Development
    (CLAD) teaching credential, 66, 275–278
Cumulative files, 69–70
Curriculum compacting, 169
Curriculum guidelines, state, 91–92
Curriculum orientations influence evaluation, 314–317
Curriculum orientations, 94–96
Curriculum planning
    basic principles of, 96–97
    long-term, 100–102
Curriculum unit, creating a, 126–128

Direct instruction, 195–197
Discipline systems that build character, 46–48
Discovery learning, 263, 266–267
Discussion strategies for authentic learning, 262–264
Discussions, the teachers' role in leading, 220–221

English as a second language (ESL), 84, 168,
Enrichment in curriculum planning, 169
Enthusiasm in presentations, 190
Ethics and principles, 9–12
Evaluation procedures, involving students in, 332–333
Evaluation systems, philosophies underlying, 314–317
Evaluation
    methods of reporting, 317–333
    purposes of, 311–313
Expressive outcomes in lesson planning, 154–155

First day of school, 30–34

Gifted programs, 76–77
Goals, clarifying educational, 97–98
Good beginning for the school year, 26
Grade-equivalent test scores, 71
Grades
    authentic system for determining, 322–329
    computation of, 327–329
Group investigations, 213–214, 228–231
Group rotations using learning centers, 274–278
Grouping decisions, 74–75

High-achieving students, needs of, 76–77
Higher-level thinking, questions to stimulate, 206–210
Home visits to students' homes, 349–350

Individualized educational plan (IEP), 168

Information processing, 4–6
Inquiry training, 263, 267–268
Interdisciplinary units, sequencing objectives, 163–164
Intrinsic motivation, building, 48–57, 188–195

Jigsaw model of cooperative learning, 231

Language arts
    example of thematic unit in, 139, 143–145
    sequencing objectives in, 159–161
Language arts/social studies lesson plan, 174–176
Leadership styles, teachers', 39–40
Learned helplessness, 75
Learning centers, lesson plan using, 177, 180–181,
    274–278
Learning contracts, 300–303
Learning disabilities, varying objectives for, 168
Learning styles, 72–73
Learning styles, matched with teaching styles, 200–201
Learning teams model of cooperative learning, 231–233
Lesson plan model, 172
Lesson Plan, writing a well organized, 170–178
Limited English proficiency (LEP) programs, 66–68,
    275–278
Logical consequences, 40–41
Long-term memory, 4–6

Maine's Common Core of Learning, 92, 100–102
Mastery learning, 169, 292–293,
Mastery of outcomes and objectives, 289–290
Mathematics
    curriculum planning in, 110–111
    example of a thematic unit in, 135, 140–142
    sequencing objectives in, 157, 159
Minnesota Educational Computer Consortium, 129
Multicultural community, teaching in, 348–349
Multicultural values in curriculum planning, 102–104
Multidisciplinary thematic unit, example of, 130–135
Multidisciplinary units, sequencing objectives, 163–164
Multiple intelligences, 72–73, 201–202
Multiple intelligences, discussions using, 219–220

National Aeronautics and Space Administration
    (NASA), 287
National Assessment of Educational Progress (NAEP),
    90, 110, 285
National Committee on Science Education Standards
    and Assessment, 111
National Council for the Social Studies, 91

National Council of Teachers of English, 91
National Council of Teachers of Mathematics, 91, 110, 159
National Science Education Standards, 91
National standards for curriculum planning, 90–91
National Center for History in the Schools, 113
Natural consequences, 40
Networking, computer, 255
Norm-referenced tests, 70

Objectives
    sequencing in school subjects, 157–164
    writing to fit goals and outcomes, 152–157
Open House
    Fall, 339–340
    Spring, 352–353
Outcomes, clarifying educational, 97–100

Parent Teacher Association (PTA), 353, 356
Parent Teacher Organization (PTO), 353
Parent-teacher conferences, 340–345
Parents as volunteers, 353–354
Parents, two-way communication with, 43–46, 338–348
Peacemaking groups in the classroom, 233
Percentile rank test scores, 71
Performance Assessment Collaborative for Education (PACE), 330
Performance standards, 283
Philosophy of teaching, 21–23
Placement decisions, 74–75
Planning time, 58–59
Planning web for thematic unit, 131
Portfolio, preparing your professional, 21–23, 59–60, 86–86, 120, 148–149, 178–181, 202–203, 225–226, 248–249, 279, 307–308, 334, 359–360
Portfolios of student products, 284, 303–304
Portfolios, organization of, 330–331
Pretests, 73–74
Preventive discipline strategies, 36–43
Prewriting discussions, 218–219
Problem-solving computer programs, 255–257
Problem-solving discussions, 211–213
Problem-solving objectives in lesson plans, 153–154
Project L.E.A.P., 2

Readiness tests, 74
Record keeping and grading on computer, 257–258
Reflection-in-action, 15
Reflection-on-action, 15

Reflective action in teaching, a model of, 12–18
Reflective Actions, creating a curriculum unit, 126–128
Reflective thinking, definitions of, 7–9
Report cards, 310
Role playing, 263, 268–269
Rubric grading systems, 283, 290, 301
Rubric guidelines for student essays, 293–295
Rules and consequences, establishment of, 40–43
Rural children, meeting the needs of, 83

Scaffolding for learning, 198–199
Schedules, daily and weekly, 57–58
Schema theory, 186–187
School district report cards, 285
Science unit for high school physics, 142, 146–148
Science
    curriculum planning in, 111–112
    sequencing objectives in, 161–162
Self-fulfilling prophecy, 84
Simulations in the classroom, 263, 269–271
Social studies
    curriculum planning in, 117–118
    example of thematic unit in, 136–138
    lesson plan sample in, 175–176
    sequencing objectives in, 162–163
Socratic dialogue, 216–217
Special needs
    planning for students with, 78–82
    varying objectives for, 167–170
Standardized test results, interpreting, 70–72
Student needs assessment plan, 85–86
Student-teacher conferences, 73–74
Students at risk, meeting the needs of, 80–82
Success
    effects of, 48–49
    structuring tasks for, 199–200
Systematic classroom instruction, 195–200

Teacher empowerment, 356–357
Teacher modeling and demonstration, 198
Teacher's roles and responsibilities, 3–12
Teachers coaching one another, 357–359
Teachers' conceptions of how students learn, 68–69
Teachers' thinking, effects of, 6–7
Teaching style, 35
Teaching styles, matched with learning styles, 200–201
Technology to increase authentic learning, 252–260
Technology, managing in the classroom, 259–260
Textbook Adoption Advisory Service, 93

Textbooks, evaluation and use of, 93–94
Thematic curriculum planning, 108–110
Thematic unit topics, deciding on, 125
Thematic units
    examples of, 130–147
    how teachers plan, 124–130
Time lines in curriculum planning, 116–119
Timing in presentations, 193–194
Total quality management in classrooms, 50–51
Transitions, smooth, 192–193
Two-way communication with parents, 338–348

Underachievement, determining causes for, 75–76

Unit plans, sequencing learning experiences, 128–130
United Nations, simulation of, 270
Urban children, meeting needs of, 82–83

Variation in presentations, 194
Videotape records of student work, 306–307

Whole Language Curriculum, 104–105
Withitness, 13, 37–39
Word processing in the classroom, 253–254
Working memory, 4–5

About the Author

After receiving her first teaching credential at the University of Illinois in 1969, Judy Eby taught elementary school for several years in Elgin, Crystal Lake, and Barrington, Illinois. She coordinated gifted programs in two school districts and developed a method for identification of students for gifted programs that did not focus on paper-and-pencil tests. Instead, all students in the school were considered eligible for gifted programming and were asked to submit pretasks to demonstrate their talent, interest, and willingness to work, for each curriculum offering. She published several articles on this type of program, which develops gifted behavior in children without the stigma and exclusiveness of most gifted programs.

In 1984, Eby began to correspond with Benjamin S. Bloom about the possibilities of doing research on gifted behavior. He invited her to study with him and became her mentor and advisor as she completed her Ph.D. at Northwestern University in 1986.

In the past decade, Eby has been involved in teacher education programs at De Paul University in Chicago, National University, the University of San Diego, and San Diego State University. She has also worked in a state-supported program called Beginning Teachers Support Academy, which provides one-to-one mentoring for new teachers placed in inner-city schools for their first two years of teaching.

Currently, Judy Eby is the program director of special projects for a children's literacy program called Rolling Readers USA, based in San Diego. This program recruits and trains adult volunteers to read aloud to children and provide one-to-one tutoring for non-readers in the first three grades of school. Three times a year, volunteers are provided with new hardbound editions of children's books to give away to the children they serve. Today, Rolling Readers has more than 3,000 volunteers serving approximately 85,000 children.

Eby also works as a consultant with interested teachers or school administrators to design curriculum or establish a process for teachers to create their own professional portfolios, based on the ideas at the end of each chapter in this book.